Neighbors in Conflict

The Irish, Germans, Jews, and Italians of New York City, 1929-1941

Second Edition

Ronald H. Bayor

NEIGHBORS IN CONFLICT

Neighbors in Conflict

The Irish, Germans, Jews, and Italians of New York City, 1929-1941

Second Edition

Ronald H. Bayor

University of Illinois Press
Urbana and Chicago

Illini Books edition
© 1988 by the Board of Trustees of the University of Illinois
Manufactured in the United States of America
P 5 4 3 2 1

This book is printed on acid-free paper.

Library of Congress Cataloging-in-Publication Data

Bayor, Ronald M., 1944–
  Neighbors in conflict.

  Bibliography: p.
  Includes index.
  1. Ethnology—New York (N.Y.)   2. New York (N.Y.)—
Ethnic relations.   I. Title.
F128.9.A1B28   1988   305.8′009747′1   87-19064
ISBN 0-252-01437-5 (alk. paper)
1988   1988

For my wife,
LESLIE,
and my daughters
JILL and ROBIN

Contents

ILLUSTRATIONS

Figures

Maps

TABLES

Preface
to the Second Edition

My first thoughts about writing a study of intergroup conflict came in the late 1960s during a period when many of the nation's cities were torn by racial disorders. I wanted to determine the forces which pitted group against group and in so doing combine historical data with social-science theory to provide a model for understanding these conflicts. Although concentrating on the 1930s and 1940s, during a time when the Jews were at the center of the intergroup hostilities which involved the Irish, Germans, and Italians as well, this model could fit any group or combination of groups during other historical periods or in other cities.

This book therefore analyzes the anti-Semitism of this period but is about much more. It is a study of ethnic conflict and suggests that the intergroup friction was a product of a complex interaction of variables—a struggle over interests and values based on realistic and unrealistic elements in which both competitive, ethnic succession factors and explosive issues played a role. Most importantly, groups had to perceive a threat to their well-being, but that perception could be real or imagined or both. The study also discusses the intensity, moderation, and function of conflict.

In suggesting this model I had hoped that other historians would begin to test it by investigating the dynamics of ethnic relations in other periods and cities and for other groups, and to do so using an interdisciplinary approach. For the most part this research did not occur. Except for political scientist John Stack's *International Conflict in an American City: Boston's Irish, Italians and Jews, 1935–1944* (Westport, CT.: Greenwood Press, 1979) and various accounts of black-Jewish tensions (e.g., Joseph Washington, ed., *Jews in Black Perspectives: A Dialogue* [Rutherford, N.J.: Farleigh Dickinson University Press, 1984]), full-scale historical works on intergroup conflict have not appeared. Moreover, the few who have written on this topic have made little effort to use the models and theories offered by other social scientists. Although intergroup conflict has been briefly mentioned or implied in a number of recent books, most notably in those on New York, the focus is always on other aspects of ethnicity (see, e.g., Virginia Sánchez Korrol, *From Colonia to Community: The History of Puerto Ricans in New York City, 1917–1948* [Westport, CT.: Greenwood Press, 1983]; Deborah Dash Moore, *At Home in America: Second Generation New York Jews* [New York: Columbia University Press, 1981]; and Jeffrey Gurock, *When Harlem was Jewish, 1870–1930* [New York: Columbia University Press, 1979]).

Historians of America's ethnic/racial experience instead have concentrated their research on topics such as migration, occupational mobility, ghetto development, immigrant or black adaptation to urban America, and working-class formation. This is not meant as a criticism, for some fine work has been done, but merely as a statement that the tensions between groups and the attempt to understand this friction has been neglected. Much research still needs to be done on individual cities with combinations of various groups and on comparative analyses of different cities in diverse regions of the country or in varied time periods. A contrastive study of nineteenth- and twentieth-century Boston, for example, might reveal information on the historically constant aspects of group interaction. An analysis of Irish-Jewish or black-Hispanic relations in different cities could add substantially to understanding any local variations of the conflict model. On a more ambitious level, historians may want someday to explore cross-national differences in intergroup relations. In what way does the European (e.g., Northern Ireland) or Asian (e.g., India) intergroup experience differ from the American? Is there a common denominator in conflict situations no matter where they are occurring or has the United States developed a unique style in the manifestation and resolution of these group tensions?

While conflict was the focus of this book, clearly intergroup relations also involves cooperation and this too needs more analysis. Some recent studies have mentioned cooperative relations in passing (e.g., Ewa Morawska, *For Bread with Butter: Life-Worlds of East Central Europeans in Johnstown, Pennsylvania, 1890–1940* [Cambridge: Cambridge University Press, 1985]) but only one work concentrates on this important topic (George Pozzetta and Gary Mormino, *The Immigrant World of Ybor City: Italians and Their Latin Neighbors in Tampa, 1885–1985* [Urbana: University of Illinois Press, 1987]). While few instances of ethnic cooperation could be discerned during the New York experience covered in my book, it is obviously an element of group contact that has not received the attention it deserves.

While discussing a direction for future research, I must also comment on what I would do differently in this work if it were being written today. My original intention was to follow up this book with a history of New York's race relations in the twentieth century, thereby adding a study of racial interaction to the one on the white ethnics. I decided to approach the topic this way because racial tensions at first glance seemed to have their own causative and developmental factors, divorced from the type of friction generated between the ethnics.

Having moved away from New York, I was never able to develop this research but realize now that it would have been a better idea to include blacks within the initial work. Racial and ethnic conflict, I am now convinced, derive from the same elements—a sense of real or imagined threats to group interests and values based largely on both competitive and explosive issues. Although adding a fifth group would have further complicated an already difficult investigation, it would also have made a needed statement on the importance of merging immigration/ethnic and racial studies, especially for northern cities, in order to understand better America's pluralism. Although some books have incorporated both racial and ethnic groups in their analysis, (the best example being John Bodnar, Roger Simon, and Michael Weber, *Lives of Their Own: Blacks, Italians, and Poles in Pittsburgh, 1900–1960* [Urbana: University of Illinois Press, 1982]), most have not, and in general there has been an unnecessary and invalid split in what is actually one field—the study of America's component peoples. As editor of the *Journal of American Ethnic History,* I have tried to offer articles and reviews on all the groups which constitute North America and urge historians and other scholars to develop and nurture a broader focus in both research and course offerings.

Incorporating racial and ethnic studies has become even more important in order to understand recent urban history where blacks, Asians, and Hispanics have often been the competing or cooperating groups. Those who will be researching intergroup relations in such cities as Miami, Houston, Los Angeles, Chicago, and New York in the post-World War II period cannot make any artificial division between racial and immigrant/ethnic history. These cities now contain a variety of competing racial and ethnic groups, and the futility of looking at only some groups and not others is readily apparent.

I hope this book will continue to help others understand the complex nature of intergroup relations. As there are no simple explanations for group conflict, there are also no simple solutions. Yet historians have a special role to play in helping others, including policy makers, comprehend the forces at work. The conflict situations we study have a beginning and usually an end; therefore among social scientists, it is mainly historians who can provide the complete story, including the ramifications of a conflict situation. Since the United States, as well as other pluralistic nations, will likely experience ethno-racial conflicts many times in the future, historians must contribute their research and perspective and add their voices to the solution or amelioration of these as well as other societal problems.

Atlanta, Georgia
November 1986

Preface

This book seeks to analyze the roots, development, manifestation, and culmination of group conflict within a multi-ethnic urban setting. Studying the four major white ethnic groups in New York City during the 1930s, I have tried to weave together the various strands of a very complex but commonplace phenomenon still evident in our society today. Group conflict was significant during this period and involved all four ethnic communities in varying degrees. However, each situation, although having within it certain basic components of conflict, was different. The major clash involved the Jews, and it arose from the traditional elements of anti-Semitism as well as from pluralistic America's competitive ethnic environment.

The book is organized to provide a sense of the ethnic succession issues, related to long-term competition, interacting with explosive issues, largely emanating from concern over foreign events. The final parts of the study consider the role of political campaigns in fomenting ethnic friction and offer a look at the conflicts as they occurred at the neighborhood level. Since many events and factors took place concurrently, I have tried to tie them together in both text and notes in order to provide a coherent explanation.

As is sometimes the case with historical works, it was difficult to pinpoint the exact year with which this study should end. Rather, the intent was to follow the sources and manifestation of the 1930s conflicts to their natural conclusion. For some groups this took me to 1945 and beyond; for others the story ended earlier.

Since in many ways the subject of ethnic conflict deals with a survey of local opinions and reactions, I attempted to use only ethnic periodicals or organizational publications which had solely a New York audience or were located in the City and therefore had a New York orientation. Because the ethnic and intergroup relations situation in other cities may have varied from New York on the basis of local differences, opinion of this sort was avoided if possible. In some cases it was necessary to look beyond the borders of the City. For example, the proceedings of the New York State Branch of the Catholic Central Verein had to be used when publications of the local federations of this group could not be found.

In treating such a sensitive topic, I have tried to maintain a careful objectivity and to avoid taking up the banner for any of the involved groups. My purpose was not to criticize or blame any of the ethnic communities, but rather to explain with the hope of providing a better understanding of one of society's crucial problems. I also hope that the questions and theories discussed in this study will inspire other historians to investigate ethnic pluralism in all its parts.

Acknowledgments

Many people have assisted me in the research and writing of this book. I would first like to thank Thomas C. Cochran, of the University of Pennsylvania, who guided this work through its dissertation stage. Seymour J. Mandelbaum, University of Pennsylvania, also provided valuable help in developing the dissertation and continued to offer his keen insights as the work progressed into this book. He has always been both an astute critic and good friend over the years.

My research also enabled me to meet such fine people as Bernard Wax, Director of the American Jewish Historical Society, and Rev. Silvano M. Tomasi, Director of the Center for Migration Studies. Both men kindly interrupted their busy schedules and provided assistance in the early stages of this work. A note of appreciation also goes to Joseph B. Frechen of the St. John's University mathematics department and to William McAlpine, formerly of the Georgia Institute of Technology, who introduced me to quantitative techniques and helped in the development of the statistical data.

I would like to thank Jerome Bakst of the Anti-Defamation League of B'nai B'rith, New York; Harvey Johnson of the Central Bureau, Catholic Central Union of America; and Ward Lange of the Steuben Society of America. Their aid in finding various materials is appreciated. I owe a debt of gratitude also to the persons who granted me interviews. The personnel of a number of libraries and archives have also been helpful. I should like to express my appreciation to the staffs of the New York Public Library; the Municipal Archives and Records Center (New York); the Blaustein Library of the American Jewish Committee; the libraries of Columbia University, Brandeis University, St. John's University, and the Georgia Institute of Technology; the American Jewish Historical Society; the YIVO Institute for Jewish Research (New York); and the Franklin D. Roosevelt Library.

The Department of Social Sciences at the Georgia Institute of Technology provided necessary support which enabled me to complete this work. For this help I would like to thank Patrick Kelly, head of the Social Sciences Department.

The editors of the *International Migration Review* and the *Proceedings of the Seventh Annual Conference of the American Italian Historical Association* have kindly permitted me to use material which first appeared in their publications.

Although there have been many to thank, my wife, Leslie, deserves a special expression of appreciation. She has been a constant source of encouragement and intelligent criticism. Without her support, advice, and love, this book would never have been written.

Chapter One

The Ethnic Setting

New York City, in the nineteenth and twentieth centuries, was the main port of entry for millions of immigrants seeking a better life. As such, the City, already a multi-ethnic society, and constantly absorbing new groups, was faced with the problem of creating a harmonious atmosphere within this heterogeneous setting. This was not always easily done.

Intergroup relations based on harmony and cooperation have often not been the norm in the United States. Forever lurking beneath the surface, in all ethnic relationships, are tensions, resentments, and frictions of varying degrees which are associated with living together in a competitive society.[1] Under a certain set of conditions, these normal competitive tensions can escalate into occurrences of conflict, sometimes violent.[2] This is not to suggest, as some sociologists have through their race relations cycles, that conflict is an inevitable outcome of ethnic contact.[3] It is not, since a number of variables can influence intergroup relations, and there are many examples of different ethnic groups living peacefully together.[4] However, the possibility of conflict is always present particularly in cities where one is less likely to find an isolated niche and thus avoid contact, competition, and disagreements with others. Although the conflicts have not always been severe or violent, they have been persistent. Because of variables such as deeply ingrained status insecurities or the group's place in the occupational or political structure at a particular time, some groups have found themselves more involved in conflict situations than others. Such was the case of the Irish, the first of the immigrant groups discussed in this study to arrive in America.

By 1860 the immigrant Irish comprised 25.4 percent of the white population of New York City.[5] With the growth of this ethnic community and the increasing competitive tensions with the more established groups, conflict eventually emerged. As was noted in the definitions given in note 2, there are two elements in both competition and conflict—interests and values—both of which appear in all conflict situations to some degree. What can turn competition over either of these factors into conflict is a feeling by one group that the other poses a real or perceived threat to its present or future interests and/or values in society.[6] Periods of economic depression can have this effect by causing a loss of group position in the status hierarchy, which results in increased insecurity; or by barring those who wish to advance, thereby making them feel that their future interests are threatened.[7]

Conflict can emerge slowly, based on the increasing severity of the tensions associated with competition, or it can appear relatively quickly because of explosive issues. These are deeply emotional issues related to interests and values which often materialize with little warning and clearly and sharply pit two groups against each other, making each aware of a struggle. The development and intensity of any conflict depends on a variety of factors, such as the number of points of friction between the two groups (particularly if explosive issues interact with other competitive tensions such as those associated with ethnic succession), the absence or presence of internal or external moderating elements, and the degree of insecurity or frustration of each involved group. Conflicts which are intense are difficult to calm and move toward accommodation.[8]

In the Irish situation, during the early years of their immigration this group was seen as posing an occupational threat to the native-born Protestant working class either directly through job competition or indirectly, through depression of wages.[9] This was especially noted during periods of economic difficulty. There was also some concern about the effects of this large, impoverished group on the City's life. Conflict appeared over these issues as well as over the political rivalry posed by the Irish. The Catholicism of this group also was a source of conflict, as the Protestants were concerned that their dominance in the country would be lost. They saw in the Irish the beginning of a papal conspiracy to rule America and displace all others. Since the Protestants also viewed Catholicism as incompatible with American ideals, Irish religious beliefs indeed seemed a great threat.[10] Within this setting, explosive issues, such as the Irish challenge to the Protestant controlled public school system, sharply divided the two communities and helped to produce an intense, prolonged and sometimes violent conflict.

Although it was mainly the Irish who suffered from the nativist excesses of pre–Civil War America, the Germans, the other large immigrant group to arrive at this time, also had difficulties with the native American population.[11] These conflicts again were related to interests and values tied to ethnic succession problems, but they remained more subdued because of fewer points of friction and a number of mitigating factors. For example, while the religious practices of the Germans, both Protestants and Catholics, did inspire resentment, it was always the Irish who appeared as a greater threat. A hostile reaction to German Catholics was evident mainly in areas such as Cincinnati, where few Irish

Catholics lived. Also, the Germans arrived in America in a stronger economic and occupational position than the Irish and therefore were not as great a burden on the cities where they settled in relation to poverty and crime. Finally, there were also no explosive issues which would have contributed to an intense conflict situation.

By the closing decades of the nineteenth century, it was again the Irish who bore the brunt of nativist attacks, this time in the form of the American Protective Association. The movement of the Irish into positions of political power in a number of cities, including New York, revived the anti-Catholic crusade. The depression of the 1890s contributed an economic factor by increasing job competition. Other points of friction were also present. Catholicism once more seemed threatening and incompatible with American life. Emotional issues, such as control over the school system, again helped to produce an intense conflict.[12]

Ethnic conflict was not confined to the immigrants versus the native-born, although this was a major part of the intergroup hostilities of this period. It also involved groups that had arrived at the same time and shared the same communities and problems. The Germans and Irish, for example, often competed or conflicted with each other for political positions and jobs during the period of first arrival. A number of clashes occurred between these groups in the 1840s and 1850s as a result of economic rivalries.[13] The major rivalry, however, was for control over the Catholic Church. In the 1890s German-Americans, under the banner of Cahenslyism, sought approval for the concept that each nationality group should have its own parishes, priests, and schools as well as a number of bishops proportionate to their percentage of the Catholic population. This was an attempt both to preserve German culture in America and to escape from the domination of the Irish in the Church hierarchy. The Irish opposed this plan partly because it would fragment American Catholicism and partly because of their fear that it would dilute their power within the Church and invite condemnation by Protestants who would accuse Catholics of perpetuating foreign cultures.[14]

By the time the struggle over Church control fully emerged in the 1890s, the tensions related to job and political rivalry had largely dissipated. Therefore, the points of friction in any single period were few. Moreover, there were moderating factors at work, since both groups came to recognize that they had many common interests, problems, and rivals.[15] Ethnic conflicts, especially ones that were intense and prolonged, remained more likely either with those who came before (the native-born white Protestants) or those who came after—the Jews and Italians, who were striving to win a place in the ethnic power structure of the City and who represented a vastly different value system.

It was mainly the Irish—the group that had struggled hardest and met the brunt of ethnic hostilities—who were most conscious of the threat of the newer groups. The first indication of incipient conflict appeared during the period of immigration for the Jews and Italians, when the newer groups challenged the older ones mainly in the area of occupations and residence. In the construction and garment trades, for example, the Irish and Germans were being replaced. Fights at job sites were a frequent occurrence, particularly between the Irish and Italians (see chapter 2). Neighborhoods saw a transformation of ethnic populations as the great mass of Jews and Italians moved into formerly Irish and German sections. Street fights erupted, mainly between the Irish and Jews and the Irish and Italians.[16]

The very fact that the latter two groups were Catholic was also a major source of friction, although the German Catholics were not involved in this issue. The Irish did not consider the Italians to be good Catholics. In particular they objected to the Catholicism practiced by Italian peasants and to the anticlericalism of the educated Italians. In return, Italians entering Irish Catholic churches often discovered them to be strange and inhospitable places. To the Irish, the Italians were intruders. This was true even in relation to the parochial schools, where at times, when Italian parents did agree to send their children to these schools, they found prejudice directed against them by the Irish. In order to provide places of worship where the Italians could feel comfortable, the Church hierarchy agreed to the creation of Italian-language parishes and to train or import more Italian priests for the already established parishes. For other reasons, such as Irish hostility toward the unification of Italy, a move that would diminish the Pope's power, these two groups could not live amicably together.[17]

The attitude of the Irish is revealed clearly in an 1887 editorial in the *New York Catholic Review* which noted the disdain the Irish had for the Italians, and consequently asked for more understanding, reminding the Irish that they too had emerged from an indigent background.[18] Even in regard to the Catholic lay organizations there was a split. Italians did not feel that they could achieve equality in groups such as the Knights of Columbus as long as the Irish controlled the organization. Therefore, separate Italian associations, such as the Sons of Italy, were formed.

Since there were a number of points of friction, few conflict moderating factors, and a high level of Irish insecurity in relation to their place in society, the Irish-Italian conflict was intense and remained active for many years. The Irish-Jewish conflict, though less severe during this period, was to become the main conflict of the 1930s.

The Germans, too, engaged in conflict, but this conflict remained less intense, since there were fewer points of friction over interests and values and less insecurity based on previous experiences. For example, although Germans were also involved in sporadic street fighting with the Jews as the result of residential competition, on the whole German-Jewish relations remained relatively amicable. Jews of German background were accepted members of the German-American community and belonged to many of its organizations. Both groups were also active in the Socialist movement, and this drew them together. The outbursts of anti-Semitism in Germany prior to World War I had little effect on German-Jewish relations in New York City. Leading German-American newspapers such as the *New Yorker Staats-Zeitung* offered opposition to any appearance of anti-Semitism. German anti-Semites who visited New York found few adherents. Although anti-Semitic organizations could be found in the German-American community at this time, they were insignificant.[19]

Relatively few problems existed between Jews and Italians, too, during this period of the late nineteenth and early twentieth centuries. However, there was an awareness of competition between the two for jobs in the garment industry and for housing in such areas as East Harlem. Some early friction also existed because of Italians serving as strikebreakers in the clothing industry which the Jews were trying to unionize.[20] But this friction dissipated quickly as Italians began joining these unions, which were eager to encourage cooperation between the two groups. The leadership of the International Ladies Garment Workers Union (ILGWU), for example, conducted a conscious policy of integration in an effort to strengthen the union. Essentially, tensions between Italians and Jews remained minimal, as both groups saw others as their main rivals. In the late 1920s, as an indication of amicable relations, B'nai B'rith and the Sons of Italy discussed a plan for mutual cooperation and assistance. Each looked to the other as an ally.[21] The pattern of friendliness did not necessarily mean that the two groups would always view each other in this way. It merely meant that at this point of time the factors necessary to generate conflict were not present.

As the various ethnic communities continued to compete in a variety of ways, America moved into the World War I years. Since the insecurity of an ethnic group and its perceived status in society is an important factor in its relationship with others, the years of neutrality and war were significant in the development of an atmosphere in the City which was conducive to conflict. During the war, those groups, mainly the Irish and Germans, who had opposed American entry on the side of England, found themselves under attack. They were accused of having dual loyalties that were unpatriotic. The German-Americans, of course, suffered the most, becoming the despised Huns rather than the Americans they thought they had been. As the editor of one German-American periodical later noted: "During the World War, when propaganda was mightier than the sword or than truth, Americans of German descent were the number-one victims of that war hysteria. Truth, justice, loyalty . . . were ruled out, and with them, any recognition of free speech, free press or the right of free assemblage." The war ushered in a full re-emergence of nativism, although there had continued to be instances revealing anti-Irish and anti–foreign-born tensions as well as anti-Semitism among old-stock New Yorkers in the prewar period.[22]

Ethnic consciousness was strengthened by the war as the various groups perceived their vulnerable position in American life. If the Germans could be so easily attacked, what protection did the newer ethnics really have? The 1920s continued to increase this awareness as nativism became an active force. The explosive issue of the war and the subsequent issues such as labor radicalism, the

Red Scare, and prohibition clearly and sharply pitted native white Protestants against all or some of the immigrant groups. This was combined with severe tensions related to the competition of ethnic succession and produced an intense and often violent outburst of conflict in the United States during the 1920s. A sense of threatening competition was generated after the war by a feeling among the native white Protestants that they were becoming a minority in their own country. Jobs, political power, and neighborhoods were threatened by the new groups, whose values seemed incompatible with American ideals. In cities like New York, with large foreign-born populations, the old-stock Protestants clearly sensed their own decline.

The conflict which emerged manifested itself in many ways, all related to an attempt to curtail or eliminate the immigrant's power. On a countrywide basis the immigration restriction acts beginning in 1921 and culminating in the National Origins Quota Act limited particularly immigration from southern and eastern Europe, but also resulted in a decrease for the Irish and Germans. The re-emergence of the Ku Klux Klan, with its anti-Catholic, anti-Semitic, anti-black and anti–foreign-born crusade, drew many adherents who responded to what they perceived as a threat from these groups. In New York City the Klan organized chapters but was driven out, further proof to them of who were in control. However, in the suburbs, which were still bastions of old America, the Klan prospered.[23] The growth of this organization not only indicated the discontent among the native white Protestants but reminded Catholics and Jews of their minority status in this country and the hostility directed towards them. The Sacco-Vanzetti case was a particular reminder of this status to Italians; for the Jews, Henry Ford's anti-Semitic publications and the increasing discrimination in hiring and educational opportunities clearly illustrated their position. Also significant was the anti-Catholic and anti–foreign-born aspect of the Al Smith defeat in 1928, which increased the fears of all the groups but was especially symbolic to the Irish as a challenge to their Americanism and ability to assimilate. For the Germans and Irish, the war and the 1920s destroyed whatever hope they might have had that America had finally accepted them.

New York's ethnic groups brought with them into the 1930s an increased insecurity combined with a continuation of the ever-present ethnic tensions; they were unsure of their place in American life and fearful of any more threats to their position. Since the older groups, who had thought acceptance was within their grasp, had received the greatest shocks during the war years and its aftermath, it was they who were particularly aware of their lowly status and desirous of maintaining or expanding upon what they had. An indication of Irish attitudes is contained in a 1929 editorial in the *Irish World* which warned its readers that "we see all around us, the peoples of other races forging ahead." The paper hoped that as a result the Irish would experience a "reawakening of self-consciousness." Throughout the 1930s, efforts were made to ensure that the contributions of Irish-Americans to the United States were stated in school textbooks. There were also attempts to introduce Gaelic into school curriculums. The Irish wanted to be reassured of their value to America. The Germans reacted with a sensitivity to criticism of anything German and a desire to protect themselves in the future. Organizations such as the Steuben Society were formed to protect the German name.[24] The Italians and Jews were also disturbed by the nativist events of this period and were determined to forge ahead, to win their proper place.

While the conflicts of the 1920s had raged, the immigrant groups had been at relative peace with each other, but the setting for a renewed conflict between these ethnic groups had been provided.

Chapter Two

Economic Collapse

The first jolt to harmonious ethnic relations in New York City came from the economic system. When prosperity existed and jobs were plentiful, it was easier to accept the rivalry of other groups. As a result of the Depression and other factors, competition became sharp for increasingly scarce resources. The result, although different for each group depending on their particular place in the occupational structure, was an increase in the ethnic tensions and hostilities which had remained relatively submerged during the 1920s. To understand fully the economic aspect of conflict, one must consider not only the degree of unemployment during the Depression but also the occupational patterns of the period, which would have indicated problems for certain groups even if there had been no economic collapse.

PRE-DEPRESSION TRENDS

In the period from 1910 to 1930 the trend both in the United States and in New York State was away from unskilled labor. A study published by the State University of New York in 1937 notes a 67.3 percent increase in the white-collar and proprietary group during this period, while manual workers had increased by only 21.7 percent. (The rate of increase for all gainfully occupied workers in New York State was 38 percent.) Moreover, the percentage of manual workers among all gainful workers had declined from 64.4 percent in 1910 to 56.8 percent in 1930. Skilled workers showed the smallest decline within this category. The study also found that, within the grouping of manual workers, unskilled workers had increased by 5.4 percent, semi-skilled by 23.4 percent, and skilled by 34.3 percent. This shows that white-collar and more highly skilled manual occupations were the expanding fields. Within the white-collar and proprietary group, clerks and kindred workers showed the largest increase (106.3 percent). Professional persons indicated an increase of 85.8 percent and nonfarm proprietors, managers, and officials showed the smallest increase in this category, with 39.7 percent.[1]

The same trend away from unskilled labor can be noted by looking at the occupational structure by census occupational divisions combined with the above data on socioeconomic groups. The declining occupational categories in New York State for the period 1910–1930 were agriculture, mining, the manufacturing and mechanical industries, and domestic and personal service.[2] Agriculture and mining can be disregarded, since they do not apply to New York City; but the figures for the remaining two categories are revealing. In the declining manufacturing and mechanical industries the trend was for skilled labor to supplant the less skilled. Skilled manual occupations increased more rapidly (32.6 percent) than the semi-skilled (5.6 percent) or unskilled (16.5 percent). Most of the semi-skilled workers were factory operatives; most of the unskilled were factory laborers. This occupational division also showed an increase in its white-collar and proprietary category, although less than in other fields owing to a significant decrease in builders and building contractors between 1910 and 1920. However, even this declining industry indicated a trend toward white-collar and skilled manual labor. The domestic and personal service division noted a decline because of the shift of women away from this occupation to clerical and professional positions. The only part of this category which showed an increase was the proprietary group (e.g., lunchroom and restaurant keepers).

The expanding census occupational divisions also exhibit a trend toward white-collar work. The clerical field increased enormously (130.2 percent) during this period, especially owing to the movement of women into occupations such as stenographers, typists, and clerks.[3] This took place mainly during the World War I years. There was also a sharp rise in the professional service occupations (mostly professional persons), which increased at the rate of 95.6 percent during these twenty years. This figure included increases among such occupations as teachers, lawyers, and social workers. The public service occupations also were growing rapidly, at the rate of 77.2 percent, for the 1910–1930 period, with increases in white-collar as well as manual occupations. Taking the state and municipal civil service separately, the rate of increase (104 percent) was greater than that for most of the other occupational divisions. This was one of the most rapidly expanding categories. Trade also showed growth during this period (56.1 percent). Clerks and proprietors were increasing the fastest in this field (73.2 percent and 49.7 percent respectively), while manual workers increased at the slowest rate (11.5 percent). In the transportation and communication category the increase was 57.7 percent, with the same pattern emerging.

This was the situation in New York State up to the time of the Depression—a continuing increase in the white-collar and proprietary fields and, among manual workers, in the higher-skilled positions. There was also a particularly substantial growth in clerical, professional service, and civil service occupational divisions. The expanding socioeconomic and occupational categories, which provided greater job opportunities up to 1930, for the most part also did so during the Depression.

THE DEPRESSION TRENDS

Of the industrial divisions for New York City (see table 1), the manufacturing and mechanical exhibited the highest percentage of unemployment at the beginning of the Depression.[4] The majority of people in this industry were manual rather than white-collar workers, although it cannot be determined whether it was the skilled, semi-skilled, or unskilled workers who formed the bulk of the unemployed. Specifically, within this category, the building industry showed 18.6 percent of its gainful workers out of a job. Public service, at 1.1 percent, had the smallest percentage of its workers unemployed and was the most stable industrial grouping, the least affected by the Depression at this time. This category included all civil service occupations. Professional service and trade also proved to be relatively stable.

In terms of persons laid off from their jobs, the manufacturing category was again the highest (2.1 percent), public service the lowest (.1 percent). Relief figures for 1934 substantiate this picture of selective unemployment. Using data from the 1930 census and an urban relief survey of 1934, the Works Progress

Table 1. Unemployment by Industry in New York City, 1930

Industry	% of gainful workers unemployed and seeking work
Manufacturing and mechanical	10.1
Transportation and communication	5.8
Domestic and personal service	5.3
Trade	4.1
Professional service	4.1
Public service	1.1

SOURCE: United States, Department of Commerce, Bureau of the Census, *Fifteenth Census of the United States, 1930: Unemployment*, 1:709–10.

NOTE: Nonurban industries such as mining and agriculture were excluded from this table, although they were included in the census data.

Administration (W.P.A.) was able to produce statistics which indicated how various industries were affected by the Depression[5] (see table 2).

As table 2 shows, the manufacturing and mechanical industries indicated a much higher proportion of workers on relief than would be expected from their percentage of all gainful workers. This was the most severely affected industrial category. Public service, professional service, and trade were under-represented in the relief column. The others were approximately the same as their share of all gainful workers. More specifically, within these general categories, only the building and construction industry (part of the manufacturing and mechanical division) showed a particularly disproportionate percentage of workers on relief (20.2 percent of all workers on relief but only 7.5 percent of all gainful workers).[6] This is not to say that some occupations were unaffected by the Depression. By the end of the 1930s all had been affected, although in varying degrees.[7]

According to the 1940 census which surveyed the labor force in New York City (see table 3), the industry with the largest percentage of its experienced workers seeking employment was construction (considered separately in this survey), with 31.3 percent.[8] Professional and public service (government) were still relatively secure. Within the professional category, the educational services reported a figure of 6.1 percent of their workers seeking employment. Within the government category, state and local government reported a figure of 3.5 percent.

It is also necessary to look at occupational groupings to determine how severely each industry and worker was affected. The 1934 relief survey indicated that certain occupations in New York City were more adversely affected than others by the Depression.[9] All occupations (white-collar and manual) associated

Table 2. Relief by Industry in New York City, 1934

Industry	% of all gainful workers, 1930	% of all workers on relief, 1934
Manufacturing and mechanical	35.3	49.8
Transportation and communication	10.9	10.2
Trade	24.2	17.4
Domestic and personal service	14.1	15.5
Professional service	8.8	4.8
Public service	2.3	.7

SOURCE: United States, Works Progress Administration, Division of Social Research, *Urban Workers on Relief: The Occupational Characteristics of Workers on Relief in 79 Cities, May, 1934* (by Katherine D. Wood), part 2 (Washington, D.C.: Government Printing Office, 1937), p. 99.

NOTE: Nonurban industries were excluded from this table although they were included in the relief survey.

Table 3. Unemployment by Industry in New York City, 1940

Industry[a]	% of experienced workers seeking work
Manufacturing	12.6
Construction	31.3
Transportation and communication	9.4
Wholesale and retail trade	11.7
Finance, insurance, and real estate	7.9
Business and repair services	13.5
Personal services	12.0
Amusement, recreation, and related services	25.8
Professional and related services	6.1
Government	3.5

SOURCE: United States, Department of Commerce, Bureau of the Census, *Sixteenth Census of the United States, 1940: Population: The Labor Force,* 3:460–61.

NOTE: Persons on public emergency work such as W.P.A. were not included in the census data.

[a]Nonurban industries were excluded from this table, although they were included in the census data.

with the construction industry showed a disproportionately high relief percentage in that the occupation indicated a higher proportion of all workers on relief than it did of all gainful workers.[10] All semiskilled factory operatives in such industries as clothing were also over-represented. The same was true of most unskilled laborers and workers such as longshoremen and chauffeurs and truck drivers. Occupations which were under-represented in relief included most skilled workers not associated with construction, including bakers and tailors, and most white-collar and proprietary positions such as clerks, salesmen, proprietors and retail dealers in trade, and teachers. Public service workers also were under-represented. The vulnerability of certain occupations, of the manual more than the white-collar and proprietary, and of the unskilled more than the skilled is further illustrated by the 1940 occupational statistics.

Table 4 shows that unskilled laborers fared the worst, while those in the protective service and proprietary category were least subject to unemployment during the Depression. Most occupations in professional work also indicated low percentages, although musicians and entertainers showed a high rate of unemployment within this category and drove this figure up. As the trend has already indicated, all occupations (white-collar and manual) associated with construction had higher percentages of its workers unemployed. For example, among proprietors, managers, and officials, those in manufacturing (3.3 percent) and in wholesale (4.1 percent) and retail trade (4.2 percent) were in a better position than those in construction (8.6 percent). In the craftsmen category, machinists and toolmakers (9.5 percent) and tailors and furriers (14.8 percent) were in a

Table 4. Unemployment by Occupation in New York City, 1940

Occupation[a]	% of experienced workers seeking work
Professional and semiprofessional workers	9.5
Proprietors, managers, and officials (excluding farm)	4.6
Clerical, sales, and kindred workers	11.5
Craftsmen, foremen, and kindred workers	16.9
Operatives and kindred workers	14.5
Domestic service workers	11.9
Protective service workers	8.9
Service workers (other than domestic and protective)	11.8
Laborers	27.1

SOURCE: United States, Department of Commerce, Bureau of the Census, *Sixteenth Census of the United States, 1940: Population: The Labor Force*, 3:363–65.

NOTE: Persons on public emergency work were not included in the census tabulation.

[a]Ncnurban occupations were excluded from this table although they were included in the census data.

relatively more secure occupation than those with construction skills, such as carpenters (25.3 percent) and plasterers and cement finishers (30.8 percent). This was also true among unskilled laborers.

Except for a few occupations such as musicians (27.2 percent) and some fields in clerical and sales such as shipping clerks (16.9 percent), the white-collar and proprietary categories and those who could be identified in civil service indicated the lowest percentages seeking work. This would include teachers (5.4 percent), proprietors, managers, and officials in retail trade (4.2 percent), and firemen and policemen (1.6 percent), classified in protective services. By the 1940 census, skilled workers did not fare better than the semiskilled except in the service fields, but both were in a better position than the unskilled. The Depression therefore mainly struck hardest at the industrial, occupational, and socioeconomic categories which had offered fewest opportunities before. However many workers in all occupations were adversely affected. For example, the proportion of the total population of the City who were gainfully employed declined from 46 percent in 1930 to 38 percent in 1940. In 1935 one out of every three workers who had been gainfully occupied in 1930 was unemployed. Relief figures also indicated the extent of the economic collapse. The peak period for relief in New York City was October 1935. After this date a downward trend began, continuing until the end of 1937, when relief figures again began to rise and continued to do so into 1938 during the so-called Roosevelt Recession. Relief numbers, however, never again reached the 1935 peak.[11] Not until the Second World War period could the Depression be considered over. By 1943 there was a substantial increase in the number of factory wage earners, and essentially in the employment of practically all the employable labor.[12]

With this background, we can now look at where the various ethnic groups fit into the occupational structure and determine whether this had any effect on the development of conflict.

ITALIAN AND JEWISH OCCUPATIONS: THE EARLY YEARS

The Italians, predominantly of peasant background, found themselves mainly in the unskilled laboring class during their early years in America. According to reports of the Immigration Commission in 1911, of 1,471,659 Italian immigrants admitted to the United States in the 1899–1910 period and reporting an occupation, 34.5 percent were considered in the category of farm laborer and 42.5 percent as general laborers. Only 14.6 percent were classified as having a skilled occupation. A 1903 immigration study noted that only .2 percent of Italian immigrants had been engaged in professional occupations in Italy; 12.7 percent had been employed in trades or industry and 64.9 percent had worked in agricultural positions. The remaining 22.2 percent were women and children.[13]

According to an analysis of the Immigration Commission's data from the 1900 census, among the foreign-born Italian males in the United States who were skilled, the concentration was strongest in the occupations of tailor and mason (brick and stone). This would indicate movement into the clothing and building fields. For all immigrant Italian males (skilled and unskilled) the occupation of greatest over-representation was that of peddler. Laborers also showed a significant overconcentration of Italians.[14]

The Immigration Commission reported in 1911 that among the ethnic groups in the City, the Italians had the highest proportion of common laborers, with the Irish in second place. It has also been noted, however, that by 1911 Italians made up more than a majority of the City's barbers and "more than one-third of the [City's] boot and shoemakers and repairers," both skilled trades. Growing numbers of this ethnic group also entered the longshoremen trade. In addition many Italians were becoming merchants who operated fruit stands, bakerys, or wine shops in the early years of the twentieth century. There was also a slight entry into clerical positions by the Italian second generation as of 1905.[15]

The Jews, arriving at essentially the same time, were more ably fitted for entrance into an occupational structure that was becoming more oriented to the higher-skilled and white-collar positions. The Immigration Commission reports of 1911 noted that of 590,267 Jewish immigrants admitted between 1899 and 1910 and reporting an occupation, 67.1 percent were considered skilled, while only 13.7 percent were either farm or nonfarm laborers. The Jews were skilled or semiskilled in industrial work and entered the United States in such occupations as furriers, tailors, dressmakers and seamstresses, watchmakers, and milliners. Almost half of the skilled were in the garment trades. An analysis of the Immigration Commission's data from the 1900 census revealed that foreign-born Russians (Jews) were over-represented as tailors, peddlers, tobacco and cigar factory operatives and merchants (except wholesale). Also the proportion of this group "in the professions was high for the non-English speaking immigrants." A view of the 1905 New York Eastern European Jewish occupational structure further indicates their movement into clerical work (by both first and second generation) and their involvement in various skilled trades such as housepainting and carpentry.[16]

One historian who traced Italian and Jewish individual occupational mobility from 1880 to 1915 noted that although both groups were upwardly mobile, the Jews were moving faster into white-collar positions and had a larger percentage of their workers in this category than the Italians. The background of the Jewish and Italian immigrants is important for understanding their occupational position within the City during the 1930s.[17] The Jews, more so than the Italians, were the group who emerged as the major competitors for some of the more stable upper-level jobs held by the older ethnics. This is explained both by differences in the occupational positions of the Jews and Italians upon their arrival in America and by differences in their attitudes toward education.

JEWISH AND ITALIAN EDUCATIONAL VIEWS

The Jews have traditionally considered education and scholastic achievement to be of great value. Because learning has given the Jewish individual an enhanced status within the community, the school was always an important institution to this ethnic group. Even during the early settlement period, school officials considered Jewish children to be excellent scholars.[18]

In the southern Italian culture, however, a different sentiment existed toward schools and formal education. The agricultural economy of this region made the child's labor important to the sustenance of the family. Therefore, there was no time or need for schooling. Education represented an alien undertaking intended only for priests and the upper class. While education did not benefit the peasant in any way, it could threaten him by jeopardizing family unity. For example, since priests were removed from their families for schooling, the desire to keep the family intact militated against extensive education in this direction. Beyond this, the school system in southern Italy was inadequate and controlled by people who had little interest in uplifting the peasantry. Therefore, many South Italians who entered America were illiterate.[19]

The fears did not abate when Southern Italians arrived in America. They held the same hostilities to schooling, for basically the same reasons. Schools prevented children from securing jobs and therefore from contributing to the family income. The number of unskilled jobs available during the early years of Italian arrival made both children and parents consider schooling to be unnecessary. Moreover, many Italian immigrants still felt concern that school would alienate the child from the family and inculcate him with ideas "contrary to all Italian codes of proper family life." (This, of course, was experienced to some degree by all immigrant families who were concerned about the schools' Americanizing influence and its contempt for the immigrant culture.) It was also feared that education might have the effect of diminishing a boy's masculinity by precluding him from working, since nonmanual jobs were not considered work.[20] This attitude toward nonmanual jobs was particularly significant in relation to the preponderance of Italians in manual rather than white collar jobs in the 1930s.

Whatever the motivation for the Italian response to education, the effects were notable. In the early settlement years, the Italian child was considered a poor student who had difficulty with academic subjects. Truancy among this ethnic group was significant. The problems with schooling continued. A Board of Education study in 1926 noted that only 11.1 percent of Italian-Americans who entered high school graduated.[21] Efforts to increase the level of education among Italian children met with continued apathy in the Italian community. An Education Committee of the New York State Sons of Italy was set up in the late 1920s, yet no money was forthcoming from the state body. An attempt by the City to change the plans for a school in an Italian community from academic to vocational was met with apathy among the Italians, who did not care whether the school was academic or vocational. Yet there was interest in education by those in the Italian community who were already well-educated, as well as a feeling of inferiority concerning educational achievement. This is best illustrated by an article in the *Casa Italiana Bulletin* (associated with Columbia University), which noted that "students of Italian origin are attending High School in ever increasing numbers. They are learning to hold their own very effectively not only on the athletic field but in scholarship as well." The article went on to declare that two Italian boys graduated from DeWitt Clinton High School with a grade average above 90 percent. "We have evidence," the article noted, "that this is neither an accident nor an isolated fact."[22]

The effects of the Italian and Jewish attitudes toward education were illustrated by a Welfare Council of New York study in 1935 based on a sample of the population of the City in the 16- to 24-year-old age group. The report stated that the "youth of Italian parentage deviate considerably from youth of native parentage as regards . . . the extent of school attendance. . . . Both boys and girls of Italian stock have the smallest proportion of any white group attending school." The same report noted that the foreign stock Jews have almost as high a proportion of their youth in schools and colleges as those youth with native parents. A part of this 1935 survey which was published earlier commented that the rate of college graduation was four times greater among Jewish boys than among non-

Jews.[23] The Italian and Jewish attitudes toward education and their involvement with the schools had a direct effect on their occupational positions.

Also important in determining the Italian's place in the occupational hierarchy was the initial desire of many immigrants to return to Italy, thereby preventing them from taking an active interest in improving their lot in America. Italians, unlike the Jews, did not at first join the growing unions which were striving to provide better living conditions, although many did so later on. While self-help mutual benefit societies, organized to aid the immigrants, were found in both Italian and Jewish communities, the Jews, with financial support from earlier German Jewish immigrants, were able to extend more benefits to their population.

THE DEPRESSION YEARS: ITALIANS AND JEWS

The basic weakness in the Italian occupational structure was obvious during the initial immigration period as well as in the 1930s. Tables 5 and 6, which list the occupations of Italian-born fathers of children born in New York in 1916 and 1931, suggests the significant percentage of unskilled laborers dominating the

Table 5. Occupations: Italian-born Fathers of Children Born in New York City in 1916

	Number	Percent
Laborer	15,905	50.4
Tailor	1,697	5.4
Barber	1,667	5.3
Shoemaker	909	2.9
Carpenter	651	2.1
Longshoreman	596	1.9
Driver	546	1.7
Coal man	325	1.0
Businessman	289	.9
Mechanic	278	.9
Other[a]	8,663	27.5
Total	31,556	100.0

SOURCE: John J. D'Alesandre, "Occupational Trends of Italians in New York City," *Italy America Monthly* 2 (1935):15.

[a]Includes a series of twenty-eight occupations such as cook, baker, painter, bricklayer, and printer, none of which amounts to more than 0.8 percent.

Table 6. Occupations: Italian-born Fathers of
Children Born in New York City in 1931

	Number	Percent
Laborer	5,321	31.4
Barber	850	5.0
Tailor	713	4.2
Shoemaker	633	3.7
Chauffeur	608	3.6
Carpenter	429	2.5
Ice dealer	392	2.3
Painter	379	2.2
Mechanic	363	2.1
Plasterer	306	1.8
Other[a]	6,951	41.2
Total	16,945	100.0

SOURCE: John J. D'Alesandre, "Occupational Trends of Italians in New York City," *Italy America Monthly* 2 (1935):15.
[a]Includes a series of twenty-nine occupations such as longshoremen, clerk, salesman, baker, and bricklayer, none of which amounts to more than 1.5 percent. Proprietors were only 0.5 percent.

Italian occupational scene in both years.[24] In 1916 laborers represented 50.4 percent of the list; by 1931 the largest category was still that of laborer, although it had decreased to 31.4 percent. This decline may have been the result of the Depression, which, by devastating the construction industry, decreased the need for laborers in this field and caused an unwilling exodus into other occupations. It is also notable that more Italian-born fathers were found in skilled occupations by 1931. Plasterers (1.8 percent) and painters (2.2 percent) appear in the top ten occupations by 1931. Mechanics, who in 1916 made up .9 percent of the total, were 2.1 percent in 1931.

By indicating a higher percentage of workers in skilled positions than before, the Italian immigrant occupational structure in 1931 fits the general City and State pattern. However, as compared to the City's other ethnic groups, as will be noted later, the Italian position was still not an economically strong one. Immigrant Italians classified as laborers or as workers in the construction trades numbered 41.6 percent of this list. Nearly half of the Italian-born fathers in 1931 were in occupations which were severely affected by the Depression.

Other studies reveal that during the 1930s the Italians were mainly in skilled, semiskilled, and unskilled manual occupations, while the Jews were represented not only in skilled and semiskilled work but also in managerial and employer positions.

The Welfare Council of New York, through their 1935 study, was able to determine the usual occupations of the fathers of the youths in the sample. Of those fathers born in Russia (whom the survey identified as Jewish), 3.8 percent were professionals and 31.8 percent of the 1,642 in the sample were proprietors, managers, and officials.[25] The clerical division made up 6.8 percent, the skilled 23.1 percent, and the semiskilled 29.8 percent of the Jewish sample. Jews in service occupations numbered 2.1 percent. Only 2.6 percent of the Jewish fathers were listed as unskilled. In the same study, 1.1 percent of a sample of 1,964 Italians were listed as professionals, 17 percent as proprietors, managers, and officials, 2.8 percent in clerical positions, 23.3 percent as skilled, 27.8 percent as semiskilled, and 23.4 percent unskilled. There were also 4.6 percent in the service category. It is evident on the basis of this study that the Jews were strongly represented in managerial and proprietary positions as well as in skilled and semiskilled occupations. The Italians also had concentrated in skilled and semiskilled work but still had many in the unskilled category. The Welfare Council report noted that "almost twice as many of the youth of Italian parentage as of the other foreign stock has fathers whose usual occupation was in unskilled labor."[26]

Similar conclusions could be reached by considering just the youth. With data based on the 1935 survey, it was noted that "Jews, both male and female, had a greater proportion of employed youth in professional, clerical, and managerial work than did non-Jews." For example, although the Jewish youth comprised 33 percent of those in the 16- to 24-year-old age group who were employed, they represented "56 percent of the youth of this age group employed in proprietary and managerial work, 43 percent of those in clerical and sales positions, [and] 37 percent of youth in the professions." Among the skilled and semiskilled, Jewish youth comprised 24 percent, with 10 percent unskilled and 5 percent in service occupations. The study also noted that the Jewish youth were more likely than the non-Jews to be working at a job "of a higher socio-economic grade than that of the parent."[27] All reports on Jewish employment, for youth and others, indicated a predilection for white-collar positions, particularly in proprietary, clerical, sales, and professional occupations.

The effects of these occupational choices can be seen in the unemployment and relief figures. There was less unemployment among Jewish youth than among the non-Jews—a situation attributed to the higher educational position of the Jews. Italians, among all white groups, had the highest proportion of their youth unemployed. Similarly, Jewish youth on relief numbered 12.2 percent of the total Jewish sample, while relief among Italian youth reached 21 percent. Looking at families on relief, we see that 12 percent of the Jewish youth were in such families, compared with 15 percent of the non-Jewish white youth.[28]

This, of course, does not indicate that Jews as a group were unaffected by the Depression. Since Jews were found in many industries, particularly the apparel trades, which were hard hit by the Depression, they also suffered. In fact, by December 1937, during the recession, Jewish gainful workers, comprising 27.4 percent of all gainful workers in the City, were 33.3 percent of the total gainful workers unemployed.[29] However, the advantageous position of the Jewish youth and the fact that many Jews were in the relatively more stable white-collar and proprietary positions and in skilled rather than unskilled work gave the impression to some that the Jews were not affected by the Depression. Also notable in perpetuating this impression was the fact that many Jews were employers, controlling or dominating a number of industries in the City.

The Jewish occupational structure of New York City was studied further in 1937 by the Committee on Economic Adjustment of the American Jewish Committee and the Conference on Jewish Relations, using figures obtained from trade associations and labor unions. The report revealed that 25.4 percent of the 924,258 Jewish gainful workers, both immigrants and native-born, were engaged in manufacturing. The other major categories included 25.7 percent in trade, 10.9 percent in domestic and personal service, 7.4 percent in professional work, 5.2 percent in construction, and 13.5 percent unemployed. Small percentages of Jews were scattered in such categories as finance, transportation, public service, amusement, and public utilities.[30]

These figures become more meaningful when it is noted that Jews predominated as employers rather than as employees. While the Jews owned almost two-thirds of the 34,000 factories in New York City, they composed only one-third of the workers. In trade, the Jews were the proprietors of two-thirds of the 103,854 wholesale and retail establishments, but only 37.8 percent of the workers were Jewish. The Jews also constituted two-thirds of the owners of 11,000 restaurants and lunchrooms (classified under domestic and personal service) but only 15 percent of the workers were of this group. Even in construction, 4,000 of the 10,000 builders were Jewish, although this group made up only 14.4 percent of the gainful workers in this field. The study concluded that there was a concentration of Jews in employer and semi-employer categories "where they have at least a measure of independence."[31] A number of these businesses were small enterprises.

In a number of situations, Jewish employers dominated industries which employed an increasing number of Italian workers. For example, in the men's clothing industry by 1938 the Italians represented the largest single group of workers, while the executives and foremen in the factories were predominantly Jewish. This situation was also true in other areas of the clothing industry. Many unions which had large numbers of Italian members found their work to be dependent on Jewish contractors and manufacturers. This was true in such unions as the Painters Brotherhood local 874, the International Ladies Garment Workers Union local 89, and the Bedding local 140 of the United Furniture Workers of

America. Of course there were also a number of unions and industries dominated by Italians with little dependence on Jews. These would include the Transportation and Communications workers (particularly longshoremen) and the barbers union. However, the occupational areas in which Italians were dependent on Jews and saw themselves in lower status positions was plentiful enough to have caused an undercurrent of Italian resentment based on envy of Jewish success. Resentment related to general Depression frustrations may also have existed as a product of the widespread unemployment among Italian youth during the economic collapse. Some Jewish resentment against Italians was evident too because of the competition between the two groups for jobs in such areas as the ladies garment industry. As the number of Italians in the union and industry grew and the number of Jews decreased, the resentment increased.[32]

While Jews predominated as employers, they also dominated certain areas within specific occupational categories such as professional work. Jews in professional service, according to the 1937 study, made up 7.4 percent of the total Jewish gainful workers, while only 6.6 percent of all gainful workers were in professional service in New York. Jews especially were concentrated in medicine, law, and dentistry. A study of Jewish lawyers in New York notes that in the period 1930–34 there was an increase in the number of Jewish lawyers admitted to the bar, with the most being admitted in 1931; these people had begun their law studies before the Depression. Specifically, while 27.9 percent of all lawyers admitted to the bar prior to 1935 were admitted in the 1930–34 period, 41.5 percent of the Jewish lawyers were admitted during this period. An upsurge of Jews entering the law profession occurred at the same time the Depression was forcing some lawyers into unemployment.[33] However, these Jewish lawyers were able to enter readily the expanding civil service, which, because of admission changes brought about by Mayor Fiorello La Guardia, was increasingly open to people with an education.

Although Jewish occupational success caused some difficulties in intergroup relations with their co-arrivals, it posed a more serious problem to relations with the already established and older ethnic groups who were watching their hard-won gains being destroyed by the Depression.

GERMANS AND IRISH: A COMPARISON

The Depression had seriously affected all the ethnics, but the older groups, because they had worked for so long to attain their position in society, felt the shock of the economic collapse more severely. One of the great misfortunes of this period was that the Jews, and to a lesser extent the Italians, emerged once again as strong competitors at about the same time that the country was hurled into the Depression.[34]

In the early years of Jewish and Italian immigration, and continuing into the twentieth century, both the Irish and Germans had faced job competition from the newer groups. In the construction trades, as unskilled laborers and as longshore-men, the Irish and Italians were rivals for positions. Italians had also competed with the Irish for unskilled city jobs. In the apparel trades German and Irish workers became less important in an industry increasingly dominated by Jews and Italians. However, because the Germans as a group were in a stronger occupational and economic position than the Irish, less friction with the new-comers was generated by the economic issue, even with increasing job competition.[35]

Even during the period of first settlement in the mid-nineteenth century, the Germans exhibited a superior occupational level.[36] A report of the Immigration Commission substantiates this point for a later period by noting that of the Germans entering in the 1899–1910 period and reporting an occupation, 30 percent of the 458,293 immigrants were skilled, as compared to only 12.6 percent of the 376,268 Irish arriving and reporting an occupation. There were other indications of German and Irish occupational positions as well. An analysis of the 1890 census, which indicated the occupations of the foreign-born workers, revealed that the Germans (males) were particularly concentrated in the manufac-turing category as brewers, food industry workers (for example, bakers and butchers), clothing workers (tailors, seamstresses), and skilled craftsmen such as basket- and cabinetmakers, gunsmiths and locksmiths, trunk makers, and piano makers and tuners. There was also a significant German concentration in the occupation of saloon keeper.[37]

The foreign-born Irish (males) in 1890 were mainly concentrated "in domestic and personal service, as watchmen [and policemen], nurses, soldiers, janitors, laborers, sextons, [and] servants." Other occupations with a significant Irish concentration were porters, foremen, hostlers, saloon keepers, and gas works and street railway employees. The Irish in general were under-represented in the skilled occupations, although they did have some concentrations in such skilled positions as stone masons and plasterers. Compared to the total white population and to the other immigrant groups, the Irish also had a higher propor-tion of their workers in government work; they were well represented in factory labor, too.[38]

Analysis of the Immigration Commission's data from the United States census of 1900 provides similar information. The German male immigrant was mainly employed in manufacturing; the Irish male immigrant's main employ-ment was in domestic and personal service. In terms of specific occupations (listed in order of concentration), the German immigrants were found in the category of tailors, saloon keepers and bartenders, tobacco and cigar factory operatives, and boot- and shoemakers and repairers. The Irish immigrants (again in order of concentration) were found in the categories of servants and waiters, masons (brick and stone), saloon keepers and bartenders and laborers. This employment pattern for the Germans reveals a stronger occupational structure which was better geared to the coming trend toward more highly skilled occupations. Second-generation Germans in 1900 show a continued concentration in skilled and semi-skilled labor, and second-generation Irish indicate a movement into the skilled and semi-skilled fields. The Germans (in order of concentration) were found in the categories of tobacco and cigar factory operatives, saloon keepers and bartenders, printers, lithographers and pressmen, and salesmen. They had also shown increases as bookkeepers and accountants, clerks, and in the building trades. The Irish noted great diversification in occupations by the second generation and were found in a number of skilled occupations. In order of concentration, they were primarily in the categories of building trades, both skilled and unskilled, saloon keepers and bartenders, textile mill operatives (except cotton), and teamsters. There were notable increases in such occupations as bookkeepers and accountants, clerks, and salesmen. However, the Irish also continued to show a generally weaker occupational structure than the Germans. For example, although Irish concentration in the unskilled laboring class had decreased, laborers were still slightly more common among the second-generation Irish than among the total second-generation population. Among Germans, the figure indicated an under-representation in this occupational division. The same pattern was true for both groups in the category of servants and waiters.[39] Both ethnic communities were to find many of their workers in upper-level and skilled occupations by the Depression era, although the Germans, as a group, still seemed to be in a stronger position by the 1930s. The Irish, however, had entrenched themselves in such sought-after areas as civil service.

The Welfare Council study on the youth of New York offers some proof of this assertion by providing data on foreign-born fathers in 1935. Of 272 German-born fathers in the sample, 4 percent were professionals, 26.5 percent were proprietors, managers, and officials, 9.5 percent were clerical, 11.8 percent were service, 28.3 percent skilled, 16.9 percent semi-skilled, and 2.6 percent unskilled. Among the 388 Irish in the sample, only 1.3 percent were professionals, 9.8 percent proprietors, managers, and officials, 6.2 percent clerical, 6.2 percent service, 36.8 percent skilled, 27.6 percent semi-skilled, and 12.1 percent unskilled.[40] If these figures can be taken as an indication of the general German and Irish occupational structure, then a larger percentage of Germans were in the more stable occupational categories during the Depression era, especially as professionals and proprietors, managers and officials; and a smaller percentage were in the devastated unskilled area. Although census data on what specific industries or occupations the manual workers of each group were concentrated in is not available, other evidence notes a strong Irish presence in the hard-hit construction industry and in longshoremen and teamster positions.[41] On the basis of the 1935 data, the Germans compared well with the Jews, and both showed a stronger occupational structure than either the Irish or Italians. The only difference was the presence of the Irish in such relatively stable fields as teaching and civil service.

This general picture, however, does not fully explain the ethnic tensions associated with the economic factor. One cannot assume that all Germans were in a better economic position than all Irish simply because the overall occupational level of the Germans was superior. Many Germans were in job categories severely affected by the Depression. Moreover, some German-American neighborhoods in the City, such as Ridgewood, Queens, were poorer (classified as lower-middle- and lower-class) in 1940 than areas such as Fordham in the Bronx, where many Irish lived (classified as middle- and lower-middle-class).[42] Both areas had been downwardly mobile during the 1930s.

Interestingly, in even the poorer German communities little evidence of an economic factor in the conflict with the Jews could be found, while it was noticeable in all Irish neighborhoods. Although surely some German economic resentments existed, for various reasons it did not find expression on a group level or in the press. The Nazi German-American Bund tried to make an issue of Jewish occupational gains, but it seemed to arouse no interest in the German community. Jews were criticized a number of times in the German-American press, but no mention was made of Jewish occupational competition or success. Although there was evidence of conflict with the Jews in German neighborhoods, there is no basis for stating that these actions were directed against the Jews because of economic resentments. Other issues, such as the anti-Nazi boycott discussed in chapter 4, form the basis of German-Jewish conflict. To understand why even the poorer Germans did not react to this issue, one must note that there was little direct economic competition between these groups and therefore little identification of the Jews as realistically threatening the German economic position. However, even general Depression resentments were not aimed at the Jews. After the "Roosevelt Recession," when bitterness over the new economic collapse brought to the surface the realistic and unrealistic components of the economic factor in the conflict between the Irish and Jews, the Germans as a group did not express these feelings.[43] Perhaps by 1938 sensitivity to the Nazi issue and to expressing overt anti-Semitic statements muted these attitudes. Fearful of being labeled Nazis at a time when American public opinion was reacting against Germany and its policies, and having within their City both a vocal and embarrassing Bund chapter and a large and powerful Jewish community ready to retaliate against those thought to be Nazis, most German-Americans, while perhaps sharing with the Irish these resentments, did not express them or otherwise act them out. There was also, in contrast to the Irish community, no respectable leader of the Germans who voiced the economic grievances. Of course, some German-Americans expressed these attitudes by joining anti-Semitic organizations, but few were involved.

DISPLACEMENT OF THE IRISH AND OTHER ETHNIC PROBLEMS

The Irish on the whole not only were harder hit by the Depression than the Germans but also were more concentrated in jobs which were particularly sought after by the newer ethnics. The Irish had a definite penchant for civil service jobs, politics, law, and the church. Caroline Ware, in her study of Greenwich Village, notes that the Irish who lived there had a definite rating scale of occupations. Janitors, watchmen, and scrubwomen were at the nadir of the economic and social ladder. At the next level were longshoremen, auto mechanics, truckdrivers, and some occupations within the building trades. Policemen, firemen, office workers, and other civil service posts were considered superior to positions at the longshoremen and artisan level. White-collar and city jobs were regarded as better than blue-collar positions. The occupations of politician, lawyer, real estate man, doctor, and clergyman were regarded as the pinnacle of the social ladder. For women, the most prestigious occupation was the teaching profession. According to Ware, "economic and occupational position gave a recognized status within the Irish community," and "all were constantly seeking to climb, or at least to maintain the position on the ladder which they had." Civil service jobs were recognized as a particularly important step upward and something to be desired for their children.[44] The close ties between the Irish and politics provided a steady flow of civil service jobs into the Irish community. However, the Irish were soon to lose their hold on these valued and relatively stable positions.

The election of Fiorello La Guardia as Mayor in 1933 provided a change in civil service appointments. Before the advent of La Guardia, Jews, Italians, and blacks had been discriminated against when applying for civil service jobs; most of the positions had gone to the Irish. Mayor La Guardia, however, increased the number of civil service jobs in the competitive category. In 1933, 54.5 percent of the city workers were in the competitive class; by 1939, 74.3 percent were within this group. The number of exempt (appointive) and noncompetitive jobs (requiring only a qualifying exam) were reduced. Furthermore, to take a minimum entrance exam for certain positions, a high school diploma was needed. According to one individual who was prominent in the Irish community during the 1930s, the educational requirement had the effect of eliminating many Irish, particularly of the first and second generations, who did not have the necessary schooling but nonetheless desired civil service jobs. Thus La Guardia managed to increase the number of non-Irish, notably the better-educated Jews, in the City's civil service. The working class Irish bore the brunt of this job loss, which came at a time when employment was hard to find. It was natural for them to feel resentment toward the Jews, who were the major competitors for these positions.[45] The La Guardia administration also made an effort to eliminate political influence and ethnic discrimination for those already in the civil service. Through job ratings and exams, employees were given the opportunity to rise in the civil service more on the basis of their abilities than political connections.

Within the teaching profession, so highly regarded by Irish women, there is also evidence to suggest that the Jews were displacing the other groups. One study based on a random sampling of teacher's names in the New York City school system noted that "the majority of teachers entering the system in the early years of the century were of Christian backgrounds and the majority of teachers entering the system since the late thirties have been of Jewish background.'' The study concluded that in 1914 only 22 percent of the teachers entering the school system were Jewish. The Jewish percentage had increased to 26 percent by 1920, 44 percent by 1930, and 56 percent by 1940.[46] It is clear, if this study's findings can be accepted, that teaching was one profession which the Jews were entering in significant numbers.

Who were the Christian teachers in the early years of the century? An Immigration Commission study in 1908–09, through the use of questionnaires, classified elementary school teachers in the City by nationality background. The report concluded that the first- and second-generation Irish made up 20.7 percent of the 14,900 teachers. The German foreign stock was 8.7 percent; the southern Italians were .12 percent; and the Jews made up 11.3 percent of this occupational group. The Jews and Irish were therefore the two main ethnic groups (excluding third-generation native-born of undetermined ethnic background) involved in the teaching profession in 1908–09.[47] Certainly the influx of Jews into this occupation served as competition for the Irish and others who wanted such jobs. Table 7 corroborates the other studies by noting when teachers who were serving in the Manhattan School system in 1937 first entered that system. While the majority of Jewish teachers received their jobs after 1920 (70.8 percent), the majority of Irish and German teachers entered the system before 1920 (57.5 percent and 60.7 percent respectively). By the 1920s and 1930s, not only were Jews entering the teaching profession as never before but (because of a declining birth rate, a population shift to the suburbs, decreased immigration, and the Depression) there were fewer teaching jobs available. The majority of jobs, however, as noted in the Cole study, were going to the Jews. What this meant, in terms of schools, can be illustrated by an example drawn from the South Bronx, an area which exploded in anti-Semitic hostilities in the late 1930s. At Public School 9 (138th and 139th streets, west of Brook Avenue), while only 7 percent of the student body was Jewish, 75 percent of the teachers were of this ethnic group. The area surrounding the school was mixed but predominantly Irish.[48]

Since the Irish were concerned about occupational status, the increased competition from the Jews in such areas as teaching, civil service, and law contributed to their resentments. Cultural differences also played a role in increasing tensions. There were also no mitigating factors, as with the Germans, which would have muted the expression of hostility on this point. The Irish were the main older group both to lose economic status because of the Depression and to face severe competition from the newer ethnics. According to various studies, the process of downward occupational mobility, by those who are concerned about status, results in "hostility feelings toward minority groups, who are engaged in bettering a lower social position or maintaining a newly-won higher status." These status-oriented, downwardly mobile individuals tend to be the most prejudiced. There is also a high degree of prejudice among those who are

Table 7. Sample of Teachers in Manhattan Public Schools in 1936–1937, by Ethnicity and the Years Entered into Teaching

Years of Entry into Teaching	% and number of Jews entering teaching before 1937		% and number of Irish entering teaching before 1937		% and number of Germans entering teaching before 1937		% and number of Italians entering teaching before 1937	
1890–1899	5.2	(8)	10.6	(17)	8.1	(5)	0	
1900–1909	10	(15)	22	(35)	31.1	(19)	0	
1910–1919	14.3	(22)	25	(40)	21.3	(13)	25	(6)
1920–1929	39.6	(61)	30	(48)	31.1	(19)	50	(12)
1930–1937	31.2	(48)	12.5	(20)	8.2	(5)	25	(6)
Total number in sample		154		160		61		24

SOURCE: New York City, Department of Education, *List of Members of Board of Education, Local School Boards, Officials, Employees and Supervising and Teaching Staff*, May 1936–March 1937 (New York: 1938) pp. 41–69.

NOTE: In this sample, ethnic identification of the teachers was based on their names. Any ethnically doubtful names were not counted. As an aid to ethnic name identification, the following were used. American Council of Learned Societies, *Report of the Committee on Linguistics and National Stocks in the Population of the United States*, in American Historical Association, *Annual Report, 1931* 4 (1931): 232–48, 271–305; Edward MacLysaght, *A Guide to Irish Surnames* (Baltimore: Geneological Book Company, 1964), and a list of 106 distinctive Jewish names kindly furnished by Dr. Fred Massarik, scientific director of the U.S. National Jewish Population Study. In this computation approximately every fifth Manhattan Public School was counted and included: P.S. 1, 5, 12, 31, 39, 50, 58, 72, 78, 84, 89, 94, 102, 121, 151, 160, 169, 188, 193, and J.H.S. 20, 65, 115, 136.

status- or mobility-oriented but who have failed to advance.[49] The increasing economic frustrations of the Irish and their attitudes towards the Jews were well reflected in their press and indicated an awareness of the struggle.

The *Brooklyn Tablet,* official diocese paper of Brooklyn, complained repeatedly during the 1930s that Catholics were being discriminated against and that anti-Christianity, not anti-Semitism, was the real problem in New York.[50] One editorial in the *Tablet* noted that Catholics in Brooklyn were underrepresented in the Emergency Relief Bureau and in many situations had been replaced or not hired.[51] Patrick Scanlan, managing editor of the *Tablet,* also urged Catholics to apply for civil service jobs in greater numbers in order to drive out the leftists. In the Irish press Leftists, Communists or Reds frequently meant Jewish liberals. Scanlan also stated that local people "without diplomas or fancy salaries" should administer relief.[52]

The fact that some jobs were going to the better-educated Jews irked the Irish, who found themselves at an occupational disadvantage just when jobs were scarce. In 1934 the *Gaelic American* appealed to Irish-American parents to let their children stay in school. The editorial stated that it was a mistake to consider a person educated when he finished elementary or high school. "To the credit of our Jewish fellow citizens," the paper continued, "it must be said that they take full advantage of these free educational facilities [city colleges]." In another instance of resentment and awareness of Jewish education, *Social Justice,* a paper read by many Irish, complained that the New York police, largely Irish, would soon have "Reds" placed over them by the Civil Service Commission. These "Reds," according to the paper, were college graduates who would now be given preference for promotion within the force. *Social Justice* continued by wondering whether now "a man must be up on his Greek, mathematics, zoology, astronomy and Hebrew before he can be a good cop." One interesting letter to the editor of the *Tablet* noted that of 2,734 names on a civil service eligibility list for the position of Social Investigator, "over 1,700 or 62 percent of these names are obviously Jewish. Less than 100 names are Irish. Such a result should give Catholic leaders pause for thought." The writer continued by asking whether anything could be done "or are Catholics doomed to exclusion from the field of Public Welfare as they have gradually been excluded from the field of Public Education?"[53]

The *Tablet* also complained about the lack of Catholics in the professions. Essentially, the Irish were upset that they had been in the City longer yet the Jews were surging ahead in the higher and more stable occupations. "Just look at the doctors' shingles in any neighborhood and behold how few Catholics are indicated," commented the *Tablet.* Scanlan asked, on one occasion, what the Jews had to complain about when "in the professions, civil service, schools and public life they are represented out of all proportion to their numbers." One Irish writer to the *Tablet,* noting that the Jews seem to control 75 percent of the professions, asked what Catholics can do to improve their lot.[54]

In the late 1930s one of the frequent complaints of the mainly Irish and violently anti-Semitic Christian Front, when they held their street-corner rallies, was that the Jews controlled all the good jobs and businesses. This thought was echoed by many of the anti-Jewish vandals, most of whom were Irish, who were arrested in the early 1940s.[55] It is clear that there was a feeling of displacement among the Irish, coupled with a growing resentment of Jewish success. The Depression, making certain occupations such as civil service more valuable, made the Irish all the more aware of Jewish competition and their own failings.

The Jews also had occupational problems at this time, but theirs were related primarily to discrimination. They had experienced discrimination many times before, but the 1930s was a unique era. A study conducted by the American Jewish Congress in 1938 noted that the frequency of anti-Jewish specifications in help-wanted ads was at an all-time high.[56] Attempts to limit the number of Jews in medical and other professional schools also increased during the 1930s.[57]

The discrimination of this period put the Jews into an extremely defensive and worried position. One Jewish periodical, noting that Jews were crowding into law and medical school, suggested that Jewish youth look to other professions.[58] It was thought that a dispersion of Jews into different fields would result in a decrease in occupational discrimination.

Because of these factors, as well as others, the Jews began to feel increasingly insecure and eventually reacted accordingly. The same feeling was evident among the Irish, who were also on the defensive. For the Germans, who were challenged less by the newer groups and seemingly hurt less by the Depression, economic resentment, for these and other reasons, remained muted (though probably present to some degree) and therefore less of a source of intergroup tension. The Italians, although still offering an economic challenge to the Irish in certain areas, posed a lesser threat than the Jews. Also the fact that this group had been seriously hurt by the Depression did not seem to evoke significant feelings of frustration and anger toward others, since, even with the economic collapse, they were showing signs of economic advancement.[59] The two main antagonists in relation to the tensions associated with ethnic succession, based on the economic factor, were the Irish and Jews. The economic situation was to be just one of the many points of friction which contributed to the intense conflict which emerged between these groups during the decade of the Depression.

Chapter Three

La Guardia and the New Ethnic Order

At the same time that economic rivalries between the ethnics became more severe, significant political changes were taking shape that were also to serve as a source of conflict. The Irish were beginning to realize during this period that new groups were assuming control of the City's power structure. The Irish sense of displacement increased as the Jews and Italians became more threatening. What was happening in the 1930s had occurred before. In the nineteenth century, it had been the Irish who challenged the older groups for political control. The New York Democratic party, and particularly Tammany (the Democratic party organization of New York County) which controlled it, became an Irish-run organization, and they remained its undisputed rulers until well into the 1930s. The Irish enjoyed their hard-won gains and came to feel that their political position was the natural order of things. George Olvany, who became Tammany leader in 1924, noted that "the Irish are natural leaders. The strain of Limerick keeps them at the top. They have the ability to handle men. Even the Jewish districts have Irish leaders. The Jews want to be ruled by them."[1] However, dissatisfaction with Irish control had been brewing for many years and reached its climax as a result of the Depression, which increased the desire for new leadership and a redistribution of political power. Seeing the Irish with the still lucrative and stable civil service positions was enough to generate discontent among the out-groups.

30

JEWISH AND ITALIAN DISCONTENT

The Democratic party in New York had made some concessions to the Jews and Italians, but as they grew in voting strength, they demanded more. The Jews particularly had been given a number of positions in an effort to prevent their defection to the Socialists and Republicans, and they were the first new group to be recognized by Tammany.[2] It was not unusual to find some Jewish district leaders (in Assembly districts similar to wards), state assemblymen, or senators and congressmen. The position of Borough President of Manhattan was usually given to a Jew after 1909 and they were also able to secure the governorship in 1932 with the election of Herbert H. Lehman. However, the Irish clearly dominated the party leadership and decisionmaking structure, and they determined which political positions the Jews would receive.

New York's minority parties provided more and earlier recognition as they bid for the new ethnic vote. Thus it was the Republican party which first supported an Italian for congressman and mayor (Fiorello La Guardia in both cases) and for U.S. senator (Edward Corsi in 1938). The Jews achieved prominence in the Socialist party and to a lesser extent in the Republican party. From 1911 to 1932 a Jew (Sam Koenig) was New York County Republican leader. This party also was the first to nominate Jews for governor (Albert Ottinger in 1928) and U.S. senator (George Z. Medalie in 1932). The Jews were also the main force behind the American Labor Party, which emerged in 1936. However, these parties remained in the minority category, and until the new groups secured more positions of power within the dominant Democratic organization based on what they considered their fair share, a great deal of discontent continued to be expressed.

The *Jewish Examiner* aptly noted in 1933 that the Jews, who constituted a significant percentage of the City's population, should be given more political positions or "the Jews awakening to a realization of the facts . . . will . . . correct it." An article in the *Brooklyn Jewish Center Review* unhappily noted that although the Jews composed 47 percent of Brooklyn's population, only 11 percent of the public officials were Jewish. A number of complaints were voiced about the lack of representation in district leader positions in various boroughs, judgeships, and particularly positions in the educational power structure. One letter to Mayor James J. Walker from a prominent Jewish leader complained that there were only two Jews among the thirty-six district superintendants of schools, although "there are over 6500 Jewish teachers." The *Jewish Examiner* noted that "by conservative estimates, one-third of all children attending the public schools in the metropolitan district are of Jewish parentage. . . . Putting it bluntly there should be more high school principals of Jewish faith." Some Jews were suggesting simply that a proportional representation in all city positions be based on ethnic population figures. The desire for more recognition continued throughout the 1930s, especially in the middle to latter part of the decade, when the increased anti-Semitism made Jews very sensitive to any hint of political discrimination in the selection of party nominees. Jewish discontent resulted in a persistent effort to secure greater power in the party by capturing the district leadership positions in areas with a majority Jewish population.[3]

While the Jews wanted increased political power, they already held considerable influence compared to the Italians, who were virtually left out of the political power structure. The Italian's lack of recognition was a product of the pre-1930 period, when this group was not as well-organized politically as the Jews. Although the dissatisfaction which pervaded both the Italian and Jewish communities interested Democratic party leaders, the Irish bosses were unable to satisfy both groups without giving up most of their own power, so they responded mainly to Jewish discontent in these early years. They simply were more fearful of the defection of the politically organized and regularly voting Jews. Italians, they found, were also more likely than Jews to give the Democrats a majority of their vote. Therefore their support did not have to be cultivated as much as the Jews, whose vote was split among a number of parties. The Italian vote went only to the Democrats and Republicans.[4] The result was a very slow political recognition of the Italians as well as some movement by them into the Republican party.

Although some Italians were placed in important political positions, this was usually done by the Irish bosses only in areas where there was serious competition for the Italian vote from the Republicans and where the community's discontent could not be assuaged in any other way.[5] For example, the Democrats chose James Lanzetta as their congressional candidate in 1932 in Italian East Harlem in order to oppose the popular La Guardia. Even with this policy, Italian involvement in important positions remained minimal, and they continued to lag behind the Jews. Alfred Santangelo, an Italian political leader, commented on this neglect when discussing his own background.

> Staten Island, where I grew up, was dominated by the Irish. The Congressman, the Senator and one or two Assemblymen were Irish. The other Assemblyman and the City Councilman were of German extraction. All the judges were Irish. No judge was of Italian descent. No Italian-American was considered for public office, although the Italian-Americans constituted about 25 per cent of the Staten Island population.

Not surprisingly, the Italians too desired some form of proportional representation based on ethnicity. *Il Progresso Italo-Americano*, New York's leading Italian-American newspaper, called for the appointment of an Italian-American to the position of Justice on the New York Supreme Court in the first judiciary district "in an effort to re-establish the just proportion according to our electoral strength in the District." The Italians also wanted their fair share. The main Italian thrust in the 1930s was an attempt to secure district leaderships in their population centers. This was an old ambition begun with little success in pre–World War I days. The Italians had long been eager to secure some political power.[6] During the 1930s, Italians did begin to move slowly into important positions until eventually, with Jewish help, they drove the Irish from their control of the party.

THE LA GUARDIA IMPACT

The political awakening of this group was tied closely to the career of one man—Fiorello H. La Guardia. Along with such men as Edward Corsi, the future mayor began organizing the Italians during the early 1920s into Republican clubs and eventually into his own political machine, the F. H. La Guardia Political Club.[7] Political organization, even as Republicans, led to political organization and recognition by the Democrats, but only after many years. Increasing ethnic awareness among Italians allowed La Guardia to secure office and eventually convinced the Democrats that they had to compete for this group's support. For example, when La Guardia ran for mayor in 1929, he did not get the endorsement of the pro-Tammany *Il Progresso*. By 1933, however, the newspaper was indicating support for him by urging the election of all candidates with Italian names.[8] The change had come as a result of the proof of corruption within Tammany ranks and the effect of the Depression.

La Guardia was able to convince the Italian-American community that in electing him they too would achieve recognition and power. It was a successful tactic, since many Italians, particularly after the Depression began, saw in La Guardia a possible solution to their political and economic frustrations. For example, when La Guardia was running for mayor in 1933, the *Sons of Italy Magazine* noted that "in helping to elevate one of our race to an important public office it must be remembered that we are helping ourselves and our individual aspirations for future realization.[9]

La Guardia did emerge as something of a solution for this group's problems, but moreso for the Jews, whose vote was initially more difficult to capture and therefore required special attention. In his 1933 mayoralty campaign, La Guardia, running on a Republican–City Fusion party ticket against a split Democratic party, supported an ethnically balanced slate of candidates in contrast to the predominantly Irish nominees that Tammany usually picked. With an Italian running for mayor, Bernard Deutsch, president of the American Jewish Congress, was chosen as the nominee for president of the Board of Aldermen, and W. Arthur Cunningham, a prominent Irish figure, was selected as the candidate for comptroller. Also for the first time, an Italian was given the nomination for a borough presidency: Joseph A. Palma, a Republican-City Fusion candidate, was soon to be the City's first Italian-American borough president (Staten Island).

La Guardia's tactics forced both the Democratic party and the Recovery party, made up of anti-Tammany Democrats, to balance their tickets; but they did so only in relation to the Jewish vote, which seemed the more significant and unstable.[10] While both the Tammany and anti-Tammany Democrats chose Irish mayoral candidates—John P. O'Brien and Joseph V. McKee respectively—the Jews were given the next highest position. The Democratic party nominated Milton Solomon as their candidate for president of the Board of Aldermen, and the Recovery party chose Nathan Straus, Jr., as their Jewish nominee for this post.[11] Italians also appeared on these tickets, but in lesser positions. For example, Ferdinand Pecora was the Recovery party's candidate for district attorney of Manhattan.

Even at the lower level of city posts, however, it was clearly La Guardia's Republican-Fusion slate that carried a larger number of candidates from the newer ethnic groups (although with the Jews predominating). For example, there were sixty-five positions open for the New York City board of aldermen. Twenty-five of the Democratic party nominees could be identified as Irish, six as Jewish, five as German, and three as Italian. The Republican-Fusion ticket carried only six who could be identified as Irish, fifteen as Jewish, three as German, and six as Italian. McKee's Recovery party, which only contested thirty-four out of the sixty-five aldermanic posts, nominated twelve Irish, four Jews, three Germans, and one Italian.[12] La Guardia was making his bid for the votes of the Italians and Jews. It also shows that these groups may have had easier access to candidacy than in the Irish-controlled Democratic and Recovery parties, where the Italians especially were still largely disregarded.

The election of La Guardia, the first Italian-American mayor of New York City, brought jubilation to the Italians. Torchlight parades and bonfires lit the streets of Italian neighborhoods. *Il Progresso* noted that La Guardia's victory was an Italian victory: "only a few years back we were in last place; today the Italians are able to decide the outcome of a great contest and bring Fiorello La Guardia to one of the highest and most valued public offices of this country."[13] Truly the Italian colony in New York felt it was beginning to arrive, and La Guardia was the one who was bringing them there.

The Irish reacted differently, and viewed with suspicion the elevation of an Italian to the post of mayor. A *Gaelic American* editorial sadly lamented the victory of an Italian over an Irish-American in "this most Irish of cities." In a very small article on the bottom of the first page the newspaper begrudgingly declared "La Guardia Elected Mayor of New York." Thus ended an era in the Irish control of New York politics—or at least this is how some of the Irish began to feel. In fact, some members of this ethnic group had already felt that they were not getting their fair share of patronage under John F. Curry's Tammany machine.[14] What would become of them under a Fusion Italian mayor?

The increasing political power of the new groups became apparent immediately, with some indication that the Irish were beginning to lose control. In 1926, at the start of Mayor Walker's administration, the board of estimate (including the mayor, comptroller, president of board of aldermen, and the five borough presidents) had consisted of five Irish, one German, and one Jew (identified out of eight members). By 1934 the ethnic composition of the board was three Irish, two Jews, and two Italians (again identified out of eight members). La Guardia's effort to provide openings for Jews and Italians—often at the expense of the Irish—which was evident in his campaign, continued into his years as mayor. One study of mayoral cabinet appointments noted that while the appointees of the two previous mayors (Walker and O'Brien) were approximately 25 percent and 41 percent Irish, respectively, La Guardia's were only 5 percent Irish. The Jews meanwhile dropped from about 9 percent of the appointees under Walker to 7 percent under O'Brien, and then rose to 15 percent under La Guardia. For the Italians, recognition was beginning. While Walker's appointees were only 1 percent Italian and O'Brien's were 3 percent, La Guardia gave about 5 percent of his appointments to Italians.[15]

Although both new groups increased their representation under La Guardia, the Jews, as under Tammany, continued to receive the larger share of upper-level appointments because of the importance of their vote and because of La Guardia's apparent over-confidence with his Italian support. By 1938 six out of nineteen department commissioners could be identified as Jewish and only one as Italian. Of course, La Guardia also provided new political recognition for the Italians. Among the lower-level city posts, such as deputy commissioner, or in the appointive court positions, Italians notably increased their representation. By his third term, for example, La Guardia had decided the appointments of all the city magistrates (since these officials served 10-year terms, it took this long for all the Tammany appointees to be replaced). As a result of the mayor's court appointments, seven Italians were serving as city magistrates by 1944, whereas in 1925, under Tammany, there had been only one. Jewish representation in these posts remained the same as under Tammany; however, the number of Irish decreased sharply.[16]

Elective offices, which were still largely dominated by the Democratic party, indicated a somewhat different pattern, since the Irish were able to retain their positions longer because of their continuing control of the Democratic organization. However, as with appointive positions, the Jews rather than the Italians received, as earlier, more of the important elective offices. For example, from 1922 to 1942 only four Italian Democrats from New York City served in the state senate, but in 1934 alone, six Jewish Democrats from the City were in the senate. By 1938 on the state executive level, the Democrats had allowed an Italian (Charles Poletti) to secure the lieutenant governor's position, but the state had had a Jewish governor since 1932.[17] Also the New York City congressional delegation in 1938 consisted of four Jews and only one Italian (all Democrats). Since the Irish retained their dominance in the delegation, as they had for a number of years, neither new group was able to increase their representation for a long time. However, the Jews continued to be awarded more positions than the Italians. Thus while the Irish held on to many of the elective positions, the Jews were still favored by the Democrats as the second-place group; the Italians, although moving up, still maintained a definite third place in representation. As for the Germans, in all areas of political life, their role had diminished significantly since World War I.

The mayor was quick to make political use of the changing ethnic-political scene, especially in his appeals to the Italians, who, moreso than the Jews, were starved for the positions which he now controlled. As his Italian Re-election Committee noted in 1937, "In New York City, the biggest Italian city in the world, we have with the Fusion administration begun to achieve the first genuine measure of representation in government. . . . A new day has arrived!" The Democrats were accused of shoving Italian candidates into the background.[18] In the early years of La Guardia's administration, this was the accepted view, since the Italians appreciated any recognition.

However, the Democrats, becoming more aware of Italian voting strength after La Guardia's victory, and desirous of wooing this vote away from the mayor, began to offer Italians some choice positions which previously had been denied. One of La Guardia's most significant achievements for the Italian community was in forcing the Democrats to acknowledge this group. Italian votes now became important enough to be rewarded with better positions. Of course, for the Irish this meant a further sharing of scarce political jobs; but it was unavoidable if they wanted to regain control of the mayor's office. Therefore, Peter Brancato, after being recommended by Frank Kelly, Democratic leader of Brooklyn, was appointed by Governor Lehman in 1935 as the first Italian county judge. Ferdinand Pecora, also appointed by Lehman in 1935, became only the third Italian in New York's history to serve on the State Supreme Court. In 1936 President Franklin D. Roosevelt, upon a recommendation from Kelly, appointed Matthew Abruzzo to the position of federal judge—the first time for an Italian to hold this post.[19] The more important district leaderships, with their patronage and decisionmaking powers and the higher-level nominations such as mayor or U. S. senator, were not forthcoming as easily, since the Irish hoped to satisfy Italian demands with as little as possible and thus retain complete control in their own hands. By the 1937 mayoral election the Democrats, using the recent appointments as proof of their future intentions, tried to move the Italians away from La Guardia by noting that the mayor was not providing enough positions for the Italian community. Only the Democrats, it was claimed, could secure for the Italians a just representation.

Although this tactic had little effect in 1937, by 1941 (for a variety of reasons to be explained later) it hit a responsive chord among Italians, that cost La Guardia some votes.[20] Although Italians were elated at having a mayor of their ethnic group, he was considered just a beginning. They expected much more to come and perhaps were too optimistic concerning what one Italian mayor could do for his people. As *Il Progresso* noted earlier: "We do not yet have a State Governor; we do not yet have a representative to the Federal Senate." The paper went on to assure its readers that such goals would shortly be secured.[21] For the most part they were not, and La Guardia, being the most powerful and well-known Italian-American politician, naturally received more than his share of the blame for this failure.

The Italians remained eager for political recognition throughout the 1930s and frequently called for the election or appointment of members of their group to office. Although they obviously were desirous of more positions, there are also indications that they were pleased that they were finally being recognized at all, and this tended to mute their anger and frustration. However, these feelings were at times revealed, as with the La Guardia vote or in cases where they demanded from the Democrats and others the representation that other groups, such as the Jews, were achieving in politics.[22] However, ethnic political competition between Italians and Jews was mild, since both were struggling for control and saw a common political opponent in the Irish, the group which was most affected by the political changes in the 1930s.

The Irish came to perceive two things about the new political scene. First, that La Guardia was anti-Irish, and second, that they were losing their power to other ethnic groups who cared little about Irish Catholic opinion and represented different cultural values. These attitudes were initially voiced because of the mayor's appointment in 1934 of Dr. Charles Fama as medical examiner for the City's Employee's Retirement System. Fama, an Italian Protestant, was accused of having written two anti-Catholic articles in 1925; furthermore, at the time of his appointment he criticized the Irish Catholic control of New York. The Bronx County Division of the Ancient Order of Hibernians, the United Irish-American Societies of New York, the *Brooklyn Tablet,* and the *Gaelic American* all called for Fama's dismissal on the basis that he was anti-Irish, anti-Catholic or both.[23] When La Guardia refused, claiming that Fama did his job and that was all that concerned him, the Irish press feared the worst. "It is very evident," roared an editorial in the *Gaelic American,* "that our Mayor has little regard for the opinions of people of Irish blood." After Bernard Deutsch, the Jewish president of the board of aldermen, supported La Guardia's decision on Fama, the *Gaelic American*'s editorial asked, "Would Mr. Deutsch be so liberal in his views if his own co-religionists had been the subject of Dr. Fama's attacks?" Patrick Scanlan, of the *Tablet,* commented that "it is equally unfortunate that a subcommittee of the Board of Estimate, composed of Aldermanic President Deutsch of the Bronx and Borough President Levy of Manhattan, who have regularly denounced prejudice against the Jews, should have recommended such a man to any office, or that they will keep him there."[24]

The board of aldermen, after an investigation, sustained the charge of religious intolerance against Fama and voted to dismiss him. Only the board of estimate, however, had the power to dismiss an appointee officially. Passing the buck, they decided to allow La Guardia to make the decision. The mayor continued in his refusal to dismiss Fama. Although it was only a minor event in which the mayor could easily have yielded, he chose not to. La Guardia seems to have had two motives for his action. First of all, he continued to feel that Fama was the right man for the job and, therefore, desired to retain him. However, La Guardia's obvious neglect of Irish opinion also indicates that he wished to do few favors for this group. Since the Jews and Italians already saw the Irish as controlling too much power in New York, the mayor was not eager to identify himself in any way with a continuance of that power. The retention of Fama, therefore, satisfied both of La Guardia's desires in this case.

The Fama incident made the Irish even more suspicious about the mayor. Later in the decade the Irish press repeatedly charged that La Guardia and his appointees discriminated against Irish Catholics. The origin for these later charges was in the Fama incident. The Irish had come to distrust La Guardia not only for the Fama appointment, but for what they saw as his anti-Irish attitude in relation to the civil service, which brought new groups into positions there. They were further worried by the notable decrease of Irish strength in the mayor's cabinet and other appointed offices. Even La Guardia's supporters acknowledged these Irish concerns. The Irish-American Non-Partisan Committee for La Guardia in 1937 made sure to note all of the mayor's Irish appointments and stressed that La Guardia did give many Irish-Americans positions in his administration and was not prejudiced. This was an apparent attempt to counter the pervasive feeling among the Irish that La Guardia had snubbed them in an effort to win support from other groups. The *Tablet,* as well as others representing the Irish viewpoint, called for more representation and claimed that they were losing to other groups under the La Guardia administration. Some of the Irish who did support the mayor were in his camp only in order to regain a place for their ethnic group in the City. Eileen Curran, secretary of La Guardia's Irish-American Non-Partisan Committee noted in 1937 that "a La Guardia victory seems certain, but it is important, for reasons you understand, that Irish-Americans shall have a prominent part in that victory."[25]

Other facets of the Mayor's administration bothered the Irish. For example, Paul Blanshard, considered by many to be an anti-Catholic crusader, was appointed commissioner of investigation and accounts. La Guardia's supposed ties to Communism were also seen as a particular rebuke to the Irish community and were used by the Democrats to win Irish votes.[26] Moreover, many Irish Catholics were upset about the selection of Paul Kern as chairman of the municipal Civil Service Commission in 1938, for Kern had supported the Loyalists in the Spanish Civil War and had approved of the appointment of a Communist to a position in the City government.[27]

The attitude of many Irish toward La Guardia is well revealed in a statement made by Father Edward Lodge Curran, a prominent Irish Catholic cleric closely associated with the Coughlin movement. Incensed that the mayor had not answered a letter which he had sent in complaint about the appointment of Communists, he asked if this was the way "in which Mayor La Guardia handles communications addressed to him by Rabbi Stephen Wise or by the Rev. John Haynes Holmes? . . . Or is this treatment on the part of the Mayor limited to communications received from Catholic priests and from Catholic editors?"[28]

As the voting statistics in chapter 7 suggest, the Irish were convinced that they could expect little from the mayor and saw in his administration and in the state leadership an effort to permit other groups to secure power at the expense of the Irish. Many statements reflected this feeling and indicated an increasing awareness of displacement and competition. For example, in 1938 Daniel Danaher, secretary of the Federation of Irish Societies, noted that the Irish,

> as a race are, to put it bluntly, being pushed aside to make room for other more aggressive and better organized races. True, some of our people still hold high places in the various phases of our city, state and national life, but what about the hundreds of thousands who are never heard from, who are the backbone of our race? There was a time when a large majority of them were found in the personnel of our various city departments, but not today.[29]

Even Al Smith made reference, although jokingly, to this political shift when he spoke at a 1934 fund-raising dinner to aid the Jews in Germany. "All my life," he said, "I've been hearing about the plight of the poor Jews some place in the world. . . . As I look around the room tonight, I see the Governor here, Herby Lehman. He's Jewish. Take the Mayor, he's half Jewish. The President of the Board of Aldermen, my old job, Bernie Deutsch, he's Jewish and so is Sam Levy, the Borough President of Manhattan. I'm beginning to wonder if someone shouldn't do something for the poor Irish, here in New York."[30] In 1937, Jeremiah Mahoney, the Democratic candidate for mayor, stated that "when it comes to politics, I don't know where I'd be but for my Jewish friends."[31] These were significant comments which illustrated a definite Irish attitude. These statements also did damage in an atmosphere where, for example, many of Roosevelt's opponents had been stressing what they considered to be excessive Jewish influence in the government. "The New Deal is a Jew Deal," was a familiar cry.

Yet the question remains: how extensive and severe was this Irish decline? While La Guardia's changes in civil service regulations and his ethnic appointments, as well as the Democratic party's increasing need to satisfy the other groups, did dilute Irish power, they nevertheless remained in control in many areas of political life well into the 1930s. For example, although Tammany's power in the party declined, the Irish continued to control all the other Democratic county organizations throughout this period. Therefore even though less federal patronage went to Tammany, because of political disputes between them and Roosevelt, it did go to Edward Flynn's organization in the Bronx and Frank Kelly's in Brooklyn. Irish politicians continued to hold many elective offices and were also prominent in the Democratic party hierarchy. James Farley, the national and New York State chairman of the party, exerted great power as a close Roosevelt adviser and as his Postmaster General.[32] After Farley resigned as national chairman in 1940, Flynn took the position. Roosevelt also brought more Irish Catholics into the cabinet than any of his predecessors, and appointed more Catholics, mainly Irish, to the federal judiciary than the three presidents before him serving an equal twelve years in office.[33] The Irish therefore still seemed strong in many ways.

THE AMERICAN LABOR PARTY

Beyond these indications of strength, there remained serious threats to Irish power that transcended in importance even La Guardia's ethnic appointments. By the late 1930s the balance began to shift slowly against the Irish. The American Labor party (ALP) did much to weaken, albeit temporarily, Irish political influence by challenging the strength of the Democratic party in New York State. The ALP had been formed in 1936 in an effort to provide a line on the ballot for those Roosevelt adherents who did not want to support the Democratic party.[34] Jews and Italians were prominent in the leadership of this new party. The nucleus of this organization was Sidney Hillman's Amalgamated Clothing Workers Union and David Dubinsky's ILGWU. The state chairman was Luigi Antonini, vice-president of the ILGWU. It also included as its leaders Alex Rose of the Hatters, Cap and Millinery Workers Union, Andrew Armstrong of the International Printing Pressmen's Union and Michael Quill of the Transport Workers Union as well as politicians such as Vito Marcantonio.

By 1938, Communist elements also moved into the ALP and soon gained control of the Manhattan branch. The state committee and the other borough organizations were under non-Communist domination. Although a large segment of the Party's rank and file remained non-Communist, the Communists did eventually gain more control over the organizational structure of the ALP by the early 1940s. The ALP therefore came to represent various threats to the Irish, who were solidly tied to the Democratic party. The fact that the ALP did well in elections reaffirmed the view of many, particularly those inclined to Coughlinism, that the Communists were indeed taking over City and State politics. At the same time it threatened the hold that the Irish had on New York politics through their power in the Democratic party.[35] The Tammany organization recognized the strength of the ALP when, during the 1940s, they formed an alliance with Marcantonio, head of the Manhattan branch of the party. Marcantonio provided Tammany with favors such as ALP endorsements of some of their candidates, thereby insuring victory, in return for no Democratic opposition to him at election time. Through the use of these endorsements, Marcantonio also had some influence over Tammany nominations and on one occasion requested that a Negro or Italian be nominated for a City judiciary post. This alliance was strictly a political one, and the fact that Marcantonio was a leader of the left-wing faction of the ALP was temporarily disregarded.[36]

Voting returns (see table 8) for the presidential, gubernatorial, and mayoral elections between 1936 and 1941 indicate that the ALP also signified mainly a Jewish challenge to Irish Democratic control over politics.[37] Jews were more inclined to vote ALP than were the other ethnics, and they consistently gave this party a sizeable percentage of their vote. Jewish election districts (New York's voting divisions) which had previously given the Democrats the large majority of their votes now began to vote heavily for the ALP. Although the party was to be only a temporary danger, since it remained a powerful force in city politics for a relatively short time, it did threaten Democratic control and no doubt contributed to a feeling of waning power on the part of the Irish.

TAMMANY AND THE CONNECTION WITH ORGANIZED CRIME

More significant than this transitory party was the situation within the Democratic organization. The Irish had less to fear from the ALP than from the desire for change in their own party, particularly on the part of the Italians. La Guardia's Italian support and appointments had forced the Irish Democratic leaders to bid for this group with token positions while retaining control in their own hands. By the late 1930s the Italians wanted the decisionmaking posts, and because of the weakness of the Democratic party as a result of the long reign of a Fusion administration and the changes La Guardia made in the City government, the Italians were able to get what they wanted.

The most vulnerable of the Democratic county organizations was Tammany, for it had suffered the most during the 1930s. Tammany's anti-New Deal stand in the early part of the decade had hurt it in relation to federal and state patronage. The loss of civil service and appointed court positions during La

Table 8. ALP Percentage of Ethnic Groups' Vote in
New York City, 1936–1941

	Irish	German	Jewish	Italian
1936 presidential	3.2	2.3	19.9	6.3
1936 gubernatorial	2.7	2.1	19.4	6.0
1937 mayoral	10.3	8.1	40.9	22.6
1938 gubernatorial	6.8	4.5	32.1	9.7
1940 presidential	5.3	3.5	20.4	5.9
1941 mayoral	8.4	7.8	39.3	13.8

Guardia's administration left Tammany weakened in City patronage. Furthermore, the courts had formerly provided income either from appointments or protection, both of which were sold. Through his county reform proposals and new city charter, La Guardia was also instrumental in abolishing certain posts, such as commissioner of records, which had been Tammany patronage jobs. All that remained for Tammany as a source of income and patronage were mainly the elected court positions. Tammany's precarious situation eventually led to its control by underworld figures who could provide money at the right time. As William O'Dwyer, the Democratic nominee for mayor in 1941, answered when asked about the appeal of a certain gangster to politicians, "It doesn't matter whether it is a banker, a businessman, or a gangster, his pocketbook is always attractive."[38] In the late 1930s many mobster leaders were Italian, and therefore Italians slowly filled the positions of power in the Democratic Party because of this gangster support.

This shift in politics was preceded by shifts in the criminal world.[39] New York has seen the rise of many neighborhood gangs whose members were Irish, Jewish, Italian or whatever immigrant group was struggling to move up the economic ladder. Prohibition and labor-management conflicts during the 1920s gave many gangsters the ability to expand their operations beyond their neighborhoods and become wealthy. Although all ethnic groups participated in organized crime to a certain extent, Jewish and Italian mobsters, often allied with each other, became the dominant ethnic element by the 1930s. Forging this alliance in the New York area and dominating the city underworld was Salvatore (Charles "Lucky" Luciano) Lucania, who by 1931 had achieved prominence in the Italian gangs. Luciano believed in cooperation with non-Italian mobsters and by 1934 had helped to form a loose syndicate made up of such Italian and Jewish gang bosses as Francesco (Frank Costello) Castiglia, Meyer Lansky, Louis (Lepke) Buchalter, Jacob (Gurrah) Shapiro, Benjamin (Bugsy) Siegel, and Joseph (Joe Adonis) Doto. Each had his own specialities, but all cooperated to some extent in governing organized crime in the City.

Most important for this study was the criminal connection with politics. For many years Tammany politicos offered protection to gangs for a price. On the west side of Manhattan James J. (Jimmy) Hines, a powerful Tammany district leader in the eleventh assembly district, protected a number of mobsters such as Arthur (Dutch Schultz) Flegenheimer, Luciano, Lepke, and Costello. On the east side, Tammany men had long been safeguarding Italian gangs. A number of district leaders, mostly Irish, thereby grew rich out of this arrangement. While this political-criminal alliance was acceptable to both sides during the 1920s, by 1931, Luciano decided to oust one of the east side Irish district leaders and put in one of his own ethnic group, perhaps for reasons of ethnic pride or perhaps just to put a more trusted man in that position.[40]

In 1931 Albert Marinelli, supported by Luciano, declared that he was a candidate for the district leadership of Manhattan's second assembly district, west, then held by Harry Perry, half-brother of later Tammany chieftan Christopher Sullivan and a solid member of Tammany's Irish regime. According to one political observer, the succession was accomplished when members of Luciano's gang threatened Perry and "convinced" him not to run for reelection. This was not known to the general public. For example, in the aftermath of the Perry ouster and Marinelli entry, the *New York Times* editorialized on how Tammany makes room for new ethnic groups: "As the type of resident changes, Tammany is quick to recognize the fact. . . . Deference to popular feeling in such matters is one of the secrets of its [Tammany's] strength."[41] In 1934 Marinelli also became county clerk of New York and emerged as a powerful figure in Tammany.

Therefore it was Italian gangsters who helped their fellow Italians take one of the first important steps up the Democratic party ladder. Other Italians, without gang backing, also began to run for district leader positions. In 1935 Paul Rao ran for one such vacant post in Yorkville's fourteenth assembly district, but the election went to Edward V. Loughlin, an Irish politico. However, in 1937 Paul Santangelo defeated Joseph A. Greenfield, the Tammany candidate, in Manhattan's first assembly district, east, a heavily Italian area. Santangelo became the second Italian district leader in Manhattan, but only Marinelli had managed to replace a reigning Irish politician. When Santangelo was defeated in 1939, another Italian, Paul Sarubbi, took his place, thereby securing this district for the Italians.

A change in the criminal-political alliance which gave the gangsters more control and aided the Italian drive for political power came after a number of exposés and arrests. Thomas Dewey, special prosecutor appointed by Governor Lehman, and as of 1938 the District Attorney of Manhattan, was responsible for ending Luciano's reign in 1936 by successfully prosecuting him for his role in the prostitution racket. Lepke and Gurrah later met the same fate as a result of an investigation by Dewey and federal agents of their industrial racketeering and Lepke's involvement with narcotics. The political link was revealed when Dewey exposed Marinelli's sordid connections during the 1937 campaign and in 1938 implicated Hines as the protector of Dutch Schultz's enterprises.[42] Hines was sent to prison in 1940.

The disclosure of Marinelli's activities and the arrest and conviction of Luciano, Lepke, Gurrah, and Hines, combined with La Guardia's changes, resulted in a shaken Tammany which was in need of money. Frank Costello emerged to fill Luciano's leadership position in the underworld and soon became the power behind Tammany. This increase in Costello's influence was the result of the financial support he provided to the income-starved Tammany. Eventually he decided that rather than working through the customary system of buying protection, he would simply take control. In some areas, he used threats of force to get district leadership resignations and then used similar tactics to secure these openings for his supporters.[43] Through his district leadres and the use of well-placed financial and other types of "persuasion," Costello controlled the largest bloc of votes on the Tammany executive committee by 1941. With this power in Tammany, Costello was extremely influential in 1942 in ousting Christopher Sullivan as Tammany leader and securing the post for Michael J. Kennedy. With Kennedy's election, Costello shifted fully into position as the power behind the throne.[44]

In 1943 a wiretap placed on Costello's phone by Manhattan district attorney Frank Hogan revealed that Thomas Aurelio, a city magistrate recently nominated as a candidate for the state supreme court, had called Costello to thank him for his help in securing the nomination and to promise his loyalty to the gangster. Costello's comment was that "when I tell you something is in the bag, you can rest assured." Costello had used his influence with Kennedy, his district leader friends, and Bert Stand, secretary of the Tammany executive committee, to get the nomination for Aurelio. At one point Kennedy was reported to be "cooling off on an Italian candidate" and was going to nominate an Irish-Catholic instead (Joseph A. Gavagan, who had been suggested by Roosevelt). Costello, when informed of Kennedy's attitude, approached the Tammany leader and strongly pressured him to make a decision, to declare himself; he decided in favor of Aurelio, thereby rejecting the President's choice. After the taped conversation was made public, Kennedy repudiated Aurelio. This angered Costello, who then helped engineer in 1943 the ouster of Kennedy as Tammany head and the entry of Edward Loughlin into that position.[45]

Costello remained the dominant influence in Tammany throughout the 1940s. He was a significant force in bringing Italians into Tammany district leadership positions and judgeships as well as decreasing the influence the Irish had in the organization. Italians who wished to advance in politics often went to Costello for help. In the 1943 Aurelio-Costello conversation it was also revealed that an Italian assistant district attorney of Queens, who wanted to be nominated for either county judge or district attorney, had contacted Costello to ask for his aid in making contact with Tammany leader Kennedy. Costello was involved in at least three situations involving Italians who secured judgeships.[46]

Even before Costello secured a dominant role in Tammany, his growing influence contributed to ethnic changes as Italians were placed, whenever possible, into prominent political positions. For example, in 1940, in order to devote his time to the Tammany leadership, Christopher Sullivan decided against seeking re-election to his U.S. congressional seat, which he had held since 1916. In his place Louis J. Capozzoli was nominated.[47] Tammany's decision to bring Italians into higher office was not based only on Costello's rise; other factors worked in conjunction with his role. In 1940 the Democrats wished to secure Italian support for Roosevelt after his offensive "stab in the back" remark about Italy's invasion of France; and they also desired to continue their previous policy of wooing Italians away from La Guardia. Roosevelt at this time began appointing more Italians to federal office.[48]

Gangster influence did not occur only in Tammany. Since all county Democratic machines lost patronage positions, the mobsters increased their power in the others also. In Brooklyn politics, Joe Adonis wielded great influence. His financial assistance to various politicos obligated a number of them to him. Adonis's presence was also felt in citywide affairs, since he had given La Guardia financial help and protection at election time in 1933, presumably because of ethnic pride. He probably aided Italians in Brooklyn local politics as well. Consequently, La Guardia did not bother Adonis until 1937, when the gangster supported La Guardia's opponent, Royal Copeland, in the primary.[49]

THE DESAPIO CASE

Extremely important at the same time was the rise to power of Carmine DeSapio, who in 1949 succeeded in becoming the first Italian leader of Tammany. His political career provides a good example of Irish resistance to the ethnic changes. In certain areas considered to be Irish territory, Irish political families looked upon their district leaderships as an inheritance, and the Irish Tammany leaders considered these positions as permanent possessions of their ethnic group. These areas the Irish refused to surrender. In 1939 DeSapio challenged Daniel E. Finn, Jr., for the district leadership of Manhattan's first assembly district, west (Greenwich Village), where the Finn family had been in control for many years and where there was a significant feeling against having an Italian leader in territory which the Irish had ruled for so long.[50] According to Tammany's rules, a district leader was chosen by the county committeemen from his area. Thus the election held was to pick county committeemen pledged either to DeSapio or Finn. DeSapio's supporters (and therefore DeSapio) won the election, but Sullivan, the Tammany leader, refused to recognize the victory, insisting that Finn was still district leader and thereby still entitled to his seat on the Tammany executive committee.

Very likely Sullivan's actions were based on his unwillingness to surrender the position to an Italian. As with general Irish resistance to any advancement of the new groups, more was involved here than simply competition for political positions. Cultural differences, and animosities left over from previous years, played a role in Irish opposition too. Also involved in this particular case, according to one political observer, was the fact that Sullivan was still angry over the ousting of Perry, his half-brother, by Luciano in 1931.[51]

DeSapio's supporters began to picket Tammany Hall and finally took the case to the courts, which ruled in favor of the Italian leader. However, he was still denied the executive committee position by Sullivan, and thus was denied the patronage power entitled him as district leader. In 1941 DeSapio lost to Finn, although the election had to be settled by the courts after DeSapio charged fraud. By 1943, however, with Costello dominant in Tammany and with Sullivan no longer in control, DeSapio was recognized as the de facto leader of his district and shortly thereafter, with Tammany backing, officially won the district leadership. He was then given his rightful place on the executive committee. Finn, who had first intended to fight DeSapio again in 1943, was stopped when the courts removed his name from the ballot by invalidating the designating petitions of his candidates for county committeemen. He then decided to retire, and closed his political club.[52] Thus Irish control of this much-desired area was destroyed.

DeSapio came to lead Tammany's Italian bloc, which also included Jews and which remained friendly to Costello. This group, consisting of district leaders DeSapio, Harry Brickman, Francis X. Mancuso, and Sidney Moses, continued to battle with the Irish and eventually defeated them in the late 1940s.[53] In 1948 Hugo Rogers became the first Jewish leader of Tammany, and in 1949 DeSapio finally took control. In the other boroughs, however, the Irish retained more power.

MORE DISPLACEMENT:
ETHNIC POLITICS ON THE STATE LEVEL

On the national level, which will be discussed later, and on the state executive level, the Irish also saw signs that either the politicians remained deaf to new demands or that Irishmen were being displaced. Certain issues gained new meaning when they were interpreted as indications of political neglect. One such issue occurred in 1935 when Lehman vetoed legislation endorsed by the Catholic Church which would have provided public transportation for parochial school children. Commenting on this action, the *Irish World* noted in an emotional outburst that "President Roosevelt smiles at protests against the persecutions of Catholics in Mexico. Governor Lehman... denies the rights of Catholic-Americans in New York State. And we used to think that bigotry was a thing of the past." The paper urged Catholics to fight for their rights. In addition to the school bus issue, Lehman was attacked by Father Charles Coughlin for his association with the ALP, and by other Catholics for having ties to Communists. According to one political observer, the school bus issue and the forthcoming gubernatorial election marked the beginning of an Irish-Jewish split in the Democratic party.[54]

The Republicans did try to take advantage of Irish dissatisfaction with Lehman by nominating an Irish Catholic, William Bleakley, for governor in 1936. While all ethnic election districts except the Jewish ones showed a decrease in support for Lehman from 1932 to 1936, the Irish districts indicated the largest percentage of decline[55] (see table 9). When one considers just the Democratic party vote, the Irish areas were the only ones to fall below 50 percent in 1936, an odd occurrence for a group that was traditionally Democratic. With approximately the same number of people in the Irish election districts voting for

Table 9. Ethnic Vote for Lehman in New York City, 1932–1938

	Lehman-Democratic party vote by percentage	Lehman-All parties' vote by percentage (includes ALP vote in 1936 and 1938)
City, 1932	69.7	69.7
City, 1936	56.9	65.3
City, 1938	49.6	64.6
Irish, 1932	75.6	75.6
Irish, 1936	49.4	52.1
Irish, 1938	53.8	60.4
German, 1932	62.4	62.4
German, 1936	51.1	53.2
German, 1938	40.6	45.1
Italian, 1932	78.9	78.9
Italian, 1936	60.9	66.9
Italian, 1938	50.0	59.7
Jewish, 1932	79.7	79.7
Jewish, 1936	66.4	85.8
Jewish, 1938	56.3	88.4

president and governor in 1936, there was a considerable drop in votes from Roosevelt to Lehman, much greater in this community than in the others.[56]

Voter support for Lehman in German areas was also below the City average and indicated the impact of the school bus issue as well as other Catholic concerns.[57] In addition, Lehman may have lost some votes among the Germans due to the Nazi issue and the conflict between the Jews and Germans on this point. However the majority support for the governor in this community suggests, as with the Irish, that many did not think of him in ethnic terms, were not unhappy with him, and voted on the basis that he had provided a good administration. The *New Yorker Staats-Zeitung und Herold* supported him on this basis—although it should be noted that Roosevelt and Lehman, keen on obtaining the German vote for their party, had recently made some significant appointments. Victor Ridder, publisher of the *Staats-Zeitung* was appointed by Roosevelt in 1935 as New York City Administrator of the Works Progress Administration and by Lehman in 1936 as chairman of the State Board of Social Welfare, which controlled relief activities in the state. Finally, Lehman had not been associated with the attacks on German-Americans in which other politicians were indulging.[58]

The Italian vote, while decreasing, still remained above the City average.

This decrease, too, may have been due to the same issues affecting other Catholics.

By 1938, Lehman, now facing Thomas Dewey as his opponent, attempted to win back his general Catholic supporters by opposing certain New Deal ideas, such as the Supreme Court packing proposal, unpopular with segments of this group, and by supporting an amendment to the state constitution which would permit the public busing of parochial school children. His effort did not assuage everybody. Evidence of open and hostile opposition to Lehman appeared in Irish areas showing signs of incipient conflict with the Jews. To combat this, the Democratic party sent prominent Irish figures such as William O'Dwyer (who was then Democratic candidate for district attorney of Brooklyn) into various Irish neighborhoods around the City to speak on Lehman's behalf.[59]

Some of the Irish discontent in this election related to ethnic and ideological political displacement. When the Democratic and American Labor Parties met to select candidates, they both endorsed Lehman, but the Democrats disregarded Lt. Governor M. William Bray, a conservative Irish Catholic, and chose instead as their nominee Charles Poletti, a liberal Italian Protestant.[60] The ALP supported the Democratic ticket, except for their candidate for attorney general, John J. Bennett, a conservative Irish Catholic. The ALP objected to Bennett because he was supporting the Franco side in the Spanish Civil War and was felt to be a conservative.[61] They chose instead Joseph V. O'Leary, another Irish Catholic, as their candidate.

These actions incensed many conservative Irish, particularly the Coughlinites. They were angry at the substitution of liberals like Poletti and O'Leary for conservatives and the switch by the Democrats from an Irish Catholic to an Italian Protestant for lieutenant governor. Bennett's failure to secure the ALP nomination was also seen as an indication of anti-Catholic prejudice. Since he belonged to the ALP, O'Leary was not considered a Catholic by some. There were also rumors that Poletti had been born a Catholic but had converted. Justice Herbert O'Brien, a leading Coughlinite, issued the first open complaint by noting that the Catholics were being ignored, as indicated by the Poletti situation. He suggested that they begin voting on behalf of their own interests and for their own group rather than making a fetish of party regularity. O'Brien particularly pointed to the fact that there were thirteen Jewish assemblymen in New York City, although the Catholics were mainly in a majority there; this, he said, indicated how Catholics had unwisely supported other groups in the past.[62]

Leaders of the state and local Democratic organization were so concerned about a Catholic, and especially an Irish, bolt from the party that they took special action to ensure that it would not happen. In the City, Irish Catholics were conspicuously brought into the campaign structure: John C. Kelley was appointed chairman of the Lehman-Poletti Independent Citizens Committee; John Lynch, secretary of the Emerald Association of the Brooklyn diocese, vice-president of the St. Patrick's Society of Brooklyn, and a member of the Ancient

Order of Hibernians and Knights of Columbus was appointed as Kelley's assistant.[63]

However the problems were not solved. Father Edward Lodge Curran, a prominent cleric, now suggested that Poletti and the ALP were anti-Catholic and Communist in leaning. O'Leary had to assert in a telegram to Curran that although he was a member of the ALP, he was still a Catholic. Poletti also, fearing the loss of Catholic votes, had to assuage Curran through a long public letter stating the reasons for his political and religious beliefs. He noted that he was not a radical, explained why he was a Protestant, and denied any responsibility for the ALP nominee selections.[64]

Although the attack on Poletti seemed to be due more to his political beliefs rather than his ethnic background or religion, some Italians saw it as part of an Irish attempt to thwart Italian political aspirations. One letter which was forwarded to Poletti by Paul Rao, chairman of the Italian-American Division of the State Democratic Campaign Committee, illustrates this well. The letter was addressed to Archbishop Amleto Cicognani, the Apostolic Delegate to the United States, and stated that

> You undoubtedly have read of the attacks which have been made by the Irish Catholics upon the Democratic Candidate for Lieutenant-Governor of New York, Hon. Charles Poletti. . . .
>
> I believe that I express the sentiments of thousands of Italian Catholics in this State, when I say that all are proud to be of the same race as Charles Poletti. The attacks and insidious remarks made against Charles Poletti by the Irish Catholics are unwarranted and untrue. . . .
>
> I have heard at first hand the opinions expressed by non-Irish Catholic Americans in New York City, and it is to the effect that the Irish Catholic is using the Catholic Church to further their [sic] political purposes. . . .
>
> I sincerely trust that your Excellency will communicate with the proper authorities in New York to the end that the responsible persons involved be instructed to cease their political activities in the name of the Catholic Church.

Rao commented that he was ''sure the way has been paved to put certain people in their place.'' Shortly afterward, Rao, who as president of the Italian Holy Name Society had some influence in the Church, arranged a private meeting between Poletti and Bishop Steven Donahue, temporary head of the New York Archdiocese. Rao stressed to the bishop that Poletti was being unfairly treated. Father Curran, either due to Church pressure brought on him or to Poletti's letter of explanation (or both), soon switched to unqualified support of Poletti and fully endorsed him. While O'Brien still offered some criticism of Poletti, the attacks on him virtually stopped.[65] This incident indicates another aspect of the political conflict between Italians and Irish which was so evident on the district leader level.

The special overtures made by Lehman and the Democratic party to retain the Irish vote, and the pressure put on certain Irish Catholic leaders, were successful in bringing their vote back to the party. To a group which was feeling neglected, special attention, as well as carefully placed pressure, was important. Lehman therefore was able to recapture some of his Irish support. However, owing to the issues of Nazism, Fascism, and the coming war, along with various Catholic concerns, he began to lose his German support and slip slightly among the Italians (see chapter 4 through 6 for further discussion of these factors).

Except for the recapturing of the Irish vote in 1938, the 1936 gubernatorial contest marks the beginning of an Irish-Jewish split in the Democratic party. They were no longer supporting the same candidates to the same degree as they had up to this point, with the exception of the 1933 mayoralty (see figure 1). Since many Jews ''defected'' to the ALP, if one adds that party's vote to the Democratic party vote for elections in which they endorsed the same candidates, the split is more obvious (see figure 2). When the votes of one group increase, the votes of the other decrease. The Germans, and to a lesser extent the Italians (see figures 3 and 4) were also starting to disassociate themselves from the Jews in political choices after 1936, but most notably beginning in 1938. Explosive issues, discussed in later chapters, in combination with a feeling of displacement and neglect on the part of some groups and a disagreement over certain New Deal policies, began to rip apart the Democratic ethnic coalition.[66]

THE GERMAN DISCONTENT

The Irish, of course, were not the only group to sense political displacement. The Germans also complained about their lack of representation.[67] However, their reaction did not come as the result of Tammany's decline or the emergence of the Jews and Italians. It was due to World War I, which resulted in a temporary German withdrawal from politics, and the Nazi takeover of Germany, which convinced many German-Americans that to protect themselves from future anti-German hysteria, they needed to increase their political power. German Catholics were also reacting to a feeling that Catholic opinion was being neglected. One of the aims of the Steuben Society, founded in 1919, and the main goal of the Roland Society, consisting of German-American Democratic party clubs, therefore was to win political recognition in an effort "to renew the reputation of our German-Americans, and achieve for us, what other nationalities have accomplished by their efforts." The Roland Society urged that German-Americans get their proportional representation in government. The Steuben Society noted that the neglect of politics by the German-American community made it easier for them to be attacked. At times the American reaction to the Nazi issue increased the fears of German-Americans that they were reentering a period of anti-German hysteria, and they reflected this anxiety in their votes. La Guardia, who at first was greeted by the Germans as an answer to Tammany corruption, did much to encourage this fear.[68] However, it was not until 1938, when America fully reacted against Nazism, that this feeling began to permeate the whole German community, including those who had been indifferent during most of the 1930s to the issues involving Germany and Nazism.

For humanitarian as well as ethnic political reasons, the mayor immediately entered into the controversy over Nazism and eventually, along with other politicians, turned it into a New York political issue. La Guardia initially illustrated his intentions by endorsing the controversial Jewish anti-Nazi boycott which had begun in 1933 and by becoming vice-chairman of one of the boycott organizations, the American League for the Defense of Jewish Rights (later renamed the Non-Sectarian Anti-Nazi League to Champion Human Rights).[69] Some German-Americans saw the boycott as a weapon against them rather than against Germany and were upset at La Guardia's decision. The Jewish community, however, was delighted with La Guardia's interest and support. Jewish leaders, as well as other Americans, were constantly urging prominent citizens to protest against the policies of Nazi Germany.[70] It was important to the Jews to have a man of La Guardia's stature prove to them that someone in their government cared. It is unfortunate that a positive response to the Jews during this period often seemed like a rebuke to the German-Americans.

By 1935 the situation for the Jews in Germany had worsened, and La Guardia again voiced his protest against Nazi Germany. He refused to grant a masseur operator's license to a newly arrived German immigrant who had shown no intention of becoming an American citizen. In defense of his action, the mayor stated that because American Jews were being discriminated against in Germany, German citizens would receive no special privileges here. He was referring to a treaty signed by Germany and the United States in 1925 stipulating that American and German citizens had equal rights to work in their professional occupations in the other country. Some German-Americans in New York saw La Guardia's action as a direct attack on them. "We Americans of German extraction," said a letter from the General Custer Unit (Brooklyn) of the Steuben Society, "believe ourselves to be, as a rule, good citizens—upright and honest, thrifty and frugal, attending to our daily duties, and we know that we are entitled to a great deal more consideration and attention, and yes, more respect from you, for we consider ourselves, as good, as loyal, as sincere citizens as any other group in this great city and country of ours." The Roland Society recognized that La Guardia's action did nothing but antagonize the German population of New York. Protest meetings were held by organizations which were either Nazi-controlled, sympathetic to the Nazis, or non-Nazi (neither pro- nor anti-). This included such groups as the United German Societies, German-American Conference, United Bavarian Societies, and the United Singers Society of New York. Prominent New Yorkers of German extraction such as Victor Ridder urged the mayor to change his mind about the German masseur. An editorial in the *Staats-Zeitung* asked La Guardia to act in the interest of the whole city and not

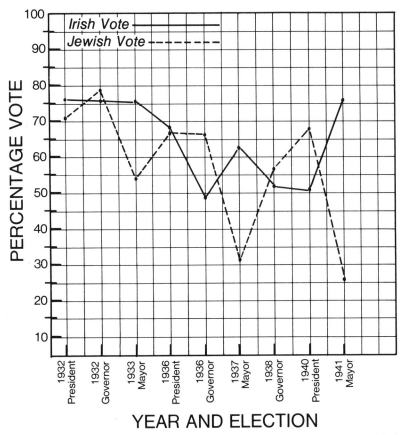

Figure 1. Irish and Jewish percentage vote (Democratic), 1932–1941. For 1933 the McKee vote is considered to be part of the Democratic vote.

follow his personal feelings. A headline on the front page of the newspaper screamed, "Mayor Acts in Spite of all Protests."[71] La Guardia's Corporation Counsel, Paul Windels, suggested that the mayor's actions were not legal. "A mayor has no right to invalidate a United States treaty," said Windels. On the question of whether American Jews were being denied the right to practice their profession in Germany, Windels, after contacting the State Department, claimed no such discrimination was in evidence. Therefore, the treaty was still in effect and under it La Guardia had to give the masseur his license. In a letter to the General Custer Unit of the Steuben Society, the mayor answered his critics: "The citizens of German extraction were not at all involved in my action or in anything that was officially or otherwise stated by me." However, La Guardia refused to change his decision, still claiming that the actions in Germany against American Jews voided the

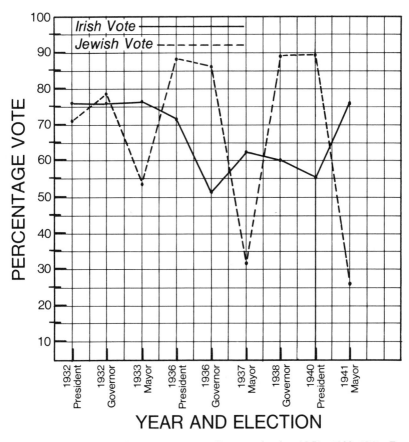

Figure 2. Irish and Jewish percentage vote (Democratic plus ALP), 1932–1941. For 1933 the McKee vote is considered to be part of the Democratic vote. The ALP vote is included in the 1936, 1938, and 1940 elections.

treaty. This was a relatively minor incident in which La Guardia could easily have changed his mind to soothe the ruffled feathers of many German New Yorkers. The mayor, consistent with his boycott decision, was protesting against what he felt was a reprehensible regime, while, at the same time, gathering Jewish votes.[72]

The German-American reaction probably would have been more severe at this time had it not been for other evidence that their interests were being protected. The elevation of prominent members of their group to important positions mitigated their fears of political weakness. This included Victor Ridder's appointments by Roosevelt and Lehman in 1935 and 1936. Also William Brunner, Chairman of the Manhattan district council of the Steuben Society, was elected President of the board of aldermen in 1936, although the board was to

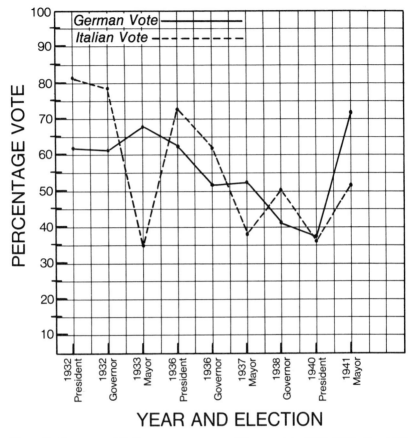

Figure 3. German and Italian percentage vote (Democratic), 1932–1941. For 1933 the McKee vote is considered to be part of the Democratic vote.

function only one more year before it was to be replaced by the new city council. Most important was the presence of Robert F. Wagner as U. S. senator from New York from 1926 to 1947. Although Wagner had not hesitated to criticize Germany, his high and influential position, while certainly not everything the German community wanted, kept their political discontent and insecurity to a minimum until the years just before World War II; it also robbed the American Nazis of a potentially powerful issue.[73]

The German-American Bund tried repeatedly to arouse the German community to a sense of outrage at their lack of political power and the strength of the Jews, using La Guardia as an example of an anti-German, pro-Jewish politician. They even considered Wagner not a true German because of his support of Jewish causes. Although some votes were surely affected by this feeling of political displacement and insecurity—and there were occasions when many in

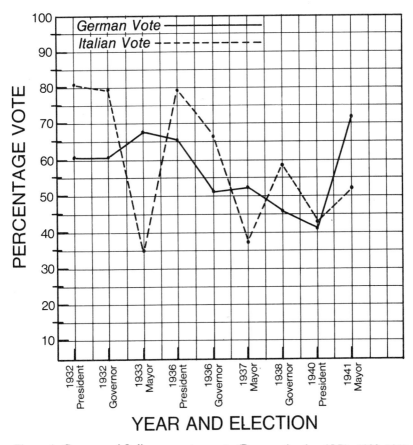

Figure 4. German and Italian percentage vote (Democratic plus ALP), 1932–1941. For 1933 the McKee vote is considered to be part of the Democratic vote. The ALP vote is included in the 1936, 1938, and 1940 elections.

the German community were upset—there is little indication that it became a major factor until 1938. There is also little indication that it was a major source of German-Jewish friction or conflict. Only minor references appeared in the non-Nazi German press which indicated resentment against the Jews in relation to political power.[74] There were no attacks on the Jews on this issue.

Unlike the Irish, who saw their political empire crumbling and were unable to surrender peacefully to the other groups, the Germans were not involved in the political succession battles, having already lost many years before. Instead they were concerned basically with securing enough representation to protect themselves from an outburst of anti-German hysteria. Wagner, Ridder, and others somewhat satisfied this desire, at least until 1938. The antagonists in the political arena were the Jews and Irish, and Italians and Irish. Conflict was evident between the latter two groups in areas such as DeSapio's district, where the Irish were engaging in efforts to injure, thwart, or eliminate this ethnic rival. Competition was evident between the Jews and Irish with a full awareness of the struggle, and it became a factor in the intense and prolonged conflict in which these two groups became involved. The Irish were indeed correct in fearing a loss of political power. Even when the Democrats regained control of the mayoralty in 1945 with the election of William O'Dwyer, the Jews and Italians were in too secure a position in the higher levels of the party to be displaced. While the Irish percentage of cabinet appointments increased under the new administration, so too did that of the Jews and Italians.[75] The Irish were never again to achieve the dominance in New York City and State politics that they once had. They knew it, and that was the problem.

Chapter Four
The Old World Influence

Fights between Mussolini's supporters and opponents, and huge Nazi rallies honoring Hitler, were taking place not only in Rome and Berlin but also in New York. One could watch brown-shirted Nazis marching down the streets of Yorkville and black-shirted Fascists meeting in East Harlem in the 1930s. Mussolini's and Hitler's rise to power, which did so much to disrupt life in Europe, also caused problems in New York. The emergence of Nazism in Germany, for example, provided the explosive issue which threw New York's Jewish and German communities against each other, and made each aware of a struggle.

Both groups, as well as the Italian-Americans, were deeply affected by the events in Europe and considered their fate and status in the New World to be dependent on the American reaction to the Old World dictatorships. Since greater prestige for Germany and Italy would enhance the status of German- and Italian-Americans in the United States, these groups were reluctant to criticize any aspect of their ancestral homes, and they took pride in these countries' achievements. The Jews, however, felt their interests threatened by a favorable American and world response to Germany and, later, Italy and were highly critical of these countries and their supporters. With such vital interests at stake, the Germans and Jews, and eventually the Italians and Jews, in New York found themselves in disagreements over their responses to Nazism, Fascism, and related issues which could easily lead to conflict.

GERMAN-AMERICANS AND NAZI GERMANY:
THE INITIAL RESPONSE

Although Italian Fascism was the first to appear on the world scene, Nazism was by far the more disruptive force in America because it emphasized anti-Semitism and exaggerated the decline of the German-American's status in the United States. Moreover, many German-Americans found it difficult to look at Nazism and Germany objectively. They were reluctant initially to criticize, especially publicly, anything German, unwilling to believe what was really happening to the Jews in Germany, and slow to react to the dangers of the American Nazis.[1] A number of factors, each of which could operate separately, contributed to this reluctance. One was a fear of reviving in any way the traumatic World War I experience in which German-Americans had been abused so unfairly. A renewed anti-German crusade seemed a possibility in New York in 1933 and continued to be of concern to some German-Americans throughout the decade. The American Nazis made effective use of this point, claiming that an attack on them was an attack on all German-Americans. Other factors were the desire not to malign the ancestral home without full knowledge of what was happening there, plus a pride in the new respect Germany had secured among the world's nations. As Albert Zimmer, a Cincinnati Nazi leader, said: "Of course, most of these people [Germans in Cincinnati] do not agree with Hitler, but at the same time Hitler represents Germany to them. And they will not tolerate any criticism, verbal or written, of Germany. They consider it a reflection on themselves."[2] Finally, one must also note that the German government probably pressured the German-American organizations to avoid criticism of Germany and Nazism.

Although there was fear of a new anti-German crusade in 1933, mainly in New York, for most German-Americans, particularly those who did not belong to the German organizations, were less ethnic conscious and less concerned about Nazi issues unless it directly threatened to affect their lives, this fear did not appear again as a serious one until 1938. At that time, when America began to react hostilely toward Germany, all German-Americans began to feel that their vital interests were at stake and they became sensitive to the issues involving Germany.

German-American statements on Nazi atrocity stories illustrate this ethnic group's reaction to criticism of Germany in the early 1930s. The *Steuben News* stated that "we recognize in the authors of these reports the same elements which were extremely venomous during the period both before and after the World War in creating a feeling of hatred and contempt for the German people." Theodore Hoffmann, national chairman of the Steuben Society, on returning from a visit to Germany in 1934, commented that the reports of oppression against the Jews were exaggerated. Hoffmann thus helped to perpetuate the belief that Nazi Germany was receiving unfair criticism. Even German-Americans who strongly stated their opposition to any Jewish persecutions in Germany could not accept the news from the Old World. Bernard Ridder, copublisher of the *New Yorker Staats-Zeitung,* while admitting that anti-Jewish actions had occurred, noted that these events were very likely exaggerated and the work of a "small group of young fanatics" who mistakenly thought that the Nazi party wanted this. Ridder claimed that Germany would solve this problem, and therefore he urged Jews not to overreact. One German New Yorker said, "I believe there is not a German-American in New York whose pride has not been hurt by the apparent willingness of many Americans, especially the people of the Jewish faith, to regard as truth the sensational atrocity accounts coming from sources outside of Germany."[3]

Some Germans also asked whether other Americans had any right to question Germany's choice of government. German-Americans wanted their fellow Americans to regard Germany as just another country, disregarding the Nazi government there. Therefore, they were angered when the Jews attempted to keep the Olympics from being held in Berlin in 1936 or to keep Germany out of the World's Fair in 1939.[4]

NAZISM COMES TO AMERICA

While the advent of Hitler and Nazism in Germany alone would have caused problems for Germans in the United States, a greater difficulty was faced in determining how to respond to Nazi organizations set up in this country. The first of these groups appeared in the 1920s and was the seed which eventually blossomed into the German-American Bund.

The organized Nazi movement began in the United States after World War I when many Germans, some belonging to Hitler's National Socialist German Workers' Party (NSDAP), emigrated to America. A local unit of the Nazi party was formed in the Bronx in 1922, but the more important of these early Nazi efforts came in 1924 with the formation in Detroit of the National Socialist Teutonia Association, led by Fritz Gissibl and others. This organization was made up of newly arrived German immigrants, most of whom did not belong to the NSDAP. By the early 1930s chapters had been set up in Cincinnati, Chicago, Milwaukee, New York, and other cities with a declared membership of over 500. The aim of Teutonia was not to convert the German-American community to Nazism but rather to present Nazi ideas to German citizens living in America.[5] Although this group represented the beginnings of Nazism in this country, it attracted little attention. Hitler had not yet come to power in Germany, and the people of the United States, German-Americans as well as others, did not at this time regard Nazism as a serious concern.

Teutonia prospered until 1931, when it failed to receive the designation as the official unit of the Nazi party in the United States; shortly thereafter it was dissolved. Instead the seal of approval went to a New York City Nazi party cell established by members of the NSDAP. This cell was now named a Gau (department) of the German Nazi party. Divisions of the New York Gau were then organized in other cities, but the hub of the Nazi movement remained in New York. Many of the German nationals belonging to Teutonia soon affiliated with the Nazi party Gau. Some Americans, mainly of German ancestry, also joined this group, but by 1933 had formed in New York the Friends of Germany (a separate Nazi society for American citizens). This organization was led by Colonel Edwin Emerson, an early German-American supporter of Nazism and a man with important connections in the Yorkville German community, and particularly in the United German Societies, a federation of German-American organizations.[6]

The Nazi party organization in the United States was dissolved in 1933 due to intra-party dissension which caused unfavorable publicity for the Nazis. To rebuild the movement, Heinz Spanknoebel, originally a member of Teutonia, was sent to the United States by the foreign bureau of the German Nazi party in 1933. In July 1933 he created the Friends of the New Germany, which was an amalgamation of the supporters of many of the earlier Nazi organizations. Also joining with this new society were the Friends of Germany under Colonel Emerson, who now became the head of the American Section of the Friends of the New Germany.[7] Like the earlier Nazi party, the Friends were also plagued with problems. In 1934 Hubert Schnuch, leader of the Friends, and Anton Haegele, assistant national director, engaged in what was mainly a power struggle which resulted in a well-publicized court case and the formation of a separate American National Socialist League by Haegele. This damaged the reputation of the Friends, although the organization retained most of its members. In 1936 the name of the Friends was changed to the American German Bund, or German-American Bund, and came under the control of Fritz Kuhn, who was thought to be someone who could provide stable, effective leadership to the strife-torn organization.[8]

The Bund made a concerted effort to capture German-American support. This appeal was aimed at any discontent felt within the German-American community. In 1933 this organization issued a platform which indicated its direction. The goals, which were two-fold, fit very well into Nazi ideology. First, the American Nazis were to awaken German-Americans to the fact that they had been denied their proper position of power in American society and consequently should unify racially to correct this wrong. Secondly, Jews were the enemy, the ones who had taken an unfair amount of power and barred the German's rise to his proper place. Anti-Semitism, emphasizing an exaggerated portrayal of Jewish economic and political power, and chauvinistic Germanism, picturing an oppressed and humiliated German-American community, were the two main elements of the American Nazi program. The Bund also stressed a Jewish alliance with Communism and therefore pictured itself as saving America—and particularly German-Americans—from the all-powerful and communistic Jews.[9]

Any grievances, however small, within the German-American community were emphasized and exaggerated within the above framework in order to create discontent and win support. The *Deutscher Weckruf und Beobachter* (the Bund's newspaper) claimed that the Bund was made necessary ''by the persistent anti-German propaganda of a violent and all inclusive character that has been waged since 1914." A Bund pamphlet stated that "our movement is not a pilgrimage; it is a defensive war, a last call for you to rally to the rescue. . . . What German immigration brought to America in cultural values and contributed to the cultural fructification of their new home, should have sufficed to insure our pioneers of toil and intellect a merited place in the history of the country." This place, the Bund claimed, was denied to the Germans. Although this propaganda appealed to some, the membership remained relatively small and, most important, did not attract very many German-Americans who had emigrated before World War I.[10]

Although the exact size of the Bund is not known, its numbers have been estimated. The Justice Department suggested that Bund strength was 8,500 in 1938. Kuhn claimed it numbered 20,000, with 40 percent of its members in the New York City area. The German Ambassador to the United States in 1938 said it was 6,000. Local leaders of the Bund in New York City put the number at 3,000 in 1939 for the metropolitan area. Finally, the American Legion arrived at a figure of 25,000 for their estimate of Bund membership, as did the House Committee on Un-American Activities.[11]

More important is that occupationally the Bund was drawn from the middle to lower economic classes. A Department of Justice description of Bund officers in New York noted that most of them were "mechanics, restaurant workers, clerks, odd-job men and the like, with a scattering of technicians such as draftsmen, chemists and so on." A description of a Brooklyn Bund meeting in 1939 noted that 90 percent were working class and 10 percent were business people. An observer at a 1941 Bund meeting asserted that the poor quality of German spoken by the members suggested that the Bundists did not have a great deal of education. A study of the Bundists who in the late 1930s returned to Germany stated that they were mostly skilled workers. "More than half of the returnees had been trained as skilled industrial workers or artisans before emigrating to America." The occupations included locksmiths, carpenters, and other skilled jobs. Many, however, were thwarted in their attempt to practice these skills in the United States and had to take other jobs such as waiters or dishwashers when the Depression struck. Many of the returning Bundists had found themselves out of work at various times during the economic collapse.[12]

Sociological theory indicates a connection between a concern with status, downward occupational mobility, and prejudice.[13] The Bund members who returned to Germany certainly had been downwardly mobile, and many had been mobility- or status-minded (in the sense that they had higher occupational class orientations). However, others in the German-American community who also fit this description did not join the Bund. The difference may lie in the fact that most of the Bundists had recently arrived in America (during the 1920s), and many of these had been identified with right-wing anti-Communism and anti-Semitism in Germany and therefore already were prone to see the Jews as a source of their economic and other problems. The acceptance of anti-Semitism was already there; the Depression simply gave it new reason to emerge.

The ethnically conscious members of the older German-American community as a group, although experiencing some of the same economic difficulties, were not, in their American experience, inclined toward an anti-Jewish attitude. They were also increasingly sensitive to charges of Nazism and anti-Semitism—particularly in a city where a large and well-organized Jewish community could retaliate—and were reluctant to join an organization which, as the 1930s progressed, appeared more and more to be un-American. The few members of the older German-American community who joined the Bund apparently did so mainly out of fear of an anti-German crusade in America: they looked to the Bund as a protector. Fear of or anger at the Jews was not a motivating factor at first, but was later absorbed along with other points of Nazi propaganda. There were also those who joined because of pride in Germany's new, powerful position in Europe.[14] However, these people were few. Bundists and the Bund were products of Germany and its ethnic environment rather than that of the United States. The Bund therefore was not at all similar to that other 1930s anti-Semitic organization which operated in New York—the predominantly Irish Christian Front, which grew out of the intergroup frictions in America.

The rank and file of the Bund, of whom the returnees were representative, were mainly recent immigrants, Catholics, from the South German states and were either German citizens or newly naturalized. The membership of a Brooklyn local in 1934 consisted of 126 citizens and 332 aliens, with most of the citizens recently naturalized. The Manhattan unit in the 1936–38 period had no citizens out of an estimated 115 members, although some of the members had begun the process of attaining American citizenship. The leaders of the Bund, including Kuhn, were predominantly naturalized Americans. A Justice Department report stated that "in the majority of cases the leaders of the Bund have come to the United States from Germany since the World War." Spanknoebel, Ignatz Griebl, Gissibl, Reinhold Walter, Schnuch, and Kuhn, all leaders of the Bund or predecessor organizations, were German-born. The last three and Griebl were naturalized Americans who were chosen as leaders in order to emphasize the American character of the Bund.[15]

Persistent efforts were made to make the Bund appear more American. For example, in 1935 and again in 1938, the German government directed that German citizens withdraw from the organization. This order was also given so that German citizens in the Bund would not embarass the German government nor jeopardize its relations with America. The orders were ignored, and German nationals continued to join the American Nazi organizations.[16] Furthermore, the Bund attempted to promote itself as within the American mainstream. "Who are these so-called Friends of New Germany?" asked the *Deutscher Weckruf und Beobachter*. "They are the kind of people who have helped to build up this country, who have done their share in fighting for true democracy, and the right it implies." The Bund claimed that it sought mainly to defend the Constitution, combat Communism, and reawaken German-Americans. The goal of the organization, the leaders said, was not to establish National Socialism in the United States or weaken American institutions. "We German-Americans," stated J. Wheeler-Hill, the National Secretary of the Bund, "are unequivocally committed to the defense of the Flag, Constitution and Sovereignty of our United States." By 1938 the Bund had replaced its cry "Sieg Heil" with "Free America." Bund gatherings were referred to as pro-America meetings, patriotic American songs were sung, and English was used at all rallies and more extensively than before in the Bund's newspaper.[17]

The German-American community never saw the Bund as an American organization—a fact which kept citizen membership low. The Bund's superficial changes convinced only a few that the Bund was American. German-Americans remained very conscious of the questionability of the Bund's Americanism. Still smarting from the alien label applied to them in World War I, German-Americans were reluctant to get involved with a foreign organization. The Bund's ties to Germany were always suspected and later proved.[18] Its activities in America were constantly attacked as treasonous. Therefore, although some second-generation German-Americans and those of more remote ancestry did join the Bund, it stayed basically an organization of the newly arrived who had not gone through the searing World War I experience in America. Of course, members of the older German-American community could have joined extremist groups with more American roots; some did, but very few.

PENETRATING THE GERMAN-AMERICAN COMMUNITY

However, the Bund still achieved much influence through its penetration of established German-American societies, and it is here that the older German-American community was criticized for being too lenient and foolish with the Nazis. Conflict involving the older German-American community and the Jews in New York did not arise as the result of any active and strong pro-Nazi element among these Germans; it came instead because of a lack of a strong anti-Nazi response.[19] While the organized and leadership elements among the non-Nazi German-Americans avoided contact with the anti-Semitic component of Nazism—which immediately would have put a Nazi label on them—their silence and willingness to work with the American Nazis did virtually the same. Some German-Americans understood the Nazi danger early. For example, in 1934 Eugene Grigat, a prominent anti-Nazi German-American, noted that "it is . . . surprising that the major protests and other counteractions [against Nazism] were launched by our Jewish friends with the magnificent support of Christians here and everywhere; but with no notable German-American endorsement." He went on to warn the German-American community that if they did not speak out against the Nazis, "our fine friendships formed here with our Jewish fellow-citizens and neighbors, social and otherwise, are bound to suffer. If we do not raise our voices in sincere and determined protest—coupled with action—we deserve to be suspect of being tacit Hitler admirers.''[20]

This was the German-American dilemma of the 1930s: how to prevent being labeled Nazis while expressing pride in the achievements of the Fatherland and avoiding all criticism of anything German. The initial response of the older German-American organizations was either silence or an attempt to minimize the significance of the Nazis. Herman Kudlich, chairman of the political committee of the Steuben Society, questioned as late as 1937 whether the Bund should be considered important. He asked that "if these young fellows find pleasure in playing at soldiering, what harm is that? Why take them seriously?" There was also the feeling that the right of the Bund to hold meetings should be protected.[21] Although the Bund was a nuisance to some Germans because of its tactics, little attempt was made to criticize its ideology, since this represented the new Germany.

Since the older German societies were often lax in ostracizing the American Nazis from their community, the societies sometimes found themselves the captives of the Nazis, as in the case of the United German Societies of Greater New York (UGS), an important German-American organization in the City. The Bund was not a member of this federation, nor was it likely to be admitted to an organization which included many Jews and had voted against flying the swastika flag or inviting the German ambassador to its German Day celebration in 1933 (a yearly event held by the UGS marking the arrival of German settlers in America). Nevertheless, the Nazis penetrated the UGS by capturing control of two minor organizations which were members, the Stahlhelm, a German veterans group, and the Commercial Society of 1858. Spanknoebel, the Bund leader, appealed to a number of UGS officials on the basis of their emotional ties to Germany and was able to secure the calling of a special meeting to reconsider the actions concerning the German flag and an invitation to the ambassador. As a delegate from the Stahlhelm, Spanknoebel attended the special meeting held in September 1933. He also was placed on the program with the aid of Colonel Emerson's pro-Nazi connections in the UGS such as Ignatz Griebl (soon after chosen leader of the Bund). Spanknoebel then packed this poorly attended meeting with his supporters and, with threats of physical harm, forced his changes through. The anti-Nazi President of the UGS was compelled to resign; Spanknoebel was put on the organization's board of directors; the German ambassador was invited to the German Day celebration; and the meeting exploded into a vicious tirade against the Jews. Once the Nazis had gained control of the leadership, they began to oust many of those who had opposed them. Others resigned, as did the German Jewish groups. Therefore the Nazis, both members and nonmembers of the Bund, were able to capture at least the name and machinery of one of the largest and most prestigious German-American organizations. At the next meeting, when Bernard Ridder attempted to denounce the Nazis, he was shouted down. The Ridder brothers, Bernard and Victor, were expelled from the UGS, and as a final act the flying of the German flag was approved.[22]

The UGS never did hold its German Day celebration in 1933. Mayor John P. O'Brien, fearing that violence would erupt at the Nazi-controlled event, threatened to revoke its permit to meet at a city armory, so the organization cancelled the festivities. A belated celebration (held under the auspices of the Steuben Society) to which the German ambassador was invited to speak, took place in December. However, the UGS, still under Nazi control, planned the German Day event through most of the 1930s. The Bund took part in all the celebrations from 1934 to 1937, except the one in 1935. In that year, because of a dispute over tactics between the Nazis in the Bund and those in the UGS leadership who were not Bundists, the Bund was not invited to participate.[23] Essentially the UGS leadership came to accept a more moderate approach toward fostering Nazi principles among the German-American community. Also the Bund was considered too divisive, since it had attacked other German-American organizations. In 1936, however, the reorganized German-American Bund was invited to take part in German Day.

The Nazis also attempted to infiltrate and control many other German-American societies and newspapers.[24] The German-American Conference of Greater New York (a larger federated group than the UGS to which all German-American organizations, including the UGS, belonged) was taken over by the Nazis in 1934. Earlier, the Nazis had attempted to eliminate the influence of Victor and Bernard Ridder, who had been active in challenging the American Nazis in various German-American societies. In July 1933 Spanknoebel presented the Ridders with letters from Dr. Robert Ley, head of the German Labor Front, and Ernst Bohle, chief of the foreign division of the German Nazi party, notifying the Ridders that their pro-Jewish articles must cease and giving Spanknoebel the authority to take control of the *Staats-Zeitung*. Although Spanknoebel thought the letters would be enough to frighten the Ridders into compliance, it was not—he was thrown out of the office. The newspaper remained in the hands of the Ridder family, although it did not speak out against Nazism until much later. The Steuben Society of America also was threatened as the Nazis attempted to infiltrate the organization. Some Steubenites joined the Bund, and some Bundists joined the Steuben Society. Even the Roland Society (made up of German-American Democratic party clubs) was forced to expel members—including a former president in 1933—for Nazi sympathies and for advocating race prejudice. Also a number of very small German-American social, sport, and cultural societies began to affiliate with the Bund because it promised them funds. Throughout this period the Nazis continued their tactic of penetrating other German-American groups with the intent of taking over the name and machinery of the organization. In the late 1930s they concentrated on smaller societies, such as singing groups, or on setting up such groups within the Bund in order to draw in new members.[25]

At their peak the Nazis actually controlled only a few German-American organizations, but their influence was felt in all. As the impression began to be created that German-Americans were not willing to destroy fully the Nazi influence, efforts were made to limit the Bund and other Nazi influence. For example, Nazi control of the German-American Conference was short-lived. The split in the Bund movement in 1934 permitted the older German-American groups to rally and regain their dominance of the conference, although, even with Victor Ridder as the new president, some Nazi sympathizers remained in positions of power. The New York State chairman of the Steuben Society, Gustav W. M. Wieboldt, not only publicly attacked the Bund but refused to allow Nazi doctrine to be discussed at meetings and threatened to withdraw the charter of any unit which had Nazis within its ranks. In 1936 a charter revision specifically forbade membership to Nazis and others who were against the American form of government.[26]

Although an attempt was made to fight for control of these organizations, there was still, with few exceptions, no open criticism of Nazi ideology or Germany and only muted criticism of the Bund until later in the decade. For instance, the German-American Conference, although no longer pro-Nazi after 1934, still was willing to participate in German Day celebrations with the UGS and the Bund until 1938. The Steuben Society, whose leadership had offered one of the few open attacks on the Bund and which had refused to participate with them in the German Day celebrations in 1934, soon changed its attitude. Perhaps because of pressure from the German government, an unwillingness to continue public denunciations of a German organization, or the split over this issue within the society itself, the Steubenites no longer publicly criticized the Bund and after 1934 agreed to attend the German Day celebrations with them. Their position on German Day was explained simply that they wanted to honor their German-American ancestors, and this should not be inferred to indicate a desire to establish Nazism in the United States. However, this was the impression created. Some German-American organizations were so torn over the issue of criticism of Nazism that they voted to prohibit any political discussions at their meetings.[27]

The editorials in the *Staats-Zeitung* also illustrate the dangerous and misunderstood ambivilence which prevailed; at the same time the Ridders were fighting the Nazis for control of the organizations, their newspaper avoided criticism of Nazism and actually offered glowing praise of Hitler's Germany. In a 1934 editorial which looked at what a year of National Socialism had meant for Germany, the paper noted that "the union of the German tribes, the apparent complete setting aside of class hatred—if not also of race hatred—the economic successes as claimed on Sunday by Propaganda Minister Goebbels . . . , the recession of unemployment, the revival of industry, [and] the stablization of the financial picture speak on behalf of the new regime.'' The increasing racial abuses of the Hitler regime were largely ignored by the *Staats-Zeitung* during the early to middle 1930s, as they hoped that these practices would subside. They noted in 1934 that since the National Socialist Revolution was not tied to a rigid doctrine, and therefore might evolve, this should give hope to those who deplored certain features of it. Therefore when riots against Jews in Berlin occurred in July 1935 and the infamous Nuremberg laws (which delineated the Jews' status in Germany) were passed in September 1935, the *Staats-Zeitung,* although reporting these events, offered no editorial comment on them.[28]

However, a small segment of the German-American community had immediately condemned Nazism. They opposed Hitler and his ideology for political or humanitarian reasons—or because of an early recognition of the danger inherent in remaining silent. The most prominent of these early opponents was Senator Robert F. Wagner, who in March 1933 had strongly criticized the Nazi government and its anti-Semitic activities. The German-American Socialist newspaper *Neue Volkszeitung* in 1933 had been the sponsor of a large anti-Nazi meeting. Eugene Grigat also had spoken out forcefully against Nazism, warning his fellow Germans not to give the impression of siding with Hitler. In 1935 he organized the Friends of German Democracy, a German-American society devoted to fighting Nazism in the United States.[29] However, the general German-American response was a non-Nazi one; that is, either favorable toward Germany for non-ideological reasons or indifferent.

JEWS AND GERMANS

Whatever the reasons for the various delays in the German-American response against Nazism, the effect of this on Jewish-German relations was profound. Both the Jews and those Germans who were ethnically conscious were aware of their incompatible opinions on Germany. Although a sense of this existed, the only conflict which immediately emerged was that between the Jews and the Nazis (mainly the Bund). Each wanted to injure or eliminate the other. Although the Jews had every intention of striking out at only the Nazis, it became increasingly difficult for them to determine who was a Nazi and who was merely reluctant to criticize Germany. This was particularly true after the Nazis gained entry into or secured control over various German-American organizations. At times the distinction was not made, and therefore non-Nazi elements of the German-American community were brought into the conflict. While the expanding conflict was a natural consequence of the division over the Nazi issue, it was also unintentional, and was based on misconceptions of each other's opinions and motivations.[30]

The Jews, of course, were aware of their threatened position in the world during the 1930s and were very worried about the emergence of Nazism in the

United States and the fate of their brethren in Germany. Concern was also expressed about the general increase in anti-Semitic activities and sentiments in America. As one Jewish New Yorker, after seeing a Nazi poster, commented to his newspaper's editor, "I thoroughly agree with you that this incident is only a beginning, and that in the future we may well expect other types of defamatory propaganda, up to and including bombs." The *Jewish Examiner* in 1934 warned Jews not "to be lulled into a false sense of security. . . . Less than a year ago the leaders of German Jewry were making light of the Hitler peril."[31] They therefore sought to fight Nazism, although there was no consensus among the major Jewish organizations on how to do this. In general the American Jewish Congress and the Jewish Labor Committee were more activist, favoring demonstrations and boycotts, than were the American Jewish Committee or B'nai B'rith. The principal tactic of response which eventually emerged was the anti-Nazi boycott of German goods; however, not all Jews supported this initially.

The Jewish War Veterans, in March 1933, were the first group to support a boycott of German goods. The event which caused more Jews to become interested in this response was the Nazis' April 1, 1933 general boycott of Jewish businesses in Germany. The American Jewish Congress, working separately from the Jewish War Veterans, soon became active in the anti-Nazi boycott. In addition an ad hoc boycott organization called the American League for the Defense of Jewish Rights was formed in May 1933. This organization was later taken over by Samuel Untermyer, a prominent Jewish lawyer and civic leader, and renamed the Non-Sectarian Anti-Nazi League to Champion Human Rights. The American Jewish Congress, failing to amalgamate its boycott effort with Untermyer's organization, joined with the recently formed Jewish Labor Committee and set up a Joint Boycott Council in 1936. Thus at one point there were three boycott organizations. In 1937 the three agreed to partial union through an Actions Committee designed to investigate possible boycott violations. However, no real union of all boycott agencies ever was secured, and the boycott movement therefore was not as strong as it could have been.[32] B'nai B'rith, which did not participate in the boycott until 1939, and the American Jewish Committee both opposed this tactic in 1933, feeling that such action would only lead to retaliation against Jews in Germany. This was part of the great controversy going on within Jewry on what to do about anti-Semitism. Jewish- as well as German-Americans never represented a monolithic community with one opinion. Although the majority might be in favor of one thing, there always would be others supporting something else. However, by the end of 1938, according to a Gallup Poll, 96 percent of the Jews supported the boycott, along with 64 percent of the Catholics and 61 percent of the Protestants in America.[33]

The Jews who did favor the boycott were often fervent in their support, considering it to be a great moral as well as material weapon. However, the problems associated with it were numerous. German-American merchants, both those who sold and those who did not sell German-made goods, were affected by the boycott. For example, the *Jewish Examiner* reported a story of a German-American storeowner in Brooklyn who lost all of her Jewish customers when it was rumored falsely that she had Nazi ties. The article warned its readers to be careful how they used the boycott. This event probably was not an isolated case, since there were attempts in various Jewish papers throughout the decade, and from anti-Nazi German-Americans, to emphasize that Jews should not think that all Germans were Nazis and to remind them that the fight was only with the Nazis. Essentially, though, if the German-American was not explicitly anti-Nazi, he was thought of as a Nazi. Moreover, rumors were plentiful. The Joint Boycott Council received many letters urging the organization to investigate rumors that various companies were selling German goods.[34] There were, of course, reasons why some German-Americans were affected. German merchants who continued to carry goods from Germany because of Nazi sympathies, indifference, or a reluctance to take part in a campaign against their ancestral home were candidates for the boycott.

As a result various German-American leadership elements began to complain about unfair treatment. Bernard Ridder protested to Samuel Untermyer that the boycott increasingly was being directed against the German-Americans in the City, especially grocers and delicatessen owners, and noted that the friendly relations between Germans and Jews could be affected. Untermyer insisted that the "boycott is directed against German goods and German ships" and not against German-Americans as long as they did not handle German goods. Since this was not always the case, the protests continued. The National Council of the Steuben Society of America claimed "that a widely advertised boycott of articles of German manufacture was extended to a concerted attack on everything German-American, and as a matter of course retaliation would be preached." In contrast, the Bronx County District Council of the Steuben Society was upset that the boycott was finding its true mark. They reported that people were being prevented from entering stores that sold German goods and asked for an end to the boycott.[35]

Nazi sympathizers in the German-American community took advantage of the increasing bitterness over the anti-Nazi boycott and planned a retaliation aimed at the Jewish community. The United German Societies in December 1933 established the German-American Business League (DAWA), which organized an anti-Jewish boycott and encouraged German-American merchants to import German goods. Businessmen who belonged to the league put its emblem on their store windows and were included in a shoppers' guide. Handbills and stickers with mottos such as "Buy German" urged German-Americans to buy at these stores. Although the league was initially a product of the UGS, the Bund, through the intervention of Colonel Emerson and the German consulate, became active in DAWA and by 1935 had absorbed the organization.[36] The German Consumers' Cooperative (DKV), a Bund subsidiary since its inception, also took part in the anti-Jewish boycott. DKV stickers appeared in shop windows carrying messages such as "Don't Buy from Jews."[37] The German-American Board of Commerce (in Yorkville) also operated on behalf of the boycott; by the mid-1930s this organization was controlled by the German consulate. At the inception of the anti-Nazi boycott, while some merchants actually became Bund members as a response, DAWA was the most successful of the various organizations in appealing initially to non-Nazi German-American merchants who were affected by and wished to protest against the boycott. A DAWA emblem on their shop windows could possibly increase sales from Nazi and Germany-oriented customers.[38]

Jewish merchants and other Jews in German sections of the City now began to feel the effects of the Nazi-planned anti-Jewish boycott. Jewish merchants lost customers, and some even were forced to close up their shops. According to one report, Jewish doctors, dentists, and lawyers were moving out of German areas in Queens because of a loss of German business.[39] As an article in the *Jewish Examiner* stated, "Sharp lines are being drawn between German and Jew, . . . and the blind bigotry that burns in Germany is being ignited in this country." A pamphlet issued by the American Jewish Congress commented that the peace and harmony which used to categorize relations between Germans and Jews was now a thing of the past, as Germans had taken up the slogan "Boycott the Jews of America!"[40]

Another effort was now made by Jewish leaders to explain the anti-Nazi boycott to the German-American community. In an open letter addressed to "our patriotic German-American Fellow-Citizens," Samuel Untermyer tried to explain that Jews were compelled to undertake the boycott as their only available weapon. "Why," he asked, "should decent German-American citizens seek to retaliate upon the American-Jewish storekeepers for this boycott?" and he urged German-Americans not to be misled by Bund propaganda. Understanding the mood of the German-American community, Untermyer stressed that "*to love one's Fatherland does not mean to love or support Hitler, or to condone his monstrous cruelties.*"[41]

Although Untermyer tried to make a distinction between German-Americans who simply refused to criticize Germany and those who were solidly pro-Nazi, for many Jews it was increasingly difficult "to distinguish friend from foe." Incidents other than the boycott revealed this clearly. For example, in 1934 during an election for a state committeeman in Brooklyn the *Jewish Examiner* noted that "malicious rumors have been spread to the effect that because [John H.] Gerken is of German descent he is racially prejudiced." While the conflict between Jews and Nazis continued unabated during the 1930s, eventually fewer non-Nazis were involved. The anti-Jewish boycott was short-lived owing to a lack of continued non-Nazi participation.[42] As the pressure to declare oneself to be against Nazism increased, more German-Americans did so. By 1938 some distinction between those who were or were not Nazis could more readily be made.

THE GERMAN-AMERICAN SHIFT

At the beginning of the decade (except in New York, where the Jewish community was large and the Nazis were very active) the Bund and Nazi Germany had been largely ignored by the American people. However, anti-Germany attitudes began to increase slowly during the 1930s as the result of Germany's hostility toward the Jews (as seen by the world in such events as the Berlin Riots) and the beginning of attacks on the Catholic Church. Because of this shift in the American outlook, as well as out of concern for co-religionists in Germany, there were some new responses from the German-Americans. The New York State Branch of the Catholic Central Verein of America protested Germany's treatment of Catholics in 1935. While expressing hope for a change in policy, the Verein resolution condemned Germany for its actions against Catholics and for "innumerable actions of a like nature." The Roland Society, which up to 1936 had refrained from discussing foreign politics, now joined the anti-Nazis and noted that it was time for German-Americans to "decide whether we want to be German-Americans or Germans." The Federation of German Workers Clubs in 1936 initiated a signature campaign "demanding the disbanding and disarming of the Nazi Bunds in Yorkville and other centers." Particular pro-Nazi events now brought a German-American response. For example, in 1936 an anti-Nazi German Day celebration was held to protest Bund participation in the regular ceremony.[43]

The most significant change in German-American opinion toward Nazi Germany and the Bund eventually came in 1937–38 as the result of a growing American awareness of the threat of Nazism. Because of Bundist activities, what little concern most Americans had at first felt about Nazism had centered on this organization. However, by 1938 various events in Europe were increasing the awareness of a threat from Germany (and subsequently also the Bund) and brought the burgeoning anti-Germanism to a point where America's Germans had to speak out. They became by this time much more fearful of an anti-German response from other Americans.[44] The first event was the annexation of Austria in March 1938, which strengthened Germany's position in Central Europe. American press opinion reacted hostilely to the takeover, and there was renewed criticism of Nazism in the United States. Anti-Nazi articles began appearing with frequency in several national magazines. The general feeling that had emerged by this year was that Nazism was for export and consequently a serious threat to America. Increasing this fear were the arrests of some German nationals in 1938 for espionage against the United States. The growing awareness of the Nazi threat also manifested itself in attacks on the Bund. Disorders occurred when Bund leaders tried to speak at mass meetings in 1938. The government began a series of investigations into Nazi activities in the United States. In May 1938 the House of Representatives voted to set up a committee, under Martin Dies, to investigate un-American activities, including, of course, Nazism. New York State organized a similar committee under State Senator John J. McNaboe which looked into Communism and Nazism. In New York City, Mayor La Guardia ordered an investigation of the Bund in an effort to destroy the organization. The Sudetenland problem later in 1938 and the subsequent penetration and takeover of Czechoslovakia in 1939 further increased this new awareness of the Nazi danger from abroad and from within.[45]

German-American press and organizational opinion also continued to shift, although slowly. The initial thrust of their shift was in relation to the American Nazis. Although the non-Nazi organizations such as the Steuben Society met with the Bund in German Day celebrations in 1937, there was uneasiness at this time about doing so. Kuhn was not allowed to speak at the 1937 meeting, and the Steubenites objected to the wearing of Nazi uniforms by some of Kuhn's followers. By August 1938 the Steuben Society was publicly hinting that it was reappraising its relationship with the Bund and that a break was imminent.[46] In October 1938, in an effort to correct the impression the general public had of German-Americans, the society lashed out at the American Nazis. The Steubenites claimed that their earlier silence had been the result of an unwillingness to attack members of their own race and a desire to keep the disagreements of the German-American community within the confines of the societies involved. The Bund was now accused of being un-American and having caused dissension among German-Americans during a difficult and dangerous period. Particularly the Steubenites were upset by Bund attacks on their society. "The attacks and vilification on the part of the American-German Bund have become so violent and arrogant, the taunts of cowardice so ruthless, the situation so intolerable," declared the *Steuben News,* "that it is now deemed the better part of wisdom to speak up now in order to clarify a situation that has become unbearable." The German-American Conference also decided that the time had come for a public attack on the Bund and castigated them for undermining a united front of German-American organizations during an especially critical period. The conference proclaimed that they did not and never would recognize Fritz Kuhn, the Bund Fuhrer, as their leader, "not only for political reasons but for other weighty and important reasons." At the insistence of the German-American Conference and the Steuben Society and with the approval of the German consulate in New York, which suggested that German societies not connected with the Bund refrain from joint activities with that organization, the American Nazis were left out of the plans for German Day in October 1938. The celebrations, however, found Hoffmann, of the Steuben Society, noting his contentment with Germany under Hitler and with its expansion into Austria and the Sudetenland.[47] Increasing fear of being labeled Nazis would eventually force a change in the attitudes of the German-American community toward aspects of Nazism other than the Bund.

The next major shift for the German-Americans came just one month later as the result of repercussions from an event which occurred on 7 November 1938. On that day a young Polish Jew, Herschel Grynszpan, assassinated Ernst vom Rath, third secretary of the Germany Embassy in Paris. What followed this incident was the Kristallnacht (night of broken glass) pogrom in Germany, in which many Jews were injured and a number of synagogues and Jewish-owned stores were destroyed. The Nazi government also levied a one-billion-mark fine on the Jewish community and passed new anti-Semitic decrees. Although the earlier anti-Jewish policies and actions had adversely affected Germany in world diplomatic and economic circles as well as in public opinion, and some German government officials had expressed concern over this, there was no indication whatsoever, especially now, that the anti-Semitism would end in the foreseeable future.[48]

The reaction in American public opinion to these excesses was noteworthy. There were protests against Germany from a number of labor, religious, political, and social groups as well as newspapers. The United States ambassador to Germany, Hugh Wilson, was recalled, and Roosevelt, at a press conference, expressed surprise that such barbarity could still occur in the twentieth century. Hans Dieckhoff, the German ambassador to the United States, in a communication to the German foreign ministry, noted the anger in America over this incident. He stated that "any expression of public opinion is without exception incensed against Germany and hostile toward her. And as regards this, the outcry comes not only from Jews but in equal strength from all groups and classes, including the German-American camp." The Ambassador also remarked that "the good prospects for a gradual spread of anti-Semitism has suffered a serious setback . . . ; even the most bitter anti-Semites are anxious to disassociate themselves from methods of this kind." The *Forward,* a Jewish newspaper, also noted the impact of the anti-Semitic excesses at this time: "The savagery involved is so horrible that this time the Christian world has been shaken up deeper than by any of the previous Nazi brutalities against the Jews. . . . prominent Christians in all walks of life, statesmen, writers, clergymen, political leaders, have come out with the strongest words of condemnation against the regime of darkness." A Gallup poll of 9 December 1938 on Nazi persecutions of Jews revealed that 94 percent of the American people disapproved of Germany's anti-Jewish activities.[49]

The German-American community was forced at this time to take a stand not only against the American Nazis but also against Germany's anti-Semitism. Silence at this emotionally tense moment could easily be construed as signifying a pro-Nazi position. The Steuben Society offered its first criticism of the Nazi government with a rank-and-file–supported declaration condemning the Nazis' anti-Semitic activities. On 15 November 1938 the *Staats-Zeitung,* in an editorial entitled "Cold Terror," also strongly attacked the anti-Semitic practices of the Nazi Government. An unwillingness to believe that the German people could engage in such acts still existed, and the paper therefore again preferred to blame the excesses on fanatics within the party. However, no attempt was made to suggest that the party did not really support anti-Semitism or that the Nazis would mellow with time. No attempt was made to belittle the anti-Semitism or to claim that the reports were exaggerated. There was only disgust and a plea that it stop.

> We enter a protest against the dark powers which now make an assassination a welcome occasion to turn loose the lowest and most degraded instincts against defenseless people....
> All of us still have parents, brothers, and sisters, and other relatives in the old country whom we love and respect. All of us cannot and will not permit a beautiful dream, indestructible memories, to be torn from our hearts and trampled underfoot and soiled by those who are unworthy to be called Germans. And, therefore, in the name of our loved ones over there, we protest the defamation of the German name by fanatics, by those elements in the ranks of the party in power... who want to drag a great people into the mud of their sadistic meanness.

In another editorial, the paper proclaimed that "all those upright and good citizens of this land who bear the good name of Germany, the good name of the German people, as a sacred legacy in their hearts must realize that what is going on in the Reich today cannot be reconciled with American ideals ... just as little as it can be reconciled with what is truly German."[50] Statements favorable to the Nazi government no longer appeared in this paper. The *Staats-Zeitung* now began to carry articles describing protests against the Third Reich on this issue.

The motivating force behind a strong German-American anti-Nazi stand was the fear that silence would inspire a revival of the anti-German excesses of World War I.[51] The presence of the Bund became more and more an embarrassment and liability, especially after the American Nazis defended the November pogrom. The non-Nazi German-Americans therefore had to speak out. Other efforts of the non-Nazis to cleanse the German-American name included a radio address on WNYC by Victor Ridder and Gustav Wieboldt on 22 November 1938 in which both excoriated the Bund and Hitler. A few weeks later Ridder was a speaker at a Carnegie Hall meeting to protest racial and religious persecution. In an editorial in the *Staats-Zeitung* he noted that his presence at this gathering was the result of his feeling that German-Americans must either reject what was happening in Germany or be classified as supporting the Nazis and therefore face rising anti-German prejudice. "Woe to us," Ridder said, "if an enraged American public opinion turns against the German-American element in the mistaken opinion that we agree with the harassment which is now being promulgated in Germany. We would pay a terrible price for this error."[52]

Ridder also made a special effort to improve German-Jewish relations in the City during this period. Speaking at a synagogue shortly after his November 15th editorial (quoted earlier) appeared, he urged both Jews and German-Americans to eschew the spread of racial prejudice. He tried particularly to make others understand what German-Americans were going through at this time. "Our element," he stated, "is having a difficult time. They find it hard to believe what they are now slowly being compelled to believe, and that is that things are going on in their old Motherland which shock them and which they would have believed impossible.'' Ridder pleaded with the Jews to consider this and avoid any hatred or economic discrimination against German-Americans.[53]

Those in the German-American community who had earlier declared themselves to be against Nazism stepped up their attacks on the Third Reich during this time in an effort to avoid the Nazi label. Anton Weidman, president of the Roland Society, stated in July 1938 that ''we German-Americans who are loyal to the United States . . . are practically on trial before the American public'' and therefore must show their loyalty. The Rolanders were also very worried about anti-German discrimination, particularly in relation to jobs. The Roland Society later asked the Dies Committee for a chance to testify in an effort to counter the image of German-Americans created by the Bund, which was causing the public to take ''a discriminatory attitude toward German-Americans in general.'' *Volksfront,* organ of the German-American League for Culture (which had been created by the Socialist German-American newspaper *Neue Volkszeitung*) commented that since the Nazis were turning the American people against everything German, it was crucial for German-Americans to declare against Nazism ''in order that you may not yet be knocked on the heads as traitors to your own country.''[54]

The increasingly hostile attitude toward the Nazis in the German-American community, especially from those who had not declared themselves before, brought a favorable response from the Jews. For example, the refusal of the German-American Conference to allow the Bund to participate in German Day celebrations in 1938 caused the *American Hebrew* to state that this was ''an indication of a definite trend away from Nazism on the part of Germans in America.'' The *Jewish Examiner* gave front page headlines to this repudiation of the Bund. Further German-American condemnations of the Nazis brought renewed feelings of friendliness on the part of the Jews. After the *Staats-Zeitung* editorial condemning anti-Semitism, the *American Hebrew* commented that this German newspaper, ''heretofore generally regarded as sympathetic to the Nazi regime,'' had now denounced that regime. The *American Hebrew* went on to note that ''the Jews of America want to live in peace and harmony with the Germans of America and the Germans of Germany who feel, with them, that the Hitler regime is a blot upon civilization.'' Other indications of change in the Jewish attitude were evident. In 1939, a New York Lodge of B'nai B'rith presented an award to Victor Ridder, citing him as an outstanding protector of human rights, presumably for his statements and actions against the Nazis.[55]

While an intense conflict continued between the Jews and Nazis, the actions of the non-Nazis in 1938 helped to clarify their position. Had the non-Nazi segment of the German-American community not taken an anti-Nazi position after 1938, certainly the intensity of their conflict with the Jews would have increased. An anti-Nazi response after the pogrom of November 1938 was extremely important in controlling this conflict. The reaction of the non-Nazis was based simply on their realization that what they feared the most—a revival of anti-Germanism—would happen if they did not speak out and remove the Nazi and anti-Semitic labels. Their vital interests now compelled them to move in this direction and served as the main mitigating factor in this conflict situation. However, not all difficulties between Germans and Jews were eliminated. Many German-Americans continued to take pride in Germany's foreign policy and military accomplishments. Therefore, although a willingness to attack Nazism existed, there was still a reluctance to criticize Germany and her increasing power in the world. While this reluctance produced less ethnic friction than the original failure to condemn anti-Semitism and Nazism, relations remained strained between Jews and Germans, and some conflict still occurred over the continued use of the anti-Nazi boycott. The *Staats-Zeitung,* for example, favored the annexation of Austria, convinced that this was something which both the German and Austrian people desired and which would right the wrongs of the World War. The headlines in this newspaper on 15 March 1938 stated that "Hitler has Triumphant Entry into Vienna" and noted that there were "a million people in the streets in undescribable jubilation." The paper was merely reflecting the sentiments of the German-American community. In Ridgewood, Queens, where the Bund chapter was not strong, a local editor remarked that "Ridgewood glowed with pride at the annexation of Austria." These people, the editor noted, were not Nazis, yet continued to take pride in Germany's victories. Even after the German army had marched into Czechoslovakia and the nation was absorbed, the *Staats-Zeitung* could not accept that Hitler would do such a thing and continued to believe the best. Their editorial asked, "who or what has forced [Hitler] to begin this attack?" The paper hoped that Hitler was not bent on aggression, and it tried, when possible, not to interpret his motives unfavorably. The ambiguity of the *Staats-Zeitung* in relation to German foreign policy led to Victor Ridder's loss of a 1945 libel suit in which he branded as liars three writers who accused him of supporting a pan-German conspiracy. The jury decided that Ridder could not prove that he was not in favor of pan-Germanism. The Steuben Society and its officers also found it difficult not to endorse Germany's foreign policy successes.[56]

NAZISM AND THE OTHER ETHNICS

Although Germany presented problems for Jewish-German relations, it had little effect on the Irish or Italians. The Irish press, being hostile toward England and sympathetic toward Germany, could therefore generally agree with the German-American newspapers on foreign policy.[57] The concordat signed between Germany and the Pope in 1933 did much to satisfy Irish Catholic opinion and take their attention away from that country to other matters, such as the

Spanish Civil War or anti-Catholicism in Mexico and Russia.[58] However, after the Vatican expressed dissatisfaction in July of 1935 with Germany's infringements of the condordat and in March 1937 issued an encyclical to Germany's Catholics castigating the Nazi government for its attempts to undermine Christianity, the Catholic press, including the *Tablet,* began to criticize Germany. Also some Irish Catholics criticized Germany's anti-Semitic policies. Still, many continued to hold the attitude that if Hitler would cease his anti-Catholic activities, he would be acceptable. Communism remained the real enemy which Hitler was helping to fight.[59] The issue of Nazism then was diminished as a point of contention, and the Irish and Germans were not involved in conflict over it. The end of the decade even saw cooperation between the Bund and Irish anti-Semites which Bund leader Fritz Kuhn encouraged. Bundists, Christian Fronters, and other kindred spirits often went to each other's meetings, and at one point a merger was discussed between the Bund and the Christian Mobilizers, a largely Irish group similar to the Front. However, after the arrest of Kuhn the Bund's new leaders dropped all ideas of merger.[60]

A similar situation developed for the Italian community. Nazism was not a major issue to the Italians, although they did note to other Americans the differences between Hitler and Mussolini, with the intent of showing Italian Fascism in a favorable light. However, at the beginning of the decade, when Italy and Germany were competitors in Europe, *Il Progresso* was critical of Hitler, referring to him at times as "dictator Hitler" and objecting to various foreign policy moves such as Germany's attempted union with Austria in 1934. As Italy and Germany drew closer as allies, comment in the Fascist Italian-American press became favorable toward Germany. England and France were now accused of causing all the trouble in Europe.[61] This response to Germany continued until American entry into World War II.

In the United States, Bundists and Italian Fascists collaborated as their ideological homelands drew together. In 1937 the Bund and the Italian Blackshirts held a joint meeting at Camp Nordland, a Nazi Youth Center, in New Jersey. The Bund also met with other Italian Fascist organizations, such as the Associazione Italiano All'Estero (Association of Italians Abroad). The issue of Germany's anti-Semitism did bring adverse comment from the Italian anti-Fascists such as Marcantonio, La Guardia, and Luigi Antonini. However, concern with the fate of Germany's Jews was not widespread in the Italian-American community until later in the decade, when efforts were made to respond to Italy's anti-Semitism.[62] La Guardia probably did the most damage to Italian-German group relations in the United States by singling out Germany for attack a number of times while saying nothing about Mussolini and Italy. The Nazis and non-Nazis in the German-American community thought La Guardia to be unfair, but their attitude toward him was never extended to include hostility toward Italian-Americans. Nazism and other matters involving Germany remained mainly a German-Jewish issue.

ITALIAN-AMERICANS AND FASCISM

While Nazism was an immediate source of intergroup friction, the initial impact of Fascism came within the Italian-American community, where it was the cause of much in-fighting. Only later, and in muted form compared to the Nazi issue, did it contribute to group conflict. Even in New York, Mussolini was less a danger than Hitler.

Italian-Americans supported Italy for very much the same reasons that German-Americans supported Germany. The achievements of their ancestral home enhanced the prestige of the Italians in America and inspired pride in the accomplishments of the Mussolini regime. As one Italian-American noted: "Whatever you fellows may think of Mussolini, you've got to admit one thing. He has done more to get respect for the Italian people than anybody else. The Italians get a lot more respect now than when I started going to school. And you can thank Mussolini for that."[63] Moreover, the agreement signed between Mussolini and Pope Pius XI in 1929, ending a long dispute between the Vatican and the Kingdom of Italy, made Il Duce appear as a champion of the Church.

While the German-Americans were called upon immediately to declare either for or against Nazism, and then were regarded suspiciously by other Americans if they hesitated, Italians faced no such ordeal. Americans in general tended to react much more favorably to Mussolini than to Hitler throughout the 1930s. Therefore it was easier for Fascism to gain a foothold in the United States and for Italian-Americans to support it—which the majority of them did. However, for the most part, this support was nonideological, since they were actually only expressing support for Italy.[64]

Organized Fascism first appeared in America in the 1921–23 period with the emergence of a number of independent Fascist clubs. One of these was the Fascist League of North America, which, with the help of the Italian government, was able to absorb the other clubs. The league met with some opposition within the Italian-American community from anti-Fascists and from those who were apprehensive that an obvious Fascist presence would allow hostile nativist sentiment to emerge. By 1929 an exposé of the league in *Harper's* and the expression of some concern in Congress about this organization finally convinced the Italian government, which wanted to keep a low profile on Fascist activities in the United States, to abolish the league.[65]

To replace the league, a number of smaller organizations arose with the help of Italian consular officials in the United States. These new groups included the Lictor Federation, established by Dominic Trombetta, a man who played an important role in the ethnic conflict of the late 1930s; and the Dante Alighieri Society, originally founded in 1890 but taken over by the Fascists in the 1920s. This organization disseminated Fascist propaganda through its cultural centers. A group that later became active in the Fascist cause was the Committee Pro-Italian Language, which propagandized Italian neighborhoods under the pretext of promoting the Italian language. The activities of the Dante Alighieri Society and the

Committee Pro-Italian Language were coordinated by the National United Italian Associations, an organization believed to be under the control of the Italian consulate in New York City. This coordinating body also worked with the United States section of the Association of Italians Abroad under the direction of the Italian Ministry of Foreign Affairs. These organizations for the most part discarded the tactic of violence which their predecessor, the league, had used against anti-Fascists. However, the American Union of Fascists, a Blackshirt group similar to the German-American Bund, did not disclaim the use of physical assaults.[66]

Efforts to penetrate legitimate Italian-American fraternal societies caused an emotional reaction in this ethnic community. A particularly bitter battle erupted in the Sons of Italy during the mid-1920s over the issue of Fascism. Irreconcilable differences resulted in the splitting of the New York State section, led by La Guardia and State Senator Salvatore Cotillo, from the national body and the establishment of an anti-Fascist American Sons of Italy Grand Lodge.[67]

Among the Italian-Americans there was a vocal anti-Fascist opposition represented by men such as Salvatore Cotillo and Luigi Antonini, president of Local 89, the Italian Press and Waist Makers Union of the ILGWU, and by such events as the split within the Sons of Italy. Antonini, for example, lashed out in weekly radio talks against the Fascists and received many threats for his stand.[68] In 1923 the Anti-Fascist Alliance of North America was created. This organization received support from the ILGWU and the Amalgamated Clothing Workers Union of America. The ILGWU also endorsed *Il Nuovo Mondo,* an anti-Fascist newspaper which began publication in 1925.[69]

However, those that were outright Fascists or sympathizers with the Mussolini regime were numerically stronger within this community. The major Italian-American newspapers, including the formidable *Il Progresso,* supported Mussolini. An indication of the weakness of the anti-Fascist opposition occurred during the Italian-Ethiopian War of 1935–36 when the leadership of the Italian labor unions criticized Mussolini's invasion but won little support among the rank and file for their views.[70]

FASCISM AND THE OTHER ETHNICS

Since most Americans, including the other ethnics, did not yet regard Mussolini as a threat, the battles within the Italian community and the pro-Mussolini sympathies of the majority of Italian-Americans concerned few. In the Irish press, for example, there was no criticism of Italian Fascism. The settling of the Vatican-Kingdom of Italy dispute had perhaps satisfied many Irish Catholics that Mussolini was acceptable. Later in the 1930s the Coughlinite Irish would heap praise on Mussolini and Fascism. Indeed, when Hitler began his attacks on the Catholic Church in Germany, Mussolini looked even better. The German-American press at first responded differently. At the beginning of the 1930s, when Germany and

Italy were competitors in Europe,the German-Americans were critical of Mussolini. The *Staats-Zeitung* clearly blamed the Ethiopian War on Italy and was quick to point out Italian atrocities committed in that struggle. References were also made to Mussolini as a dictator. However, this attitude quickly changed as relations between Italy and Germany improved, and by the end of the 1930s the troubles in Europe were being blamed not on Italy but on the English and French.[71] However, even with the early criticism of Italy, there is no indication that this issue impaired relations between the Germans and Italians in New York.

The Jews, who offered the most vehement opposition to Nazism, had a different reaction to Fascism until the late 1930s, when anti-Semitism became a factor. The Jewish press constantly compared Italian Fascism favorably to the degenerate German Nazism. "As Mussolini has gained in the respect of the world, the obsessed Fuhrer has won the odium of enlightened mankind," commented one Jewish paper in 1934. Nazism was described as "counterfeit Fascism." The Jews in Italy were pictured as enjoying a renaissance under Mussolini. Statements in Italy's newspapers critical of Hitler's racial dogmas were given prominent space in the Jewish press. A full-page article in the *Jewish Examiner* described how Mussolini was aiding Jewish refugees from Germany and Jews in Italy. In 1933 a poll taken of forty-three Jewish newspaper editors to choose the twelve greatest Christian champions of the Jews in the previous year produced the name of Mussolini. Il Duce was chosen because he "took pains to demonstrate that Italian Fascism does not tolerate racial and religious persecution."[72]

Some Jews in New York, of course, were opposed to the Italian government on an ideological basis. The Jewish leadership of the ILGWU and the Amalgamated, along with the Yiddish socialist newspaper *Forward,* were prominent in anti-Fascist ranks. Rabbi Stephen Wise was a member of the American Friends of Italian Freedom, an early anti-Fascist organization.[73] However, Italian Fascism did not evoke any hostility or even concern from the majority of the Jewish community in New York during the 1920s or early 1930s.

The Italian-Americans were very pleased not to antagonize the Jews and made a major point of showing the differences between Italian Fascism and German Nazism. Until 1938 Italy was pictured as a society where all could live in peace. "In Italy everybody is equal: Catholics, Protestants, and Jews, all Italians," commented one Italian-American newspaper (which was later to become rabidly anti-Semitic). Mussolini himself noted in 1933 that "it is impossible to imagine in Italy . . . any persecution of Jews."[74]

MUSSOLINI AND ANTI-SEMITISM

However, Italian Fascism did eventually emerge as an explosive issue as Mussolini gradually drew closer to Germany and introduced racial policies which fit the

Nazi model. This shift began slowly. As late as 1936, when German and Italian "volunteers" were aiding Franco in Spain and the Rome-Berlin Axis was forming, the Italian delegate to the World Jewish Congress could still refer to his country as the "noblest example of perfect equality for Jews." By 1937, the year when Italy joined the German-Japanese anti-Comintern pact, indications of change appeared as Mussolini's Milan newspaper, *Popolo d'Italia,* asked Jews to give total support to Fascism or leave Italy. The paper stated that any opposition to Nazi ideas would be "irreconcilable with the friendship that binds us to Germany, which has objectives far more vast and fundamental than the Jewish question." The paper noted, however, that Italy did not wish to rid itself of its Jewish population. Mussolini also indicated that a definite policy toward Jews had not yet been formulated when in July 1937 he venerated an Italian Jewish soldier killed in the Spanish Civil War and refused to accept the resignation of Italy's Jewish communal authority, the council of the Union of Israelitic Communities in Italy.[75]

By 1938, however, the racial policy had been set. During this year, the world witnessed the German takeover of Austria and the Munich Conference. With these events came Italy's anti-Semitic decrees. On 14 July 1938 ten Fascist university professors issued a government-sponsored manifesto charging the Jews with ruining the qualities that made up the characteristics of the Italian race. By the end of July Jews were gradually being removed from high office. This action served as the immediate prelude to the actual decrees, the first of which was promulgated on September 2. This anti-Semitic order prohibited Jewish teachers and students from entering the schools. It also ordered all Jews who had come to Italy since 1919 to depart within six months. Throughout September, October, and November in 1938 decrees were passed which restricted marriages between Jews and non-Jews, land and business ownership, Fascist party membership, and service in the armed forces or government. Later decrees in 1939 prohibited Jewish professionals from serving anyone but fellow Jews. The simultaneous establishment of a privileged class of Jews who were excluded from the restrictions softened these edicts. This group originally included the families of men who lost their lives in Italian wars or for the Fascist cause, who volunteered in wars or received the military cross, or who were members of the Fascist party in the early years of its growth. The privileged category remained until 1943, when the Germans occupied Italy after the overthrow of Mussolini. The Italian public, in contrast to the higher levels of Mussolini's government, did not entirely endorse the anti-Semitic decrees. The result was an effort to soften the provisions through nonenforcement or by placing Jews in the privileged class.

As far as Italian-Jewish relations in New York were concerned, however, the most important fact was that the decrees had been passed at all, amid a great deal of publicity, and that a number of Jews in Italy were affected by them.[76]

REACTIONS TO THE DECREES

Some Jews were aware as early as 1936 that the edicts might be forthcoming in the near future. For example, in 1936 Rabbi Stephen Wise, President of the American Jewish Congress, suggested to a number of prominent Italian-Americans that they contact Mussolini "so that he may know of the value of Jewish citizenship to America. If that were done, it might avail to avert that anti-Semitism in Italy which up to this time has not been, but which seems to be foreshadowed by [Roberto] Farinacci's recent attack."[77] However, there remained in the Jewish community an unwillingness to believe that Italy would really follow Germany's sordid policies. Consequently many Jews were unprepared for the events of 1938. One Jewish periodical commented that "Fascist Italy's ruthless campaign against the Jews in Italy came as a shock to many Jews and non-Jews, who somehow associated Jew-baiting with Nazi Germany alone and who thought that Italian Fascism was above the taint of anti-Semitism." However, the *Forward,* an early critic of Mussolini, expressed no surprise and reminded its readers that "there is no good Fascism."[78]

Aware of the problems that Italy's actions could cause, the Jewish press immediately attempted to calm the situation by urging continued harmony with all Italians. Evident, however, in the frantic pleas for harmonious relations, particularly with Italian-Americans, was the fear that ethnic relations were already, or soon going to be, deeply strained. The *New York Jewish News,* for example, commented that "to allow this black poison of hate, imported from abroad, to interfere with the mutual respect the Jews and Italians now feel toward one another would be a grave mistake." The *American Hebrew* pleaded that Jews "should be careful not to be so blinded by fury that they strike at innocent persons who happen to be standing nearby." The editorial continued with the hope that Jews would "not transfer our quarrel with the Italian government to this country by undertaking boycotts against Americans of Italian extraction." An article in the *Jewish Examiner* urged Italians and Jews to work together in America in order to avoid repercussions from events in Italy. The newspaper also noted that "Italian sentiment in America is definitely opposed to Mussolini's newly formulated 'Aryan' theory and its implications of anti-Semitism." One writer in the *Jewish Veteran,* perhaps trying to convince himself as well as his readers, stated that "the insane situation in 'Aryan' Italy will not affect the friendly relationship existing between Jews and Italians in our country."[79]

Besides urging and pleading with Jews not to retaliate against Italian-Americans, the Jewish press attempted to mollify tensions by exonerating Italians abroad for their actions. In an open letter to Mussolini, the *American Hebrew* stated that "we want to believe—our former admiration and respect urges us to believe—that what you have done in recent days you have not done of your own free will." An article in the *Jewish Examiner* noted that Mussolini and the Italian people were not really in favor of the anti-Semitic campaign. Even the *Forward* commented that Mussolini had "finally caught the ugly Hitleristic disease," which they attributed to the new friendship between the two dictators. This viewpoint was supported by some Italian-Americans. Antonini, while condemning Italian anti-Semitism, stated that it was being instituted as a result of Nazi orders.[80]

The leadership of the Italian-American community did not wish to see a conflict emerge between Jews and Italians, either, and therefore it too urged harmony. Generoso Pope, the publisher of *Il Progresso*, although remaining a Fascist supporter, rejected the anti-Semitic decrees and made repeated efforts in letters and editorials to calm the situation. When Jews first became concerned about possible anti-Semitic action in Italy, Pope optimistically pointed out that Mussolini intended no harm to the Jews in Italy; after the anti-Semitism had begun, his editorials stressed that Italy had no desire to imitate Nazi policies. Pope urged that Jews and Italians in America not allow their friendship to be affected by events abroad. Letters to the newspaper echoed Pope's thoughts.[81] Other Italian-American leaders were critical of Italy's new policies and urged that there be no repercussions in America. This opinion was voiced by such notables as Marcantonio, La Guardia, Poletti, Antonini, Cotillo, Philip Bongiorno (former Supreme Master of the Sons of Italy), Santo Modica (Grand Master of the American Sons of Italy Grand Lodge of New York State), and Joseph Tigani (president of the Roman American Progressive League). These leaders were joined by many others when a number of Italian-American patriotic, civic, and religious organizations met in Manhattan in November 1938 to protest the persecution of Jews in Italy and Germany.[82]

Within six months after the beginning of Italy's anti-Semitic policy, the leadership of the Italian-American community had clearly rejected it. However, during these six months a reaction similar to that in the German-American situation developed, indicating the explosiveness of the Italian anti-Semitic issue. Essentially, before Italians expressely rejected the decrees, they were suspect in the same fashion as were the non-Nazis. Conflict was evident until the Jews were convinced of the Italian community's position on this matter. Reports from a number of sources during these months indicated an increasing friction between the two groups. Jews began to retaliate against Italians by using their economic power. A study prepared for the American Jewish Committee in November 1938 observed that fewer Jews were shopping at Italian-owned stores because of the decrees. Furthermore, in some instances Italian workers and union members had a definite feeling that work was being denied them because of Jewish discrimination. This was particularly the case in the Painters Brotherhood and the garment industry. For example, the report stated that Italian painters "resent a certain lack of work, although it has not been proven openly that this is a result of Jewish discrimination. They are, however, convinced that such a thing exists." The report continued that a number of Italian-owned garment shops, which rely on Jewish jobbers for their business, had experienced an abrupt decrease in orders. This drop in orders was perceived to be a reaction to the decrees.[83]

The concern with this problem was expressed by *Il Progresso* publisher Generoso Pope when he noted that "in my business enterprises I have faithful and loyal workers of many nationalities; I have Jews who hold high positions. . . . It never occurred to me to discriminate against anyone because of race or creed. I hope that Jewish industrialists and businessmen harbor the same sentiments." The Jews' greatest threat, and the Italians' most often-expressed fear, was that of a Jewish boycott of Italian products similar to the anti-Nazi boycott begun against Germany in 1933. Concern was expressed that any boycott would extend to all things Italian. For example, Pope noted that he had heard of a proposed Jewish boycott of Italian goods "which probably would not stop at importations from Italy." Cotillo, in a cable to Mussolini, asked that the decrees be lifted because there was "serious talk of boycotting Italy in our great city of New York where we live in close interdependent relationship" with the Jews. The Italian government also worried about a boycott and other repercussions. They saw their fears becoming reality after a decline in Italian bonds on the New York market was considered to be a reaction to the anti-Semitic events in Italy.[84]

As a result, Mussolini had little enthusiasm for pushing the anti-Semitic campaign either in Italy or America. Only a few Italian-American Fascists supported these decrees.[85] The most blatant was Dominic Trombetta, publisher of *Il Grido della Stirpe* (Cry of the Race). Trombetta's newspaper engaged itself in a defense of the Nazis and began to repeat the accusations against Jews found in the German-American Bund newspaper in New York. While the newspaper claimed that reports of anti-Semitism in Germany were exaggerated, it emphasized the plight of Italians in America and Catholics in Mexico, Spain, and Russia. Jews were described as Communists and anti-Fascists whose goal was to destroy Italian Fascism. In addition, the paper defended the German-American Bund, noting that "it is needless to say that the Bund is a patriotic organization determined now more than ever to fight the world's worst parasite, namely Communism." The intent of the newspaper seemed to be to coordinate activities, including anti-Semitic propaganda, between Fascists and Nazis in New York City and to convince Italian-Americans to support Nazi Germany.[86]

Partly because of Trombetta's rhetoric and the initial Jewish response to the decrees, anti-Semitism soon began to appear among Italians. One study focusing on Italian East Harlem indicated that the area was seeing the growth of overt anti-Semitism, especially among "Italians who worked in Jewish sweatshops." Another study mentioned a burgeoning anti-Semitic movement among Italians in the Amalgamated Clothing Workers Union and an "increasing coolness" between Italians and Jews in the Painters Brotherhood. The Italians drawn to anti-Semitism were mainly those who were working in Jewish-dominated industries and affected by the Jewish reaction to Italy's decrees. Also involved here was some Italian resentment of real or perceived Jewish success. For example, one Italian-American garment worker who joined an anti-Semitic organization at this time complained that in the Jewish-dominated ILGWU "65 percent of the union is Sicilian and we don't hold one office."[87] As with the non-Nazi experience, the conflict expanded as retaliation was preached.

RESOLVING THE CONFLICT

Many Italian-Americans were concerned that the conflict would grow more intense if it were not checked quickly. Marcantonio remarked in February 1939 that "there is existing the danger of the spread of anti-Semitism among our people" and urged that a conference of Italian-American leaders, to which Jewish representatives were invited, be held soon. This, he felt, would "help destroy once and for all the misunderstanding which is being engendered by dishonest people between Jews and Italians." By June 1939 a circular sent out by the American Sons of Italy Grand Lodge noted that "anti-Semitism in Europe, unfortunately, has had a repercussion in America, particularly in the City and State of New York, causing a spirit of hatred and resentment between Italians and Jews that can only culminate in a daily struggle." This organization set up a Bureau of Good-Will Between Italians and Jews in America whose main purpose was to "promote brotherhood and settle any dispute caused by discriminatory acts." Members were requested to notify the bureau regarding grievances involving the loss of business or employment due to the Italian-Jewish conflict.[88] As with the explosive issue involving non-Nazi German-Americans and Jews, conflict had developed out of misunderstanding. However, the effort of the Italian leadership to repudiate anti-Semitism and to work to improve relations with the Jews helped to mitigate the conflict.

The desire of the Italians to avoid conflict with the Jews was the result of many factors. Foremost was a concern over Jewish economic power. Being more vulnerable to Jewish economic retaliation than the Germans, the Italians expressed particular concern about this aspect of conflict. Even the anti-Semitic *Il Grido della Stirpe* expressed this concern. At the same time that the newspaper was calling Jews Communists, it also reported cases of Jewish economic discrimination against Italians. The result was that the paper requested that Jews maintain their friendship with Italians in America and disregard the events in Italy. "We wish to live in peace with others" said the anti-Semitic journal. The Jews, of course, were not unaware of their power in this respect. The *Jewish Examiner* claimed that the two largest Italian-American newspapers in New York had remained neutral on Mussolini's decrees because Jewish businesses provided three-fourths of their advertising.[89] Whether or not the claim is true, it indicates that some Jews perceived that economic power kept the Italians in New York from supporting the decrees.

Jewish economic power was certainly not the whole explanation, however. Italians were also more willing than Germans to castigate certain aspects of the Fatherland, for the German's World War I experience made them extremely uneasy about criticizing anything German. Even pro-Fascist Italian-Americans were willing to repudiate the anti-Semitic decrees while maintaining support for Mussolini's government. Furthermore, the racial theories which were such an integral part of Nazism were not a vital part of Italian Fascism and could therefore be more easily rejected.

The point in time at which this conflict emerged also must be noted. By 1938 American public opinion was showing an awareness of the German threat, thereby forcing German-Americans to declare themselves to be against Nazism; there was also a budding awareness of the danger of Italy. Starting in 1937 a number of exposés of the Italian Fascist movement in the United States began to appear in American periodicals.[90] Gradually, pressure increased on Italian-Americans to state their position or be suspect as enemies of America. In this changing atmosphere, and with the response of the Jews, most segments of the Italian community moved relatively quickly to declare themselves against anti-Semitism. Had there been no repudiation of the decrees, the conflict would have continued. Again, a group's vital interests eventually had compelled them to shift their position and speak out against their ancestral home and the sources of the conflict.

The Jews also moved away from the conflict situation for a number of reasons. They were under attack during the 1930s not only by German Nazis but also from organizations operating in New York, such as the German-American Bund and the largely Irish Christian Front. As problems with the Bund and Front increased toward the end of the decade, Jewish leaders began to focus their attention on these groups. The much less vocal Italian anti-Semitism faded into the background of Jewish concern. The relatively small number of Jews in Italy and the mildness of Mussolini's anti-Semitism also aided the Jewish effort to suppress conflict. Il Duce was never fully identified in the Jewish mind with anti-Semitism; Hitler occupied this position, and the Jews concentrated on him. The forthright denunciation of the decrees by Italian-American leaders eventually convinced enough Jews that the Italian community was not hostile to them. It was extremely important to have major Italian and Jewish leaders urging harmony. Although some difficulties between Italians and Jews remained because of continued Italian-American support for Mussolini, the main point of friction had been eliminated.[91]

Explosive issues that can easily lead to conflict can also easily be moderated. In the case of both the German-Americans and Italian-Americans, a group's vital interests had compelled a stand which led to conflict, and then, by a turn of events, these same interests were responsible for the elimination of the main source of conflict. For a group to survive in America's competitive society, it is only natural that it behave in this way.

Chapter Five

Communism, Coughlinism, and the Church

"REDS WILL CONTROL NEW YORK UNLESS BLOCKED."[1] This often-repeated prophecy of the 1930s and '40s sent fear through the hearts of many New Yorkers who honestly believed a Communist takeover was imminent. Communism, like Fascism, was not a problem to intergroup relations in the early 1930s, but it became one of the major explosive issues later. As the fear of this "-ism" grew, and as one group, the Jews, became identified with it, ethnic conflict over this issue appeared. Interacting with the other points of friction of the day, the Communist issue played an important role in the emergence of a very intense, prolonged, and often violent Irish-Jewish conflict. The Communist question and the attendant conflict also affected other intergroup relations as well, but in a different way from that of the Irish and Jews.

For many years Communism had been considered the foe of Catholicism and had symbolized all the forces seen as threatening the Church's teachings and power. During the 1930s the battle with Communism seemed to be reaching a climax. Not only was the Communist party growing in strength, but the many changes in American society after World War I and particularly during the New Deal indicated to many that Communism was sweeping the country. Warnings of this threat were issued from Rome itself. In 1930 Pope Pius XI urged Americans to be wary of the rise of Communism during their economic difficulties. In 1932 the Pope further noted the danger of militant atheism, which was using the media and political parties to achieve its goals. The Pope's major statement came in an encyclical (Divini Redemptoris) in 1937 which warned that Communism was the greatest menace to the world and called for a Catholic crusade against it.[2]

ENTER COUGHLIN

In America an important figure echoing the Pope's statements was Father Charles E. Coughlin, the radio priest of Royal Oak, Michigan, who in his Sunday broadcasts and later through his newspaper, *Social Justice,* attracted a large audience. Coughlin first began preaching anti-Communism in 1930. Although his appeal had other aspects, such as attacks on the New Deal and on the wealthy—an approach which won followers—the anti-Communist theme remained a central one in his rhetoric throughout the 1930s and was particularly important to his Catholic supporters. In a sense Coughlin became a spokesman for the Church, since he was acting out the Pope's warnings (albeit according to his own interpretation). Rather than converting others to his beliefs, the radio priest instead was able to lead those with similar sentiments. He provided an explanation for his followers' economic problems, an understanding of who were the sources of their frustrations, and a rationalization for their group hostilities. Moreover, while Coughlin's appeal was strong among Catholics attuned to the threat of Communism, it also had a class basis.[3]

Although Coughlin had middle-class support in the early stages of his movement, this declined as he lost prestige by involving himself in extremist politics. By 1938, according to two Gallup polls, the radio priest received his strongest support from the lower economic levels. One study of the priest noted that "as economic status decreases, approval of Coughlin increases," regardless of occupation. However, some occupational categories gave the priest stronger backing than others. Farmers, skilled and unskilled manual workers (more so among the unskilled), those on relief work (W.P.A.), and the unemployed provided the highest rate of approval of Coughlin. Among Catholics, however, white-collar workers (especially unskilled) also had a predilection for the priest. Professionals and businessmen indicated the least approbation of Coughlin. On every economic level the priest's followers exhibited certain basic traits. They were unhappier with their economic position, with America's economic situation, and with the outlook for the future than were those who disapproved of Coughlin. More supporters than opponents perceived that their own economic position was deteriorating for various reasons. Therefore Coughlin was able to receive his strongest support in the cities from economically discontented Catholics of the lower income classes who were manual, relief, or white-collar workers or who were unemployed. Of course it must be noted that there were other reasons besides economic, religious, or ideological ones for the support for Coughlin. For example, the radio priest also may have attracted those who for psychological reasons were drawn to his authoritarian movement.[4]

While Coughlinites were mainly Catholics, this group also had an ethnic dimension. A number of studies have revealed the Irish and German Catholic base of Coughlinism. Although it seems that Coughlin's support in New York City during the 1930s came more from the Irish than from the German community, it is only important to note, for the purposes of this study, who was attracted to his appeal, including his anti-Communism, when it took an anti-Semitic turn.[5] In New York overt support for Coughlin's anti-Semitism was found mainly among the Irish.[6] In order to understand the relationship between Coughlin and the emergence of an anti-Semitic response, it is first necessary to look at the awareness and fear of Communism which permeated the German and Irish Catholic communities.[7]

THE COMMUNIST THREAT

Enough evidence of Communist party activity existed in both the City and nation by the late 1930s to upset all Catholics and convince them that the Communist threat was real. For example, in December 1937 Simon Gerson, a member of the state executive committee of the Communist party, was appointed to the staff of Stanley Isaacs, borough president of Manhattan. The Catholic community protested bitterly to officials such as Governor Lehman.[8] Gerson, however, was retained because Isaacs was unwilling to fire him on the basis of his party membership.[9] Clearly, Catholics saw this as evidence of the Communists' power in the City government. La Guardia was already suspect because of the charges of Communism leveled against him during the mayoralty campaigns; his refusal to intercede in this case only seemed to confirm his Communist sympathies.[10] On the national level, there was a strong suspicion that the New Deal also showed Communist leanings—a view stressed by Coughlin and other influential Catholics such as Al Smith.[11] A number of events had occurred during the decade which slowly increased Catholic dissatisfaction with Roosevelt and made this group more susceptible to anti-New Deal rhetoric. The recognition of Russia, the neglect of Catholic persecution in Mexico, the president's tolerant attitude toward unions engaged in sit-down strikes, his court-packing plan, the appointment of former Ku Klux Klan member Hugo Black to the Supreme Court, the "Roosevelt Recession," and the Reorganization Bill created the picture of an inept, possibly anti-Catholic, president bent on assuming dictatorial powers. Beginning in 1938 the Dies Committee investigations, which noted Communist infiltration into the federal government, helped to join these fears with those of a Communist takeover of America. All of these conditions seemed to threaten the position of Catholics in the United States and certainly increased their insecurity. Furthermore, prominent government officials such as Victor Ridder, George U. Harvey (borough president of Queens) and Congressman Hamilton Fish noted that Communists were employed in the relief agencies. Similar pronouncements by other highly placed individuals indicated the same for the unions, particularly the newly formed Congress of Industrial Organizations (C.I.O.). Finally, Earl Browder, general secretary of the Communist party, remarked in 1938 that Communism had penetrated into the schools, civil service, relief and other agencies. Therefore the evidence was strong enough to convince many that the Communist party was a real threat which had infiltrated various important American institutions by the late 1930s. Of course, Communist party members were active during this period, so to some extent the fears were warranted.[12]

However, the strength of Communism was exaggerated, primarily because its definition was not limited to party membership or Marxism. *Communism* meant *change*—from birth control to increasing divorce rates to a general disrespect for authority.[13] The unions, and especially the C.I.O., were classified as Communist both for actual party influence and for their methods. The C.I.O.'s militancy and use of sit-down strikes in 1937 disturbed the status quo and, according to the *Tablet,* indicated "a link to Communism." Coughlin even claimed that Catholics should not join this union since it was incompatible with Catholicism. Relief, too, was attacked, not only because party members were in the welfare agencies but also because the relief system greatly increased the government's power and could possibly be used as a weapon against the Church. As the *Tablet* warned, "It was thought that seventy million citizens claimed no church. But, if the Washington giving goes on, that number will be swollen largely each year" because the poor will no longer look to the clergy for help.[14]

Fear of change, of increasing government power, especially with the liberals in control, and of an attack on Catholic values and institutions was evident among all Catholics, but it was stronger among the Irish, who saw particularly their own power and values being challenged in New York. A speech by Father Robert Gannon, president of Fordham University, to the Friendly Sons of St. Patrick illustrates this theme. He remarked how the United States and especially New York had changed over the years. Instead of harmless politicians who would perhaps just steal some money, now

> there is a swarm abroad in the land. They call themselves 'liberals'.... They are not as crude or as simple as the ward-heeler with the big cigars. What they want is not so much our money as our children. They want our schools and colleges. They want the key positions in the civil service. They want control of relief and all the social agencies and they are getting what they want. Later they hope, when they have the youth of the nation in their power, to eliminate all religion and all morality that does not conform to their peculiar ideology.[15]

Journals identified as liberal, such as the *Nation* and the *New Republic,* were often referred to as anti-Catholic and Communistic in the Irish press. Scanlan, of the *Tablet,* noted that they really were "intellectual Kluxers."[16]

Foreign events, such as the persecution of Catholics in Mexico and especially the Spanish Civil War, also contributed to Catholic fears about Communism and change.[17] The threat to the Church in Spain during the Spanish Civil War was of great concern to many Catholics. Since Russia was aiding the Loyalist forces, and Communist Front groups in America were doing the same, many Catholics interpreted the war as a battle between Christianity and Communism and therefore wished to defend the faith. Stories relating Loyalist anti-Catholic persecutions filled the Catholic press. Most Church leaders, including Patrick Cardinal Hayes of New York and Bishop Thomas Molloy of Brooklyn in addition to Father Coughlin, castigated the Loyalists and supported a Franco victory. Coughlin stressed the Communist support for the Loyalist side, and prominent Catholic laymen such as Al Smith repeated these arguments, warning that unless atheism were defeated, Spain's situation would be repeated in America.[18]

Despite urgings from their leadership, Catholics in general were not overwhelmingly behind Franco. However, stronger support for Franco could be found in this community than in others. A Gallup poll taken in December 1938 indicated that 39 percent of all American Catholics favored Franco and 20 percent favored the Loyalists; for Protestants the figures were 40 percent for the Loyalists and 10 percent for Franco. Among Catholics and Protestants who took sides (discounting those who favored neither side or had no opinion), 58 percent of the Catholics supported Franco and 42 percent supported the Loyalists, while 83 percent of the Protestants favored the Loyalists and 17 percent were for Franco. Among those who approved of Coughlin, the Catholic Coughlinites gave stronger support to Franco than the Protestant Coughlinites. However, even among the Catholics, Franco's support was not a majority: about 42 percent of the Catholics favored Franco and only 11 percent of the Protestants; the rest were either Pro-Loyalist, neutral, or of no opinion. Greater support for Franco was found among those who approved of Coughlin than among those who disapproved of the radio priest.[19] By ethnic groups, stronger support for Franco is indicated among those groups which were heavily Catholic, although again not necessarily a majority. A Gallup poll in February 1939 (see table 10) asked those who had been following the civil war which side they favored.[20] It must be noted

Table 10. Attitudes toward Spanish Civil War, by Ethnic Group, February 1939

Ethnic Group[a]	Loyalists	Franco	Neither	No Opinion
Irish	28.2	48.7	17.9	5.1
German	35.0	27.5	30.0	7.5
Italian	20.0	55.0	15.0	10.0
Russian[b]	52.8	17.0	20.8	8.6

SOURCE: American Institute of Public Opinion [Gallup] Poll 147 (2 February 1939).
[a]By country of birth of father.
[b]Many Jews would be expected to be found among this group.

that this poll can only be taken as suggestive, since the number of respondents was very small and it was based on a national rather than a New York sample. However, when this information is coupled with opinions evident in the ethnic press,there is an indication of support for Franco by many individuals in each of the Catholic ethnic communities of New York.[21]

The domestic and foreign attack on the Church inspired a militant response which was strongest among the Irish-Americans. This group saw themselves as defenders of the faith, militant Catholics who would protect the Church, which in itself was a symbol of their power and status.[22] The Irish-Americans also saw themselves as the defenders of American institutions and interpreted the attack on Catholic values as an attack on America—patriotism and Catholicism had become intertwined in Irish minds. Editorials in the Irish press stressed the Americanism of the Irish and their duty to fight Communism and defend America. The *Irish World* commented that the Irish were "the pillars of American life, the very backbone and the certain security of Americanism in every phase," and it was their responsibility to defend American ideals. Coughlin's *Social Justice* affirmed that the Irish were true Americans who would rid the land of Communism.[23] At a time when other Americans were challenging and rejecting Irish-Catholic values, it was gratifying to become the real Americans.

JEWS AND COMMUNISM

The increasing fear of Communism and change in both domestic and foreign affairs by the late 1930s would not necessarily have been a factor in intergroup relations had not one group—the Jews—been identified as the Communists. A number of elements led to this identification and made it mainly an Irish response.

There was first an immediate Catholic-Jewish division on the Communist issue which can be related to differences over values and interests. Most Jews did not see Communism as a great threat; rather, they considered fascism (including Nazism) to be the major danger to America. "In the event of its [fascism's] success," claimed the *Jewish Examiner,* "nothing but the most dire consequences could befall American Jewry." In short, fascism represented to the Jews what Communism did to the Catholics: everything that threatened their existence. In some cases, that which the Catholics defined as Communism was seen by the Jews as progressivism and social awakening. What was a threat to one group could be seen as the basic social philosophy of the other. It was for this reason that Father Edward F. Brophy, a priest sympathetic to Coughlinism, questioned how the *Jewish Examiner* could claim to be opposed to Communism and still attack men like Coughlin, whom Brophy saw as one of the leading anti-Communists in the country. Compounding the problem was the fact that some Jews accepted Communists as allies in their fight against fascism and anti-Semitism, just as some Catholics accepted fascists in their fight against Communism and anti-Catholicism.[24] Misunderstanding existed on both sides.

Many Jews were attracted to Communism because of social beliefs which were grounded in a history of discrimination. As Rabbi Stephen Wise noted, the "Communism of most young Jewish boys and girls is not anti-democratic nor anti-American, but a poor, misguided expression of their own will to achieve a more just and equitable social order."[25] To some Jews, Communism offered a better order of things, a system lacking the oppression of traditional society. In the Communist society all were supposed to be equal. (Russia, for example, had outlawed anti-Semitism.) This appealed to Jews upset by the discrimination and intolerance of the 1920s and 1930s.

In a sense, this attraction to Communism was merely a continuation of earlier Jewish attempts in eastern Europe to work for a just society. The General League of Jewish Workers in Russia, Poland and Lithuania (Bund), active at the turn of the century, had much the same desire to create an equitable social order. This background of revolutionary, socialist activity made the Jews a susceptible target for the rhetoric of Communism in the 1930s. In the same way, the conservative, authoritarian orientation of Catholics lowered their resistance to fascist appeals.

Many Jews had been drawn to revolutionary activities in eastern Europe by the actions of society against their people. This was especially true of Jewish students in Czarist Russia who had found many of their dreams shattered when they were barred from the Russian universities. Anti-Semitism also impeded the upward social mobility of Jews in America, particularly those of the second generation, and they, like those before them, were attracted to the people who fought it—in many cases this appeared to be the Communists. Therefore, many Jewish professionals of the second generation found themselves tempted by Communism. Teachers, doctors, lawyers, and social workers were especially drawn into the party. Their affiliation came not from love for the Soviet Union but merely from a desire to bring about a more equitable social order. In New York City, therefore, the Communist party membership was mainly Jewish, although most Jews in the City were not Communists.[26]

On the basis of their background and their situation in the 1930s, the Jews also tended to support the Loyalists in the Spanish Civil War—an understandable position, since Hitler was aiding Franco. To this ethnic group the battle in Spain was not one between Communism and Democracy, but rather between fascism, with its accompanying radical theories, and Democracy. A Loyalist victory would diminish Hitler's power and prestige in the world. Although not all Jews felt this way, support could be seen in such actions as the Central Conference of American Rabbis in 1937 endorsing a resolution which castigated Franco's side in the Spanish conflict and a statement by Rabbi Wise excoriating prelates who had prayed for Franco's victory. The Abraham Lincoln Battalion, made up of American volunteers who fought for the Loyalists, was 25 percent Jewish.[27]

THE IRISH, COUGHLIN, AND ANTI-SEMITISM

Given the Jewish position on the Spanish Civil War and their different orientation toward Communism, the ethnic situation was conducive to an anti-Semitic response by the Catholic community on the Communist issue.[28] That it was mainly the Irish who made this response is based on their Catholic militancy, their relationship with the Jews, and the absence of mitigating factors which would have prevented it.[29] The fact that the Jews were perceived as opposing Catholic interests and values closely identified with Irish status, were found in Communist party ranks, and were the major threatening competitors to Irish economic and political positions during a difficult period helped to lead many of the militant and discontented members of the Irish community, aided by Coughlin, into anti-Semitism on this issue and into a more broadly based, intensive conflict as well. This conflict contained both realistic and unrealistic components. The unrealistic elements included historical tradition in the form of religious anti-Semitism, which played a minor role; deflected hostility related to Depression frustrations; and erroneous judgements concerning, for example, the extent of Communist activity among the Jews.[30]

Although the German and Italian Catholics could also identify the Jews as opposing Catholic interests and values, they were less militant in their defense. They did not, as much as the Irish, react to the Communist factor as a personal threat and an indication of waning power.[31] Other elements also muted their anti-Jewish hostility on this and other issues. As noted previously, the Jews were much less an economic and political threat to the Germans and Italians than to the Irish. Moreover, the Germans were not as hard hit by the Depression. Finally, there was a reluctance on the part of the Germans and Italians, particularly by 1938, to involve themselves in anti-Semitism. Neither the Italians, including the Fascists, nor the non-Nazi Germans in New York wished to be identified with Hitler's racial policies. In this City, with its large and powerful Jewish community capable of retaliation, this identification would not have been in the interests of either the Germans or Italians. Both groups were vulnerable to attack because of their increasingly unpopular Old World sympathies, or economic position, or both. Although some support for anti-Semitism existed in these communities, it remained minimal and subdued. Coughlin's anti-Semitic rhetoric appealed to mainly the Irish.[32]

Ethnic tensions in New York increased as a result of Coughlin's influence. His chief contribution to conflict was to increase the awareness of a struggle with the Jews and to encourage a hostile response to them. Since Jews signified to Coughlin the two main dangers to the world—Communism and plutocracy—an attack on this group represented to him both a way of fighting the rise of radicalism and the causes of the Depression, as well as winning support. Although for several years he had indicated an anti-Jewish sentiment in his speeches and private statements, Coughlin did not emerge fully as an anti-Semite until July 1938, when he began to publish in his *Social Justice* the spurious *Protocols of the Elders of Zion* (an account of a Jewish plot to rule the world). His newspaper increasingly emphasized its concern about the rise of anti-Christianity (or anti-Catholicism) in the world while at the same time playing down anti-Semitism and calling attention to the great power of the Jews.[33]

Coughlin also began to use radio broadcasts as an avenue for his increasingly outspoken attacks. On 20 November 1938, just after the Kristallnacht pogrom in Germany, Coughlin offered a defense of the Nazi position. In a radio address over New York City's WMCA he explained and justified the Nazi persecution of Jews as a defensive response against Communism. (He also accused the Jews of financing and organizing the Communist Revolution in Russia.) In essence, Jews and Communists were regarded as synonymous in this speech.[34] In response to this attack, WMCA decided that henceforth Coughlin would have to provide the station with a copy of his speech 48 hours before he was to read it on the air. Coughlin refused and, as a result, was barred from the station. However, he was able to secure an outlet at a smaller station, WHBI, Newark, and proceeded to repeat his accusations against the Jews.

The WMCA action opened up a major controversy between Coughlin's supporters and opponents. The Irish (although not the German or Italian) press defended Coughlin's statements. The *Irish World* declared that Coughlin had been denied freedom of the air "because he dares to speak the truth—and in this instance the truth hurts." Coughlin, the paper continued, was "one of the foremost exponents of Americanism in its soundest form and . . . undoubtedly one of the most erudite and saintly priests in the United States." Apparently the *Irish World* accepted Coughlin's statements about the Jews. So did Scanlan, of the *Tablet,* who defended Coughlin in his assertions that a large proportion of Communist leaders were Jews. An article in the *Tablet* further claimed that Coughlin was barred from certain radio stations because these stations were controlled by Jews. Both the *Irish World* and the *Tablet* printed letters to the editor which agreed with this analysis.[35]

Many Irish-Americans and others were concerned not with what Coughlin said but instead with his right to speak. T. Fitzpatrick, president of the County Down Social, Athletic, and Patriotic Association of New York, said in a letter to Coughlin that "as a patriotic organization comprised of Irish and Irish-American Catholics, we have adopted a resolution to protest the unjust attitude of station WMCA toward your radio program. We inform you of our action because we want to express our sympathy with you for the unjust action you have received from WMCA." Similar statements came from the Galway Men's S and B Association and from Irish-Americans meeting in the Bronx. The *Catholic News,* in a small article, referred to a rally to secure Coughlin radio time as one for "free speech and Americanism." However, the paper showed no agreement with Coughlin's position; rather, it gave prominent coverage to clerical and lay critics of the speech.

An ad hoc group, the Committee for the Defense of American Constitutional Rights, was formed to support Coughlin. Its speakers at one rally included such prominent New Yorkers as Justice Herbert O'Brien of the Queens County Domestic Relations Court, State Senator John J. McNaboe, and Borough President George U. Harvey. Demonstrations against WMCA began on 18 December 1938 and continued until September 1939. Pro-Coughlin picket lines were formed in front of the station's offices and were removed only when La Guardia ordered that all such inflamatory and divisive actions be stopped due to the outbreak of war in Europe. The number of pickets had already been limited by the mayor because of fighting between opposing forces outside the station. Anti-Semitic posters and statements were common among the protesting Coughlinites.[36]

The barring of Coughlin from WMCA was a further indication to the Irish of their loss of power in New York and of the strength of the Jews, and it served to increase ethnic animosities in the City. The incident fit well into a theme already running through the Irish press and in *Social Justice:* that anti-Christianity, not anti-Semitism, was the real problem in the world and particularly in New York. This sentiment was first expressed during the early 1930s as a result of the persecution of Catholics in Mexico and the indifference shown by non-Catholics to this situation. As this attitude grew during the decade, it was accompanied by a tendency to belittle the anti-Jewish events in Germany and to wonder why only the Jews seemed to be able to gather support. The *Irish World,* for example, asked why those who had protested against the persecution of Jews in Germany had not spoken out "against the far greater persecution of Catholics in Mexico." The *Tablet* later complained that the Jews were concerned only about Jewish persecutions and had overdramatized the situation in Germany. Scanlan commented that while a great deal was being done by the government to protest against anti-Semitism in Germany, little was being done "to assist the far worse persecuted Catholics of other nations." In this country, too, according to Scanlan, "the anti-Christian movement is far more prevalent . . . than the anti-Semitic campaign." The paper subsequently carried articles noting how Jews were the troublemakers who were involved in attacks on Christians. The *Tablet* finally concluded that the issue of anti-Semitism was "nothing more than a 'Red' herring used by Communists and their 'liberal' dupes and stooges to spread strife, discord and confusion throughout the land."[37] These sentiments were evidence of the insecurity felt by the Irish, who saw themselves as powerless and rejected in a society unconcerned with the plight of their co-religionists. Such expressions were also an indication of their resentment of perceived Jewish power on the basis that the Jews were the ones who were able to get a government response. The WMCA incident engendered bitterness and frustration, for it confirmed what the Irish felt they already had known.

Although Coughlin tried to defend himself during this period by noting that he was attacking only Communistic and atheistic Jews and that he had no quarrel with the religious Jews, this distinction was really never made either by him or his followers.[38] All Jews appeared threatening. Consequently, Coughlin's statements and writing could have only one effect: to encourage an anti-Semitic response among those already susceptible to this appeal. The fact that the priest continued to receive support from prominent elements in the Catholic community lent respectability to his movement as it moved into its anti-Semitic phase and helped to win recruits.[39]

THE CHRISTIAN FRONT

The best example of Coughlin's influence can be seen in the formation of the Christian Front. Coughlin was interested in Pope Pius XI's suggestion of a Catholic Action program which would spread the doctrines of Catholic social principles and provide a Catholic response to a number of social problems.[40] Picking up the Pope's appeal, Coughlin turned it into a call for a Christian Front, which did little to bring society back to basic Christian concepts or to create a just world, as the Pope had desired. Instead it served only to intensify the Irish-Jewish conflict in New York.

Inspired by statements in *Social Justice* during May, June, and July of 1938 which warned of a Communist takeover of America and called for a Christian Front, and spurred by the economic and political climate of the period, the organization began to take form.[41] Late in June of 1938, at the corner of Flatbush Avenue and Albemarle Road in Brooklyn, a militant anti-Communist and anti-Semite named Russell G. Dunn began speaking against the Communist elements among the refugees from Germany. A number of young Catholics who were already involved in anti-Communist activities soon began appearing with Dunn at his streetcorner rallies. The result was the formation of two organizations—the Flatbush Anti-Communist League and the Flatbush Common Cause League—which were involved in arranging weekly anti-Communist and anti-Semitic meetings and which received favorable publicity in the *Tablet*. The locations for these gatherings were usually the corners of Flatbush Avenue and Albemarle Road, and Kings Highway and East 17th Street, both of which were in Irish-Jewish neighborhoods and were places where Communist meetings had previously been held.[42]

From these local Brooklyn rallies, and from meetings held in the rectory of the Roman Catholic Church of St. Paul the Apostle in Manhattan, the Front emerged.[43] The first meeting of an organization with the name Christian Front came on 14 July 1938 at the Church of St. Paul. ''Most of the men who joined the Front during this period were Catholics recruited by other priests and laymen'' in the vicinity of the Paulist church. However, a connection existed between the Brooklyn and Paulist meetings, for John Cassidy, a leader of the Brooklyn group, spoke at the first Paulist meeting.[44] The early gatherings centered on discussions of Communism and the Jews and were addressed by various people, including Bundists. The specific topics covered issues such as Jewish involvement with Communism, the anti-Catholic position of the Jews during the Spanish Civil War and Jewish control of labor unions and jobs. One participant at the first meeting who complained about Jewish control of the ILGWU was an Italian-American garment worker.[45]

The WMCA controversy in November 1938 involving freedom of speech for Coughlin helped to increase the Front's membership.[46] Shortly thereafter, John Cassidy, who had continued his anti-Semitic street meetings, organized a Brooklyn unit which eventually came to dominate the citywide movement and through which Cassidy was to become national director of the Front. As it grew, the Front developed into both a membership and a coordinating organization. Branches of the Front eventually included the Christian Labor Front, which was designed to infiltrate unions in order to oust Jewish-Communist leaders, and the Greater New York Committee for Christian Action, which supported an "employ Christian only" campaign as well as an effort to boycott Jewish merchants. The Front also coordinated its activities with groups that shared its philosophy, such as the Flying Squads for Americanism and the Committee for the Defense of Constitutional Rights.[47]

Most members of the Front were Irish Catholics, although some German, Italian and other Catholics were also in the group.[48] The appearance of an organized and relatively long-lasting anti-Semitic society which engaged in planned violence indicated the increasing intensity of conflict as explosive issues interacted with those associated with ethnic succession. That it was mainly the Irish rather than the Germans or Italians who were drawn into this organization reveals that the most serious conflict of this period involved the Irish and Jews.

The Front was an ethnic organization; even its occupational and class breakdown illustrates this point. Its rank and file were mainly blue- and white-collar workers of the lower class and lower middle class. Among these were workers facing and/or fearing job competition from the Jews. Many Front members were also described as people who had suffered from the Depression. According to a survey ordered by La Guardia in January 1940, 407 policemen had applied for and received membership in the Front. (However, only twenty-seven were still reported to be Front members at the time of the survey; the others claimed they had joined the organization because of its anti-Communist nature but had quit when they became aware of its anti-Semitism.) At one meeting of the Front, a Transport Workers dance was announced; at another meeting, in September 1939, longshoremen, truck drivers, policemen, and school teachers were seen in attendance.[49] The Front's leaders, however, represented a different element from most of the rank and file. John Cassidy and other young leaders of the organization were college graduates, mostly from local Catholic colleges. Cassidy, moreover, had recently graduated law school. Priests and politicians also were active in the leadership of the group. Thus the Front, with its lower class and lower-middle class cadres and its lawyer, priest, politician, and college-educated leaders represented a cross section of any New York Irish community. In its membership, then, nothing distinguished the Front from any other Irish organization.

The individual Irish who joined this organization came out of the larger Coughlinite group but exhibited more militancy on the issues of anti-Communism, anti-Semitism, and a defense of Christianity. The Frontists saw themselves as patriots rather than rabble rousers—citizens resorting to self-defense units in order to fight what were perceived to be alien and anti-Christian influences in America. As Cassidy said, "we are a militant group of men . . . determined to use every means at our command to guarantee to the Christian people of America, that they shall never be subjected to the misfortune that befell their Christian brothers in Russia, Mexico and Spain." The Front served those who were convinced that force was "immediately necessary to defend Christian civilization."[50] Some also may have joined because of individual psychological needs which drew them into an authoritarian movement.

Although Coughlin's anti-Communist rhetoric was the organizing spark for the Front, it addressed itself to all the points of Irish-Jewish friction and offered itself as the only effective response. On the economic grievances, as was noted earlier, the Front organized boycotts against Jewish merchants. At one meeting a plan was discussed to go to New York City department stores and demand that at least 60 percent of the workers be Christian. In general, at Front meetings "an extravagant picture of Jewish success in a setting of exaggerated Christian failure" was emphasized.[51] Politically the Front was committed to fighting against those politicians with whom they disagreed. Since the Front saw Communism as sweeping the country, they were determined to destroy this movement. However, to Frontists (as to the general Irish population) Communism meant more than party membership. As one Front pamphlet noted, there were "political moves and social changes . . . now taking place which, tending to throw this country off its traditional course, are rapidly weakening our institutions and threaten to end in chaos and anarchy." The Roosevelt administration was seen as encouraging these changes, and the Jews were thought to be controlling not only the City, State, and Federal government but also the press and radio. The Front, Cassidy stated, was organized with the purpose of preserving the United States government "and the Christian social order on which it was founded." To save America from Communism the Front attempted to oust Jews from positions of leadership in organizations such as labor unions; they worked to prevent what they saw as the infiltration of government by alien influences; and they opposed "government by willful minorities."[52] The Spanish Civil War issue was brought up repeatedly in Front literature and at their meetings, with most of the discussion on this issue taking an anti-Jewish theme. One pamphlet asked, "Are they [the Jews] not all actively supporting a cause [i.e., Loyalist/Communist] whose purpose is to crush Christianity out of the earth?'' Thus, to the Front, anti-Communism became "Christian Self-Defense." Finally, on at least one occasion, a Front speaker attacked the Jews as Christ-killers.[53]

As the ultimate response to Jewish Communist control and influence in society, the Front engaged in numerous physical attacks on the Jewish community. Front streetcorner meetings were also marked with violence, both from the anti-Semites and their opponents.[54] Street fights between Frontists and Jews occurred often. This organization therefore was a product of and a response to the many points of ethnic friction, based on realistic and unrealistic factors, between the Irish and Jews. The Front also grew partly as the result of the general anti-Semitic climate of the period which was encouraged by foreign and local propagandists for Nazism and Fascism.

The growth of this organization was related not only to the ethnic issues and anti-Jewish climate of the times but also to the respectability it gained by associating itself with prominent public figures. John Cassidy spoke on the same platform in September 1939 with U. S. Senator Pat McCarran of Nevada, and the Front sponsored rallies at which, for example, Queens borough president George U. Harvey spoke. These meetings helped give the impression that the Front was well thought-of in high places. Most important, however, was the involvement of Catholic religious and lay leaders. Father Coughlin, as a priest and national figure, lent respectability to the Front. His *Social Justice* often defended the organization and implied that its opponents were Communists. Other priests, such as Fathers James Keeling of the Bronx, Edward Lodge Curran of Brooklyn, Peter Baptiste Duffee of Manhattan, and Edward F. Brophy of Queens, supported the Front, thereby helping to convince many that the Catholic Church in New York looked favorably upon the organization. A relative of Christian Fronter Michael Bierne observed that "the fact that Father Coughlin was a priest of the Church led Michael to think that the Catholic Church had given its blessing to the Christian Front movement.'' The *Brooklyn Tablet* (official diocese paper of Brooklyn) gave a great deal of favorable coverage to Front meetings and praised and defended the group. Patrick Scanlan also appeared with Cassidy in pro-Front rallies.[55] The initial support that the Front received at the Paulist Church also lent credence to this idea. Moreover, the silence of the Church hierarchy only encouraged this belief. The failure of the Church to repudiate the Front and the obvious clerical support it received helped it to secure members. Also, a number of the Front leaders and other prominent Coughlinites had been involved in Catholic study and discussion groups suggested by the Catholic Action program. It is easy to see why the more militant and discontented supporters of the radio priest, with a twisted idea, based on Coughlin's preachings, of what Catholic Action was supposed to be and with the Pope's warnings on Communism in mind, would be drawn to this organization in the belief that it was a positive, respectable response and that they were good Catholics by becoming involved.[56]

As the Front grew, it faced competition in the Bronx and Manhattan from another organization—the Christian Mobilizers. This group, organized in July 1939, was similar to the Front in every way, except that its members thought that the Front program was too timid, and therefore favored more violence against the Jews and Communists. On the advisory board of the Mobilizers were Thomas Monaghan, Joseph McDonagh, Joseph Hartery, James Stewart, James Downey, and Edward Burke, all former Front members.[57] The leader of this group was Joseph McWilliams, who had also belonged to the Front. He had split from the Cassidy organization because he had felt it was not going far enough and because he had disagreed with Front leaders over acknowledging and welcoming aid that the German-American Bund had given to the Front. McWilliams had spoken openly of this aid, thereby embarrassing the Front.[58] When the Mobilizers formed, they had a close and open association with the Bund, even against the wishes of their spiritual leader, Coughlin, who at the time of the Nazi-Soviet Non-Aggression Pact in August 1939 urged his supporters to break completely with the Bund. Cassidy's group followed Coughlin's advice, but McWilliams announced that the Mobilizers would not break off relations with the Nazis. This statement followed a huge joint rally he had held with the Bund. Coughlin then repudiated the leadership of the Mobilizers because of their Nazi ties, although he continued to refer to the rank and file as ''good people and friends of Social Justice.'' The Front, which had already repudiated the Mobilizers, refused to have anything to do with them after this. Because of the rejections by Coughlin and the Front, and as a result of McWilliams' presence at a Ku Klux Klan rally, the Mobilizer's Catholic support began to dissipate. At this point the *Tablet* began printing a number of letters to the editor criticizing McWilliams for being anti-Christian and for cooperating with anti-Catholics.[59]

For the most part, however, the Mobilizers supported the same goals as the Front, and stressed the power of the Jews and their ties to Communism. The membership application of this group stated that ''Christian civilization can only be maintained if Christians get a fair share of the business of the city, state and nation. Christian schools, Christian culture and the Church can only be supported when Christian business is flourishing.'' Members of the Mobilizers pledged to ''buy Christian until such time as the Christian people attain a fair share of the economic power of this nation.'' They also supported a ''vote Christian campaign.'' Speeches at Mobilizer meetings emphasized that American Jews and Jewish refugees were taking jobs away from Christians and that the Jews were rich while the Christians suffered. Consequently the Mobilizers engaged in anti-Jewish boycotts and violence in an effort to achieve their goals. Actually, to a certain extent the leaders of this group represented a criminal element, since a number of them had prison records. However, the rank and file were the same as in the Front—mainly Irish Catholic small tradesmen, clerks, artisans, and others of the lower class and lower-middle class.[60]

Although it was the Mobilizers who supported more violence on the streets, it was the Front that was linked to what might have been the climactic violent incident of the period. On 14 January 1940 the Federal Bureau of Investigation arrested eighteen people, most of whom belonged to the Front, and charged them with conspiring to overthrow the government of the United States.[61] The plot, a complex one, involved the bombing of the *Forward* building, the *Daily Worker* offices, the Cameo theater in Manhattan (where Russian-made films could be seen), Jewish neighborhoods, and Jewish businesses.[62] This was to be accompanied by the assassination of several Jewish congressmen who had voted for a repeal of the arms embargo, which had been part of the pre–World War II neutrality legislation. It was hoped that this terrorist activity would initiate a significant anti-Semitic movement in America, thus forcing the government to use the army to safeguard the Jews. The Front would then be able to claim that the government was protecting just one special group, indicating therefore the powerful influence of Jews in the government. While the anti-Semitic drive was commencing, the Frontists expected a period of disorder and street-fighting and then an uprising of Communists and Jews, assisted by some government officials—the long-expected Communist Revolution. The Front would then organize a counterrevolution, set up a right-wing dictatorship, and eliminate the Jews.[63]

The events leading up to the arrests began when William Bishop (later to be one of the defendants) suggested to John Cassidy the formation of a military training group whose members would be recruited from the Front's rifle club (the Sports Club). A subsequent disagreement over this proposal broke up the rifle club. Soon afterward, in July 1939, as the Mobilizers were organizing (and criticizing the Front for being too timid), Bishop, with Cassidy's help, established a secret military group which included some non-Frontists; it was known variously as the Sports Club, the Country Gentlemen, and the Action Committee. The members of this group were to be trained as squad leaders and were to recruit people who believed that a Communist Revolution was impending, that the government was partial to Communism, and, consequently, that they should overthrow the government. Munitions were obtained from members in the National Guard who had access to the stores at a local armory.[64]

Of the eighteen originally arrested, eleven were Irish, five German, one Austrian, and one of unknown ancestry. The Germans included two who had been born in Germany, one of whom was a member of the Bund. Those who actually were Front members included ten Irish and three Germans, one of whom had been born in Germany and was recently naturalized.[65] Occupationally they included three salesmen, three clerks, and one each of the following: baker, tailor, lineman for the telephone company, chauffeur, elevator mechanic, swimming instructor, W.P.A. worker, and one who was unemployed. The occupations of the other 4 were unknown.[66]

After a long and well-publicized trial in which the defense stressed that the plot was too fantastic to be true, given the number of people involved and the number of weapons they had, nine of the seventeen brought to trial were acquited on both counts; one committed suicide during the trial; charges against two were dismissed for lack of sufficient evidence; and a mistrial was declared for three on both counts and two on one count. The jury simply could not agree that there had been a real conspiracy to overthrow the government, plus there was confusion over who had actually been involved. The government decided to proceed no further on the case since the prosecutor found it too difficult to prove to the jury that an organization which had only a few guns and some homemade bombs was planning to overthrow the United States government.[67] However, the trial had firmly established that the defendants were strongly anti-Semitic and that many had found the plot an appealing idea.

The reaction to the arrests and trial by Irish and other ethnic newspapers helps to illustrate the feelings of the communities. The *Tablet* noted that the only thing the Frontists were guilty of was their "excessive patriotism" and remarked that the anti-Christian forces must be rejoicing now. The paper went on to state that the whole affair seemed to be an effort to smear the Christian Front and Father Coughlin. The *Irish World* gave a prominent place in its paper to a speech by Coughlin which referred to those arrested as these "Christian Young Men." The Frontists were pictured in the Irish press as patriots defending their country and the Christian way of life. In a special article on one of those arrested, the *Tablet* noted that "in every conflict this country has ever had, his family has defended this country." The *Gaelic American,* in a favorable article entitled "Conspiracy to Railroad 17 Young Men Exposed," made sure to state that John T. Prout, Jr., one of the accused, was the "son of Major Prout of the old Sixty-ninth Regiment [the Fighting Irish]." The *Irish Echo* called the arrests an insult to the loyalty of the Irish-American population and compared them to the British raids on the homes of Irish patriots in the old country.[68] The arrests, of course, helped to increase insecurity among many Irish Catholics, since it was yet another example of who really controlled the City.

In contrast to the Irish reponse, the *Staats-Zeitung* took this occasion to note that: "One seems to be dealing here once more with one of those cases in which the small people are caught because one cannot get hold of the big ones. And the big ones are those elements who let loose on Sundays on the radio and in their printed organs in the name of misunderstood freedom of speech, and press their demagogic and intolerant phrases on a mass of people who are close to despair because of the industrial problems of the time." This was, of course, an obvious attack on Coughlin, suspected of being behind the Front and encouraging it all along.[69] The *Catholic News* remained editorially silent on this situation. It did print an article on Coughlin's views of the arrests but buried it on page twenty-six. The paper also continued to offer stories favorable to the Jews. *Il Progresso* gave brief coverage of the event in small articles outlining just the basic facts of the case.[70] Only the Irish rose to the defense of those arrested.

The Front itself held no more street meetings during 1940 and went temporarily underground. However, it reappeared again in 1941, stressing an anti-war and anti-Semitic theme.

RESPONDING TO COUGHLINISM

The Jews were naturally aware of and hostile to the anti-Semitism of both Coughlin and the Front. Jewish awareness of Coughlin's rhetoric is indicated by a December 1938 Gallup Poll which concluded that Jews, of the various major religious groups, showed the highest percentage of disapproval of Coughlin and the lowest percentage with no opinion. Voting behavior also gives a good indication of Jewish attitudes toward Coughlin. In 1938 Congressman John O'Connor of the sixteenth congressional district on Manhattan's East Side was defeated in the Democratic primary. According to his campaign manager the fact that *Social Justice* endorsed O'Connor, particularly in the same edition that ran excerpts from the *Protocols,* lost the Congressman a significant amount of Jewish support. The Jews also retaliated against the Front in street fights and through a boycott of merchants suspected of working with the Front's Greater New York Committee for Christian Action.[71] However, the boycott never developed into a major response in the Irish-Jewish conflict for a number of reasons. First of all, the Front was a home-grown movement; a boycott of Ireland's goods, similar to the one of Germany's goods would have had no effect. Secondly, the Jews often identified their opponents in a religious rather than an ethnic way: because of the perceived ties between official Catholicism and the Coughlinites as well as a tendency to regard Irish and Catholic as synonymous, the Jews often saw their opponents, although mainly Irish Catholics, simply as Catholics. A boycott against such a large and powerful group would have been impossible. Instead, the main Jewish response was to appeal to the politicians for help and to urge others to speak out.

Although Coughlinism remained strong in the Irish community, there were Catholics, including Irish Catholics, who did offer a vigorous opposition to the radio priest. In December 1938, in response to Coughlin's November 20 address, George Cardinal Mundelein of Chicago stated that the radio priest was not a spokesman for the Catholic Church and that his views did not represent those of the Church, although as a citizen he did have the right to voice his own opinions. Frank Hogan, a prominent lay Catholic and president of the American Bar Association, condemned anti-Semitism in December 1938 and quoted Pope Pius XI's earlier statement which noted that Christians must not get involved in such a movement since spiritually Christians are Semites. Cardinal Hayes was responsible for the publication of a pamphlet refuting various lies about the Jews. The Bishops of the Administrative Board of the National Catholic Welfare Council also attacked racial bigotry and cited the Pope's thoughts on the matter. Catholic periodicals such as *Commonweal* and the *Catholic Worker* often expressed their opposition to Coughlin, the Front, and anti-Semitism.[72]

However, only Coughlin's superior could discipline him, and Bishop Michael Gallagher had rarely done so. With Gallagher's death in 1937 the radio priest had had to contend with Archbishop Edward Mooney, who had attempted to bring greater control over Coughlin's activities. Rather than yield to censorship, Coughlin had removed himself from the radio in October of 1937, at which time *Social Justice* had begun a campaign to restore Coughlin's independence. This had resulted in numerous letters to Mooney and the Vatican, as well as rallies protesting the archbishop's actions. After a meeting between Coughlin and Archbishop Amleto Cicognani, Apostolic Delegate to the United States, it was announced that on 9 January 1938 Coughlin would return to the radio. Mooney, disturbed by the public reaction to his discipline of Coughlin, and perhaps also yielding to changes in the Vatican's desire to control the radio priest, was afterwards more cautious in his relations with Coughlin. Mooney was also concerned that further action might cause even more trouble; for example, he became aware of the threats of the New York Coughlinites to attack the Jews if *Social Justice* were censored. Thus Coughlin was again virtually free to say what he pleased.[73] Coughlin therefore entered his anti-Semitic period essentially unencumbered by censorship from his superior who had been persuaded to back down. Yet the controversy between Mooney and Coughlin, as well as the subsequent attacks on the priest by other prominent Catholics, did indicate to the Jews that not all Catholics could be considered Coughlinites or anti-Semites. It also showed that anti-Coughlinism was more than simply a Jewish movement.

Catholic opposition became more apparent in 1939, when Dr. Emmanuel Chapman, a philosophy professor at Fordham University, organized a Committee of Catholics to Fight Anti-Semitism (the name of which was later changed to Committee of Catholics for Human Rights). The committee had been formed for a number of reasons. Primarily it was designed to show the Jews that there were Catholics who were interested in their problems and to rally Catholics against anti-Semitism. The organization published a newspaper called the *Voice for Human Rights,* which focused on incidents of cooperation between Catholics and Jews and tried to explain the harm which the New York anti-Semitic group did to both Catholics and Jews. A major theme was that anti-Semitism and anti-Catholicism were closely related and that one would follow the other. The membership of the committee was heavily laden with the professionals of all the ethnic groups in the Catholic community. Attorneys, editors, politicians, labor leaders, educators, and priests abounded.[74] Unfortunately, the organization was short-lived, lasting only until 1941. It was also not very well funded and did not have the impact that the anti-Semitic *Tablet* had among susceptible groups. In addition, the committee was bitterly attacked in the Irish press. It was described in the *Tablet* as an anti-Catholic paper. Scanlan and others could not understand why this group of Catholics did not deal with the real issue of anti-Christianity and stop wasting their time on anti-Semitism, ''which scarcely exists.'' The *Irish Echo* noted that the committee was really an anti-Irish project. These themes were repeated in letters to the *Tablet.* Chapman finally disbanded the committee in 1941, expecting the war to eliminate the ethnic antagonisms. However, in 1944 in response to a wave of anti-Semitic vandalism inspired by continued Irish-Jewish friction, he reorganized it as the National Committee to Combat Anti-Semitism.[75]

Although these anti-Coughlinite actions were important, they did little to ease the conflict between the two groups. Especially disturbing to the Jews was their inability to get an official Catholic response specifically castigating Coughlin and the Front. As the *Jewish Examiner* observed in 1940:

> Sincere, fervent appeals have been made to the Catholic authorities in this country to take an official stand on the matter of Coughlin, to repudiate his hate-mongering campaign, to show indisputably that the Catholic Church regards his dangerous efforts as un-Catholic and anti-Christian. All such appeals have met blank responses; the splendid actions of some individual Catholic dignitaries and laymen and publications are, unfortunately, not enough to make it clear that Coughlin's way is no part of the Catholic doctrine.[76]

The Church in New York did not publicly condemn Coughlin or the Front for a number of reasons. Partly this was because of the prominent priests and laymen among Coughlin's supporters. It is also possible that since the Coughlinites were usually considered to be stalwart Catholics, who were in a twisted way following the Pope's encyclicals and defending the Church, there was an unwillingness to antagonize them. Francis Spellman, who became archbishop in April 1939 after Cardinal Hayes' death, found himself immediately in the midst of the New York Coughlin problem. As a newcomer he may have decided not to create an issue at a time when he was just assuming his new powers.[77] The *Catholic News*, which reflected not only the German Catholic viewpoint but also that of such moderate Irish figures as Spellman, took a neutral position on Coughlin. The paper printed his speeches but also provided prominent coverage to his critics among the clergy and laity. Spellman's position had another component. Any attack on Coughlin and his activities would be viewed as a rebuke of Bishop Molloy of Brooklyn, who obviously had given at least tacit approval to the pro-Coughlin stand of the *Tablet* and such priests as Father Curran.[78] Rather than put himself in the middle of a major controversy, Spellman remained silent. Another factor in the Church response was that Church leaders felt Coughlinism was not really a concern of the Church anyway, since the radio priest never officially spoke for the Church. Finally, although it consistently condemned Communism, the Church seemed to be willing to live with Fascism and Nazism. Fighting Communism while working with fascism—which is what the Coughlinites were doing—could actually be perceived as following Church doctrine.

This silence continued to remain a sore point into the World War II years. Catholic (mainly Irish) anti-Semitic vandalism, which did not stop with the demise of the Front, reached a climax in 1943 with physical attacks on Jews and vandalism directed against their community (see chapter 8). The Jews, naturally, were upset and called attention to the lack of response from the Catholic Church on the anti-Semitic incidents. One Jewish paper, published in an area hard hit by the anti-Semitism, commented angrily that one could "ask anybody how much cooperation the Church has given Interfaith meetings. Ask any group or club how difficult, if well nigh impossible, it has been to have the Catholic Clergy attend, to give but lip service to the cause [of interfaith cooperation]."[79]

In general, Church officials and publications remained reluctant to acknowledge the seriousness of the anti-Semitism; and because of their own insecurities, they continued to point to anti-Christianity as the true peril. For example, at the height of publicity concerning the anti-Semitic vandalism, Reverend J. Francis A. McIntyre, auxiliary bishop of New York, charged that " 'the chalk doodlings' of children have been used by paid publicity agents to conjure up 'the phantom of anti-Semitic hate' to injure the Catholic population of New York." The *Tablet* also minimized the incidents and condemned those who were making a "racket out of racism" and blaming Catholics for the attacks. They, too, saw the accusations as part of an anti-Christian response.[80] The *Catholic News* also showed sensitivity to criticism of the Church, particularly to charges that it was fascist (the paper spoke of a great increase in anti-Catholicism since Pearl Harbor). Like the *Tablet*, the *Catholic News* viewed the anti-Semitic events as another excuse for "sniping at Catholics," although it did urge New York's Catholics to keep calm and not allow current events to arouse resentment against any group; they also urged the Jews to avoid hysteria.[81]

With the anti-Semitic occurrences receiving widespread publicity in the press and already the subject of an investigation by the City government, however, some Church leaders finally felt obliged to condemn the violence. Archbishop Spellman, breaking his many years of silence on the subject, observed that "in these days Catholics are frequently accused of anti-Semitism, and doubtless some Catholics are guilty of it. That anti-Semitism is wrong from a Catholic and humanitarian standpoint as well as from an American viewpoint has been demonstrated countless times." Spellman also sent a letter to Joseph Proskauer, president of the American Jewish Committee, indicating his endorsement of any attempt to surmount racial and religious hatreds. Bishop Molloy, although not specifically condemning anti-Semitism, did continue to call for a "campaign to rid the city of hate mongering." These statements by Church leaders helped to control the renewed outbreak of anti-Semitism as well as to eliminate a disturbing point between Jews and the Church.[82]

IRISH AND ITALIANS

While the Communist and other issues embittered relations between Jews and Irish and contributed to an intense conflict, they had a different effect on other intergroup situations in the City, particularly that of the Irish and Italians. Although relations between these groups could not be considered amicable—there was considerable competition and conflict in, for example, the political sphere, and animosities still existed from previous years—certain changes were occurring.[83] Among the Irish who saw themselves fighting the Communist and Jewish menace, there was the beginning of a more friendly attitude toward the Italians. These Irish may have been eager to secure allies, particularly Catholic ones, in their battles. Therefore Scanlan, reporting on a dinner given for Bishop Molloy by the Italian laity and clergy in his Diocese, commented that "here in our Diocese a rebirth of the faith is taking place among our co-religionists of Italian origin which is promising for the future." There was also a spirited defense of Italian Fascism and an effort to encourage an anti-Jewish response among Italian-Americans.[84] In December 1938, during the controversy between Italians and Jews over Mussolini's anti-Semitic decrees, Scanlan stated that the assault on Fascism in the United States actually represents anti-Italianism and is based on "hatred of Italy" and "hatred of the Italian." He then related a story of a children's play held in a school in a Jewish section of the Bronx in which the name of Italy was booed when it was displayed on a card,but Russia received considerable applause.[85]

The Irish overtures did win some Italian-American supporters for the anti-Communist and anti-Jewish fight as noted in the following letter to the editor of the *Tablet*.

> May I, as an American of Italian descent, express my profound gratitude to you and the Brooklyn Tablet for your splendid interest in disclosing the real purpose of certain elements, particularly communistic, for their subtle endeavor to inveigh against the Italian race.
>
> Now that we have the support of non-Italians in our fight against the hidden blasphemous propaganda in the degradition of our race, there will be an increasing interest on the part of the Italians to foster and support with other racial Catholics the fight against that dreadful disease—Communism. . . .
>
> You cannot calculate the gladness and contentment that was evidenced by my Italian friends when I showed them the articles written by you and Rev. Edward Lodge Curran in defense of Italians. The Italians have an erroneous impression that other Catholics, especially Irish Catholics, who are strong and can aid us greatly are not concerned over the woes of the Italians. And now that you and Father Curran have come out and defended us so magnificently, I assure you, you will have our heartiest cooperation in fighting against atheistic creeds.[86]

However, Italians were never very interested in either anti-Communism or anti-Semitism despite the Irish attempts to involve them in these battles. The Communist issue and its interaction with other points of friction continued to remain mainly a source of Irish-Jewish conflict.

Chapter Six

Going to War

Even after the Front appeared, indicating the intensity of the Irish-Jewish conflict, other issues, which can be classified as explosive in the sense that they quickly divided the ethnic communities, continued to appear and exacerbate tensions even more. Such was the isolationist-interventionist controversy that raged in the United States prior to American entry into World War II.

THE CONTROVERSY: BACKGROUND

Beginning in 1935 the United States Congress had passed a series of Neutrality Acts designed to prevent American involvement in any war. This legislation included an embargo on arms shipments to any belligerent. President Roosevelt, who had never fully agreed with the philosophy of these acts, by 1939 became convinced that they were working against the best interests of the country. In his annual message to Congress in January 1939 the president called for a new law that, at least in the area of arms supplies, would allow a distinction to be made between an agressor nation and its victim. As the situation in Europe deteriorated because of Germany's aggressive moves into Czechoslovakia and Italy's into Albania, Roosevelt tried to secure a repeal of the arms embargo. The beginning of World War II in September 1939 forced the president to proclaim the neutrality legislation in effect but also convinced him to call Congress into special session on September 21 to consider amending the neutrality acts, particularly in relation to the arms embargo. By early November Roosevelt had his desire fulfilled; for with the passage of the Neutrality Act of 1939, the embargo clause had been eliminated.

As the war progressed and the president became concerned that Germany might win, he moved in the direction of more aid to Britain and France. After the defeat of France in June 1940, Roosevelt negotiated the Destroyer-Naval Base Deal, giving England fifty aged destroyers as rental on the lease of British bases in the Western Hemisphere. This, however, was only a stopgap measure. In January 1941 lend-lease was proposed; in this agreement the United States would become the major supplier of war materials, on a sale or loan basis to the countries fighting the Axis powers. On 11 March 1941 lend-lease became law, thus officially ending American neutrality. Within a matter of months the country was engaged in naval warfare with Germany, and soon, with the December Japanese attack, America entered World War II.

After the outbreak of war in Europe, American public opinion on how much aid England should receive gradually shifted from ambivilence to total support even at the risk of war. A Princeton Public Opinion Research Project Report noted in May 1940 that 33 percent of those Americans questioned wanted the United States to support England even if it resulted in our entry into the war; 38 percent favored aid to England short of war; and 23 percent opposed aid and military involvement. By September 1940 53 percent were in favor of aid even if it resulted in Americans fighting, and only 12 percent opposed all involvement. A Gallup poll reported in January 1941 that 68 percent of those questioned were in favor of aid even if it meant war for this country. Many Americans also saw Germany as a threat to the United States. A Gallup poll in September 1939, after the fall of Warsaw, noted that 63 percent of the American people were sure that Germany would ultimately attack the United States if Europe was conquered. The public therefore came to support Roosevelt's foreign policy; this, however, occurred only after many months of verbal battling between isolationists and interventionists for control of public opinion.[1]

THE IRISH POSITION

During the period of debate large segments of the Irish, German, and Italian communities in New York supported various degrees of isolationism. The Irish opposition to the war was based almost solely on their hostility to England. Thus they were less vitally involved in this issue than the other ethnics since for the Irish it was not a matter, for the most part, of a threat to their ancestral home or their status in America. The *Irish World* stated the major theme best when it observed in May 1941 that "it is undoubtedly the case . . . that those Americans who have a more than superficial knowledge of the centuries of impact of British imperialism on Ireland are likely to be found more resistant than some of their neighbors both to the plea for 'all out aid to Britain' as necessary to the security of the United States, and to the efficacy of slogans that proclaim British 'democracy' to be one and the same with American democracy."[2] A number of editorials in other Irish newspapers echoed the same theme—warning the United

States not to involve itself with England. Later this attitude was expanded to include noninvolvement with Russia as well. As the *Gaelic American* remarked, "It is not their [the people of the United States] business to save England."[3] Irish-American opinion was anti-English rather than pro-German.[4] The other theme, as stated by the *Tablet,* was that "the American people hate war and can see no reason for involving this country in Europe's conflict. No nation threatens our existence. Our dangers are from within, not without."[5]

The role of the Catholic Church in New York was significant in galvanizing Irish and other Catholic support for neutrality. Father Curran, who had launched his own antiwar campaign under the auspices of his International Catholic Truth Society, spoke frequently before Irish as well as general Catholic groups, calling for these people to work to keep the country out of war.[6] The *Tablet* and the *Catholic News* echoed this antiwar sentiment. Bishop Molloy also proclaimed himself in support of neutrality.[7] Constant reminders from Church officials and publications surely convinced many Irish, German, and Italian Catholics that this was the proper side in the interventionist-isolationist dispute.

Further indication of Catholic Church support for neutrality can be found in a poll of all the Catholic clergy in the United States, conducted by the Catholic Laymen's Committee for Peace in September 1941. The poll asked whether the clergymen favored "the United States engaging in a shooting war outside the Western Hemisphere," and whether they were "in favor of the United States aiding the Communistic Russian government." On the first question 91.5 percent of the clergy answered no, with only 6.7 percent yes and 1.8 percent not voting or void. On the second question, 90.1 percent answered no, with only 7.4 percent yes and 2.5 percent not voting or void. In New York City, including the Long Island counties of Nassau and Suffolk, the vote was 93.7 percent no, 3.9 percent yes, and 2.4 percent not voting or void on the first question and 93.8 percent no, 4.4 percent yes, and 1.8 percent not voting or void on the second.[8]

A counter effort was also made to move the Catholic, and especially the Irish, community into an interventionist position. Various speakers, some at the urging of the Roosevelt administration, went before Irish and Catholic associations. New York State Attorney General John J. Bennett spoke to the Ancient Order of Hibernians and Supreme Court Justice Frank Murphy did the same before the Knights of Columbus in 1941 in order to secure Irish and Catholic support for the idea of giving aid to Russia. The Hibernians responded by passing a resolution denouncing Roosevelt's foreign policy. Soon afterward the Knights were urged by Herbert O'Brien, a leading Coughlinite and active isolationist, to repudiate "Murphy of the Synagogue." The interventionist Century Group, acknowledging that the Irish were prone to isolationism because of their hatred of England and Russia, emphasized that although help to these two countries would not even have been considered before, it should now be given because of Nazism's great and present threat to Christianity. Prominent Catholics such as Chancellor James Byrne of New York University and Professor Carlton Hayes helped this group circulate interventionist petitions among leading Catholics.[9] One such petition in October 1940, which urged America to send all possible help to England, was signed by sixty well-known Catholics, including Colonel William J. Donovan, United States Coordinator of Information and Republican candidate for governor of New York State in 1932; Father Edward J. Walsh, president of St. John's University in Brooklyn; and Father John P. Boland, chairman of the New York State Labor Relations Board. The text of the petition, in keeping with Century Group tactics, noted that "whatever some of us may feel concerning the actions of England in the past, her defeat in the present war will mean the triumph of those who would usurp the things of God."[10]

The Century Group also tried to secure the signatures of Irish-Americans on an open letter to Ireland's prime minister, Eamon de Valera, urging him to allow England to use Irish ports, which would enable the British to provide more protection for the Atlantic convoys. In 1941 an organization supporting this idea appeared in the Irish community. The American Irish Defense Association (AIDA), established with help from the Committee to Defend America by Aiding the Allies and the Fight for Freedom Committee, was in favor of allowing England to use Irish bases. The Irish-American press, however, was very critical of AIDA, and a large number of Irish-American societies attacked this organization as anti-Irish and a group of propagandists.[11] Receiving more support was the American Friends of Irish Neutrality, whose chairman was Paul O'Dwyer. This organization advocated American neutrality but its main function was to keep Ireland out of war by preventing the United States from pressuring their ancestral home into allowing the British to use ports there.[12]

Significant anti-war sentiment remained in the Irish community until American entry into the war. Only a few Irish-American leaders in the City were actually involved with the interventionist groups. Also, little support was found for this position among the Irish organizations. The New York State Convention of the Ancient Order of Hibernians continued to urge neutrality and in September 1941 passed a resolution asking that the two political parties stand by their 1940 campaign promises to keep American soldiers out of foreign wars. The United Irish-American Societies of New York also remained isolationist and opposed various changes in the neutrality acts. They were especially against the lend-lease bill.[13]

ANTI-WAR AND ANTI-SEMITISM

Father Coughlin tried to direct this antiwar sentiment into an anti-Semitic response by identifying the Jews as the leading interventionists. For example, in September 1939 he asked his radio audience to use their Christian strength to fight the groups supporting an arms embargo repeal, which, it was felt, would lead to American involvement. Coughlin singled out Representative Sol Bloom, chairman of the House Foreign Affairs Committee, and his followers in New York as the major antagonists on this issue. Once again it was clear that the Jews were the enemy.[14]

It was mainly within the Irish community that this appeal found support. Predominantly Irish groups influenced by Coughlin, such as the Mobilizers and Front, took up the antiwar theme as outlined by the radio priest. For example, Joe McWilliams commented at a Mobilizer meeting in 1940 that "the Jews want to destroy Hitler to the last Irishman." The Front, reappearing in 1941, held street meetings which also joined the anti-Jewish and antiwar issues, and inspired violence.[15] Others among Coughlin's Irish supporters spoke of dire consequences if the United States went to war. Herbert O'Brien and William J. Goodwin, chairman and secretary, respectively, of the New York Committee to Keep America Out of War and leaders in the City's Coughlin movement, warned in 1941 that if America entered the war, a civil war between the various foreign-born groups in this country would probably break out, beginning in New York. As Goodwin noted, "New York is a veritable powder keg and our entry into the war might touch it off."[16] Although this prophecy was an exaggeration, the war issue, and the Irish attitude toward the Jews on this point, played an important role in the confrontations which emerged between Irish and Jews in their neighborhoods both before and after America went to war (see chapter 8).

The anti-Semitic component of the antiwar campaign was a major problem for the isolationist organizations who were trying to appeal to a broad spectrum of the population. The America First Committee (AFC), founded in September 1940 as an isolationist pressure group, had great difficulties with the anti-Jewish issue. Although the national organization and many local units of America First were certainly part of the loyal opposition, there were also many pro-Nazi and anti-Semitic elements within this committee who saw it as an excellent vehicle with which to keep America weak as well as neutral. In New York City, Coughlinites were frequently members. One official of the New York chapter, Judge Mildred Dugan, claimed that "eighty per cent of the membership is Coughlinite." The New York chapter chairman, John T. Flynn, made a strenuous effort to rid his organization of this element. America First tried to prevent Coughlinites from becoming leaders of any local units and eliminated them from the speakers staff; it was, however, impossible to prevent these people from becoming members. Flynn also attempted to stop Father Curran from presenting the invocation at an America First Brooklyn mass meeting, but failed. Curran had already been barred from the committee's platforms in other cities, but he retained his strength in New York. Curran in turn endeavored but failed to remove Flynn from the New York chairmanship of America First. Flynn, however, was successful in indicating his displeasure with the anti-Semitic isolationists when he publicly denounced Joe McWilliams and his followers who were attending a committee meeting in May 1941. Flynn declared that he did not know how McWilliams had got into the meeting, but that the committee had no responsibility for his presence. "The AFC," as Flynn stated, "is not crazy enough to want the support of a handful of Bundists, Communists and Christian Fronters who are without number, without influence, without power and without respect in this or any other community." Although McWilliams, as well as the German-American Bund, was barred from the AFC, it continued to receive and accept the more respectable Coughlinite support, thus perpetuating its problems with the anti-Jewish issue.[17]

When Germany attacked Russia in June of 1941, and American entry into the war would result in fighting as allies of the Communists, the committee made a particular bid for Catholic support, noting Papal encyclicals cautioning against alliances with Communism. AFC publications also began stressing the anticlerical persecutions in Russia. It was not unusual that many Catholics and especially Coughlinites, would be attracted to an anti-Russian appeal, given their view of the dangers which Christianity faced from Communism.[18] That the leadership of the committee was well aware of their Coughlinite support is indicated by an incident in July of 1941. General Robert Wood, national chairman of America First, castigated a *Social Justice* salesman outside a committee meeting for selling the periodical and thereby confusing the issue of neutrality. Wood, in an angry outburst, stated that he preferred not to have people of this type at meetings. A number of Coughlinites resigned from the AFC after *Social Justice* reported this event. Later in July *Social Justice* printed a letter from Wood claiming that he had not spurned the backing of the Christian Social Justice movement but, rather, welcomed their support. The fact was that a number of local and national leaders of the AFC were friendly toward the Coughlinites, and although they wished to minimize the Coughlinite presence, they did not want to lose their support.[19]

Coughlinite elements were also a problem in the American Friends of Irish Neutrality. O'Dwyer claimed that great care was taken to make certain that Irish Coughlinites and German Bundists, who were very interested in joining, were barred from the organization.[20]

THE GERMANS: AVOIDING THE NAZI LABEL

Isolationism was also strong in the German-American community, but, except for those who were in the Bund, contact with the anti-Semitic component of this issue was avoided.[21] Although the non-Nazi German-Americans had denounced anti-Semitism and Hitler in 1938 and were careful to avoid any praise of the Nazi government, it was much more difficult to criticize Germany's foreign policy and war achievements. It was also extremely important to many in this group, remembering well the World War I experience, that America not fight Germany again.

Many German-American groups and publications voiced antiwar opinions.

When the war began in September 1939, the *Staats-Zeitung* and the New York State Branch of the Catholic Central Verein were quick to call for America to remain free of Europe's hates and battles. Even earlier, in May 1939, the Roland Society had urged neutrality. The Steuben Society expressed this sentiment also, declaring that it would oppose any attempt to pull this country into a foreign war. The Steubenites sponsored many antiwar rallies during this period.[22]

Opposition to American involvement in the war remained strong into 1941. For example, both the Steuben Society and the *Staats-Zeitung* were solidly against lend-lease. When the measure was being discussed in February 1941, Ridder's newspaper charged that such an agreement would "drive us into war in 60 days." The *Staats-Zeitung* also stressed in its headlines the great power which lend-lease placed in Roosevelt's hands. After passage of the bill, the paper still continued to complain that lend-lease was essentially a give-away program that would be detrimental to the United States. The *Staats-Zeitung* also warned against tying ourselves to England and her imperialism.[23] Opposition to involvement by the Steubenites and the *Staats-Zeitung* as well as others, including the *Catholic News* and the New York State Branch of the Catholic Central Verein, changed only when America finally entered the war.

The German-American community found difficulty again in avoiding the Nazi label, as they had earlier, because of the same reluctance to criticize Germany openly. The Steuben Society continued to protest into 1940 that Germany was not an agressor and was not interested in world conquest. They charged that many of the anti-Germany stories appearing in the American press were British and French propaganda, and they asked that the United States not be fooled by this as it had been in 1917. The *Staats-Zeitung,* while calling for American neutrality, printed editorials which, though not in praise of Hitler, repeated his encouraging words on the superiority of Germany and its eventual victory over its enemies. One revealing editorial involved the paper's comment on Germany's defeat of France in June 1940. It stated that the injustice of the First World War had been corrected. "The 'Outrage of Compiègne' has been doused and at the same time the 'Treaty of Versailles.'" Observing that the next step would be the defeat of England, the paper commented that "all possible support must and will be welcomed by the Third Reich in order to achieve the final goal of the overthrow of British imperialism." Although avoiding praise of Hitler or Nazism, the *Staats-Zeitung* could not refrain from praise of Germany and defense of her foreign policy.[24]

All of these opinions made German-Americans appear suspect to many. However, the Bund was more instrumental in attaching the Nazi label to the German-American position. The American Nazis supported isolationism, opposed any aid to the Allies, and blamed both the Allies and the Jews for the war, thereby joining the isolationist and anti-Semitic themes.[25] Although the Bund was weakened by the late 1930s because of the arrest of Fritz Kuhn in 1939 and its repudiation by the leadership elements of the German-American community, it still had its supporters and, more important, continued to receive wide publicity. Therefore it was easy to identify Bund support for neutrality, which was pro-Nazi and anti-Semitic, with German-American support for this position, which was based on ancestral ties and fears of an anti-German crusade. The danger of this Bund-isolationist connection is illustrated by the fact that a July 1940 Fortune Poll reported that 70 percent of those questioned were sure that Germany had established a fifth column operation in America.[26] The German-American community, by publicly supporting what happened to be the Nazi side of this issue, was the most likely target for accusations of fifth column activities.

The Bund's endorsement of neutrality even hurt the non-German isolationists. The America First Committee, already troubled by the Coughlinite element, also experienced difficulty with the Bundists. *The Free American and Deutscher Weckruf und Beobachter* on 1 May 1941 urged all its readers to join the committee. In a letter to the Nazi paper, John Flynn repudiated their support and declared that Bundists were not welcome in his organization. He added that the AFC was against American involvement in the war not because it was pro-Nazi but because it desired to safeguard America from Europe's wars. This repudiation was placed, at Flynn's request, on the front page of the Bund newspaper. The editor of the paper, in explaining the front page prominence of Flynn's letter, stated that he did not want to see the AFC suffer from any unfair publicity about the Bund. However, the Bund's well-publicized interest in the committee added to the isolationists' difficulty in avoiding a pro-Nazi stigma. This remained a problem, since the interventionist organizations constantly drew attention to the similarity in thought between AFC and Nazi leaders.[27]

The connection between Nazism and the isolationist position, as well as the fact that America might soon be at war again with Germany, inspired trepidation in the German-American community that they might face a period of anti-German hysteria once more. Theodore Hoffmann, the president of the Steuben Society, declared in 1939 that "we will not tolerate any attempt . . . to attack our race and blood, and . . . we intend to fight . . . any and all propaganda and race discrimination, aimed at our good name and splendid record of contribution. . . . There must be no repetition of 1914 to 1917!" The *Staats-Zeitung*, in an editorial on 2 September 1939, condemned any persecution of Germans which might result from the war. By 22 May 1940 the newspaper warned that the anti-German hysteria was beginning and offered a spirited defense of the German-American name.

> With every effort not to see the picture too blackly, one cannot deny the fact that the war and hate psychosis in this country is growing from day to day. . . .
> It is only necessary today, despite long years of citizenship, . . . to bear a German name, to hold a job which reflects the fact that one is German American, in order to be looked at askance, to be harassed and discharged.
> This attitude is stirred up by those ingenious groups which see in all of those men and women who are not friendly to the allies, elements which are inimical to America.

The editorial concluded with the statement that "THERE ARE NO BETTER AMERICANS THAN THE GERMAN-AMERICANS!" and noted their many contributions to America. The *Volksfront* and the Roland Society also worried that many Americans would think that German-Americans were spies, fifth columnists, and enemies of the United States.[28] This fear convinced some of the isolationists to change their public position lest they be considered Nazis. However, for reasons of pride in Germany's foreign policy accomplishments or a stronger fear, having experienced it before, of what American entry would bring, others resisted this shift. Besides, staunch isolationists such as the publishers of the *Staats-Zeitung* could claim that they had already taken an anti-Nazi stand. The fear of an anti-German crusade also led to the creation of new and influential interventionist groups out of the older anti-Nazi societies.

The Roland Society dropped its isolationist position and began to organize interventionist opinion in the German-American community in June 1940 as German armies marched through France. The society coordinated the formation of the German-American Congress for Democracy, an umbrella organization for a number of anti-Nazi societies, which pledged itself to Roosevelt's foreign policy and the defeat of the dictators. The congress began a loyalty movement among German-Americans to counteract the massive Nazi propaganda directed at this community. This organization was also set up to aid in protecting and "clearing the German-American name" and called for the establishment of a National Committee for the Prevention of Discrimination and Persecution. Another group, the Loyal Americans of German Descent, was formed in July 1941. Robert F. Wagner, Jr., chairman of Roland's board of trustees, was named president of this association. The main aims of this body were to make all Americans aware that the majority of German-Americans were loyal and "to rally all our fellow-citizens of German ancestry to the all-out defense of America and of democracy." The Loyal Americans were quick to point out that the Nazis "try to misuse our love of the true Germany to win support for the temporary Nazi regime." This group also stressed that to repudiate everything the Nazis stood for was not "incompatible with loving the true Germany." Wagner's organization worked with and was partially funded by the Fight For Freedom Committee, which, of course, was trying to bring the German-American community into the interventionist camp. Also working with that committee was theologian Reinhold Niebuhr's American Friends of German Freedom. Senator Robert F. Wagner was influential too on the interventionist side. He supported repeal of the arms embargo and favored lend-lease and other efforts to aid England, although he had voted for the Neutrality Acts before the outbreak of war in 1939 and was opposed to sending American soldiers to Europe. His voice, however, was important in illustrating that not all Germans favored isolationism.[29]

Organizations such as the German-American Congress for Democracy were attacked by the Steuben Society, which felt that German-Americans did not have to prove their loyalty to America by organizing committees and supporting

Roosevelt's policies. Earlier the New York chapter of the Congress for Democracy had criticized the Steubenites for what it called pro-Nazi attitudes when the Steuben Society began to collect money to combat British propaganda in the United States. The congress was quick to note that the action of the society "is by no means representative of the German-American population."[30] However, the labeling of one German-American organization as pro-Nazi, when it really was not, only helped to continue the application of the Nazi tag to all German-Americans.

That this remained a problem is revealed by a *New York Times* editorial in 1941 at the time the German-American Congress was launching its loyalty drive. The paper, although observing that the great majority of German-Americans were loyal, stated that "we need to be reminded that there are Germans, both inside Germany and outside it, who hate Nazism." The status of the German-Americans in this country clearly was tied to the future of Germany, for as the United States drew closer to war, the German-Americans were regarded more and more with suspicion.[31] Besmirched first by Nazism and then by the isolationist controversy, this community did meet with some discrimination, just as it had feared. The *Steuben News,* the German-American Conference Relief Fund, the Loyal Americans of German Descent, and others pointed out the increasing discrimination against German-Americans, especially in employment.[32]

It should also be noted that the isolationist Germans had great sympathy for others caught in the same situation. An editorial in the *Steuben News* commented that "when an Italian Consul General addresses those of his own blood here in the United States, columnists abuse him as being a member of the Fifth Column, but when the British Ambassador addresses a large assemblage and bluntly urges upon Americans to consider themselves part and parcel of the British Empire, there is little criticism."[33]

THE ITALIANS: UNDER SUSPICION

The Italians did indeed share the same fate, for they were under suspicion for pro-Italy sentiments as that country drew closer to war with the United States. Although some Italian-Americans, such as La Guardia and Antonini, had been hostile to Fascist Italy for years and spoke out immediately and forcefully in behalf of intervention, a large segment of the community was on the isolationist side.[34] This attitude, as with the Germans, was mainly the result of pride in the foreign policy accomplishments of their ancestral home and fear of what American involvement in a war with Italy would mean for them. Also a strong pro-Fascist element was active in this community.

Upon the outbreak of war in September 1939, *Il Progresso,* which had remained strongly pro-Fascist and had carried many articles praising the Fascist government, urged neutrality for the United States. Although Italy was not yet a belligerent, *Il Progresso* noted its concern for the future by commenting in 1939 that "the appearance of the slightest shadow that threatens to darken the traditional friendship of the two countries [Italy and America] brings to us painful trepidations." The paper continued by hoping Washington and Rome would remain neutral and work together for peace. Mussolini's efforts to secure peace were given full and prominent coverage in the paper.[35]

The Italian-American community remained hopeful until June of 1940, at which time they too began to suffer for the sins of their ancestral home. Italy's attack on France and the entry of Italy into the war on the side of Germany brought forth from the Italian-American community a tremendous outburst of emotion motivated by fear and insecurity. This was particularly true because of remarks Roosevelt made about Italy's invasion of France. He stated that "the hand that held the dagger has struck it into the back of its neighbor." Many Italian-Americans regarded this statement as a slur against the Italian character and an indication that the President must be anti-Italian.[36]

Like the German-Americans, the Italians were deeply concerned that the war would bring a wave of prejudice against them. *Il Progresso,* just before the actual entry of Italy into the struggle, expressed this fear:

> For some time an undercurrent against the Italians of America has been making its way through the newspapers, on the radio and elsewhere. Old prejudices are put back into circulation and new resentments are encountered as a result of the situation caused by the European war.
>
> But now let it be said once and for all that the Italians of America, naturalized or merely residents, are among the best immigrants who have made this country great and powerful.

The paper went on to state that Italians were loyal—"a loyalty which is in no way undermined by the sentimental ties which bind them to their country of origin." Many Italian-American organizations and prominent individuals in the community proclaimed and reaffirmed the loyalty of Italians to America.[37] Some condemned Mussolini's actions, such as the 122 Italian-American organizations which met under the auspices of the Italian Emergency Committee. This committee was hastily formed to refute the statement of Edoardo Bertolini, Italian consular agent for several southern New York counties, that Italian-Americans secretly supported Mussolini and desired an Italian victory. The mood of the community was best expressed by one observer in a Brooklyn Italian neighborhood who commented that "the older men were bragging like hell before Italy got in. Now they're all quiet. Their sons are good Americans."[38]

Anti-Fascist Italian organizations, both old and newly formed. made greater efforts to move their community away from support of Mussolini and isolationism. The anti-Fascist newspaper *Il Mondo* and organizations such as the Mazzini Society (founded in 1940) attacked *Il Progresso's* views and brought pressure on it and others to reject Fascism and Mussolini. Exposés of Fascist activities in the United States which continued to appear in American periodicals also contributed to this pressure by making other Americans aware of the Fascist threat.[39]

Il Progresso remained resistant to any shift. Although the paper at first expressed regret that Italy had gone to war "against the side with which the American people are in sympathy," it continued to support isolationism and was filled with articles reporting Italy's military achievements. Hitler's victory over France was regarded in favorable terms, indicating the sentiment that Germany was merely correcting an old wrong. By the end of June 1940 the paper was fully defending Mussolini's actions as those which best served the interests of his country, and blaming the problems of Europe on England.[40]

By 1941 *Il Progresso*'s position began to change. Its publisher, Generoso Pope, having been too pro-Fascist in the past, was in a more vulnerable position than the Ridders of the *Staats-Zeitung,* who earlier had fought the Nazis in the organizations, denounced Hitler, and ceased to praise his regime. Concerned about a growing anti-Italianism in the United States, and under pressure both from within and without the Italian-American community, *Il Progresso* began to shift its position.[41] The passage of the lend-lease act in 1941 brought the comment from the paper that while the bill had drawn much legitimate opposition, based simply on a desire to keep our country out of war, the majority now had decided. "Everyone now responds approvingly to the President's appeal for national unity and cooperation. We must therefore banish every attitude which might impair that united front on which national defense must count in time of emergencies." Editorials in the paper began to proclaim support for Roosevelt. Influential in pressuring Pope into this shift was Roosevelt himself, who sent for Pope and apparently helped convince him that a change was in order.[42] However, although there was a noticeable change during this period, Pope was accused of taking an anti-Fascist position only in the English section of his paper. Responding to this, the publisher in September 1941 finally and completely rejected Fascism in both languages. He stated flatly that "since the European war started and Italy and the United States definitely took sides in opposing camps, and since President Roosevelt declared a state of Unlimited Emergency, I, as a loyal American citizen, took my stand for the United States." Pope noted that he was "against any government which is against the government of the United States."[43] Of course, there continued to be support for isolationism in the Italian community, but *Il Progresso*'s new position surely helped to diminish that support by 1941.

THE JEWS AND THE ISOLATIONISTS

Although certainly not all Jews were interventionists, the sentiment of the majority of this group seemed to be with this position, and was perceived so by others.

Such important Jewish organizations as the Central Conference of American Rabbis, the American Jewish Congress, Hadassah, the Jewish War Veterans, and the Brooklyn Jewish Ministers Association went on record in support of the administration's policy of aiding the Allies. Many of the major donors to the Fight for Freedom Committee, organized in April 1941, were Jewish.[44] Jewish support for intervention was motivated by two factors. First, they had long opposed Hitler and Nazi Germany because of the persecution of Jews there. Rabbi Stephen Wise summed up their attitude: "Remember the choice is between Hitler and civilization, Hitler and democracy." In 1940, in a speech urging that America not play a passive role in the world struggle, *Forward* editor Abraham Cahan declared that Hitlerism, "the great curse of the world" must be destroyed.[45] The second factor placing the Jewish community in the interventionist camp was their belief that many anti-Semites were supporting isolationism, and that many isolationists were anti-Semites.

America First was an immediate target of Jewish suspicions because Henry Ford, active in financing anti-Semitism during the 1920s, became a national committee member when the organization was formed. Other anti-Semites— especially the Bundists and Coughlinites, as already noted—either found their way into this group or conspicuously appeared at its meetings. Statements such as one made by Newbold Morris, New York City Council President, that at least 60 percent of the people present at a May 1941 antiwar rally organized by America First "were members of or sympathizers with the German-American Bund" helped convince many Jews of the anti-Semitic nature of the isolationist movement. The anti-Jewish element in the AFC was more vividly brought to the attention of the Jews when speakers at the organization's street meetings sometimes engaged in Jew-baiting arguments or questioned the patriotism of the Jews. These meetings, which were often held in already ethnically tense neighborhoods, contributed to the emergence and intensity of conflict (see chapter 8). The reappearance of the Christian Front in 1941 as an antiwar and anti-Jewish group, and the discovery in 1941 that anti-Semitic literature was being mailed out under the frank of certain isolationist senators and representatives, also helped to foster this suspicion. Therefore it was not unusual to find references in the Jewish press to the isolationist organizations as "Hitler's appeasers." In one Jewish publication, stories on America First were usually included in a section devoted to un-American activities.[46]

The one event which seemed most clearly to connect the pro-Nazi, anti-Semitic element with the isolationists was Charles Lindbergh's speech in Des Moines, Iowa, on 11 September 1941 at an AFC meeting. Lindbergh, a leading isolationist and national committee member of America First, had earlier made statements favorable to Germany and now lashed out at the groups and people he felt were leading America into war. He singled out and accused the British, the Jews, and the Roosevelt administration for "pressing this country toward war." Noting what he perceived as an excessive and dangerous Jewish influence and control of the press, radio, motion pictures, and government, he warned the Jews that they should be opposing the war, since "they will be among the first to feel its consequences." This statement suggested that the Jews would face reprisals if America entered the war. The speech, echoing Nazi propaganda, unleashed a storm of protest not only from Jews but from many other Americans who were disheartened by the attack of a national figure on an already harassed group. Roosevelt's press secretary, Steven Early, was one of the first to point out the similarities between the speech and Nazi rhetoric.[47] Many Jewish organizations such as the American Jewish Congress, Jewish Labor Committee, the Brooklyn Jewish Community Council, and Hadassah attacked the speech. It solidified in many Jewish minds the concept of isolationist–anti-Semitic collaboration, particularly after the national leadership of the AFC refused to repudiate Lindbergh. In a joint statement the American Jewish Congress and the Jewish Labor Committee described the speech as another example of Nazi tactics.[48]

Some isolationists recognized that such blatant anti-Semitic statements threatened to weaken the whole isolationist campaign and therefore castigated the speech for its position on the Jews or denied an isolationist–anti-Semitic connection. Among these were even some isolationists who either had defended anti-Semites earlier or were actively involved in anti-Semitism. For instance, Father Curran, one of Coughlin's defenders, criticized Lindbergh's attack on the Jews. The *Tablet,* too, took this occasion to print, on the front page, a speech by William Leonard, president of the AFC Brooklyn chapter, denouncing anti-Semitism and noting that charges that it existed in his chapter were "the work of warmongers trying to cause disunity."[49]

Lindbergh's speech increased Jewish insecurities, and this group therefore made an attempt to move out of the spotlight placed on them. Not wishing to be singled out as one of the main groups supporting war in a country still debating the issue, the American Jewish Congress stated that Jewish groups had not been pushing for war; rather, they had hoped all along that Hitler could be stopped without a military struggle.[50]

Although not having the impact of Nazism or Communism, the war in Europe contributed to the ethnic tensions of this period. The issue had been somewhat diluted between the German, Italian, and Jewish communities because of the Germans' and Italians' earlier rejection of anti-Semitism, their sensitivity to the loyalty issue, and their vocal interventionist elements. Its main impact was on Irish-Jewish relations as an addition to the many points of friction between these groups. Because the Irish as a group had less at stake in this issue than the other ethnics, Irish isolationists were under less pressure to prove their loyalty by moving away from their position. However, even here the issue was somewhat diluted both by the presence of Irish interventionist support and by the effort of some Irish Coughlinites to avoid any anti-Semitism that threatened the isolationist crusade. In the Irish press no mention was made of the Jews in relation to this controversy. However, as neighborhood events indicated, considerable feeling against the Jews did exist on this point. American entry into war in 1941 was to eliminate this factor as a source of conflict only for those groups sensitive to the loyalty issue.

GERMAN-AMERICANS AND THE WAR

The involvement of the United States in a war against Germany and Italy resulted in an outpouring of loyalty statements by German and Italian-Americans who now perceived their nightmare to be coming true. The *Staats-Zeitung,* the German-American Conference, and even the Bund, pledged their loyalty to the United States. The *Staats-Zeitung* also noted at this time that German-Americans, by opposing the Bund, had always indicated their rejection of Hitler. The entire issue of the *Steuben News* for January 1942 was devoted to expressions of support for America. During the war the German-American community set up various committees to organize bond drives, provide air raid wardens, and in general to prove their loyalty by rallying their community in support of the war effort. The extent of German-American concern on this issue is revealed by the large number of resignations from the Steuben Society, just before and after American entry, by those who were afraid that their patriotism would be questioned if they remained members in a German, and previously isolationist, organization. There was now a greater reluctance to be associated with anything German. These were not, however, reactions to mere fantasy, since discrimination against German-Americans was a problem at this time. The *Steuben News,* for example, complained of employers refusing to hire members of their society.[51] There was also the situation of non-citizen Germans being required to register as enemy aliens.

During the war a good deal of space in former isolationist German-American periodicals such as the *Steuben News* was devoted to defending their isolationist past, pointing out that they were no longer isolationists, criticizing discrimination, speaking of victory against the Axis powers, and discussing what the proper peace terms might be. An effort was also made to avoid any hint that German-Americans might be interested in anything less than total victory. The Steuben Society, for example, emphasized that it was not interested in the Peace Now movement, begun in 1944, which supported the signing of an immediate armistice with Germany and Japan.[52]

ITALIAN-AMERICANS AND THE WAR

The Italians exhibited a similar desire to reaffirm their ties of loyalty to America. In an editorial entitled "A Supreme Duty!" *Il Progresso* noted that it was the duty of Italian-Americans to confirm their full loyalty to the United States.

Within this message was the statement, perhaps the plea, that "the American people of Italian origin who are loyal to the United States need have no fear because the Government will protect them in their right to liberty and justice." The paper was filled with stories and editorials about how Italian-Americans were ready to serve their country. A number of Italian-American organizations such as the Italian Welfare League, Italian Holy Name Society in New York City, Italian Barber's Benevolent Association, and the American Sons of Italy Grand Lodge, immediately pledged support to the United States. Many of these groups also moved into such activities as war bond drives and loyalty demonstrations.[53]

Within these affirmations of loyalty were the ever-present fears of discrimination and prejudice, as expressed by *Il Progresso* and others. These fears had some reality. Italian-Americans, like German-Americans, did have difficulty securing jobs, particularly those related to defense. More significant, however, was that non-citizen Italian- and German-Americans were classified as enemy aliens in January 1942 and had to register with the police.[54] Some Fascists and Nazis in these communities who were considered dangerous were put into internment camps. Also Italian and German aliens on the west coast, if they lived within the prohibited zone, were relocated. There was a continuing threat that this would be done in other parts of the country. The Italians and Germans waited anxiously for what would follow, but they had little to fear. The government made no effort to intern all aliens from these groups. By June 1942 these enemy aliens were permitted to move back into or to work in the prohibited areas on the west coast. Although some travel and curfew restrictions remained, there were few places where they could not go. Finally, on Columbus Day, 12 October 1942, the nightmare ended for the Italians when Attorney General Francis Biddle announced that non-citizen Italian-Americans would be exempt from the enemy alien classification. However, 1942 had provided some good scares.[55]

The sensitivity of the Italian community on the loyalty issue was further revealed by their effort to play down Italy's role in the war and the support of the people of Italy for Mussolini. *Il Progresso* alluded to this theme many times. For example, a few days after Pearl Harbor, an editorial stated that "the Italian people knew that this was not their war, but Germany's war for the domination of Europe and the World, a domination which would have weighed down upon the Italians, for the alliance would have changed into subjugation." The war was blamed on Germany now, and that country was described as controlling Italy. *Il Progresso* hoped for a just peace "which will . . . liberate Italy from the Hitlerite heel." Pope also criticized Mussolini for putting Italy "under the yoke of Germany." Lieutenant Governor Charles Poletti sounded this theme too when he noted "that the Italian people have been enslaved by Hitler and Mussolini."[56]

Also, former Fascist supporters such as *Il Progresso*'s Generoso Pope, eager to have others forget the past, began working with anti-Fascists in denouncing the Mussolini regime. By 1943 *Il Progresso* was "under the influence of

[Luigi] Antonini and the IALC [Italian-American Labor Council].'' Italian-Americans were now predominantly anti-Fascist but remained divided over questions concerning the future of Italy, the peace agreements, and the leadership of their ethnic community.[57]

Stung by the loyalty issue, German- and Italian-Americans were careful to avoid anything which would classify them as un-American. This included conflict with other groups. Although interethnic tension over the war-related issues probably remained, it was submerged because of more important concerns.

IRISH-AMERICANS AND THE WAR

Certain elements within the third ethnic isolationist group, the Irish, were less inclined to drop the isolationist crusade, even after America had entered the war. As noted earlier, this group was under less loyalty pressure to shift their position. When America first entered the struggle, there were declarations from such individuals as Father Curran and newspapers such as the *Gaelic American, Tablet,* and the *Irish World* pledging support to the war effort. (And for the large majority of Irish-Americans, even the Coughlinites, this remained the case: complete support for whatever policies the government suggested to win the war.)[58] However, isolationism died hard—if at all—among some of the Irish Coughlinite spokesmen and their supporters. By 1944 Father Curran was calling for an immediate negotiated peace and speaking about rallying the remnants of America First in order to revive isolationism after the war. The *Gaelic American* commented in 1943 that it had been a mistake to disband America First and suggested that the organization be revived. Advertisements for the Peace Now movement appeared in this paper calling for an immediate end to ''this unnecessary war.''[59]

Coughlin, through *Social Justice,* remained opposed to America's policies after Pearl Harbor. More significantly, his paper accused the Jews of having been a major factor in causing the war and continued to defend the Nazi persecutions of this group.[60] Coughlin's attitude toward the Jews once again found support and expression in the Irish community. Resentment over the war and hostility toward the Jews on this issue remained a source of overt and violent ethnic conflict in Irish-Jewish neighborhoods into the war years. The war issues, and others, were not muted by a desire to prove one's loyalty or by any other factor. While the world was at war, New York's ethnic battles continued.

Chapter Seven

Winning the Votes

Although the issues which divided the ethnics caused many problems for the City, they provided for numerous politicians the means by which to stay in office. While nonethnic concerns such as corruption in government sometimes played a greater role in campaigns, an election rarely occurred in which some candidates did not make use of the ethnic issues. Campaigns frequently became battles for the ethnic vote. As a result, tensions between the groups were exacerbated as appeals were made to some at the expense of others and were designed to provoke, in some cases, a fear vote. These ethnically oriented campaigns were also a contributory factor in producing and intensifying the City's group conflicts.

THE 1933 MAYORALTY CAMPAIGN

In the mayoralty campaign of 1933, La Guardia was pitted against John O'Brien, the Democratic party's Tammany choice, and Joseph McKee, the nominee of the anti-Tammany Recovery Party.[1] Both La Guardia and McKee publicized themselves as the reform, antiboss candidates. McKee, expecting a public declaration on his behalf from Roosevelt, also labeled himself the New Deal candidate.[2] He went as far as to state that "a vote for McKee is a vote for Roosevelt." Each candidate also accused the other of being boss controlled.[3]

The three mayoral hopefuls were also very interested in securing the endorsement of the various ethnic organizations. In the early part of the campaign O'Brien received the support of many German-American societies in the City, since in the past he had sought their advice on various appointments. In an effort to secure more German support, Tammany had made specific offers of more appointments. However, statements in the *Steuben News* noting that La Guardia was well qualified and had outstanding ability indicated that he, too, had support in the German community. McKee also had some German backing, since he was endorsed by the Roland Society.[4]

The Irish organizations and newspapers split between O'Brien and McKee, even though Ed Flynn had tried to draw Irish votes to McKee by promising this group an "equal place in the sun." This remark was intended to appeal to those Irishmen who felt that Tammany had given too much to the other groups during the previous years. The *Irish World* declared for McKee, pointing out that here was an Irish public official who was not controlled by bosses, meaning Tammany. The *Gaelic American,* however, warned that McKee was really Scottish, but that a vote for O'Brien was a vote for a 100-percent Irishman. On the whole, the major Irish organizations in the City, including the Ancient Order of Hibernians and the United Irish Counties Association supported O'Brien. This is not to say that nobody of Irish background supported La Guardia. An Irish-American League for Fusion existed for those of this ethnic group who were convinced that La Guardia would make the better mayor. One letter to La Guardia from an Irish supporter revealed his reason for favoring an Italian over an Irish-American: "You are a better and nobler Irishman than Mayor O'Brien," Patrick S. Hickey wrote, going on to say how ashamed he was, as an Irishman, of the corrupt Tammany organization.[5]

The Italian citizens of New York indicated strong support of La Guardia. The normally Democratic *Il Progresso* urged its readers to vote for all of the Italian candidates. Letters from numerous Italian organizations such as the Italian-American Civic Association, the United Italian-American Democratic Club, and the Italian Medical Society of Brooklyn endorsed La Guardia with fervor. Private citizens of Italian ancestry came forth with such statements as "I have been canvassing among the Italian-American citizens of this community [Flushing], . . . and you can rest assured that 99 per cent will stand behind your party."[6] Many letters written in Italian pledged the support of entire families for La Guardia. Ethnic pride in seeing one of their own run for the City's highest office, as well as desire for recognition, motivated the Italian community.

The large Jewish vote in the City seemed to be split between the various candidates. The Jewish newspapers and organizations either endorsed nobody or spread their support among all the mayoral hopefuls.[7] Although La Guardia had championed Jewish causes before 1933, the Jewish community on the whole did not yet recognize the Italian candidate as the man who could respond to their discontents both in terms of political power and the emerging Nazi threat; therefore they were undecided.[8] For this reason, and because of the relative instability of this vote, much of the mayoral campaign was directed at winning Jewish support. The ethnic composition of the various tickets reflected this, as did the campaign tactics.[9]

McKee's supporters made the first direct bid for Jewish votes within the actual campaign by strongly hinting that an attack on Governor Lehman by Samuel Seabury, a major La Guardia supporter, was anti-Semitic in nature. Seabury had criticized Lehman for failing to prosecute some corrupt Tammany district leaders.[10] There is no indication that any anti-Semitism was intended in Seabury's remarks, but McKee needed votes and this could be developed into a good issue with which to weaken La Guardia. However, La Guardia had something better, and he now used it.

La Guardia produced an article that McKee had written for the *Catholic World* in 1915 and suggested that it bore evidence of the Recovery party candidate's anti-Semitism. He called on McKee to offer an explanation of what he had stated in the article. In 1915 McKee had called on Catholic parents to make sure that their children went to school. He compared the Catholics with the Jews, who "make up 75 per cent of the enrollment in the city high schools" and who would surely "be the lawyers, the doctors, the educators, the professional men of the coming generation." McKee charged that in their quest for material advancement the Jewish students had abandoned the moral tenets of Judaism. "Surely," stated McKee, "we cannot look for ideal results from such material." Finally, after describing the depraved, corrupt Jewish youths who would become the leaders of tomorrow, McKee urged Catholics not to let this happen.[11]

Samuel Untermyer, a prominent Jewish and Democratic party leader who had been one of McKee's important supporters, termed the article "a libel on the Jews." La Guardia, making full use of this new issue, commented that "McKee wrote a scurrilous cowardly attack on a great race and the responsibility is his." McKee, very worried about the Jewish vote, tried to defend himself in a special radio address by stating that he had also praised the Jews in his article and that it had not been intended as a condemnation of all Jews but only of those who had forsaken Judaism. He also noted that he was a director of the Jewish Memorial Hospital and had always supported Jewish movements in the Bronx. His defense, however, backfired, as Untermyer now castigated McKee for not totally repudiating his article and added that "the first impulse and the first line of defense of every anti-Semite, when charged with bigotry, is to cry, 'I have many friends among the Jews,' which has a familiar cry."[12]

Did Jews consider McKee to be an anti-Semite? Some did, as Samuel Untermyer showed. Untermyer urged other Jewish leaders to declare against McKee, remarking, "once a bigot always a bigot." Although not all Jewish leaders felt as strongly as Untermyer, there was some opinion that McKee had not offered a satisfactory explanation.[13] Letters to La Guardia from Jewish New Yorkers indicate that some considered McKee to be anti-Semitic or at least were sure that he would lose votes on this issue.[14] The *Jewish Examiner* asked whether the article was anti-Semitic and answered its own question with an emphatic YES. "We mince no words about it," stated the newspaper, "the published article in which he slandered the character of Jewish children is subject to no explanation." Other Jews, however, did not accept the accusations against the

Recovery party candidate and continued to back him, while still others objected to the injection of a racial-religious issue into a campaign that was supposed to deal with good government.[15]

Through his supporters, McKee made one last effort to use the anti-Jewish issue in his favor. La Guardia was now accused of writing an anti-Zionist letter in 1919. La Guardia, covering all challenges for the Jewish vote, released a statement to the Jewish press, using a noted Jewish newspaperman as spokesman, that in 1919 he had questioned—as indeed many Jewish leaders had—whether Zionism was the best answer, but that he had had "an open mind on the matter" and supported only "what was best for the Jews."[16]

Mayor O'Brien, meanwhile, did not leave the Jewish issue for the other two candidates. Just before the election, he threatened to revoke the permit for the celebration of the annual German Day event at a city armory because of Nazi influence in the organization planning the festivities. As a result of O'Brien's action, the scheduled event was cancelled. This was not strictly an ethnically motivated decision, since O'Brien was fearful of a riot erupting at the meeting. However, being the first strong response to the local Nazis from a government official, the action might have helped to win Jewish votes. O'Brien did announce his decision before a meeting of 500 leaders of Orthodox Jewry, and he received praise from many Jews for his action. Of course, the issue may have also cost O'Brien some German votes. Although many German-American organizations in the City had already endorsed him, there was dissatisfaction in the community with his decision in this case.[17]

The Jews were not the only group to receive special appeals. As a way of solidifying the Irish vote against La Guardia and securing German Catholic support, the Communist issue was raised briefly in the campaign. Both McKee and O'Brien accused La Guardia of being a Communist. McKee stated that he would "be an American Mayor and not a Moscow Mayor." A pamphlet from the O'Brien camp asked, "Can this little Red Demagogue [La Guardia] be true to New York City?"[18]

The important aspect of these issues is that they were used as major campaign tactics by the various parties and indicated a strong interest in winning the ethnic and particularly the Jewish vote. The constant emphasis on anti-Semitism clearly made the Jews much more aware and fearful of this movement's potential in New York City. Similarly, the spectre of Communism was constantly being held up before the Irish and German Catholics. Also, for the German community, the cancellation of their German Day celebration brought back fearful memories of World War I anti-German hysteria. In this way the ethnic issues in this campaign could only help to strain relations between the groups as insecurities and fears were emphasized and brought to the surface.

The election returns, contrary to what the politicians had hoped, indicated the importance of ethnicity mainly for the Italian-American voter (see table 11). The Italians were drawn to La Guardia in overwhelming numbers. He was able to

Table 11. Voting Percentages for 1933 Mayoralty Election, by Ethnicity and Party

	City-wide	Irish	German	Jewish	Italian
Republican (La Guardia)	20.8	12.1	18.7	18.9	27.3
City Fusion (La Guardia)	19.6	9.7	11.3	17.4	34.9
Total La Guardia	40.4	21.8	30.0	36.3	62.2
Recovery (McKee)	28.3	39.5	45.4	22.7	11.3
Democratic[a] (O'Brien)	27.2	36.9	22.5	31.9	23.7
Socialist (Charles Solomon)	2.9	1.3	1.6	5.6	2.0
Communist (Robert Minor)	1.2	.4	.3	3.3	.7
Minor parties[b]	.1	.1	.2	.2	.1

NOTE: Owing to the rounding of numbers and the exclusion of scattered votes for write-in candidates, figures may not add up exactly to 100 percent.

[a] Also includes the votes of O'Brien's Jefferson party.

[b] Includes the votes of the Taxpayers party, Five-Cent Fare party, Industrial Union party and Socialist Labor party.

secure 62.2 percent of the vote within Italian election districts, with only 23.7 percent going to O'Brien and 11.3 percent to McKee. La Guardia captured all income groups (for which information was available) within this ethnic community by large majorities, although he did better among Italians in middle-class areas (67.5 percent of the vote), than in lower-class ones (55.9 percent of the vote).[19] Democratic boss control was strongest in the lower-income sections, and therefore La Guardia's vote was slightly less there. For example, in the second assembly district of Manhattan where Tammany boss Al Marinelli ruled, one Italian election district gave La Guardia only 8.5 percent of their vote, with 89.3 percent going to O'Brien. However, in other second assembly district Italian precincts Marinelli simply could not retain control and La Guardia secured large majorities. It was difficult to keep the Italian community from voting for their Fiorello. Although La Guardia's Italian vote was basically an ethnic vote, it also included elements of Italian Republican support.

The Jews did not give La Guardia a solid vote. Jewish election districts voted 36.3 percent for La Guardia—a plurality in this three-way race but certainly not a sign of overwhelming support. O'Brien received 31.9 percent of this vote and McKee won 22.7 percent. Basically, La Guardia won the Jewish vote because the Democratic party was split. However, it is necessary to understand why La Guardia was able to receive a plurality over his Democratic opponents just a year after Roosevelt and Lehman had won huge majorities of the Jewish vote in the City.

Two issues can help to explain the Jewish vote. One is reform and the other anti-Semitism, a potent issue during a period when Jews were concerned about Nazism. La Guardia did very well in upper-class Jewish election districts, with 50.2 percent of the vote; in upper-middle-class Jewish areas, with 52.3 percent of the vote and in Jewish middle-middle-class districts with 38.7 percent of the vote. In these three class areas O'Brien and McKee finished considerably behind La Guardia. The people in these class districts were those most attracted to La Guardia's Republicanism and his good government promises, and were less likely to support a machine candidate, particularly after the Tammany scandals. As one moved down the class scale, the vote for O'Brien increased. In the lower-middle-class Jewish areas, La Guardia edged out O'Brien 34.3 percent to 31.2 percent, but in the lower-class districts the Tammany candidate was the clear winner, with 41.8 percent of the vote to La Guardia's 30 percent.[20] The lower-middle and lower classes lived in areas where machine control was still potent, and the appeal of Republican reform was less so. McKee, who finished third with all Jewish voters except those in the upper-class districts, should have done better, since he too had labeled himself as an anti-Tammany reform candidate. However, he attracted little support in the communities interested in reform. In the upper-middle-class Jewish election districts, O'Brien beat McKee 24.2 percent to 18.1 percent, and in middle-middle-class districts he won 27.3 percent to 24.1 percent. Most areas that indicated a desire for reform by going for La Guardia picked O'Brien rather than McKee as their second choice. McKee's poor showing in these areas can first be explained by noting that he simply was not as progressive as La Guardia and was not able to convince the voters that he represented a real break with Tammany.

The other explanation for McKee's Jewish vote involves the issue of anti-Semitism. That this issue probably was also a factor in the election returns is strongly suggested by the class vote and particularly by the Bronx Jewish vote. The Bronx vote was important because this borough represented the heart of McKee's machine strength. However, in almost every election district where the Jews were the majority of the voting population, La Guardia scored impressive victories over McKee. All of these districts had given Roosevelt and Lehman their votes only a year earlier, and so conceivably should have been expected to give a plurality in this three-way race to Roosevelt's supposed choice (McKee) or at least to a Democrat. Certainly it was assumed that McKee would at least substantially outpoint the Tammany candidate.[21] However, La Guardia took 36.4 percent of the Bronx Jewish vote, compared to 26.3 percent for McKee and 26.3 percent for O'Brien. The middle-middle-class Jewish vote in this borough is revealing in this case, since in these districts the voters gave La Guardia 37.1 percent of the vote, compared to McKee's 26.8 percent and O'Brien's 25.9 percent. O'Brien's decent showing in rival Democratic territory might be attributable to some Jewish support resulting from his German Day decision. McKee, the other "reformer," in his home borough and in middle-class areas barely managed to beat the Tammany candidate. He should have showed greater strength in this borough. That he did not show greater strength in this borough indicates some reluctance on the part of the Jews to vote for him. On a citywide basis the Jewish vote for McKee was below the city average, while other groups, such as the Irish and Germans, gave McKee a vote significantly above the city average. La Guardia and, to some extent, O'Brien were able to win some Jewish votes by labeling themselves as the protectors of the Jews against the anti-Semites (a tactic that would be used many times in the future, particularly by La Guardia).

The total Jewish vote for La Guardia was a combination of ethnic (anti-Semitism) and class (reform) issues at work; the Italians, in contrast, showed no major class differences and voted, it seems, on the basis of ethnic pride. The ethnic factor also played a role in the Irish community, where the Italian Republican La Guardia received his lowest vote (21.8 percent), with the two Irish candidates splitting this group's support. The Manhattan and Bronx Irish vote illustrate this split. In Manhattan, where the Tammany machine backed O'Brien, the Irish vote was 50.7 percent in his favor, with McKee securing 31.4 percent and La Guardia 16.2 percent. However, in the Bronx, where the Flynn machine worked hard for McKee, the Recovery party candidate received 45.6 percent of the Irish vote as compared to O'Brien's 32.1 percent and La Guardia's 20.5 percent. This split and the low La Guardia vote were evident across all (available) class divisions. Although there was some support for reform in this community, it was not for the type of reform offered by an upstart from a new group who was accused of having Communist sympathies. Doubtless many Irish felt it better either to vote for one of their own or to stay with Tammany.

The German vote shows a different pattern, in that McKee clearly won this community's support, with La Guardia running a poor second. That O'Brien received his lowest vote among this group probably indicates the impact of the German Day incident, particularly since O'Brien had been endorsed by many German-American organizations before that decision. The McKee victory and the lower La Guardia and O'Brien showing hold true across all (available) class divisions. La Guardia's ability to secure the second-place position in the German community was the result of their greater involvement in the Republican party, an interest in reform, less attachment to the Tammany machine than the Irish, less hysteria concerning the Communist issue, and some reluctance to vote for O'Brien.

The voting results indicated to the new mayor that the base of his support would come from the Italians and upper- and middle-class Jews. Overly confident of keeping his Italian vote, La Guardia mainly geared his administration and his campaigns toward winning a majority Jewish vote, which had eluded him in 1933. The Italians eventually came to feel somewhat neglected. Although a portion of the Irish and German communities had supported La Guardia, and continued to do so on the basis of the mayor's uncorrupted leadership, he ultimately alienated most of his Irish and German support because of policies designed to keep the newer immigrant vote. Motivated both by his own personal views on world and domestic affairs and by a desire to increase especially his Jewish vote, the mayor antagonized the older groups in the City with his decisions in such situations as the Fama and masseur cases (see chapter 3) and his involvement in the Nazi and World War II issues. Whether or not he intended it to, La Guardia's position in these various controversies helped him win more votes among the groups in which he was interested. La Guardia was willing to make this trade because he knew that the newer ethnics were now more numerous in the City and were looking for a sympathetic spokesman. However, the mayor never wrote off the votes of the Irish and Germans; if he could win these votes while holding onto the Jews and Italians, he would do it. La Guardia was adept at pitting one group against another for political advantage. Robert Moses, a prominent La Guardia aide, noted "that in exploiting racial and religious prejudices La Guardia could run circles around the bosses he despised and derided. When it came to raking ashes of Old World hates, warming ancient grudges, waving the bloody shirt, tuning the ear to ancestral voices, he could easily outdemagogue the demagogues."[22] He had done this when he had run for office earlier, and he continued the successful practice into his mayoralty years. Of course, La Guardia's opponents must also take responsibility for stressing the ethnic issues. They were often the ones to mention these issues first in the campaigns, although the mayor made more skillful use of them.

THE 1937 MAYORALTY CAMPAIGN

The mayoralty campaign of 1937 brought new ethnic appeals by the politicians, even at a time when there were signs of growing ethnic antagonism in the City. A few months before the 1937 election, in a speech before the Women's Division of the American Jewish Congress, La Guardia suggested that Hitler's figure be put into a Chamber of Horrors at the World's Fair. This brought a reaction from German-American groups. The major question on their lips was, "If Hitler is to be put into a Chamber of Horrors, what about Mussolini?" A Steuben Society of America *Bulletin* noted that

> never in all his speeches has he, this professed great lover of mankind, as far as we can learn, uttered a single word in criticism of the suppression of personal rights in the land of his Italian forbears, . . . nor did he at any time give evidence of an urge to denounce Stalin as an enemy of mankind. It does not call for much study to explain the Mayor's apparent inconsistencies. . . . Why, he reasons, estrange the Italian vote by attacking Mussolini, or the Communist vote by attacking Stalin? But on the other hand, another large block of votes can be corralled, as he calculates, by attacking Hitler.

The German-American Conference also protested, claiming that the statement only tends "to disrupt friendly relations between this country and Germany and that it breeds race hatred and ill-feeling among our citizens of different racial extractions." It was recognized, even in the general press, that La Guardia's anti-Hitler speech, as well as his earlier masseur decision, was part of an effort to win Jewish votes.[23]

The 1937 mayoralty contest between La Guardia and his Irish Democratic opponent, Jeremiah Mahoney, continued to show evidence of ethnic politics. Although there were many nonethnic issues in this campaign (such as good government, the retention of the five-cent subway fare, and rising taxes), the political rhetoric concentrated enough on the ethnic topics to be noticed by the general press.[24]

La Guardia's involvement in the Nazism controversy was an immediate issue, and one that the Bund used in their effort to win the sympathy of the German-American community. The American Nazis, while accusing La Guardia of being a Communist and a Jewish sympathizer, also stressed that the mayor was not treating German-Americans fairly. However, Mahoney was attacked, too, because he had asked for Jewish support while neglecting the "nearly 1,000,000 German and German-American taxpayers" in the City. Who, then, according to the American Nazis, were the Germans to support? The only one they could trust was the Bund itself, not the politicians. The theme of La Guardia's anti-Germanism was reflected also by a comment in the *Steuben News* which observed that "the Mayor has done more to create and foster antagonisms between racial groups than any other man in New York City. Our Society has repeatedly expressed disapproval of his persistent antagonism of everything which might have a tendency to deal justly with the rights of those of German blood."[25]

Yet not all Germans, including those who identified strongly with their background, felt this resentment. The liberal German-American newspaper *Deutsches Volksecho* endorsed the mayor. To a number of German-Americans the important factor in this campaign was not ethnicity but good government. This was particularly true for those German New Yorkers who did not at this time feel threatened by or involved in the controversy over Nazism. However, good government could also be important to German-Americans who were concerned about Germany. The *Staats-Zeitung* commented that the major question in the election should be good government, and later it viewed La Guardia's victory as a rejection of Tammany bossism and an approval of corruption-free government.[26] Ethnicity was never the sole motivating factor in either endorsements or voting.

It should also be noted, however, that the ethnic issue had been muted somewhat by the fact that Mahoney had also taken an anti-Germany stand. La Guardia, meanwhile, was careful not to antagonize the German community any further, or more than he had to. He had recently appointed a prominent German-American as city magistrate, and he tried to avoid the German issue during the actual campaign.[27] It was Mahoney who was to make use of this issue in an effort to pull Jewish votes away from the mayor. La Guardia was concerned about the votes of the German community and had the German-American division of his campaign organization actively seeking to assuage this group. Mahoney was also interested in the support of this group and was able to secure some endorsements.[28]

As in 1933, this campaign became above all a contest for the Jewish vote. The Democrats had chosen Mahoney as a candidate partially because, as president of the Amateur Athletic Union, he had opposed the holding of the 1936 Olympics in Berlin and later had suggested that the United States withdraw from the games. Mahoney also had a long association with Jewish charities. It therefore was hoped that he might counteract La Guardia's appeal among the Jews.[29]

La Guardia had by this time built up strong support in the Jewish community on the basis of his early and vigorous stand against Nazism. Mahoney was hard-pressed to find an issue with which to appeal to Jewish ethnic interests, but he tried. A pamphlet put out by the Mahoney forces in the Jewish areas stated that "the real truth is that Mayor La Guardia has been the only mayor in New York who was afraid to take a real stand, an open stand against anti-Semitism and against Hitlerism in New York." The pamphlet claimed that former Democratic mayors—and, of course, Mahoney—had done more than just verbally attack Hitler to show their support of the Jews. The pamphlet also asked for the support of Max J. Schneider, Democratic candidate for president of the city council, who also happened to be the president of the United Synagogues and Congregations in the Bronx. When this issue did not take effect, Mahoney tried other ways to prove that he was the only true friend of the Jews. He put an advertisement into the *Morning Journal* and the *Day,* both Yiddish newspapers, in which Judge Jonah J. Goldstein, a Mahoney supporter, criticized La Guardia for failing to reappoint some well-known Jews to office.[30] Although playing on the fears and desires of the Jews, these appeals were ineffective and remained so until almost the end of the campaign.

A few days before the election, however, a new incident arose. The German-American Bund had asked for and received a permit to parade in Manhattan. The permit was issued by the police, but La Guardia could have prevented it from being given. This was seemingly an exploitable ethnic issue, particularly since letter after letter poured into La Guardia headquarters from Jews protesting the parade and threatening La Guardia with a loss of votes. The Jewish vote in the Bronx was swinging to Mahoney, wrote one Jewish New Yorker, adding that "word is spreading like fire that La Guardia is a secret friend of the Nazis."[31] The Mahoney forces were quick to use this issue. A radio address by Judge Goldstein claimed that La Guardia was permitting the Nazis to march in order to secure their votes or to be the hero by cancelling the parade when the protests got too strong. Democratic mayors, according to Goldstein, never allowed such things to happen in New York. A pro-Mahoney pamphlet, put out by a nonexistent War Veterans Committee to give the impression that it was a Jewish War Veterans publication, declared "La Guardia Today Sold Out to the NAZIS!" and noted that four years earlier Mayor O'Brien had forbidden the Nazis to meet. An editorial in the *Day,* a pro-Mahoney Jewish newspaper, called for the defeat of La Guardia because he had allowed the Nazis to parade. In an editorial just before election day this newspaper stressed that New York was going to see "a Nazi parade with Nazi uniforms and Nazi flags and Nazi music; AND WITH THE FULL CONSENT OF THE NEW YORK ADMINIS-TRATION."[32] La Guardia claimed that he had not granted any permit and had had nothing to do with the whole affair; however, realizing the potential danger in this issue, he responded with a counterattack. The mayor suggested that the parade possibly may have been planned by Tammany to embarass him. There were reports that the Mahoney forces were trying to agitate the members of the Jewish War Veterans to go to the parade and create an incident, thereby bringing more protests against La Guardia.[33] The Mayor, never acting solely because of ethnic motivations, did not revoke the permit; he believed in the right of assembly and free speech for any group, but he did limit the parade route and forbade the Nazis to wear their uniforms or sing their songs, thereby turning it into an ineffective spectacle. Although Mahoney made strenuous efforts to arouse the Jewish community over this incident, La Guardia's credentials with the Jews were not tarnished; he was still looked upon as a friend for his many pro-Jewish statements and actions in the past. As the *Forward* noted in relation to the Democrats' attempt to label the mayor as a friend of the Nazis, "Nobody took them seriously; nobody believed the demagoguery of the worn-out Tammany men." The charge of Nazism against La Guardia, the paper stated, was just a false political issue designed to save Tammany. The *American Hebrew* also ridiculed the attempt to picture La Guardia as pro-Nazi. Even the *Day* noted that La Guardia was a friend of the Jews, although only for political reasons. Mahoney, this paper claimed, was simply "a truer friend." Furthermore, periodicals such as the *New York Jewish News* and the *Forward* criticized Mahoney for injecting a Jewish issue into the campaign. The *Forward* lashed out at the Democrats and the *Day* for attempting to turn the campaign "into a question of Jews and Nazis," and thereby "doing damage to the Jewish cause" by making it appear that New York was a Nazi-controlled town.[34]

By using this issue, Mahoney actually may have lost not only some Jewish votes, because they resented the ethnic appeal, but also the votes of Germans who would have preferred that the Nazi issue remain out of the campaign. However, regardless of votes lost or gained, the use of the ethnic appeal did little for harmonious intergroup relations.

Mahoney also injected the Communist issue into the campaign in an effort to win the Catholic vote. The fact that the Communist party had endorsed La Guardia made it easier for the Democrats to use this issue against him, even though the mayor had quickly repudiated the support of the Communists. An Anti-Communist party was organized to give Mahoney another line on the ballot and to indicate to voters which candidate was the real American. Mahoney declared that La Guardia was a Communist and had allowed Communists to gain control of the City and the school system. Circulars accusing the mayor of being a Communist and urging Catholics to support Mahoney were passed out in front of Catholic churches in a number of areas. One pamphlet, which also accused La Guardia of appointing anti-Catholics such as Fama to office, stated, "Vote for Mahoney, Catholics, Your Duty." Irish-Americans were specifically called on to vote for Mahoney and thereby defeat Communism.[35] The mayor was forced to fight back against these tactics. Not wishing to lose any ethnic group's vote if it could be avoided, La Guardia organized an Irish-American Non-Partisan Committee which addressed itself mainly to a defense of the mayor on the Communist charge but also noted that he had been a champion of Irish freedom and had appointed many Irish-Americans to office. Charges of bigotry against La Guardia were deemed false.[36] Mahoney's rhetoric, besides trying to secure voter support, did have one major effect; it reinforced the idea that the Communists were everywhere and powerful. This only served to increase the anxiety of groups already concerned about the threat of Communism.

Mahoney's supporters also attempted to pull Italian votes away from the mayor. A great deal of emphasis was placed on the theme that La Guardia was not providing enough political positions for the Italian community. Only under the Democrats, it was claimed, could the Italians receive a sufficient number of political jobs.[37] A pamphlet also noted that La Guardia was prouder of his Jewish blood than of his Italian. The Democrats by this time had begun to appoint more Italians to office as a way of winning back this vote and felt that they could now criticize the mayor on this point.[38] Again an obvious attempt was made to foment ethnic friction and to appeal to ethnic fears and desires to win votes.

Because of his strength with certain ethnic groups, as well as his good government image, La Guardia won an easy victory.[39] As table 12 indicates, the

Table 12. Voting Percentages for 1937 Mayoralty Election, by Ethnicity and Party

	City-wide	Irish	German	Jewish	Italian
Republican (La Guardia)	30.2	21.5	33.1	21.0	31.0
Progressive (La Guardia)	1.2	.9	.6	1.6	1.4
City Fusion (La Guardia)	7.1	4.1	4.6	5.1	7.6
American Labor (La Guardia)	21.6	10.3	8.1	40.9	22.6
Total La Guardia	60.1	36.8	46.4	68.6	62.6
Democrat[a] (Mahoney)	39.8	63.2	53.5	31.3	37.3
Minor party					
(Industrial Government party)	.1	.1	.1	.2	.1

NOTE: Owing to the rounding of numbers and the exclusion of scattered votes for write-in candidates, figures may not add up exactly to 100 percent.

[a]Includes the votes of Mahoney's Anti-Communist party and his Trades Union party, both of which received few votes.

Jewish election districts gave the mayor 68.6 percent of their vote, with large majorities among all income classes (on which data were available). Even the lower-class Jewish vote, although giving the mayor less of a plurality, went to him with 60 percent. La Guardia's percentage of the vote in Jewish election districts in 1933 correlated a high .720 ($r^2 = .518$) with the percentage of his vote in Jewish election districts in 1937 indicating that there was a consistency in Jewish support for the mayor. He also continued to hold his Italian vote, which was 62.6 percent in his favor and strong across all (available) income groupings. As in 1933, he received a slightly smaller vote in lower-class Italian districts. A consistency in support for La Guardia was noted by a high correlation of .729 ($r^2 = .531$) when his percentage of the vote in Italian election districts in 1933 was correlated with his percentage of the vote in these areas in 1937. The mayor's strategy of bidding particularly for Jewish and Italian backing was successful.

The other ethnic groups indicated less of a desire to endorse La Guardia. The vote in the Irish election districts was 63.2 percent for Mahoney, and he swept all (available) income classes. Correlation between the percentage vote for La Guardia in Irish election districts in 1933 and 1937 was .715 ($r^2 = .511$), indicating that the mayor was drawing his Irish support from the same areas— and perhaps for the same reasons: a desire among some Irish to vote on the basis of good government and a willingness to break with Tammany. One Irish New Yorker who supported the mayor noted his appreciation of La Guardia's efforts in behalf of the people of New York.[40] However, most of the Irish remained tied to the Democratic party, susceptible to the Communist issue, and resentful about what they considered the mayor's anti-Irish attitude. Mahoney therefore was their choice.

The German vote is of special interest, considering the reaction by some members of this group to the mayor's anti-Nazi statements. The 46.4 percent for La Guardia indicates that a number of German-Americans were not motivated solely by ethnic concerns. This was partly the result of the fact that both Mahoney's and La Guardia's positions were perceived as anti-German, which tended to mute the ethnic issue.[41] Mahoney's involvement in the effort to move the Olympics from Berlin had hurt him, as even his German supporters acknowledged.[42] Also, it was Mahoney who raised the Nazi issue in the campaign, allowing the mayor to assume the role of the fair-minded individual who had not interfered with the right of a group to parade. (This came at a time when some of the influential non-Nazis had not yet repudiated the Bund.) A further explanation of the vote is that the threat of a repeat of World War I anti-German demagoguery (which had seemed a possibility during the 1933 campaign, when New York's leaders began to react to Nazism) did not again appear as serious until 1938, when Germany's anti-Semitism grew more severe, when that country began drawing closer to war, and when the American people began to take a decidedly anti-German stand. It was at this point that most German-Americans fully realized the position they were in and began to vote accordingly, as illustrated by

La Guardia's low 1941 German vote. Nevertheless, it should be noted that the German vote in 1937 was 14 percent below La Guardia's citywide average. Yet this is the ethnic group that had voted heavily for McKee as a reformer and given La Guardia second place in 1933, and which therefore should have been more heavily drawn to reform's side in 1937. The McKee percentage vote in German election districts in 1933 correlated only .315 (r^2 = .031) with La Guardia's 1937 percentage vote in German election districts, indicating little identity of support. When La Guardia's percentage vote in German election districts in 1933 and 1937 is correlated, the result is .506 (r^2 = .256), showing more consistency of support but also illustrating that La Guardia did not have, as with the other groups, a strong clique of followers. Mahoney, the machine candidate, won 53.5 percent of the vote in the German election districts.

As in 1933, the importance of the campaign relates to the effect it had on ethnic tensions in the City. By stressing once again anti-Semitism, Communism, and Nazism, as well as ethnic displacement, the politicians had contributed to the emergence and persistence of conflict.

THE 1941 MAYORALTY CAMPAIGN

During La Guardia's second administration, the issue of anti-Semitism became more important, as did concern over foreign affairs. At this time the German-American Bund increased its activities in the City, and the predominantly Irish Christian Front made its first appearance. Numerous anti-Semitic street meetings were held in a number of neighborhoods throughout the City, accompanied by vandalism directed against synagogues and Jewish-owned stores and by attacks on Jews (for a full discussion of the situation in various neighborhoods, see chapter 8). The Jewish community naturally was concerned and urged that the anti-Semitic rabble-rousers be removed from the streets. Some criticized the mayor for not acting fast enough to alleviate the problem and warned of the consequences. For example, the general executive committee of the Jewish National Worker's Alliance of America warned that if something were not done to remedy it, the situation in New York "may lead to civil strife among the various religious and national groups within our city."[43] The mayor tried to do something about the meetings by putting pressure on the police and the courts to rid the streets of the agitators if they stepped outside the law. (New York City had a law which made the abuse of racial groups a violation). The number of arrests did increase—particularly after the police were accused of being partial to the Front—but the meetings continued, either as actual Front, Mobilizer, or Bund meetings, or as antiwar rallies.[44] La Guardia, remaining consistent with his previous efforts to uphold constitutional rights, tried to maintain a balance between freedom of speech and the right of minorities to be free from abuse. Acknowledging the arrests of the rabble-rousers, the mayor noted that "the City of New York will continue to remain free for all who wish to express their opinion, but the authorities will deal properly with any misguided troublemakers who, under the guise of free speech, slander or vilify peaceful groups residing in this city."[45] More damage was done to the Bund than to the others at this time because of the combined efforts of La Guardia and District Attorney Dewey. Fritz Kuhn was eventually sent to jail for larceny and forgery in December 1939, and his conviction and incarceration marked the beginning of the end for his organization.

Nevertheless, although La Guardia had taken action, the anti-Semitic problem remained and of course became a central issue in the 1941 campaign. The mayor, running this time against William O'Dwyer, district attorney of Brooklyn, was immediately accused by his opponent of being either unable or reluctant to suppress the anti-Semitic agitators. O'Dwyer even pointed out that La Guardia had appointed some of these anti-Semites to office, as well as some anti-Catholics (such as Fama).[46] Unconcerned with the mayor's explanations, O'Dwyer stated, when speaking before the Kings County Council of the Jewish War Veterans, that "we don't have to go outside the borders of our own city to find enemies." He claimed that while the mayor had done little, he, as district attorney, had not permitted any anti-Semitic orators in Brooklyn and would push the Front off the streets in New York if elected.[47] This type of campaign issue again emphasized the anti-Semitism in the City, thus reinforcing the fears of the Jewish community.

Did O'Dwyer's tactics have any effect? One Jewish New Yorker, writing to La Guardia, expressed a feeling that "we cannot understand why you permit a small group of hatemongers to hold street meetings and preach the doctrine of race and religious hatred." He continued by noting that he had supported the mayor in 1933 and 1937 and would like to support La Guardia in this election also, but that this issue was too important and that something must be done. The *Jewish Examiner* endorsed O'Dwyer claiming that the mayor had not made a sufficient effort to eliminate anti-Semitism in New York. Earlier the paper had suggested that this was perhaps because of La Guardia's desire not to lose the anti-Semitic vote.[48]

Although La Guardia may have lost some Jewish votes as a result of this issue, it did not seriously diminish his Jewish backing. One of the reasons is that La Guardia, through his subordinates, was able to smear the Irish O'Dwyer with the anti-Semitic charge. Police Commissioner Lewis Valentine denied O'Dwyer's claim that he had suppressed the anti-Semitic street meetings in Brooklyn. In a letter to one of his Jewish critics, La Guardia noted that in the past year there had been no arrests of anti-Semitic agitators in Brooklyn, although there had been 102 street meetings. After denying O'Dwyer's accusations and stating that the district attorney had done very little about the agitators, La Guardia began his attack, which revealed his able use of this issue. Louis Lipsky, former president of the Zionist Organization of America and a member of the

Citizens Committee for the Re-election of La Guardia, said in a radio address that
"instead of making pledges to the Jews that he will drive peddlers of race hatred
from the streets of the city . . . O'Dwyer . . . should address himself to the anti-
Semitic groups fighting for his election." A La Guardia pamphlet noted that "the
sinister forces of Hitlerism in America are beating the drums for La Guardia's
Tammany opponent." Even before the Lipsky statement, O'Dwyer had publicly
complained that the mayor had started a whispering campaign against him which
stated that he was an anti-Semite and a member of the Christian Front.[49] Since
O'Dwyer was Irish and it was often the Irish street corner agitators who were
disturbing the Jewish community, this issue was much more dangerous for
O'Dwyer than La Guardia.

Supporters of the Democratic candidate, meanwhile, had already moved
into action to stop these rumors. For example, Lieutenant Governor Charles
Poletti, in a radio speech, remarked upon how O'Dwyer had fought against
bigotry during the Lehman campaign three years earlier when there was an
anti-Semitic whispering campaign against the Jewish gubernatorial candidate.
Solicitor General Henry Epstein urged those who believed in racial and religious
tolerance to support O'Dwyer, noting at the same time that "you and I know that
appeals are being made to the Jewish voters in this City of New York today to
vote for La Guardia because of some mistaken idea that he is their protector
against persecution." Actually, the charges of anti-Semitism against O'Dwyer
had no foundation whatsoever, since he had worked against the Front in the past
and subsequently had incurred the wrath of the Coughlinite Irish, who accused
him of being a Jew-lover. Also, in his acceptance speech as a mayoral candidate
in September 1941, O'Dwyer had lashed out at the anti-Semitic fanatics, disavowed their support, and noted that he would continue to harass them.[50]

O'Dwyer's attack on the anti-Semitic rabble-rousers, although motivated by
more than politics, was still a shrewd political move. It enabled him to lay claim
to the large Jewish vote. At the same time he was able to secure support from the
anti-Coughlinite Irish who disliked and were ashamed of the activities of organizations such as the Front. As for the Coughlinites, many probably voted for the
Irish Tammany candidate anyway—there was nobody else for them to support.[51]
O'Dwyer also appealed to the Coughlinites, as well as others, by raising the
Communism issue and noting that Communists such as Gerson would have no
place in his administration. The Democratic candidate strongly implied that La
Guardia was a Communist. La Guardia was worried about the Communist charge
and reportedly, because of his concern over this issue, had earlier refused to
support Stanley Isaacs, the man who had appointed Gerson, for renomination as
Manhattan's borough president.[52]

Although O'Dwyer's appeal to the Irish proved to be effective, he failed to
gain the more important Jewish support. The mayor, on the other hand, was able
to explain how he was handling the anti-Semites, while hinting that his opponent
was not to be trusted. He could therefore easily emerge as the protector of the

Jews. The usually Democratic Jewish newspaper *Day,* in declaring for La Guardia, noted this theme when it stated in an editorial that "the Jewish population knows that they always have in him a trustworthy, devoted big brother."[53]

While the candidates argued over who was the greater foe of the anti-Semites, they also fought over which prominent Jews had endorsed them. O'Dwyer claimed that Louis Brandeis, just before he died, had expressed a preference for his candidacy. La Guardia denied this claim. By making an issue of La Guardia's strong criticism of Governor Lehman, for attempting to influence the election of a state controller, O'Dwyer also tried to emphasize that La Guardia was at odds with a leading Jewish political figure. Since Lehman was highly respected in the Jewish community, the Democrats hoped to turn Jewish voters against the mayor for his remarks. Some of La Guardia's supporters expressed fear that he might lose some Jewish votes because of this issue. Although many Jews were attracted by the ethnic appeals, this tactic also drew criticism. "It is the cheapest and most un-American kind of pre-election 'politics' to either scare or cajole Jewish citizens as Jews," stated one Rabbi. The *American Hebrew* asked why our politicians could not abstain from making ethnic and racial appeals.[54]

While the campaign included totally nonethnic issues, too—such as the charge that La Guardia was a part-time mayor because of his many other activities, including his job as United States Director of Civil Defense—still a great deal of emphasis was placed on issues which either directly or indirectly involved the ethnics. Of the latter, foreign policy was most important.[55] Particularly for the Jews, the anti-Semitic issue was closely linked to America's relationship with Nazi Germany. Although both candidates endorsed Roosevelt's foreign policy, it was La Guardia who, in the newspapers, had consistently called for greater American involvement in the European war. It was the mayor, for example, who became honorary chairman of the New York chapter of the Committee to Defend America by Aiding the Allies and who spoke in behalf of lend-lease and all-out aid to England and France on a number of occasions. He had also appeared at many Stop Hitler rallies.[56] In addition, La Guardia was closely identified with Roosevelt, having endorsed the president for reelection in 1940. Roosevelt in turn gave La Guardia rather than the Democratic O'Dwyer his unconditional support in 1941. The strong connection in the public's mind between Roosevelt and La Guardia and their policies, while helping the mayor in the interventionist Jewish community, hurt him with the isolationist voter. Although La Guardia had little control over foreign policy, a Gallup poll in November 1941 concluded that since there was significant support in the City for isolationism, the mayor had lost votes in his reelection bid because of his foreign policy position.[57]

Much of the isolationist opinion was based in the Irish, German, and Italian communities, and their voting reflected their response to this issue. As table 13 shows, the German election districts, which had given La Guardia 30 percent of their vote in 1933, when there were three candidates, only gave the mayor 28.3

Table 13. Voting Percentages for 1941 Mayoralty Election, by Ethnicity and Party

	City-wide	Irish	German	Jewish	Italian
Republican (La Guardia)	29.5	14.3	19.6	28.8	29.9
United City (La Guardia)	.9	.2	.2	1.4	.9
City Fusion (La Guardia)	2.8	1.0	.7	3.3	1.5
American Labor (La Guardia)	19.2	8.4	7.8	39.3	13.8
Total La Guardia	52.4	23.9	28.3	72.8	46.1
Democrat (O'Dwyer)	46.5	75.6	70.6	25.2	52.9
Socialist (Hartmann)	1.0	.4	.9	1.7	.8
Minor parties[a]	.1	.0	.1	.2	.2

NOTE: Owing to the rounding of numbers and the exclusion of scattered votes for write-in candidates, figures may not add up to exactly 100 percent.
[a]Includes votes for Workers party and Trotsky Anti-War party.

percent of their vote in 1941, with a low vote across all (available) class levels. The German following which La Guardia had won in the previous elections, although not as stable as the mayor's adherents among the other groups between 1933 and 1937, now showed no consistency of support. The La Guardia percentage vote in German election districts in 1933 correlated $-.011$ with his percentage of the German election district vote in 1941. The correlation between his 1937 and 1941 German vote was .123 ($r^2 = .015$). By this year, the German community had grown fearful of an American entry into a war against Germany, a war which might reinvigorate the anti-German hysteria of earlier days. Although important German-American newspapers such as the *Staats-Zeitung* continued to support La Guardia on the basis of good government (while acknowledging his faults), most German-Americans, feeling threatened after 1938, reacted against politicians such as the mayor whom they perceived to be unsympathetic to the needs of their community.[58]

The Irish community, in addition to feeling that La Guardia was anti-Irish for his efforts to break their political power, also reacted against the mayor on the war issue. The Communist issue also had some effect on this vote as well as on that of the German Catholics. The vote for La Guardia in Irish election districts was only 23.9 percent, and was equally low for all (available) class categories. However, while Irish support for the mayor was never strong, it remained remarkably stable. There was a small part of this community which continued to cast their votes for La Guardia. His percentage of the vote in Irish election districts in 1933 correlated .699 ($r^2 = .488$) with his percentage of the vote in these areas in 1941. Correlating 1937 and 1941 produced a figure of .818 ($r^2 = .669$). La Guardia had appealed to this group through his Irish-American Committee which stressed that the mayor had been a consistent "champion of the cause of Irish freedom."[59]

But it was the Italians, the mayor's staunchest adherents up to this point, who provided La Guardia with his most surprising losses. Italian ties to isolationism hurt the mayor, as did his criticism of Mussolini, voiced for the first time in 1940. Also important for this group was the charge, discussed earlier, that he was not doing enough for the Italian community.[60] The thrill of having one of their own as mayor had diminished by 1941, although it was certainly not gone entirely. However, there were rumblings in the community that the mayor was neglecting his people, particularly in terms of appointments.[61] With anti-Italian discrimination increasing in the United States because of Italy's entry into the war on the side of Germany, it was a natural time for Italian-Americans to perceive and complain about their lack of political power and advancement. This was a period of great insecurity for the Italian community. The issue of La Guardia's neglect, which had not caused defections in 1937, was more potent in 1941 when combined with the emotions engendered by the war. Also, the Democrats were finally opening up more positions to the Italians in an attempt to draw away votes from La Guardia at a time when he was vulnerable. Italians moving into important positions within the Democratic party were able to work against the mayor and counter his appeal in the neighborhoods since they served as proof that La Guardia was not the only one who could secure the community's political goals.

The Italian election districts, which had consistently voted over 60 percent for the mayor, dropped to 46 percent in this election, with O'Dwyer capturing the majority of the vote. That the mayor was drawing his supporters from the same election districts is demonstrated by the fact that his percentage of the vote in 1937 in the Italian areas produced a figure of .839 ($r^2 = .704$) when correlated with his percentage of the vote in 1941 in these areas. It was the same Italian constituency, but the strength of the support was much less. The Italian decrease was evident on all (available) class levels, indicating a general dissatisfaction with La Guardia within the ethnic group. However the rejection of the mayor was most notable in downwardly mobile Italian areas. Italian election districts within census tracts that had gone from middle-middle class in 1930 to lower-middle class by 1940, and from lower-middle class in 1930 to lower class by 1940, showed the greatest percentage decrease for the mayor from 1933 to 1941 and from 1937 to 1941. Although Democratic boss control was strong in some of these districts, thereby explaining a lower La Guardia vote, it must also be noted that these people were the ones hardest hit by the Depression as they fell in class status. These Italian-Americans presumably were most dissatisfied with the mayor for failing to uplift his own people.[62] These Italian areas may have been downwardly mobile by 1937, although such movement did not affect the vote then. However, by 1941 the war and the Democrats' changing attitude toward the Italian community resulted in greater dissatisfaction with La Guardia. This was still basically an ethnically motivated vote, reacting to ethnic issues (the war), but now it worked against the mayor. With this group, La Guardia, considered the master ethnic politician, made his first and almost fatal ethnic political mistake.

The mayor won this election because his policies over the years had won over one particular group: the Jews. Although the anti-Semitic street meetings issue had the potential of decreasing La Guardia's Jewish support, it seemed to have little impact, as most Jews continued to put their trust in the mayor rather than the untried O'Dwyer. On the basis of the anti-Semitic, foreign policy, and good government issues, La Guardia secured an overwhelming 72.8 percent of the vote in the Jewish election districts, offsetting his losses with the other groups. All (available) income levels in this community, from slum dwellers to residents of luxury apartment houses, gave the mayor their strong support. It did not matter whether the Jewish election districts were within census tracts that had been upwardly mobile, stable, or downwardly mobile in terms of income classes since 1930—all gave large majorities to the mayor.

La Guardia's attempts to appeal to the newer immigrant groups, was, for the most part, successful. The Italian vote brought him victory in 1933; the Italian and Jewish vote assured victory in 1937; and the Jewish vote secured victory in 1941.

However, although the tactic of the ethnic appeal was beneficial to some politicians, it was not necessarily beneficial to the City, since it also had the effect of adding to ethnic tensions and frictions. If one of the roles of a city government is that of an arbiter "whose task is to manage conflict among competing interests and to find a lowest common denominator on the basis of which a settlement or modus vivendi can be worked out," then surely the campaigns and ethnic-oriented appeals of the politicians during this era were evidence of the failure of this basic governmental function.[63]

ROOSEVELT AND ETHNIC POLITICS

It was not merely local politics which evidenced this failure to manage conflict—even national and state elections illustrated the use of this divisive tactic.[64] Examples can be drawn from the presidential campaigns, for Roosevelt, too, was an adept practitioner of the ethnic game. In 1936 and 1940 the Democratic party attempted to label its Republican opposition as anti-Semitic. Although this label was incorrect, it was easy to classify the opposition in this way, since many anti-Semites in the country were also anti-New Deal. Thus the tactic was one of guilt by association. In September of 1936 Herbert C. Pell, vice-chairman of the Democratic National Committee, remarked that the "Republican organization was 'tolerant' of wide-spread anti-Jewish propaganda in the United States." A rumor was spread that Alfred Landon, the Republican nominee, was an anti-Semite, and a point was made of the fact that Bund members had been told to vote for the Republican candidate. The Republicans were forced into a defensive position of trying to prove that they were not bigots. Landon had to call upon prominent Jewish Republicans to speak on his behalf, noting especially his support for religious liberty. The Republican presidential candidate also had to mention specifically a number of times during the campaign that he was against racial and religious bigotry.[65]

In 1940 this tactic was repeated, with some variations, by tagging Wendell Willkie, the Republican standard-bearer, as a fascist sympathizer and therefore also an anti-Semite. The Democrats emphasized that *Social Justice* had endorsed Willkie and that he was the favored candidate of America's anti-Semitic and fascist element, including the Bund. Although Willkie actually endorsed most of Roosevelt's foreign policy, the Democrats also tried to classify the Republican candidate as an appeaser. In August of 1940 Democratic vice-presidential candidate Henry Wallace stated that Roosevelt's defeat would produce great joy in Berlin.[66] The appeaser theme was repeated by others in the Roosevelt camp, such as Governor Lehman, who had great influence among Jewish voters. Furthermore, Willkie's German ancestry was made a campaign issue in the relentless effort to label him as Hitler's choice; it was even suggested that Willkie might be a German agent.[67]

The Republican candidate was put on the defensive. He had attempted to avoid making foreign policy the main issue of the campaign by supporting an interventionist policy. However, Roosevelt's efforts to use this issue had left Willkie in the difficult position of trying to convince voters that he was neither an appeaser nor pro-fascist. The Republican nominee forthrightly denounced anti-Semitism, repudiated specifically the backing of Coughlin and his followers, and rejected the votes of all who espoused bigotry or favored "any foreign economic or political philosophy in this country." He also attacked the whispering campaign being waged against him. In October 1940 the Republicans organized the Committee of 100,000 Americans of the Jewish faith to counter the anti-Semitic smear. Willkie also lashed out at Roosevelt by suggesting that the president had already made secret deals that might pull the United States into war. This forced the president in turn to promise the American people that our soldiers were not going to fight in any foreign wars.[68]

From a political standpoint, Roosevelt's tactics were good ones for solidifying the Jewish vote. However, the significance of these tactics transcends any one election. The foreign policy issue, including its anti-Semitic component, was already a divisive one; it became more so during the campaign. The Democrats had suggested that isolationists and Willkie backers were in the pro-Hitler camp, and the Republicans had hinted that Roosevelt and his supporters were warmongers. Although the differences between the candidates never became as clear-cut as some had wanted to make them, since Willkie was neither an isolationist nor against the New Deal reforms, the issue still did have a significant impact on the election. It also increased the suspicions between the ethnic groups in New York who were already divided over the war-peace issues. The campaign particularly smeared German-Americans, who, like Willkie, could be assumed to be favorable to fascism because of their ancestry—a charge which the German community feared would be accepted by the general public. The *Staats-Zeitung* condemned this slanderous tactic and partly for this reason urged its readers to vote for Willkie. Victor Ridder even allowed himself to be chosen as a Republican presidential elector at this time. The Jews were also affected, since they were presented once again with the possibility that a major political figure was an anti-Semite. As Dorothy Thompson, a well-known journalist, stated just before election day, "A vote for Wendell Willkie is a vote for fascism."[69]

The 1940 election results (see table 14), when compared with Roosevelt's previous campaigns, suggest the effect of the foreign policy issue on the various ethnic groups.[70] The largest percentage decrease in Roosevelt's votes between 1936 and 1940 (36.5 percent) came from the Italians, who had been upset by the president's speech following Italy's invasion of France in June 1940.[71] It was acknowledged at that time that Roosevelt had made a grievous political error and would probably lose the Italian-American vote. A whispering campaign in the Italian areas of New York accused the president of being anti-Italian. The Republicans, of course, used this mistake to win Italian votes for Willkie.[72] To a group sensitive about their status in America, this was a potent issue. The significance of Roosevelt's remarks, as well as the foreign policy issue in general, to the Italians is noted by the fact that *Il Progresso,* usually Democratic and strong for Roosevelt in the previous elections, endorsed neither candidate in 1940. Given the political background of the paper, this represented implied support for Willkie. Generoso Pope urged his readers to let "the supreme interests of the United States be your only guide in choosing among the candidates." Pope, however, in an effort to retain his power within the Democratic party, led the

Table 14. Roosevelt Percentage Vote in New York City, by Ethnicity, 1932, 1936, 1940

	City	Irish	German	Jewish	Italian
1932	66.4	75.7	62.7	72.2	80.5
1936[a]	73.5	72.8	65.7	87.5	78.7
1940	60.9	56.0	41.8	88.5	42.2

NOTE: Because of extensive Assembly District and election district boundary changes in 1944, which would have eliminated from my analysis many of the election districts which had retained the same boundaries since 1932, the 1944 Roosevelt vote could not be done.

[a]The 1936 and 1940 percentages include the votes of the Democratic and American Labor parties.

Democratic Councils of Americans of Italian Origin, organized by the party to rally Italian-Americans behind the Roosevelt ticket.[73] Other Italian-Americans, such as the Sons of Italy, Grand Lodge, made no pretenses and supported Willkie.[74] The president, in an effort to regain the Italian vote, tried to make amends, as did the local Democratic party (see the discussion in chapter 3, on Costello, the Democratic party, and Italians in 1940). Roosevelt, for example, after being urged to do so by various Democrats, made a major address on Columbus Day, 1940, which noted the contributions of the Italians to America. He also sent a special greeting to Pope in New York which was read at a large meeting of Italian-American community leaders.[75] However, this group was not easily won over. Many were in basic opposition to the Roosevelt foreign policy and would probably have voted Republican even without Roosevelt's offensive remarks. To the Italians the war-peace issue was much more than an idle debate. Their ancestral home and their place in America would be affected by the outcome. That more Italians did not vote Republican can be related to the fact that Willkie had endorsed the interventionist foreign policy and thereby made the choice between him and Roosevelt not a simply isolationist-interventionist one.

The Germans reacted in a similar fashion by giving the president his lowest vote and dropping 23.9 percentage points between 1936 and 1940. The slurs against Willkie's ancestry hurt Roosevelt in this community. The foreign policy issue was also important, since this group's ancestral home and status in America would be affected. The Steuben Society, which endorsed Willkie, voiced objections to Roosevelt's foreign policy and the idea of a third term. Willkie, according to the *Steuben News,* would keep the United States out of war.[76] However, there was suspicion of Willkie's intentions in this community as well, which probably decreased his support.

The Irish vote, giving Roosevelt a majority, was the result of a number of

Table 15. Roosevelt Percentage Vote in New York City, by Ethnicity and Class, 1940

	Class Levels[a]			
	Upper	Middle	Lower	Ethnic mean Roosevelt vote
Irish	—	52.5	62.0	56.0
German	—	38.6	43.7	41.8
Jews	71.2	88.8	90	88.5
Italians	—	39.3	44.3	42.2

NOTE: Includes votes of the Democratic and American Labor parties.
[a]N = 149; Irish had nine middle-class and seven lower-class voting units; Germans had eleven middle-class and eighteen lower-class voting units; Jews had two upper-class, forty-three middle-class, and thirty-one lower-class voting units; and Italians had seven middle-class and twenty-one lower-class voting units.

factors. This was a group, unlike the Italians and Germans, whose vital interests, whose place in America did not depend on the outcome of the interventionist-isolationist debate. Therefore, although foreign policy concerns did have an effect on their vote, they were less concerned about this issue than the others. This group was also traditionally Democratic. Finally, confusion existed over what each candidate represented. There was the feeling, which even the Irish Coughlinites expressed, that the two candidates were not very different. Both Roosevelt and Willkie tried to picture themselves to the Irish as the peace candidate, as noted in advertisements in the Irish press. Neither one was viewed as such, but Willkie was endorsed in some cases as the lesser of two evils. There were Coughlinites who were active in the Willkie campaign.[77] *Social Justice* supported Willkie and excused his rejection of Coughlinite support as the result of Jewish pressure. Republicans in the Bronx became so worried about Coughlinites in their campaign organization that they secured a member of the New York Co-ordinating Committee for Democratic Action, an anti-fascist group, to investigate the background of every campaign worker. A number of Coughlinites and Christian Frontists were discovered.[78] Although the Irish vote for Roosevelt did show a significant decrease (16.8 percent) between 1936 and 1940, as a result of the above factors this decrease was much less than among the other groups. Roosevelt was able to retain most of his support here.

The percentage vote for Roosevelt in Jewish election districts increased over the years and was an indication of the effectiveness of his ethnic appeals as well as the result of similar interests. Both supported aid to the allies and the strongest possible response to the fascist dictators. Although Roosevelt earlier had disappointed the Jewish community on a number of occasions when he failed to castigate Germany or to extend more help to the refugees, he remained their greatest hope to defeat Nazism.

Regardless of the voting results in these elections, the constant appeals to one group at the expense of another, and the use of issues designed to generate fear and frustration in order to win votes, worked to the detriment of harmonious intergroup relations in New York. The campaign rhetoric did much to increase ethnic insecurity and an awareness of the issues which divided the various groups.

Chapter Eight

In the Neighborhoods

The ethnic tensions and frictions felt on a citywide basis during the decade of the 1930s and afterward were clearly evident in the communities where these groups resided. Here the issues became personal, and meant that one must react not to an amorphous enemy but to one's neighbor. The areas where the Jews and Irish lived in close but unharmonious relationship were the most explosive and served during these turbulent years as the main battlefields where the ethnic conflicts became street brawls between warring tribes. These communities, which exhibited active Christian Front and Mobilizer organizations, were raked by constant anti-Semitic vandalism. The eventual elimination of such figures as Coughlin, McWilliams, and the Bundists after 1941 did not eliminate the tensions and hostilities which these individuals and organizations had helped to encourage.[1]

The two centers of Irish-Jewish confrontation were Washington Heights in Manhattan and the South Bronx area of the Bronx. Both sections were representative of the violence which caused one Jewish journal to declare, "the streets of New York have become unsafe for Jews and—who knows?—pogroms might be in the making."[2]

WASHINGTON HEIGHTS: BACKGROUND

Washington Heights was for many years an ethnically diverse but divided community (see map 1).[3] The area's first inhabitants, before the turn of the century, were upper-class Protestants of mixed national backgrounds who settled in a number of large estates.[4] However, the first major ethnic colony was that of the Irish, who came to the Heights in the 1900–1910 period, and moved mainly to the section east of Broadway. These people were middle-class, having migrated

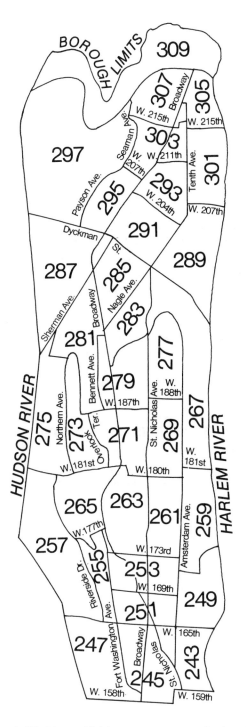

Map 1. Washington Heights, census tracts and selected streets

up Amsterdam Avenue from an earlier enclave around the City College area (Amsterdam and 140th). They were later followed by other classes of their group. Also moving into the Heights were German and English Protestants. Although no single group was ever a majority of the neighborhood, the Protestants had the smallest population.

The Jewish penetration of this area began slowly between 1910 and 1915 with middle- to upper-class Jews of German background. Jewish settlement was first made on the western side of Broadway, but then soon moved over to the Irish, German, English area on the east. Beginning about 1917 and extending into the 1920s, a much larger Jewish migration took place, made up primarily of poorer Eastern European Jews moving from their colony in lower Harlem. In anticipation of the completion of the IND subway through Washington Heights, the western section particularly experienced an apartment house building boom. The Jewish migration went primarily to this section, but again spilled over into the Eastern area.[5] An indication of the extent of the Jewish migration is found in the following figures. In 1923, 4.5 percent of the Jewish population of Manhattan lived in the Heights; by 1930, 22 percent were in the area. In other terms, the Jewish population of the Heights went from 31,500 in 1923 (27.3 percent of the Heights population) to 65,300 in 1930 (38.6 percent) to 73,100 in 1940 (35.8 percent). By 1920 all census tracts east and west of Broadway had a substantial and increasing Russian (Jewish) population.[6]

ETHNIC RESIDENTIAL SHIFTING

During this early period there was some antagonism toward the Jews because of residential competition. Relations between the Irish and Jews were particularly strained.[7] The Irish, however, did not abandon the neighborhood in response to the Jewish in-migration. In fact, census figures indicate that the Irish increased from approximately 6.5 percent (6,589) of the community in 1920 to an estimated 11.7 percent (23,900) in 1940.[8] Percentages for the total Washington Heights area would give the erroneous impression that the Irish and Jews did not move in response to each other. The shift was subtle, extending over a long period of time. Tract statistics only partially indicate what was happening. The percentage and number of Irish increased in the tracts east of and surrounding Broadway. For example, in 1920 the only tracts with an Irish population of more than 10 percent were tract 243 (14.8 percent), tracts 249 and 259 (15.8 percent), tract 251 (15.5 percent), and tracts 297 and 299 (30 percent). By 1940 a number of eastern and northern tracts indicated an estimated Irish presence of over 15 percent, including tracts 243 (21.4 percent), 245 (16.6 percent), 251 (17 percent), 253 (17.6 percent), 261 (21.9 percent), 291 (16.1 percent), 293 (16.4 percent), and 297 (22 percent). Irish presence in the Jewish tracts west of Broadway remained minimal; tract 247 was only 3.4 percent Irish (168) in 1920 and

2.2 percent Irish (169) in 1940.[9] The Irish percentage increases were not statistically the result of a total population decrease in these tracts.

Although the number of Jews decreased in tracts 243, 249, and 261, they increased in tracts 245, 251, 253, and 269, indicating that this group continued to be a significant part of the population in the tracts where the Irish lived. The area west of Broadway remained heavily Jewish, and there was some Jewish migration north. Tract 247 was 11.1 percent Russian in 1920 (620), and 20.5 percent Russian in 1940 (1,570). Tracts 255 and 257, which were only 6 percent Russian in 1920 (123), increased to 14.2 percent by 1940 (1,010). On a census tract basis, there continued to be much mixing. The Index of Dissimilarity, based on tract statistics, showed a low segregation index between the Irish and Jews in 1920 and 1940, although it was higher by the latter date.[10] However, voter registration lists reveal that segregation and shifting between the groups existed within the tracts.[11]

Essentially the Irish and Jews began to regroup along certain streets or in certain houses. For example, in 1910 the Irish were scattered along St. Nicholas Avenue, Broadway, and Amsterdam Avenue and between 160th and 170th streets. By 1920 many of the houses had begun to have their first Jewish residents. For example, at 2153 Amsterdam Avenue (tract 249) there were twelve registered voters in 1910, seven of which were identified as Irish and none as Jewish. By 1920, out of thirty-five registered voters, ten were Irish and twelve Jewish. The neighborhood experienced its greatest degree of ethnic mixing by houses and streets in 1920. However, during the decade of the 1920s, when most of the Eastern European Jews came into the area, the Irish began to shift and regroup along their own streets. The houses from 1984 to 2306 Amsterdam Avenue (159th to 174th streets) had a 23.2 percent Irish population in 1910. By 1930 the Irish made up 32.7 percent of the population of these houses, and by 1940 they were 34.2 percent. The Jewish population was minimal along these streets. Tract 243, which included Amsterdam Avenue up to 165th Street, was 14.8 percent Irish (797) in 1920 and 21.4 percent Irish (1,290) in 1940. The Russian (Jewish) population of the tract decreased from 5.5 percent (325) in 1920 to 1.3 percent (81) in 1940. Voter registration in this section of the Heights indicated a significant degree of ethnic shifting. At 434 West 164th Street (tract 243) there were forty-five registered voters in 1920—twenty-six Irish and nine Jews. By 1930 the same building had eighteen Irish out of twenty-six registered voters, and no Jews. Substantial numerical or percentage increases in either Irish or Jewish residents in a building often resulted in the other group leaving. There was some Irish-Jewish mixing in new and large apartment houses, although one group usually dominated. At 2201 Amsterdam Avenue (tract 253), an apartment house built between 1920 and 1930, there were fifty-one registered voters in 1930, thirty-two of whom could be identified as Jewish and only five as Irish, although Amsterdam Avenue was essentially an Irish street. Also common was the situation in which one house was predominately Irish and the one next door predominately Jewish. At 552, 554, and 556 West 162nd Street (tract 245), there were four Irish residents out of four registered voters in 1910. By 1930 there were six Irish out of seven registered voters in these buildings. Next door, 560 and 562 West 162nd Street, which was totally Irish in 1910, had five Jews out of six registered voters by 1930.

In the western section of the Heights, the Jews had little competition for housing. Voter registration lists for the area bounded by Broadway, Fort Washington Avenue, Riverside Drive, and 161st Street (mainly in tract 247) indicate that the Jews comprised 56 percent of the inhabitants of this area in 1920 and 68 percent by 1930. Few Irish lived in this section.

In the recently developed sections of northern Washington Heights or Inwood, as in the eastern zone, various streets and houses became either predominantly Irish or Jewish as both groups migrated to the area during the 1920–40 period. At 204 and 207 Dyckman Street (tract 291), there were only twenty-six Irish and fourteen Jews who were identifiable out of ninety-five registered voters in 1920. By 1940 the Irish made up forty-four of the 100 registered voters; few Jews were now indicated by the voter registration lists as living at this address. However, at 570 West 204th Street (tract 291) there were fifty-eight Jews and only twelve Irish identifiable out of 120 registered voters in 1940, although at the neighboring building, 590 West 204th Street, there were thirty-four Irish and twelve Jews out of seventy-five registered voters. The voter registration data suggests that in Washington Heights, streets and houses became either predominantly Irish or Jewish as both groups shifted.

Irish and Jewish migration patterns in this neighborhood can be explained by three factors. First, Washington Heights was a new and growing residential area, a desirable place to live in terms of transportation, park facilities, and new housing. The Irish as a group showed no desire to abandon this area; they instead shifted and regrouped along certain streets, and thus continued to enjoy the amenities of the community. Secondly, an economic factor was involved. Although many poor Jews lived in the neighborhood, this ethnic group on the whole was in a superior economic position, particularly as noted by their presence in the western section, where rents were higher and where the newest housing was located.[12] A 1946 neighborhood survey revealed that approximately 14 percent of the Jews were classified as being in the high-income group, compared with only 3 percent of the non-Jewish whites. One economic analysis of the neighborhood indicated in 1930 that the western Jewish area was upper-middle- to upper-class. The eastern section, containing both Jews and Irish, was classified as middle-middle-class, with a small portion along Amsterdam Avenue, where many Irish lived, as lower-middle. By 1940 a similar analysis described the western part as mainly middle-middle-class and the eastern area as lower-middle.[13] In regard to housing, one-fourth of all Washington Heights Catholics were living in dilapidated housing, "where no Jews lived." Even poorer Jews were willing to limit other expenses in order to secure a decent residence. Only two percent of the Jews were in low-rent apartments, compared with 25 percent of the Catholics.[14] Although the majority of the Catholics did live in decent housing and presumably paid rents similar to those paid by the Jews (at least in the eastern and northern sections), the greater ability and desire of Jews to live in better housing surely contributed to the two groups' living in different houses and on different streets. It also contributed to the third factor, that of hostility between the two. Ethnic friction, although remaining nonviolent during the early migration years, did seem to play a role in splitting the two communities, and setting the stage for conflict later on.

Irish and Jewish migration continued into the neighborhood. The last great influx before World War II were German and Austrian Jewish refugees, who had a significant impact on ethnic relations in the Heights. By the late 1930s the community had become a perfect setting for an intense conflict as neighborhood issues combined with those dividing Irish and Jews on a citywide basis.

IRISH-JEWISH CONFLICT
IN WASHINGTON HEIGHTS

The Christian Front began its activities in the Heights with street meetings during 1939 mainly at 161st Street and Amsterdam Avenue, 162nd Street and St. Nicholas Avenue, and at Sherman Avenue and Dyckman Street, all of which were areas of Irish concentration where many Jews lived also.[15] Agitators harangued large crowds in these and other sections of the neighborhood stressing the themes of anti-Semitism and anti-Communism. Joe McWilliams, leader of the Christian Mobilizers, was very active in this community too. The Front and Mobilizers viewed all problems as being of Jewish origin. One incident involved the transformation of an A & P supermarket into a self-service facility, thereby putting many people out of work. Front speakers blamed the loss of jobs on the Jews and held a mass street rally to protest the change. After this, a number of anti-Semitic incidents occurred. The Front also stressed that refugees, many of whom were moving into the Heights, would displace American workers.[16]

The discrediting of this organization in 1940 because of the FBI arrest of Front members did not decrease Irish-Jewish conflict in this neighborhood. As World War II began and as the United States drew closer to and eventually entered the struggle, anti-Semitic activity increased. Vandalism directed against synagogues became widespread, including stonings, painting of swastikas on doors, breaking of windows, and interruption of services by groups of boys who would yell "kill the Jews." More important to the Jewish community were the physical attacks on Jewish children by these Irish adolescent gangs. The usual scene would be a group of teenagers coming up to one or two Jewish boys and asking whether they were Jewish. An affirmative answer brought a beating. It was noted at this time that youthful anti-Semitism came from children who had heard anti-Semitism expressed in their homes. In this sense, these outbreaks were merely manifestations of anti-Jewish attitudes in the adult Irish community.[17] The vandalism and attacks were the work of two gangs—the Amsterdams and the Shamrocks. The Amsterdams lived on or near Amsterdam Avenue, the main Irish section in the Heights.[18] The beatings and vandalism usually took place in the 157th Street to 182nd Street area from Amsterdam Avenue to Riverside Drive, and in the Inwood section of the Heights around Sherman Avenue and Dyckman Street. Particular trouble spots, besides the synagogue locations, were on the borderline of the wealthier Jewish section on the west and the Irish and Jewish area to the east and north of it and/or where many Front and Mobilizer street meetings had been held.[19] The economic factor was a significant part of this conflict. Also important was the war issue. There was the feeling in the general Irish community that the Jews were responsible for the war. The vandals expressed this attitude as well as the idea that the Jews were evading their responsibilities in the war effort.[20]

CONFLICT RESOLUTION:
WASHINGTON HEIGHTS

Efforts to resolve the conflict at first proved futile. In the earlier Front-Mobilizer period, a Washington Heights and Inwood Tolerance Committee, which included Jews, Protestants, and Catholics, was set up under Congressman Joseph Gavagan. The committee, like similar ones in other troubled neighborhoods, tried to combat the Front by stressing cooperation between the Irish and Jews. They held street meetings and distributed literature in an effort to blunt the Front's appeal.[21] Most of the neighborhood tolerance committees had disbanded by the time of American entry into the war, and judging by what followed in the community their effort had not been successful. Among the Jews, the Jewish War Veterans were active in combatting the anti-Semites. Retaliation by some Jewish groups were also noted.[22]

During the entire anti-Semitic period, Jewish and other neighborhood residents often complained that the police were doing little to bring peace to the community. Many people were convinced that a strong police effort to arrest the anti-Semitic agitators and vandals would have eliminated the violent aspects of this conflict. Numerous complaints reported that the police did not respond to calls for help or else belittled the significance of the attack or showed favoritism to the agitators.[23] Jewish attitudes toward the police are best described in the following quotation from a Jewish newspaper which served Washington Heights and the Bronx. ''We are tired of approaching a police captain, hat in hand, saying 'Please Captain McCarthy (or O'Brien). . . . My boy was hit because he is a Jew. Will you send a cop?' And we are damned sick and tired of watching the sickly Hitler-like grin and hearing the usual answer: 'Ah, the boys are just playing.' ''[24] Pressure was brought on the local police to eliminate the anti-

Semitism after the Department of Investigation confirmed the general charge of police negligence in dealing with these situations. An immediate reaction was the establishment of a Precinct Coordinating Committee, composed of leaders in the community, which was to work with the local police in rooting out the anti-Semitic violence. Policemen in this and other neighborhoods were sent to guard synagogues and to investigate carefully any anti-Jewish occurrences. Also, La Guardia ordered the formation of a special detective squad to deal with these and similar incidents in other neighborhoods and offered a $500 reward for information leading to conviction of the anti-Semitic vandals.[25]

Three other responses were tried to eliminate the intergroup conflict. The Jewish community set up defensive units and began escorting Jewish children to and from school.[26] Secondly, in 1944 a large number of youths belonging to the Shamrocks were arrested for vandalizing synagogues and attacking Jewish boys. Rather than sending the offenders to jail, Judge Anna Kross, who heard the case, helped to establish an organization called Youth Aid, which was designed to work with this gang and other juveniles in an attempt to rehabilitate them.[27]

The main effort, however, and one which had long been needed, was directed at getting the Catholic clergy in the area to condemn the Front and the later anti-Semitic gangs. A persistent rumor was heard in the neighborhood that the Church approved of the anti-Jewish events. Efforts to get the cooperation of local Catholic church officials in ridding the neighborhood of the anti-Semitic agitators failed both during the Front era and when the attacks became numerous in 1943. As with the Church hierarchy in the City, there was a reluctance among local clergy to speak out against or even to acknowledge anti-Semitism among Catholics. By January 1944, however, conditions in the Heights had so deteriorated that finally the Catholic, Protestant, and Jewish religious leaders were able to join together in a Washington Heights Interfaith Committee in order to stop further intergroup violence. It was agreed that a joint statement deploring prejudice would be read in all churches and synagogues in the Heights. Furthermore, in February 1944, in the Loew's theater at 175th Street and Broadway, an interfaith rally was held at which a number of locally prominent clergy and laymen spoke. They addressed about 3,000 Protestant, Catholic, and Jewish children. It was at this meeting that the local Catholic Church formally and forcefully stated that the Church did not endorse attacks on synagogues or on Jews.[28] The combined police, Jewish, and interfaith response, plus the changes brought about in economic and world affairs by 1945, eventually destroyed the anti-Semitic violence in this neighborhood, although relations between the two involved ethnic communities remained strained for some time.[29]

SOUTH BRONX: BACKGROUND

The South Bronx exhibited a similar intergroup relations problem (see map 2).[30] The Irish and Germans migrated to this area in the late nineteenth century and

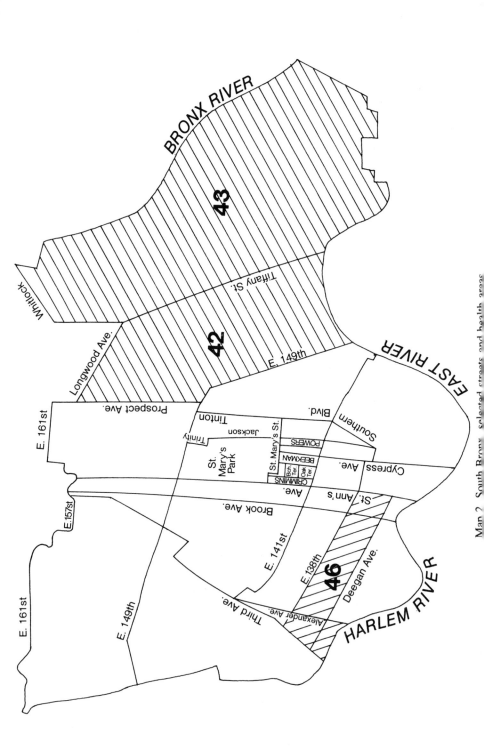

Map 2. South Bronx, selected streets and health areas

continued to do so into the twentieth century. The Jews and Italians first settled here in the 1900–1910 period.[31] By 1910 all the groups were firmly established in the South Bronx with much ethnic residential mixing in all sections of the community.[32] By the 1920s the Jews as a group had begun to migrate north into other Bronx areas. In 1923 the Jews were approximately 48 percent (98,400) of the total population of the South Bronx. By 1930 their number had decreased to 33 percent (68,400) and by 1940 to 18 percent (37,500).[33] Within this period of decline, the neighborhood developed definite ethnic dividing lines. The bulk of the Irish population was settled west of St. Ann's Avenue and predominated particularly in the area from Third Avenue to St. Ann's in the 130th and 140th Streets. Germans and Italians were also in this section, along with some scattered Jewish families. The main area of Italian concentration was in the 140th and 150th blocks west of Third Avenue, and the main German section was also in the 150th streets west of Third Avenue. The central Jewish section was in the Hunts Point area east of Prospect Avenue and 149th Street. Between 149th Street and St. Ann's was a mixed ethnic community with the Jews predominating in the area south of St. Mary's Park to 141st Street. There were also Irish residents in the Park section as well as Irish, Italian, German, Jewish, and some Spanish to the south of 141st Street, with the Irish predominating. In 1937, because of the construction of the approaches to the Triborough Bridge, a number of houses in the area below 135th Street in this section were demolished. This event may have contributed to ethnic conflict by increasing residential competition, for most of the displaced residents stayed in the neighborhood.[34] Therefore as in the Washington Heights experience, a large Irish and Jewish community was living near each other.

An economic factor also played a role in the conflict which was to emerge in this neighborhood. The heavily Jewish Hunts Point section in 1930 was mainly middle-middle-class with some lower-middle-class sections. By 1940 the area was almost totally lower-middle-class, indicating the effects of the Depression. However, it was a neighborhood of individual homes and well-kept apartment houses with no tenements. The Jewish area around St. Mary's Park was middle-middle- to lower-middle-class in 1930 and lower-middle- to lower-class in 1940. The sections that were predominantly Irish, German, and Italian were lower-middle- to lower-class in 1930 and in 1940 they were mainly lower-class.[35] Occupationally a difference also existed between the communities. A breakdown of occupations in health areas 42 and 43, predominantly Jewish, and health area 46, predominantly Irish, illustrates this point (see table 16). Although many Jews and Irish were in vulnerable Depression occupations, the Jews, especially in health area 43, indicate a slightly better economic position in that they were more heavily concentrated in white-collar positions and less in unskilled work. This fact is reinforced when it is noted that in health areas 42 and 43, 10.2 percent and 12.8 percent respectively of the Jews in the labor force were employers and own-account workers, as compared with 5.6 percent of the Irish

Table 16. Occupations of Employed Workers, by Health Area, 1940

	Percentage of employed workers		
	Health area 42	Health area 43	Health area 46
Professional workers	4.0	5.2	2.2
Semiprofessional workers	.8	1.6	.8
Proprietors, managers, and officials	8.3	11.2	7.1
Clerical, sales, and kindred workers	25.0	27.7	20.5
Craftsmen, foremen, and kindred workers	14.3	16.1	12.1
Operatives and kindred workers	30.0	25.9	25.7
Domestic service workers	1.0	1.4	1.0
Service workers (except domestic)	13.0	7.8	21.0
Laborers	2.7	2.0	8.4
Occupations not reported	1.0	.9	1.2

SOURCE: Department of Commerce, Bureau of the Census, *Population and Housing, Statistics for Health Areas, New York City, 1940* (Washington, D. C.: Government Printing Office, 1942), pp. 34–35.

in health area 46. While 3.4 and 1.7 percent of the Jews in areas 42 and 43 were on public emergency work, 7.5 percent of the Irish were so employed. Of the experienced workers seeking work, the Jews reported 16.1 and 12.7 percent respectively, the Irish 17.6 percent.[36] Therefore, although both communities were suffering, the Irish could see the Jews, a newer group, in an equal or superior economic state, which did cause resentment in this neighborhood. Deflected hostility related to general Depression frustrations also played a role.

IRISH-JEWISH CONFLICT IN THE SOUTH BRONX

With the divisive citywide issues of the 1930s and 1940s working in conjunction with the neighborhood factors, an intense, prolonged, and violent conflict soon appeared between the Irish and Jews.[37] The Christian Front and Christian Mobilizers emerged in this neighborhood in 1939 with street meetings calling for the destruction of the Jews. The German-American Bund was also active in this community and at times met with the Front or Mobilizers.[38] At one such Bund-Mobilizer meeting in the Bronx in March 1940, Kuhn's picture was displayed with American and Nazi flags on each side and underneath was a green banner with the word "Eire" on it.[39]

Anti-Semitic attacks and vandalism appeared in conjunction with these meetings and, with the emergence of juvenile agitators in the 1940s, continued well after these organizations had been disbanded.[40] During the Front period, for example, gangs often went through the streets "cursing and abusing Jewish-looking people." The windows of Jewish merchants' stores were broken, and they were picketed. Anti-Semitic posters calling for the elimination of the Jews were put up throughout the neighborhood. The Jews fought back, and a number of clashes occurred between the two in the community.[41]

Many of the Front and Mobilizer street meetings and the vandalism took place around 141st Street between Cypress and Crimmins Avenues, where many Jews lived and which was surrounded by a mixed but predominantly Irish area. The anti-Semitic vandals arrested in 1944 all came from within a few blocks of this Jewish section, in an area described as economically depressed. Most of the 1940s anti-Semitic agitators also were members of families which either were still or recently had been on home relief. The economic factor was a major one in the conflict and was expressed by the young offenders. One arrested boy noted that he had heard a great deal of resentment against the Jews in the neighborhood because "they seem to be taking everything away from them. . . . Most of the stores are owned by the Jews. Practically everything is Jewish." Others expressed the same idea: that the Jews controlled everything and had all the money.[42]

Other important factors in the conflict were the presence of the Communist party and the war issue. Between 1938 and 1941, the party held fifty meetings in this area. These meetings served to antagonize many as well as to give the impression that the fears of the growth and power of the Communists in New York were well-founded. In 1941 America First and other isolationist organizations met in the neighborhood, increasing community tensions.[43] This issue continued into the war years, since the Jews were blamed for the world struggle.

CONFLICT RESOLUTION: SOUTH BRONX

In response to the ethnic hostilities, a South Bronx Committee for Tolerance was formed in July 1939 under the leadership of Henry G. McDonough, a lawyer living in the neighborhood.[44] Counter demonstrations, stressing tolerance were aimed at the Irish Catholic population. Prominent Irish community leaders such as Bronx Borough President James J. Lyons, Assistant District Attorney Andrew McCarthy, Democratic district leader James Geraghty, and Barnaby O'Leary of the Transport Workers Union delivered speeches for the Tolerance Committee at schools and street corners. McDonough even went to a Mobilizer meeting and defended the Jews. The committee also published a local newspaper called *Good Neighbor* which encouraged a neighborly attitude in the community.[45] The local Democratic organization contributed by sending tolerance speakers out to street corners, even though, as one observer noted, "they were told that it might mean political suicide in this neighborhood which is predominantly Irish."[46]

Although the Catholic church hierarchy remained silent on the South Bronx events, one neighborhood priest, Father F.C. Campbell of St. Jerome's parish on Alexander Avenue excoriated the anti-Semitism in 1939 and became involved in an interfaith movement started by the Bronx division of the American Jewish Congress. Also the St. Patrick's Council of the Knights of Columbus in the Bronx voted in 1939 to expel any member belonging to the Front.[47]

As in Washington Heights, the police in the South Bronx were criticized for being negligent in responding to and investigating the anti-Semitic events. However, given community feeling, they had a difficult time dealing with the disturbances. For example, the arrest of some participants at a Mobilizer rally in 1939 led to a 2,000-strong protest march to the police station.[48] Obviously, breaking up the anti-Semitic meetings was not popular with many in the neighborhood.

The end of the overt conflict came by 1945 and was again a product of the interfaith work, the increased police activity, and the changed economic, political, and social conditions of the time.

IRISH-JEWISH CONFLICT
IN OTHER NEIGHBORHOODS

Hostilities also were noted in a number of other Irish-Jewish neighborhoods especially on Manhattan's upper west side, the Fordham and Highbridge areas in the Bronx and Flatbush in Brooklyn.[49] The Front was active in all these communities and anti-Semitic vandalism was reported during the war years.[50] Flatbush, of course, bears the dubious distinction of being one of the first neighborhoods where the Front began its activities. John Cassidy lived in this section. The same factors as in Washington Heights and the South Bronx were present. One boy who attended some local Front meetings in the Fordham area noted that he had heard people observe that "the Jews have all the good jobs." Communists had been very active in Flatbush, and there were numerous complaints about their meetings. The war issue also was significant. America First rallies were held in these sections, and the Brooklyn Jewish Community Council and others in 1942 noted persistent rumors that the "Jews had an inordinate number of conscientious objectors" and were not doing their part in the war.[51]

Combatting the Front and later vandalism involved a number of tactics. In Flatbush the Jewish War Veterans on one occasion drove the anti-Semitic orators, who were soon to become the Brooklyn unit of the Front, out of the area in the autumn of 1938. Attempts were made to get the Catholic church to intercede, although with no success at first. Later efforts in various communities involved the establishment of interfaith organizations and programs in the schools.[52] Eventually, as in the other neighborhoods, the hostilities ceased.

OTHER NEIGHBORHOODS
AND INTERGROUP RELATIONS

Although Irish-Jewish communities were marked by an intense, prolonged conflict during this period, this was not true of other ethnic neighborhoods. Irish and German relations remained good. Nothing pitted them against each other. In Irish-Italian neighborhoods, such as Greenwich Village, there was definite evidence of conflict in the political sphere. However, relations between these two groups never deteriorated to what it was between Jews and Irish or, for a time, Jews and Italians. The Jews and Italians, as noted, also experienced conflict related mainly to Mussolini's decrees, but this was quickly resolved.

German-Jewish neighborhoods witnessed hostilities during the pre-1938 era because of the influence of the Bund, but remained calm afterwards as overt conflict was submerged. In Yorkville, for example, the anti-Nazi boycott and subsequent retaliation by the Bund and other German-Americans caused problems between the two groups and strained relations for a long time. Anti-Semitic orators and pamphlets were frequent in the neighborhood, although no vandalism was reported, not even against the synagogue which was right near Bund headquarters.[53] By 1938 most German-Americans had repudiated the Bund and anti-Semitism. An indication of this rejection was noticeable in the German-American response to Joe McWilliams' Bund-supported attempt to stir up trouble and launch a political career in Yorkville by running for Congress in 1940 on an anti-Semitic and isolationist platform.[54] He lost in the Republican primary by a vote of 2,573 to 674, receiving 20.7 percent of the vote. In the predominantly German election districts, in the center of Bund strength and activity in the City, he lost by a vote of 568 to 242 (29.9 percent), even though the community was agitated by the war issue.[55] McWilliams' campaign was marked by constant verbal attacks on the Jews; however, there was no violent repercussions from this and little support. Other Nazis or their sympathizers who had run in Yorkville before had also lost.[56] Support for Coughlin was also evident in this neighborhood, but during his anti-Semitic period this came particularly from the Irish community in Yorkville. The Front chapter in the area was also mainly Irish.[57]

As Washington Heights, South Bronx, and other areas have shown, neighborhood conflict and tensions were very much reflections of intergroup relations in the City and serve as good case studies of the larger problem.

Chapter Nine

On Ethnic Conflict

Although the conflicts discussed in this study involved different sets of groups and different situations, certain features common to all represent the basic components of ethnic conflict. In all cases a struggle over interests and values, based on realistic and unrealistic factors, was present.[1] The key element in initiating these conflicts was a sense of threat. Groups which felt threatened in a number of areas, and had no reasons for moderating their hostilities, found themselves in the most intense conflicts.

The Irish-Jewish conflict offered the best example of the interaction of variables which can produce such an intense and hostile struggle. There were a number of points of friction between these groups based on both long-term competitive issues and explosive issues which, acting together, produced a severe conflict. The Irish saw the Jews as serious threatening competitors in both the economic and political spheres. Jews competed for jobs which the Irish held and which they valued highly, especially during an economic depression. At the same time, Irish political power was threatened by the desire of the Jews to share that power. Added to these ethnic succession issues were the explosive issues. "Communism" (including the Spanish Civil War) and, to a lesser extent, American entry into World War II clearly and sharply pitted the Irish and Jews against each other, making each aware of a struggle. Within the interaction of these issues both realistic and unrealistic components relating to interests and values were evident. This conflict was a product of a real threat to certain Irish economic and political positions and to certain cultural values. However, it also included unrealistic elements, such as erroneous judgements about the extent of Jewish involvement in Communism, deflected hostility related to general Depression frustrations, and historical tradition in the form of religious anti-

Semitism, although this last element played only a minor role. Simply stated, the Irish felt threatened by the Jews for both realistic and unrealistic reasons. The emergence of the Christian Front illustrated the intensity of this conflict. This organization indicated the attempt by some of the Irish to deal violently with the threat from the Jews. Quite naturally, the Jews retaliated against the Front, as they, too, felt threatened.

However, the violence of the Irish-Jewish conflict never equaled that of the native white Protestant-Irish conflict during the nineteenth century in certain cities. A few factors can explain this difference in the degree of violent activity. Although the politicians of the 1930s had much to gain by playing on ethnic fears and frustrations, they also did not want to see the ethnic tensions become so severe that votes would be lost and party unity weakened. Both La Guardia and the Democrats made use of ethnic appeals but also tried to limit ethnic violence. La Guardia, for example, did take action to prevent and control anti-Semitic violence both during the Front-Bund period and afterward. During the nineteenth century, however, the election, at times, of city and state politicians who were nativist-supported or who sympathized with the anti–foreign-born movement put into office individuals who either had much to gain from a violent and prolonged conflict or were uninterested in controlling the clashes. Therefore, very often little was done to protect the Irish or discourage the Protestants until the violence had become extreme. In the twentieth century the FBI also may have had a role in preventing more violence from emerging when they arrested the individuals connected with the January 1940 treason plot. During the 1940s wave of anti-Semitic vandalism, the police and Catholic church also helped to control the violence, although not at first. Social tensions and hostility can be prevented from leading to violence if outside forces intervene. External control can prevent the emergence of physical violence between groups.[2]

Although the violence was controlled, the conflict itself was difficult to resolve because so many serious factors produced it. Furthermore, it developed and remained active for a number of years because of the absence of moderating elements. There were no vital interests or self-preservation factors which would have moved the Irish away from the conflict. The end of this conflict was partially a product of the tolerance committees, interfaith work, and increased police surveillance in various communities. However, these forces for tolerance and accommodation would not have been effective if the issues producing the conflict had continued to agitate the involved groups. By 1945 the Depression and World War II were over. The Spanish Civil War had ended earlier, eliminating this struggle as a source of friction. O'Dwyer, an Irishman, rather than La Guardia, was now mayor. Anti-Communism, although still strong, no longer had an anti-Semitic emphasis. Perhaps the revelations of the Nazi atrocities at this time muted this and other anti-Jewish feelings. Finally, although the Irish might not have fully accepted the new Jewish position in the ethnic power structure of

New York, by 1945 they were no longer resisting it. The fight had been given up and an adjustment had been made. For example, efforts to revive the Christian Front after World War II failed.[3]

The other conflicts of this period also represented an interaction of factors but, except in the Irish-Italian struggle, involved the ethnic succession and long-term competitive issues to a much lesser extent. In the German-Jewish and Italian-Jewish conflicts, explosive issues played the major role. As with the Irish-Jewish clash, these conflicts also involved threats to interests and values based on realistic and unrealistic factors. For example, the conflicts were a product of the real threats to each group's interests and values in America posed by the rise of Nazism and Fascism in Europe. Unrealistic elements included, for example, erroneous judgements. In the German-Jewish conflict, the Jews misunderstood the motivations of the non-Nazi German-Americans who were not Nazis yet could not criticize Germany. The Jews perceived the German's reluctance to declare against Hitler's Germany as a hostile response. Similarly, the motivations of the Jews, who were reacting to their own threatened position in the world, was also misunderstood. They were attacking not the German-American community but those whom they viewed as possibly anti-Semitic Nazis. Until they were convinced of the German's anti-Nazi position, conflict was evident.

The German-Jewish and Italian-Jewish conflicts indicate the role that foreign events can play in producing domestic conflicts. These conflicts also reveal how easily conflict can be resolved if a group's vital interests direct them away from a clash. Although it is true that these vital interests were responsible for making the explosive issues significant at first, they were also able to eliminate or mute these issues eventually along with other points of friction. In both the German and Italian cases, the various elements producing conflict were moderated by what these groups perceived as the need to avoid and then to declare against anti-Semitism for the purposes of their own self-preservation. Although there was some German and Italian involvement in New York's anti-Semitism, it remained minimal. Similar motives forced a German and Italian stand against Nazism, Fascism, and the foreign policies of their ancestral homes. The Jews in turn were mollified by this changing opinion.

New York's conflicts, with various realistic factors being an important element, illustrates the type of struggle most likely to emerge in areas where the groups are in actual contact. Conflicts can also arise in places where there is little or no contact. The emergence of anti-Semitic organizations in rural or small-town areas where few or no Jews live reveals more clearly the unrealistic components of conflict. In these cases deflected hostility and historical tradition (for example, religious anti-Semitism) are major elements. Another notable unrealistic factor in no-contact conflict is ignorance, a complete ''unawareness of other groups' characteristics'' which can make one group see the other as a threat, based on misinformation having little to do with reality.[4] During the 1930s the

Nazi government was influential in this respect by constantly providing hostile propaganda about the Jews.

Anti-Semitism in the United States was at a high point during the 1930s. If all instances of group conflict involving anti-Semitism during this period were studied, one would likely find that threats to interests and values, based on realistic and unrealistic elements in varying proportions, were involved. Furthermore, I suggest that the various group conflicts in American history can be understood in this way. As such, the conflicts of the 1930s fit into the pattern of earlier group conflicts described in chapter one. No matter whether nativism (majority-versus-minority conflict) or minority-versus-minority conflict is involved, the elements producing it remain the same. This is true whether one feels it is one's country which is being threatened, one's own group, or a combination of both. To the Irish in the 1930s and the native white Protestants of the nativist periods, country and group were seen as synonymous terms. A threat to one was a threat to the other. Conflict emerged with those elements (immigrants, Catholics, Jews, etc.) perceived as the threatening force. Too often the very complex phenomenon conflict has been explained only in terms of irrational prejudice or other single factors. What is really involved is "the interlocking and mutual reinforcement" of various factors.[5]

Those conflicts which contain significant realistic elements can bring something positive in their wake. As some social scientists have suggested, new social relationships and ethnic adjustments to changed conditions can result from conflict.[6] The Irish conflict with the Jews involved a desire to maintain the dominance of Irish interests and values in the City and to limit the threatening Jewish presence. After years of struggle, the Irish adjusted to the new Jewish position. In this sense, conflict cannot be regarded as necessarily serving a dysfunctional purpose. It should also not be regarded as a deviant phenomenon, especially in highly competitive multi-ethnic urban areas, but rather as part of the social process. All groups compete with each other to some degree. Thus there are constant ethnic tensions which provide the setting for conflict. Although conflict is not inevitable, it can easily emerge if competition reaches the point where a group feels threatened. This sense of threat can be caused by a variety of factors, as noted in this study. Economic depressions, foreign events, or simply periods of change can produce the necessary sense of threat to create conflict. Furthermore, this feeling of threat can exist for majority as well as minority groups, as indicated by other group conflicts which have occurred in American history. Therefore, although efforts can possibly be made to limit the intensity and violent aspects of conflict, the elimination of conflict itself would be an impossibility in a society where there is strong competition for scarce resources and where each group remains insecure and protective of its own position. Under such circumstances, America will probably see these conflicts, in varying degrees of intensity, wax and wane many times in the future.

Notes

CHAPTER 1. THE ETHNIC SETTING

1. An ethnic group is defined as a number of people "who conceive of themselves as being alike by virtue of their common ancestry, real or fictitious, and who are so regarded by others" (Tamotsu Shibutani and Kian Kwan, *Ethnic Stratification* [New York: The Macmillan Company, 1965], p. 47).

2. *Conflict* is defined as a struggle over scarce (real or perceived), interests and values "in which the immediate aims of the opponents are to neutralize, injure, [thwart] or eliminate their rivals" in order to preserve or secure the interests (status, jobs, political power, etc.) and provide for the dominance of certain values. *Value conflict* can include a struggle over standards of conduct, the preferred state of affairs, or the criteria of choice. Since only one value system can dominate, this too can be thought of as a scarce object. Although all conflicts involve interests and values, one factor may play a more important role than the other. *Group conflict* should not be considered only in its most overt form, that of physical violence. It can manifest itself in many other ways, such as assaults or threats in the ethnic press or the use of economic or political power as a malicious force (e.g., boycotts). The goals of all its forms, violent and nonviolent, overt and subtle, are the same. Although *conflict* requires at least two parties with an awareness of the struggle, it can be initiated by only one and can remain essentially unilateral. The agressor is the one who feels more threatened. *Competition,* on the other hand, is defined as a struggle over scarce (real or perceived) interests and values in which the main objectives are the interests and values rather than the elimination or injury of the rival. It is regulated by rules which "limit what the competitors can do to each other in the course of striving." Since the groups may be independently striving to secure these interests and to provide for the dominance of certain values, there may or may not be a conception of the struggle or a conception that the possible future positions of the two groups will be incompatible. (Robin M. Williams, Jr., *The Reduction of Intergroup Tensions* [New York: Social Science Research Council, 1947], Bulletin 57, pp. 40–43; Raymond W. Mack and Richard C. Snyder, "The Analysis of Social Conflict—Toward an Overview and Synthesis," *Journal of Conflict Resolution* 1 [June 1957]: 217–19, 233; Burton B. Silver, "Social Mobility and Intergroup Antagonism," *Journal of Conflict Resolution* 17 [December 1973]: 607; Quincy Wright, "The Nature of Conflict," *Western Political Quarterly* 4 [June 1951]: 197; Brewton Berry, *Race and Ethnic Relations,* 2d ed. [Boston: Houghton Mifflin Company, 1958], p. 122; Kenneth Boulding, *Conflict and Defense* [New York: Harper and Row, 1962], pp. 4–5, 154).

3. See discussion of race relations cycles of Robert Park, E.S. Bogardus, and others in Berry, *Race and Ethnic Relations*, pp. 151–58. Some of these theorists do not feel that their cycles fit all occasions.

4. If, for example, only an insignificant degree of competition exists between two groups, or outside factors pull the two groups together, or the cultures are not inimical to each other, conflict can possibly be avoided. However, if these variables change, conflict may emerge (Ibid., pp. 115–17).

5. Oscar Handlin, *The Newcomers: Negroes and Puerto Ricans in a Changing Metropolis* (Cambridge, Mass.: Harvard University Press, 1959; reprint ed., Anchor Books, 1962), p. 134.

6. Conflicts are based, in varying proportions, on realistic and unrealistic components. Realistic factors would involve an actual rivalry for scarce resources. Unrealistic factors include, for example, deflected hostility related to feelings of frustration. In this case the hostility cannot be directed at the real source of frustration or threat and is therefore deflected to a suitable (vulnerable and visible) substitute, a scapegoat, who is now perceived as an opponent and the source of the group's problems. This cause of conflict is most obvious in a situation in which a rural area experiences an outburst of anti-Semitism although few Jews live there (Robin Williams, *Reduction*, pp. 40–41, 52–53; Hubert M. Blalock, Jr., *Toward a Theory of Minority Group Relations* [New York: John Wiley and Sons, 1967; reprint ed., Capricorn Books, 1970], pp. 42–44).

7. Silver, "Social Mobility," pp. 606–9. *Status* is defined as a group's acknowledged place in society determined by a number of diverse factors such as length of time in country, economic or political power, and perceived loyalty to one's country.

8. *Accommodation* is defined as a temporary lessening of hostilities in which intergroup disagreements remain but are disregarded.

9. Information on the pre–Civil War Irish–native white Protestant conflict in New York is from Robert Ernst, *Immigrant Life in New York City, 1825–1863* (New York: King's Crown Press, 1949; reprint ed., Port Washington, N. Y.: Ira J. Friedman, 1965), pp. 101–3, 135, 271; Ray Allen Billington, *The Protestant Crusade 1800–1860* (New York: The Macmillan Company, Quadrangle Books, 1964), pp. 36, 58–59, 97, 132, 143–56, 199, 201–2; Louis Scisco, *Political Nativism in New York State* (New York: Columbia University Press, 1901).

10. This reveals another unrealistic component of conflict: historical tradition, in which, for example, the resentments and hates of the old world would play a role in the conflict occurring in the new land. The Protestant-Catholic friction over religion was the continuation in America of the historical antipathy between these groups which had convulsed Europe so often. The groups in this case still see each other as rivals based on old conflicts which may no longer have any "relevance to current situations." However, barring this unrealistic element, cultural differences such as religious beliefs are not necessarily a major factor in competition or conflict unless these values are seen as incompatible with or threatening to another group's values (Robin Williams, *Reduction*, p. 41).

11. On the Germans see Ernst, *Immigrant Life*, pp. 56–58; Billington, *Protestant Crusade*, pp. 328–30; Emmet H. Rothan, *The German Catholic Immigrant in the United States (1830–1860)* (Washington D.C.: Catholic University of America Press, 1946), pp. 113–18; Maldwyn Allen Jones, *American Immigration* (Chicago: University of Chicago Press, 1960), pp. 131–32, 154–55.

12. Donald Kinzer, *An Episode in Anti-Catholicism: the American Protective Association* (Seattle: University of Washington Press, 1964), pp. 146–47, 180, 257; John Higham, *Strangers in the Land: Patterns of American Nativism 1860-1925*, 2d ed. (New Brunswick: Rutgers University Press, Atheneum, 1965), pp. 59–61, 80–87.

13. Seymour J. Mandelbaum, *Boss Tweed's New York* (New York: John Wiley and

Sons, 1965), p. 135; Roy V. Peel, *The Political Clubs of New York City* (New York: G. P. Putnam's Sons, 1935), p. 256; Ernst, *Immigrant Life*, p. 107.

14. Ernst, *Immigrant Life*, p. 137; Richard O'Connor, *The German-Americans* (Boston: Little, Brown and Company, 1968), pp. 354-59; Colman J. Barry, *The Catholic Church and German Americans* (Milwaukee: Bruce Publishing Company, 1953); John B. Duff, *The Irish in the United States* (Belmont, California: Wadsworth Publishing Company, 1971), pp. 80-81. See also Jay P. Dolan, *The Immigrant Church: New York's Irish and German Catholics, 1815-1865* (Baltimore: Johns Hopkins University Press, 1975), pp. 72, 89-90, 93.

15. Caroline F. Ware, *Greenwich Village, 1920-1930* (Boston: Houghton Mifflin Company, 1935), pp. 141, 217; O'Connor, *German-Americans*, p. 394.

16. George E. Pozzetta, "The Italians of New York City, 1890-1914" (Ph.D. diss., University of North Carolina, Chapel Hill, 1971), pp. 157-58; Moses Rischin, *The Promised City: New York's Jews 1870-1914* (Cambridge, Massachusetts: Harvard University Press, Corinth Books, 1964), p. 91; Alter F. Landesman, *Brownsville: The Birth, Development and Passing of a Jewish Community in New York* (New York: Bloch Publishing Company, 1971), pp. 58-59; Ware, *Greenwich Village*, p. 130; Pozzetta, "Italians of New York City," p. 157.

17. Ware, *Greenwich Village*, pp. 131-32, 311; Pozzetta, "Italians of New York City," pp. 283-89; Phyllis H. Williams, *South Italian Folkways in Europe and America* (New Haven: Yale University Press, 1938), p. 147; Rudolph Vecoli, "Prelates and Peasants: Italian Immigration and the Catholic Church," *Journal of Social History* 2 (Spring 1969): 221-22, 224, 228, 230, 249-50; Henry J. Browne, "The 'Italian Problem' in the Catholic Church of the United States, 1880-1900," *Historical Records and Studies* 35 (1946): 67-68; interview with Leonard Covello, New York City, 20 February 1969; copy of interview with Gregario Morabito by Rev. Silvano Tomasi, New York City, 28 March 1969. (See also Herbert Gans, *The Urban Villagers* [New York: The Free Press, 1962], pp. 111, 113). Covello, principal of Benjamin Franklin High School in Italian East Harlem from 1934 to 1956, helped to organize the Italian community for La Guardia and has been for many years an influential figure within this group. Morabito was Grand Secretary of the New York State Order Sons of Italy in America.

18. Cited in Browne, "The 'Italian Problem'," p. 52.

19. Rischin, *Promised City*, pp. 263-64; Landesman, *Brownsville*, p. 26; Ernst, *Immigrant Life*, pp. 119-20; Nathan Glazer, *The Social Basis of American Communism* (New York: Harcourt, Brace and World, 1961), p. 20; John Higham, "Anti-Semitism in the Gilded Age: A Reinterpretation," *Mississippi Valley Historical Review* 43 (March 1957): 575, 577.

20. Irving R. Stuart, "A Study of Factors Associated with Inter-Group Conflict in the Ladies' Garment Industry in New York City" (Ph.D. diss., New York University, 1951), pp. 103, 172; Rudolph Glanz, *Jew and Italian: Historic Group Relations and the New Immigration, 1881-1924* (New York: Ktav Publishing House, 1970), pp. 71, 137-38; Ware, *Greenwich Village*, p. 137; Thomas J. Jones, "The Sociology of a New York City Block," *Studies in History, Economics and Public Law* 21 (1904): 24-25, 106; Pozzetta, "Italians of New York City," pp. 355-56.

21. Interview with Charles S. Zimmerman, New York City, 30 March 1973; Glanz, *Jew and Italian*, pp. 25, 49-52; Rischin, *Promised City*, pp. 249-50; interview with Morabito. Zimmerman was a Communist leader in the ILGWU until he broke with the Party in 1929; in the 1930s he was vice-president of this union.

22. Higham, *Strangers in the Land*, p. 208; Frederick C. Luebke, *Bonds of Loyalty: German-Americans and World War I* (DeKalb, Ill.: Northern Illinois University Press, 1974), pp. 249, 251, 253; *Steuben News*, August 1937, p. 1; Rischin, *Promised City*, pp.

265–66; John Higham, "Social Discrimination Against Jews in America, 1830–1930," *Publication of the American Jewish Historical Society* 47 (September 1957):7–19.

23. Kenneth T. Jackson, *The Ku Klux Klan in the City 1915–1930* (New York: Oxford University Press, 1967), pp. 175–78, 240–46.

24. *Irish World and American Industrial Liberator*, 5 October 1929, p. 4, and 9 October 1937, p. 4 (hereafter cited as *Irish World*); *Brooklyn Tablet*, 25 March 1938, p. 12; Charles Corcoran to editor, *Brooklyn Tablet*, 15 April 1939, p. 5 (after 1939 the *Brooklyn Tablet* was called the *Tablet*). For further discussion on German political displacement, see chapter 3.

CHAPTER 2. ECONOMIC COLLAPSE

1. The data on New York State occupational trends for 1910 to 1930 were secured from Bradford F. Kimball, *Changes in the Occupational Pattern of New York State, 1910–1930*, Educational Research Studies No. 2 (New York: The State University of New York, Division of Research, 1937), pp. 26, 37–38, 41, 50, 66–67, 72, 86, 89–94, 98–100, 104, 110, 120–21, 133–34, 146–48, 151.

2. *Declining* means that these occupations exhibited a smaller percentage of the total gainfully employed workers in 1930 than in 1910, although they increased in numbers from 1910 to 1930. Their percentage of numerical increase, however, was the smallest for all the occupational categories in this period (17.7 percent for the manufacturing and mechanical industries and 29.3 percent for domestic and personal service).

3. The percentage of the gainfully occupied who were employed in this division increased from 8.0 percent in 1910 to 13.6 percent in 1930. In the other categories the percentage increases were professional service, 5.7 percent to 8.1 percent; public service, 1.7 percent to 2.2 percent; trade, 13.6 percent to 15.6 percent; transportation and communication, 8.1 percent to 9.2 percent.

4. See United States, Department of Commerce, Bureau of the Census, *Fifteenth Census of the United States, 1930: Unemployment*, 1: 709–10. One study determined that it was the inability to employ more people in manufacturing that accounted for the large amount of unemployment in the City as late as 1940. See Regional Plan Association, *The Economic Status of the New York Metropolitan Region in 1944* (New York: Regional Plan Association, 1944), p. xvi.

5. Comparison of the census and relief survey data is limited but strongly suggestive and is "the best available index of the intensity of relief" in 1934. See United States, Works Progress Administration, Division of Social Research, *Urban Workers on Relief: The Occupational Characteristics of Workers on Relief in 79 Cities May 1934* (by Katherine D. Wood), part 2 (Washington, D.C.: Government Printing Office, 1937), pp. 1, 65–66.

6. Ibid., p. 99.

7. An unemployment census of 1937 proved to be unusable, since it only recorded the number of unemployed in each industry and occupation without giving the number of gainful workers or employed workers in each category. It was therefore impossible to secure from this compilation data on the percentage of unemployment in each industrial or occupational category. The 1940 census had to be used instead.

8. The 1930 and 1940 figures (tables 1 and 3) are also not directly comparable and must be taken as suggestive. For example, the industrial classifications are not exactly the same. Moreover, the 1930 unemployment census included persons ten years old and over; the 1940 labor census included persons fourteen years old and over. The 1930 census is

based on gainful workers, those reported as having a gainful occupation and who have previously worked full-time, "regardless of whether they were working or seeking work at the time of the census." The 1940 figures in these tables are based on employed workers, not including those on public emergency work, and experienced workers who were seeking work. The difference involves such factors as retired workers, who were included in the 1930 census but not in 1940. However, although the data is not exactly comparable, a good indication of the industries and occupations most affected by the depression can be secured by using both tables. See United States, Department of Commerce, Bureau of the Census, *Sixteenth Census of the United States, 1940: Population—The Labor Force,* 3:2–5.

9. The part of the survey dealing with occupations considered only unemployed workers on relief. The section on industries considered both unemployed and employed workers on relief (those whose earnings were inadequate to support their families). This last group probably included many who were forced into part-time work.

10. United States, W.P.A., *Urban Workers on Relief,* pp. 206–7.

11. Regional Plan Association, *Economic Status,* pp. xv, 9; City of New York, *Report of Mayor La Guardia's Committee on Unemployment Relief* (New York, 1935), p. 9; City of New York, Department of Welfare, *Public Assistance in New York City, Annual Report, 1939–1940* (New York, 1941), pp. 12, 109.

12. Regional Plan Association, *Economic Status,* pp. xx, 58.

13. United States, Congress, Senate, *Abstracts of Reports of the Immigration Commission,* S. Doc. 747, 61st Cong., 3rd sess., 1911, 1:101; Leonard Covello, "The Social Background of the Italo-American School Child" (Ph.D. diss., New York University, 1944), p. 437.

14. Nonurban occupations such as mining were not included in my study, although they were listed in the 1900 data. Many occupations, however, were omitted by the Immigration Commission analysis. See E. P. Hutchinson, *Immigrants and Their Children, 1850–1950* (New York: John Wiley and Sons, 1956), pp. 174, 178.

15. George E. Pozzetta, "The Italians of New York City, 1890–1914" (Ph.D. diss., University of North Carolina, Chapel Hill, 1971), pp. 305–17; Thomas Kessner, "The Golden Door: Immigrant Mobility in New York City, 1880–1915," (Ph.D. diss., Columbia University, 1975), pp. 88–89, 91, 131, 133.

16. *Abstracts of Reports of the Immigration Commission,* p. 101; Moses Rischin, *The Promised City: New York's Jews, 1870–1914* (Cambridge: Harvard University Press, Corinth Books, 1964), pp. 59, 61, 67–68; Samuel Joseph, *Jewish Immigration to the United States from 1881 to 1910* (New York: 1914; reprint ed., New York: Arno Press, 1969), p. 141; Hutchinson, *Immigrants and Their Children,* pp. 175, 179; Kessner, "Golden Door," pp. 101, 103, 143–44.

17. Kessner, "Golden Door," pp. 172, 181, 188, 191, 194, 204, 235, 270–73, 275. The data in my study does not indicate rate of occupational mobility for each of the groups to the 1930s since that would have required information on individuals and their occupational movements, a task that would in itself require a book. Instead the information presented tries to note each ethnic group's occupational position in the 1930s, while at the same time giving some background information on the period of first arrival and afterward, which would help to explain that position. The stress is on their occupational level at various points in their history.

18. Fred L. Strodtbeck, "Family Interaction, Values, and Achievement," in *The Jews: Social Patterns of an American Group,* ed. Marshall Sklare (New York: The Free Press, 1958), p. 150; David C. McClelland *et al., Talent and Society* (New York: D. Van Nostrand Company, 1958), pp. 149–50; Selma Berrol, "Turning Little Aliens into Little Citizens; Italians and Jews in New York City Public Schools, 1900–14," *Proceedings of*

the Seventh Annual Conference of the American Italian Historical Association (November 1974): 34–35.

19. Scholars have disagreed as to whether the lack of enthusiasm by Italians toward schooling was the result of deeply ingrained cultural traits or was a temporary response to an economic position in society which forced them to concentrate on the struggle for existence rather than the luxury of going to school. It was probably a combination of the two. Schooling had come to have less meaning in the peasant Italian culture, and this was reinforced by their economic position both in Italy and America as well as by the inadequacy of the schools. See McClelland, *Talent and Society,* p. 150; Strodtbeck, "Family Interaction," p. 150; Covello, "Social Background," pp. 432, 625; Joseph Lopreato, *Italian Americans* (New York: Random House, 1970), pp. 152–57; Mary Fabian Matthews, "The Role of the Public School in the Assimilation of the Italian Immigrant Child in New York City, 1900–1914," in *The Italian Experience in the United States,* ed. Silvano M. Tomasi and Madeline H. Engel (New York: Center for Migration Studies, 1970), pp. 127–28, 137–38.

20. Of the various ethnic groups, Italians had the largest percentage of their first generation children working rather than at school (Berrol, "Turning Little Aliens," p. 33); Covello, "Social Background," pp. 458, 495; Interview with Leonard Covello, New York City, 20 February 1969; Phyllis H. Williams, *South Italian Folkways in Europe and America* (New Haven: Yale University Press, 1938), pp. 133–34; Matthews, "Role of the Public School," p. 140; Herbert Gans, *The Urban Villagers: Group and Class in the Life of Italian Americans* (New York: The Free Press, 1962), pp. 123, 129, 205, 207; Humbert Nelli, *The Italians in Chicago 1880–1930* (New York: Oxford University Press, 1970), pp. 66–69.

21. Covello, "Social Background," p. 450. Truancy was also evident in the Jewish community, but on a much smaller scale (Berrol, "Turning Little Aliens," pp. 32–34).

22. Interview with Covello, 20 February 1969; *Casa Italiana Bulletin* 2 (December 1931): 7.

23. Nettie P. McGill and Ellen N. Matthews, *The Youth of New York City* (New York: The MacMillan Company, 1940), p. 62; Nettie P. McGill, "Some Characteristics of Jewish Youth in New York City," *Jewish Social Service Quarterly* 14 (December 1937): 258. The Jewish youth were predominantly native-born of foreign parents.

24. These figures are not meant to indicate lack of significant upward occupational mobility but rather to show that the weaknesses in the Italian occupational structure were evident in the early settlement years as well as during the Depression.

25. Proprietors included owners of small businesses.

26. McGill and Matthews, *Youth of New York City,* table 5, pp. 62, 45.

27. McGill, "Some Characteristics," pp. 263–64.

28. Ibid., p. 265; McGill and Matthews, *Youth of New York City,* table 5, pp. 62, 45; McGill, "Some Characteristics," p. 255.

29. Dorothy Helen Goldstein, "The 'Disproportionate' Occupational Distribution of Jews and Their Individual and Organized Reactions" (M.A. thesis, Columbia University, 1941), pp. 23–24.

30. While only 2.2 percent of the Jewish gainful workers were in public service, they made up 21.4 percent of the total gainful workers engaged in this field (ibid., p. 20). Much of the 1937 report is included in the Goldstein study.

31. Ibid., pp. 18–24; *New York Jewish News,* 4 February 1938, p. 4.

32. United States, Works Progress Administration, Federal Writers Project, *The Italians of New York* (New York: Random House, 1938), pp. 64–65; Joseph W. Anania, "Report on the Interdependence of Italians and Jews Living in New York City and the Effects of the Recent Italian Governmental Decrees on Relations between Italians and

Jews in New York City,'' prepared for the American Jewish Committee, November 25, 1938 (in the files of the committee, New York City), pp. 4, 25–26; W.P.A., *Italians of New York,* pp. 65–66; interview with Covello, 20 February 1969; Irving R. Stuart, "A Study of Factors Associated with Inter-Group Conflict in the Ladies' Garment Industry in New York City" (Ph.D. diss., New York University, 1951), pp. 173, 175, 194. See also the discussion on Italian anti-Semitism in chapter 4, below.

33. Goldstein, "The 'Disproportionate' Occupational Distribution," p. 23; Melvin M. Fagen, "The Status of Jewish Lawyers in New York City," *Jewish Social Studies* 1 (1939): 84–85; *New York Times,* 20 November 1935, p. 19.

34. The Italians, while also emerging as competitors in such areas as civil service, did not seem to pose as great a threat as the Jews. At least there was no evidence of hostility toward them based on the economic factor. Also Italians were very hard-hit by the Depression and therefore did not inspire resentment on this point.

35. Stuart, "A Study of Factors," p. 50; Paul O'Dwyer, "Reminiscences" (Oral History Project, Columbia University, 1962), 1:40–42; Pozzetta, "The Italians of New York City," pp. 157–58, 309, 311–12; Rischin, *Promised City,* p. 67; Kessner, "Golden Door," p. 91. Studies which detail the occupational mobility of the ethnic groups in various cities note that the Germans moved up the occupational ladder at a faster rate than the Irish. See Stephan Thernstrom, *The Other Bostonians: Poverty and Progress in the American Metropolis, 1880–1970* (Cambridge, Mass: Harvard University Press, 1973), pp. 111–44; Clyde Griffen, "Workers Divided: The Effect of Craft and Ethnic Differences in Poughkeepsie, New York, 1850–1880," in *Nineteenth-Century Cities: Essays in the New Urban History,* ed. Stephan Thernstrom and Richard Sennett (New Haven: Yale University Press, 1969), pp. 80–81.

36. In 1855, when the Irish constituted almost 80 percent of the foreign-born servants and waiters residing in Manhattan, the Germans composed only about 15 percent. One-fourth of the Irish gainful workers were servants, as compared to "one-tenth of the German workers." The Irish also were 87 percent of the immigrant laborers in the City. This occupational group made up more than one-fifth of the Irish working population, while among the Germans only approximately 5 percent of their workers were laborers. The Irish were also concentrated in the construction trades; the Germans less so. The reverse was true in the apparel trades. Germans also dominated as cabinet makers and piano makers and were numerous as butchers and bakers. Robert Ernst, *Immigrant Life in New York City, 1825–1863* (New York: King's Crown Press, 1949; reprint ed., Port Washington, N. Y.: Ira J. Friedman, 1965), pp. 66, 69, 73–79, 87–88, 97; For similar conclusions using other cities see Theodore Hershberg *et al.,* "Occupation and Ethnicity in Five Nineteenth-Century Cities: A Collaborative Inquiry," *Historical Methods Newsletter* 7 (June 1974): 197–202.

37. *Abstracts of Reports of the Immigration Commission,* 1:101; Hutchinson, *Immigrants and Their Children,* pp. 123–28. Nonurban occupational categories such as agriculture or mining were not considered. All figures are based on the United States and not New York State or City.

38. Hutchinson, *Immigrants and Their Children,* pp. 123–28.

39. Ibid., pp. 173–74, 177–78. Both the Irish and German second generation also showed concentrations in the position of messengers and office and errand boys. This information was omitted, since it was assumed that this included mainly the very youngest members of the second generation (census figures listed all those ten years of age and older).

40. McGill and Matthews, *Youth of New York City,* table 5.

41. Paul O'Dwyer, "Reminiscences," 1:41–42. O'Dwyer places the Irish in the

longshoremen occupation as late as 1929. See also Caroline F. Ware, *Greenwich Village, 1920-1930* (Boston: Houghton Mifflin Company, 1935), pp. 67-68.

42. New York Times, Daily News, and Herald Tribune, *New York City Market Analysis* (New York: 1934); New York Times, Daily News, Mirror and Journal-American, *New York City Market Analysis* (New York: 1943). This does not necessarily mean that all Germans and Irish in these neighborhoods fit this description. However, in all probability one can say that there were Irish residents of the city who were in an economically superior position to some Germans during the Depression. For an explanation of how I determined population and economic data for these neighborhoods see chapter 3, note 37, and chapter 7, note 19.

43. Frederick Franklin Schrader, ed., *The New Germany under Hitler* (New York: Deutscher Weckruf und Beobachter, n.d.), p. 28; *Deutscher Weckruf und Beobachter*, 16 July 1936, p. 6. In the period from 1934 to 1943, the largest number of relief cases handled by the German-American Conference Relief Fund was in 1938, indicating many Germans were affected by the recession (German-American Conference Relief Fund, *Annual Report*, 1943).

44. Ware, *Greenwich Village*, pp. 67-68, 210, 214-15.

45. Civil service news was an important segment in the Irish press but was not found in the Jewish, Italian, or German papers. S. Burton Heath, "Investigation by Innuendo," *Survey Graphic* 30 (October 1941):502; *New York Sun*, 5 August 1941; Charles Garrett, *The La Guardia Years: Machine and Reform Politics in New York City* (New Brunswick, New Jersey: Rutgers University Press, 1961), pp. 132-34; interview with Paul O'Dwyer, New York City, 9 August 1973; Paul O'Dwyer, "Reminiscences," 2:186-89. O'Dwyer was president of the American Friends of Irish Neutrality and the United Irish Counties Association. He was also a brother of the 1941 Democratic Mayoral candidate.

46. Stephen Cole, "The Unionization of Teachers: Determinants of Rank and File Support," *Sociology of Education* 41 (Winter 1968):85.

47. *Abstracts of Reports of the Immigration Commission*, 2:52, 60. See also Alter F. Landesman, *Brownsville: The Birth, Development and Passing of a Jewish Community in New York City* (New York: Bloch Publishing Company, 1971), p. 158.

48. Bronx Council of Social Agencies, "A Study of the Lower Bronx," September 1939, p. 5. Also, see below, chapter 8, discussion on South Bronx.

49. Joseph Greenbaum and Leonard I. Pearlin, "Vertical Mobility and Prejudice: A Socio-psychological Analysis," *Class, Status, and Power*, ed. Reinhard Bendix and Seymour Martin Lipset (Glencoe, Illinois: The Free Press, 1953), pp. 487-91; Fred B. Silberstein and Melvin Seeman, "Social Mobility and Prejudice," *American Journal of Sociology* 65 (November 1959): 258-61; Walter C. Kaufman, "Status, Authoritarianism, and Anti-Semitism," *American Journal of Sociology*, 62 (January 1957):382. Prejudice is defined as a "prejudgement of individuals on the basis of some type of social categorization." Prejudice, of course, is not conflict. However, prejudices which exhibit negative attitudes toward others, which is in many cases accompanied by discrimination, can serve to benefit the prejudiced group or individual in its competitive struggles. More important, an antipathy toward another group may make a group or individual more conducive to engaging in conflict. Quote is from Robin M. Williams, Jr., *The Reduction of Intergroup Tensions* (New York: Social Science Research Council, 1947), Bulletin 57, pp. 36-39. See also George E. Simpson and J. Milton Yinger, *Racial and Cultural Minorities: An Analysis of Prejudice and Discrimination*, rev. ed. (New York: Harper and Row, 1958), pp. 113-15.

50. Although the *Tablet* during this period was ostensibly a general Catholic newspaper, it actually represented mainly an Irish viewpoint. This is illustrated by an editorial

in 1919 welcoming home the "fighting Irish" (the 69th regiment) which noted with pride that "we are Irish-Americans as were the majority of the Sixty-ninth." There is also substantiation from the leadership of the Irish community for classifying the paper in this way. Paul O'Dwyer noted that the *Tablet* was the militant organ which appealed and spoke to mainly the Irish Catholics. For the purposes of this study, this is also revealed by the *Tablet's* blatant support of Father Charles Coughlin's anti-Semitism, which began in 1938, and its belittling of Jewish persecutions in other lands. The *Tablet's* attitude is very similar to that found in the press of the Irish community, the *Gaelic American* and the *Irish World*. At the same time, the leading German and Italian-American papers were specifically rejecting anti-Semitism, had avoided it up to this point, and were sympathetic to the plight of the Jews in other countries. Only the Nazis, a very weak element in the German-American community, particularly by 1938, attacked the Jews in its press, although it did not agree with Coughlin and the *Tablet* on all other matters. The Christian Front, a grass-roots extremist organization directly inspired by Coughlin's rhetoric and endorsed by the *Tablet,* also indicates this. The Front, like the *Tablet,* was strongly pro-Coughlin and anti-Semitic. Its leadership and rank and file was mainly Irish. The *Catholic News,* official organ of the archdiocese of New York and published by Henry and Charles H. Ridder (uncle and cousin of the Ridders who published the *New Yorker Staats-Zeitung und Herold,* the leading German-American newspaper in New York) also offers an illustration of mainly the German-American viewpoint, although it also expressed the views of more moderate Irish figures such as Patrick Cardinal Hayes and Archbishop Francis Spellman. This paper condemned anti-Semitism and spoke favorably of the Jews at the same time that the German papers were doing so (*Brooklyn Tablet,* 26 April 1919, p. 4; Interview with Paul O'Dwyer). See the discussion on anti-Christianity in chapter 5, below, and also chapter 4, note 59, and chapter 5, notes 5 and 32.

51. *Brooklyn Tablet,* 30 March 1935, p. 1; 4 February 1939, p. 13.

52. Patrick Scanlan, "From the Managing Editor's Desk," *Brooklyn Tablet,* 25 March 1939, p. 11; 4 August 1934, p. 9.

53. *Gaelic American,* 6 October 1934, p. 4; *Social Justice,* 11 September 1939, p. 1; George Johnson to editor, *Brooklyn Tablet,* 10 February 1940, p. 8.

54. *Brooklyn Tablet,* 3 September 1938, p. 8; Scanlan, "From the Managing Editor's Desk," 24 February 1940, p. 11; Ignatius Byrne to editor, *Brooklyn Tablet,* 17 September 1938, p. 6.

55. See the discussion on the Christian Front in chapter 5, below, and the discussion on South Bronx and Fordham in chapter 8. Some Jews recognized the economic factor in this conflict. See *American Hebrew,* 28 July 1939, p. 1. (From 1932 to 1935 this paper was called the *American Hebrew and Jewish Tribune*).

56. *Jewish Examiner,* 30 December 1938, p. 1 (the *Jewish Examiner* was called the *Brooklyn Jewish Examiner* from 1930 to 1933); *New York Times,* 28 December 1938 p. 5. Ads of this type would ask for Christian help or would note that the firm was a Christian one.

57. New York, N.Y., Mayor's Committee on Unity, *Report on Inequality of Opportunity in Higher Education,* July 1, 1946, pp. 15–17; Alfred L. Shapiro, "Racial Discrimination in Medicine," *Jewish Social Studies* 10 (April 1948): 103, 105; *Jewish Examiner,* 19 October 1934, p. 1.

58. *B'nai B'rith Magazine,* December 1933, p. 83. From 1934 to 1938 this journal was called the *B'nai B'rith National Jewish Monthly,* and after 1938 the *National Jewish Monthly.*

59. There was a feeling among the Italians that they were progressing. See, for example, *Casa Italiana Bulletin* 2 (December 1931): 7.

CHAPTER 3. LA GUARDIA AND THE NEW
ETHNIC ORDER

1. Quoted in Alfred Connable and Edward Silberfarb, *Tigers of Tammany: Nine Men Who Ran New York* (Holt, Rinehart and Winston, 1967), p. 274.

2. Before the 1920s the Jewish vote was often divided between the Democrats, Republicans, Socialists, and Progressives. Although the Democrats usually received the largest vote, it was often not a majority. During the 1920s Jewish voting somewhat stabilized, and a majority of these votes often went to the Democrats. This was the result both of a decline in the Socialist Party's strength and the attempts by Tammany to support liberalism. However, Jews continued to support reform and liberal candidates. See Thomas Henderson, "Tammany Hall and the New Immigrants, 1910–1921" (Ph.D. diss., University of Virginia, 1973), pp. 24, 109, 112, 147–49, 230–32, 239, 247, 262–66. This study provides an ethnic voter analysis for Manhattan.

3. *Jewish Examiner,* 28 July 1933, p. 12 (see also 23 February 1934, p. 1); Elias Godofsky, "No Unity in Local Jewish Life," *Brooklyn Jewish Center Review,* December 1933, p. 10; Samuel Untermyer to James J. Walker, 17 March 1930, James J. Walker Papers, Box 575, Municipal Archives and Records Center, New York City; *Jewish Examiner,* 4 October 1929, p. 40 (see also 19 January 1934, p. 1); 20 September 1935, p. 20; Nicholas Pinto to Fiorello H. La Guardia, 28 October 1939, Fiorello H. La Guardia Papers, Box 2538, Municipal Archives and Records Center, New York City (La Guardia Papers hereafter cited as LGP). For information on district leadership fights in the early 1930s see Roy V. Peel, *The Political Clubs of New York City* (New York: G.P. Putnam's Sons, 1935), pp. 287, 289–90.

4. Henderson, "Tammany Hall," pp. 42–43, 112, 118–19, 231–32, 261, 267–68. Italian political organization was slowed by the large number of returnees to Italy and the high illiteracy rate in Italian-American communities. Although they might constitute a majority of the population in a particular assembly district, they were not always a majority of its voting population since fewer Italians had gained citizenship. See Henderson, "Tammany Hall," pp. 48–49, 114, 132–36, 249–50, 257–59.

5. Ibid., pp. 38–39, 42–43, 58–59; George E. Pozzetta, "The Italians of New York City 1890–1914" (Ph.D. diss., University of North Carolina, Chapel Hill, 1971), pp. 375, 380, 382–85; Interview with Paul P. Rao, New York City, 7 August 1973. Rao was president of the Italian Holy Name Society of the Archdiocese of New York, chairman of the United Italian-American League, organizer of the Italian-American Democratic Club of Yorkville (which later became the city-wide Paul Rao Association), chairman of the Italian-American division of the New York State Democratic campaign committee in 1938, and chairman of the Italian-American division of the Democratic mayoralty campaign in 1937.

6. Alfred E. Santangelo, speech delivered to the American Italian Historical Association, 26 October 1968, p. 1 (mimeographed); *Il Progresso Italo-Americano,* 6 November 1938, editorial page; 1 November 1934, p. 1; 13 January 1939, p. 1; 24 August 1939, p. 1 (hereafter cited as *Il Progresso*); Peel, *Political Clubs,* pp. 287, 289–90; Henderson, "Tammany Hall," pp. 38–39, 43, 58–59; Caroline F. Ware, *Greenwich Village, 1920–1930* (Boston: Houghton Mifflin Company, 1935), pp. 282–84.

7. On La Guardia's political organization of the Italian-American community see Arthur Mann, *La Guardia: A Fighter Against His Times, 1882–1933* (Philadelphia: J. B. Lippincott Company, 1959).

8. *Il Progresso,* 5 November 1933, p. 1. Although La Guardia did well in Italian areas in the 1929 mayoralty election, it was not until after his victory in 1933 with very

strong Italian support that the Democrats became seriously concerned about this ethnic vote (Mann, *La Guardia*, p. 279; Henderson, "Tammany Hall," pp. 267–68).

9. Quoted in Arthur Mann, *La Guardia Comes to Power, 1933* (Philadelphia: J.B. Lippincott Company, 1965), p. 136. See also the discussion on Italians and the 1933 mayoralty campaign in chapter 7, below.

10. In the previous mayoralty election, Jews gave significant support to Morris Hillquit, the Socialist candidate (Ibid., p. 142).

11. Nathan Straus, Jr., was offered the mayoral nomination on the Fusion ticket before La Guardia, but he refused to accept, on the advice of other Jewish leaders who feared that having Jews as both governor and mayor might inspire anti-Semitism (Nathan Straus, Jr., "Reminiscences" (Oral History Project, Columbia University, 1950), pp. 74–75, 77.

12. Ethnic identification of aldermanic candidates was based on their names. I wish to thank Dr. Fred Massarik, scientific director of the U.S. National Jewish Population Study, for the use of his list of 106 distinctive Jewish names. The following works were also used as an aid to identification: American Council of Learned Societies, *Report of Committee on Linguistics and National Stocks in the Population of the United States* in American Historical Association, *Annual Report, 1931* 4 (1931): 232–48, 271–305; Edward MacLysaght, *A Guide to Irish Surnames* (Baltimore: Genealogical Book Company, 1964). Any ethnically doubtful names were not counted.

13. *Il Progresso*, 8 November 1933, p. 1; *New York Times*, 8 November 1933, p. 2.

14. *Gaelic American*, 2 December 1933, p. 4; 11 November 1933, p. 1; *New York Times*, 7 October 1933, p. 17.

15. All figures are close approximations based on a bar graph. See Theodore J. Lowi, *At the Pleasure of the Mayor* (New York: The Free Press of Glencoe, 1964), pp. 34–39, 41.

16. The information on La Guardia's department commissioners, board of estimate, and others is based on an ethnic study of their names and on obituary notices. Any ethnically doubtful name was not counted. See also note 12, above. For Jews appointed or elected to various positions see "Appointments and Elections," *American Jewish Year Book*, vols. 24–39, September 1922–September 1938.

17. The Irish Tammany bosses at first opposed the Lehman nomination, mainly owing to political rather than ethnic differences, but were forced to give in because of pressure placed on them by Roosevelt, various Jewish Democrats, and other Irish leaders such as Al Smith and Edward Flynn, head of the Bronx organization. See Allan Nevins, *Herbert H. Lehman and His Era* (New York: Charles Scribner's Sons, 1963), pp. 127–30.

18. Italian Non-Partisan Committee for the Re-Election of Mayor La Guardia to Generoso Pope, 13 September 1937, LGP, Box 2721.

19. Both the Brancato and Pecora appointments were temporary ones given to fill some vacancies. However, both men won easily in the elections for these positions that same year with the support of the Democratic County organizations (*New York Times*, 6 January 1935, p. 1; 11 January 1935, p. 1; 16 January 1935, p. 1; 2 October 1935, p. 2; 4 February 1936, p. 11.

20. For more on the use of this tactic and an analysis of the vote, see chapter 7.

21. *Il Progresso*, 5 November 1934, p. 1.

22. Ibid., 5 November 1936, p. 1; 11 November 1941, p. 6; 19 January 1939, editorial page; D. Spadafora to editor, 5 July 1938, editorial page; 1 November 1934, p. 1; 2 November 1937, editorial page; 3 November 1938, editorial page; 6 November 1938, editorial page; 13 November 1939, p. 1; 24 August 1939, p. 1. J.C.M. to editor, *Brooklyn Tablet*, 23 July 1938, p. 6. Telephone interview with Alfred E. Santangelo, 5 July 1972. Santangelo was district leader, state senator, and congressman from the East Harlem area

during the 1940s and 1950s, and brother of Paul Santangelo, district leader of Manhattan's 1st A.D. East from 1937 to 1939.

23. *New York Times,* 15 June 1934, p. 18. *Gaelic American,* 6 October 1934, p. 1; 3 November 1934, p. 1. *Brooklyn Tablet,* 26 May 1934, p. 7. While German Catholics also protested against the Fama appointment, it remained primarily an Irish concern, since they were the group singled out for attack by the doctor (New York State Branch, Catholic Central Verein of America, *Proceedings of the Annual Convention,* 1934, p. 16).

24. *Gaelic American,* 27 October 1934, p. 4; Scanlan, "From the Managing Editor's Desk," *Brooklyn Tablet,* 19 May 1934, p. 11.

25. Irish-American Non-Partisan Committee for La Guardia, Publicity Releases, 1937, LGP, Box 2721; *Brooklyn Tablet,* 20 March 1937, p. 11; See also 30 March 1935, p. 1; Dick O'Brien to editor, *Irish World,* 22 April 1939, p. 4; Eileen Curran to Matthew Troy, 24 October 1937, LGP, Box 2721.

26. Interview with Paul O'Dwyer, 9 August 1973, New York City; Paul O'Dwyer, "Reminiscences," 1: 186–90; *Gaelic American,* 1 March 1941, p. 1. See also chapter 7, discussion on 1933, 1937, and 1941 mayoralty campaigns and the Communist issue.

27. The Communist appointee was Simon Gerson, who was added to the staff of the borough president of Manhattan in 1937. (see chapter 5, discussion on Gerson). Kern was fired in 1942, partially due to La Guardia's desire to win favor with the Catholic Church in New York in an effort to secure an army position. See Charles Garrett, *The La Guardia Years: Machine and Reform Politics in New York City* (New Brunswick, New Jersey: Rutgers University Press, 1962), p. 290.

28. Edward Lodge Curran to Editor, *Brooklyn Tablet,* 16 April 1938, p. 6.

29. Daniel Danaher to editor, *Irish World,* 3 September 1938, p. 4.

30. Quoted in Warren Moscow, *What Have You Done for Me Lately?: The Ins and Outs of New York City Politics* (Englewood, New Jersey: Prentice Hall, 1967), p. 118.

31. *New York Times,* 5 October 1937, p. 6.

32. Farley's power in the higher ranks of the New Deal began to wane by the late 1930s. His failure to be considered seriously for the Democratic presidential nomination in 1940 was partly seen as the result of anti-Catholic prejudice. This once again reminded the Irish of their insecure place in America (*New York Times,* 17 March 1940, p. 12; 5 November 1940, p. 16). Other aspects of the New Deal also disturbed the Irish. See chapter 5, discussion on Catholics, Communism, and the New Deal.

33. Samuel Lubell, *The Future of American Politics,* 3d ed., rev. (New York: Harper and Row, 1965), pp. 86–87; George Q. Flynn, *American Catholics and the Roosevelt Presidency, 1932–1936* (Lexington, Kentucky: University of Kentucky Press, 1968), pp. 50–51.

34. Edward Flynn, "Reminiscences" (Oral History Project, Columbia University, 1950), p. 21.

35. This was true even though some of the left-wing leaders of the ALP, such as Eugene Connolly, were Irish. There was also a group in the South Bronx known as the Irish Workers League, which was identified with the leftist elements in the ALP.

36. *New York Times,* 18 May 1943, p. 25; Richard H. Rovere, "Vito Marcantonio: Machine Politician, New Style," *Harper's Magazine,* April 1944, p. 392.

37. Voting statistics in this study are based on election districts (New York's voting divisions) which were over 50 percent Irish, Jewish, German, or Italian between 1932 and 1941 (a few of the election districts were 50 percent but contained no other ethnic concentration.) Census tracts in New York City were first identified ethnically for 1930 and 1940; those chosen for the voter analysis had a concentration of Irish, Jewish (Russian), German, or Italian foreign stock (first- and second-generation) population for both census years. Then those election districts or groups of election districts within these tracts

which remained the same in boundaries between 1932 and 1941 were identified. In some cases, while no single election district retained its boundary during this period, groups of election districts would maintain the same boundary and were therefore usable. The votes in these grouped districts were added together and considered as one unit, since they represented the same area in all elections. A name check, using the voter registration lists, was made of all these election districts to determine if they were over 50 percent Irish, Jewish, German, or Italian for 1932 through 1941. Care was taken to avoid election districts which fit this description but had a large concentration of another ethnic group. Therefore what was secured were 149 voting units (single or grouped election districts) which remained the same ethnically and geographically during the period under study— stable political and ethnic units which could be compared over time. There were 76 Jewish, 29 German, 28 Italian, and 16 Irish voting units. The 1930 census data was secured from the Community Council of Greater New York, which has the census tract tabulation sheets for 1930. This data, listing foreign stock by nationality group for each census tract, was never published. Also used for the 1930 information was Walter Laidlaw, ed., *Population of the City of New York, 1890–1930* (New York: Cities Census Committee, 1932), and William B. Shedd, *Italian Population in New York,* Bulletin No. 7 (New York: Casa Italiana Educational Bureau, 1934); the 1940 census data is from United States, Department of Commerce, Bureau of the Census, *Sixteenth Census of the United States, Census Tract Data on Population and Housing, New York City: 1940* (New York: Welfare Council Committee on 1940 Census Tract Tabulations for New York City, 1942), and United States, Department of Commerce, Bureau of the Census, *Sixteenth Census of the United States, 1940: Population: Nativity and Parentage of the White Population, Country of Origin of the Foreign Stock* (Washington, D. C.: Government Printing Office, 1942), p. 74. Since the 1940 census tract data contained information only on foreign-born heads of families for each nationality group, an estimate of the foreign stock population in each tract was made on the basis of ratios of foreign-born heads of families to total foreign-born, and total foreign-born to native born of foreign or mixed parentage for each nationality group, using borough and tract statistics. This ratio technique is the only possible way to secure even an estimate of foreign stock population by tracts in 1940. For both 1930 and 1940 an effort was also made to locate neighborhoods which contemporary observers had identified as Irish, Jewish, German, or Italian. This was especially useful for areas containing large numbers of an ethnic group beyond the second generation and therefore not classified by the census. In these neighborhoods, the same procedure as above was used to locate appropriate election districts. The name check was based on the City Record, City Record Supplement, *List of Registered Voters,* 1932–1941. For sources used as an aid in identifying ethnic names, see note 12 of this chapter. For election district maps, see New York City, Board of Elections, *Maps Showing the Assembly Districts of New York City, 1932–1941.* To produce the voting statistics, use was made of the Statistical Package for the Social Sciences (SPSS).

38. United States Congress, Senate, *Third Interim Report of the Special Committee to Investigate Organized Crime in Interstate Commerce,* S. Rept. 307, 82nd Cong., 1st sess., 1951, *Reports on Crime Investigation* 6:118.

39. Information on ethnicity and crime was secured from the following: Garrett, *The La Guardia Years,* pp. 152–59; William O'Dwyer, "Reminiscences" (Oral History Project, Columbia University, 1962), 2:420; Burton B. Turkus and Sid Feder, *Murder, Inc.: The Story of "the Syndicate"* (New York: Farrar, Straus and Young, 1951), pp. 81, 98–99, 109, 119; Donald R. Cressey, *Theft of the Nation: The Structure and Operations of Organized Crime in America* (New York: Harper and Row, 1969), pp. 55–56; Daniel Bell, "Crime as an American Way of Life: A Queer Ladder of Social Mobility," in *American Urban History,* ed. Alexander B. Callow (New York:

Oxford University Press, 1969), pp. 277–78; Alter F. Landesman, *Brownsville: The Birth, Development and Passing of a Jewish Community in New York* (New York: Bloch Publishing Company, 1971, pp. 331–33; Humbert S. Nelli, *The Business of Crime: Italians and Syndicate Crime in the United States* (New York: Oxford University Press, 1976).

40. Bell, "Crime as an American Way," p. 286; Garrett, *The La Guardia Years*, pp. 157–58; Warren Moscow, *The Last of the Big-time Bosses: The Life and Times of Carmine DeSapio and the Rise and Fall of Tammany Hall* (New York: Stein and Day, 1971), pp. 52–53.

41. Moscow, *What Have You Done*, pp. 169–70; Moscow, *Last of Big-Time Bosses*, p. 45; *New York Times*, 16 July 1931, p. 22.

42. Although Marinelli was forced to resign his County Clerk position after this disclosure, he remained as district leader until 1939, when he was replaced by John DeSalvio, a friend of Frank Costello.

43. Costello noted later that four district leaders who were friends of his were Paul Sarubbi of the first assembly district; John DeSalvio of the second, west; Abraham Rosenthal of the eighth; and Clarence Neal of the twentieth (*New York Times*, 26 October 1943, p. 1; Moscow, *Last of Big-Time Bosses*, p. 54).

44. William O'Dwyer admitted that in 1943 he had been to Costello's home, where he had seen Kennedy as well as other prominent Tammany figures (William O'Dwyer, "Reminiscences," 6:103, 119–20; *New York Times*, 26 October 1943, p. 1; 27 October 1943, p. 1; Moscow, *Last of Big-Time Bosses*, pp. 55–56). Generoso Pope, publisher of *Il Progresso* and a growing power in Tammany, also supported Kennedy for the leadership of Tammany.

45. *New York Times*, 29 August 1943, p. 1; 26 October 1943, pp. 1, 13; 18 November 1943, p. 25.

46. Ibid., 26 October 1943, p. 1; Senate, *Third Interim Report*, p. 123. Telephone interview with Alfred Santangelo, 5 July 1972.

47. John DeSalvio, one of Costello's district leader friends, led the effort to secure the nomination for Capozzoli (Salvatore J. LaGumina, "Case Studies of Ethnicity and Italo-American Politicians," in *The Italian Experience in the United States,* ed. Silvano M. Tomasi and Madeline H. Engel (New York: Center for Migration Studies, 1970), pp. 149–50.

48. See chapter 7, note 75, and the discussion on Roosevelt, the 1940 election, and the Italian vote.

49. Bell, "Crime as an American Way," p. 287; Turkus and Feder, *Murder, Inc.,* p. 430; Senate, *Third Interim Report,* pp. 139–40.

50. Interview with Paul O'Dwyer.

51. Moscow, *Last of Big-Time Bosses,* p. 45.

52. *New York Times,* 8 August 1943, p. 38. Finn had also opposed Kennedy for the Tammany leadership in 1942 but failed to win. The Costello-controlled district leaders, as noted, were significant in this balloting (*New York Times,* 31 October 1943, IV:12).

53. The Italians, who for a number of years had been trying to win the district leadership in the eighteenth assembly district, north (East Harlem), finally did so in 1943 with Mancuso.

54. *Irish World,* 18 May 1935, p. 4; *New York Times,* 1 November 1936, p. 48; *Herald Tribune,* 27 September 1936; tape copy of interview with Warren Moscow (Oral History Project, St. John's University, 1971).

55. Lehman had faced an Irish opponent, William J. Donovan, in 1932 also. However, in that election the Irish-Jewish political competition was not yet severe. Also, all Republicans did poorly in 1932; the traditionally Democratic Irish remained in their party.

By 1936, there were significant defections. The 1934 governor's race was not included in this study, since both candidates (Lehman and Robert Moses) were Jewish.

56. For an analysis of the Roosevelt vote see chapter 7.

57. German Catholics did protest against the Lehman school bus decision and noted resentment over this issue (New York State Branch, Catholic Central Verein, *Proceedings*, 1935, pp. 41, 48). Other Catholic concerns included, for example, the Communist issue.

58. Joseph P. Ridder, Victor F. Ridder, and Bernard Ridder to Herbert Lehman, 16 September 1938, Herbert H. Lehman Papers, Columbia University, New York City. Hereafter cited as HLP. *New Yorker Staats-Zeitung und Herold* hereafter cited as *Staats-Zeitung*. See discussion below, in this chapter, on La Guardia and German-Americans.

59. Interview with Paul O'Dwyer; *New York Times,* 15 October 1938, p. 9. See also chapter 7, note 64.

60. It was Lehman who had insisted on the Poletti nomination, but this was probably considered a good move, since the Republicans had an Italian, Edward Corsi, running for U. S. senator in this election.

61. When Bennett was nominated for governor in 1942 by the Democrats, the ALP refused to endorse him for basically the same reasons.

62. *New York Times,* 13 October 1938, p. 20; 18 October 1938, p. 13.

63. Ibid., 14 October 1938, p. 1.

64. Ibid., 15 October 1938, p. 7; 18 October 1938, p. 13; 19 October 1938, p. 1; press release, Charles Poletti to Edward Lodge Curran, 18 October 1938, HLP.

65. Julia Fuimara to Excellency Amleto Cicognani, 17 October 1938, Charles Poletti Papers in Lehman Collection; Paul P. Rao to Charles Poletti, 18 October 1938, Poletti Papers; interview with Rao; *New York Times,* 19 October 1938, p. 1; press release, Edward Lodge Curran to Poletti, HLP; *New York Times,* 5 November 1938, p. 7.

66. After 1938, as a result of the Christian Front issue, a split was noted in some Democratic party organizations, as in Brooklyn, between the Irish and Jews (William O'Dwyer, "Reminiscences," 4:670–72).

67. Interview with Ward Lange, New York City, 14 December 1972; *Roland News,* October 1935, p. 4. Lange was chairman of the Bay Ridge, Brooklyn chapter and financial secretary of the New York State chapter of the Steuben Society during the 1930s; he later became national chairman of the organization. The *Roland News* was also known during the 1930s as *Der Roland, Roland,* and, in 1939, as the *German-American.*

68. Peel, *Political Clubs,* pp. 256–57; *Steuben News,* January 1934, p. 10; *Roland News,* October 1935, pp. 3–4; January 1933, p. 3; November 1934, p. 2; *Steuben News,* January 1934, p. 10. For German-American comments on La Guardia's campaign and election in 1933 see *Steuben News,* September 1933, p. 3; *Staats-Zeitung,* 8 November 1933, p. 6.

69. For a fuller discussion of the boycott see chapter 4.

70. Richard Schween to La Guardia, 28 February 1935, LGP, Box 2564; Walter Arnold to La Guardia, 1 March 1935, LGP, Box 2564; *Brooklyn Jewish Center Review,* September 1935, p. 9; American Jewish Congress to Lehman, 18 December 1933, HLP; Bronx Jewish Democratic Club to Lehman, 22 June 1933, HLP; New Utrecht Democratic Club to Lehman, 23 March 1933, HLP: Moshe Gottlieb, "The Berlin Riots of 1935 and Their Repercussions in America," *American Jewish Historical Quarterly* 59 (March 1970): 314–18.

71. General Custer Unit of the Steuben Society of America to La Guardia, 1 August 1935, LGP, Box 2549; *Roland News,* August 1935, p. 4; *Staats-Zeitung,* 25 July 1935, pp. 1–2; *New York Times,* 30 July 1935, p. 7; 31 July 1935, p. 2.

72. Paul Windels to La Guardia, 24 July 1935, LGP, Box 2549; La Guardia to

General Custer Unit of the Steuben Society of America, 15 August 1935, LGP, Box 2549; For some Jewish comment on the masseur case see *Jewish Examiner*, 2 August 1935, p. 4; *American Hebrew*, 2 August 1935, p. 1; David Hershfield to La Guardia, 24 July 1935, LGP, Box 2549; Frank Ellenoff to La Guardia, 24 July 1935, LGP, Box 2549. The idea that the mayor had involved himself in this license dispute in order to win Jewish votes was discussed in the general periodicals of the day. See George Britt, "Will Farley Reelect La Guardia?" *Nation*, 18 March 1936, p. 342.

73. *Roland News*, November 1935, p. 2; Wagner received strong endorsements from the German press and organizations. See *Steuben News*, November 1938, pp. 5–6; *Staats-Zeitung*, 8 November 1938, p. 8; Roland Society, Yorkville Club, political flyer, HLP.

74. *Deutscher Weckruf und Beobachter*, 12 December 1935, p. 1; 28 May 1936, p. 1; 23 July 1936, p. 1. 19 August 1937, p. 3; 9 September 1937, p. 3; 25 August 1938, p. 4; German-American Bund, *Free America! Six Addresses on the Aims and Purposes of the German-American Bund* (New York: A.V. Publishing Company, 1939), pp. 3, 15–16 in American Jewish Committee Files; *American Bulletin*, 31 July 1935 in LGP, Box 2549; Bund Handbill in LGP, Box 2549; *New York Times*, 18 May 1934, p. 1; 31 July 1935, p. 2; *Steuben News*, September 1933, p. 3; September 1934, p. 5.

75. Lowi, *At The Pleasure*, p. 36.

CHAPTER 4. THE OLD WORLD INFLUENCE

1. Interview with Robert F. Wagner, Jr., 8 March 1973, New York City; interview with Ward Lange, 14 December 1972, New York City. Wagner, son of the senator, and a state assemblyman from Manhattan's Yorkville section (sixteenth assembly district), in the late 1930s, was active in German-American affairs.

2. Quoted in Donald S. Strong, *Organized Anti-Semitism in America* (Washington D.C.: American Council on Public Affairs, 1941), p. 38. Anti-Nazis always had to make special efforts to prove that they were not anti-German. See *Yorkville Advance*, 1 July 1937, p. 1.

3. *Steuben News*, April 1933, p. 1 (see also May 1933, p. 1); *New York Times*, 11 December 1934, p. 17; 28 March 1933, p. 12; Charles Oberwager to Lehman, 25 March 1933, HLP.

4. Editorial from *New Yorker Herold*, 8 December 1933, reprinted in *Steuben News*, January 1934, p. 6; *Steuben News*, July 1937, p. 1; *New York Times*, 2 November 1933, p. 11 (the *New Yorker Herold* merged with the *New Yorker Staats-Zeitung* in 1934); *Steuben News*, December 1935, pp. 1–2; February 1937, p. 7.

5. Sander A. Diamond, "The Years of Waiting: National Socialism in the United States, 1922–1933," *American Jewish Historical Quarterly* 59 (March 1970): 256–57, 261, 263.

6. Sander A. Diamond, *The Nazi Movement in the United States 1924–1941* (Ithaca, N. Y.: Cornell University Press, 1974), pp. 95–101, 110–11.

7. Ibid., pp. 111–18. Fritz Gissibl became Fuhrer of the Friends of the New Germany in November 1933 soon after a federal Grand Jury in New York indicted Spanknoebel for his failure to register as an agent of the German government. Spanknoebel subsequently fled but designated a successor before he left. Ignatz Griebl was chosen but served only from September to October 1933 since he was not the Nazi Party choice. They instead favored Gissibl. In March 1934 Gissibl was replaced by Reinhold Walter and in July 1934 Hubert Schnuch replaced him. However Gissibl controlled the Friends from behind the scenes and in 1935 again officially became leader.

8. The Friends will hereafter be referred to as the German-American Bund, since they were essentially the same organization.

9. Diamond, "The Years of Waiting" pp. 268-71; Leland Bell, *In Hitler's Shadow: The Anatomy of American Nazism* (Port Washington, New York: Kennikat Press, 1973), pp. 43-47.

10. Interview with Lange; *Deutscher Weckruf und Beobachter*, 17 October 1935, p. 1 (name later changed to *Deutscher Weckruf und Beobachter and Free American* and then to *Free American and Deutscher Weckruf und Beobachter*); Fritz Kuhn, *Awake and Act! Aims and Purposes of the German-American Bund* (New York: Deutscher Weckruf und Beobachter, 1936), pp. 3-6 (see also *Deutscher Weckruf und Beobachter*, 13 September 1935, p. 1); Diamond, *The Nazi Movement*, p. 154.

11. "Report of the Justice Department on the German-American Bund, 1939" in American Jewish Committee Files, New York City; Strong, *Organized Anti-Semitism*, pp. 30-31; United States, Department of State, *Documents on German Foreign Policy*, series D, 1:676 (hereafter cited as *DGFP*); *New York Times*, 4 April 1939, p. 8; American Legion, "Report of the National Americanism Commission" 14 March 1939 in American Jewish Committee Files; United States, Congress, House, Special Committee on Un-American Activities, *Investigation of Un-American Activities and Propaganda*, H. Rept. 2, 76th Cong., 1st sess., 1939, p. 92 (hereafter referred to as Dies Committee).

12. *New York Times*, 4 April 1939, p. 8; "Report on Bund Activities in the Bronx, Manhattan and Brooklyn," German-American Bund Folder, Anti-Defamation League of B'nai B'rith, New York City (hereafter cited as ADL); W. Phillips Davison, "German American Social Structure in New York" (M.A. thesis, Columbia University, 1941), p. 68; Diamond, *The Nazi Movement*, pp. 150-51.

13. See chapter 2, note 49, and discussion on downward mobility.

14. Diamond, *The Nazi Movement*, pp. 151, 154, 234-35; *New York Post*, 30 April 1938, in Noah Greenberg Collection, YIVO Institute for Jewish Research, New York City.

15. Diamond, *The Nazi Movement*, pp. 147, 221; Strong, *Organized Anti-Semitism*, p. 32; "Report of the Justice Department"; Strong, *Organized Anti-Semitism*, pp. 23-25.

16. The 1935 order came as a result of State Department complaints to the German government concerning Nazi activities in the United States. Information on these activities was uncovered by the House Special Committee on Un-American Activities (McCormack-Dickstein Committee), which had been created in 1934 to investigate American Nazism. United States Ambassador to Germany William Dodd also complained personally to Hitler in 1934 about Nazi activities. Hitler expressed "surprise" that this was occuring in America and promised to discontinue it. (William E. Dodd, Jr., and Martha Dodd, eds., *Ambassador Dodd's Diary* [New York: Harcourt Brace and Company, 1941], p. 88). For an illustration of the discussions going on within the German government on whether German citizens should be allowed to join the Bund, see *DGFP*, series C., 3:1113.

17. *Deutscher Weckruf und Beobachter*, 5 July 1935, p. 3; 13 September 1935, p. 2; 25 November 1937, p. 9; Kuhn, *Awake and Act!*, pp. 3-6; German-American Bund, *Free America! Six Addresses on the Aims and Purposes of the German-American Bund* (New York: A. V. Publishing Company, 1939), pp. 1-2, in American Jewish Committee Files; Leland Bell, "The Failure of Nazism in America: The German-American Bund, 1936-1941," *Political Science Quarterly* 85 (December 1970), 592.

18. The Bund itself was less under the control and direction of various departments of the German government than its predecessor, the Friends of the New Germany. However, extensive connections remained, although the Foreign Ministry, fearful of jeopardizing German-American relations, tried to sever these ties. A great deal of discussion took

place within the German government over the question of how strong the ties should be with the American Nazis. In terms of monetary assistance, the Bund did get some help. Their newspaper was partially financed through advertisements from Germany's shipping and railroad firms, and propaganda items were supplied virtually free from Germany. However, most Bund money came from dues and the sale of propaganda items and Nazi emblems (Dies Committee, *Appendix*, part 4, 77 Cong., 1st sess., 1941, pp. 1448, 1461; *DGFP*, series C., 3:1117-21; series D, 1:675-78; Bell, "The Failure of Nazism," pp. 591, 597; Diamond, *The Nazi Movement*, p. 30; Alton Frye, *Nazi Germany and the American Hemisphere, 1933-1941* [New Haven: Yale University Press, 1967], pp. 15, 82-85).

19. The German Ambassador to the United States, Hans Dieckhoff, noted in January 1938 that most German-Americans were indifferent to their German background. Even among those who had an awareness of being German, the Ambassador stated, most were unconcerned with Nazism; only a small number were Nazis. For many, this indifference and unconcern was soon to change (*DGFP*, series D, 1:667-70).

20. *American Hebrew*, 1 May 1934, p. 532.

21. *Steuben News*, February 1937, p. 3; *Roland News*, May 1936, p. 2.

22. The takeover of the United German Societies is covered in the following: United States, Congress, House, Special Committee on Un-American Activities, *Investigation of Nazi Propaganda Activities and Investigation of Certain Other Propaganda Activities, Hearings*, 73 Cong., 2d sess., 1934, pp. 113-16, 376, 387-93 (hereafter cited as McCormack-Dickstein Committee); *New York Evening Journal*, 1933, in Noah Greenberg Collection; Evelyn K. Knobloch, "The Nazi Bund Movement in Metropolitan New York" (M.A. thesis, Columbia University, 1961), pp. 11-15; Diamond, *The Nazi Movement*, pp. 122-23; Ludwig Lore, "Nazi Politics in America," *Nation*, 29 November 1933, p. 617; *New York Times*, 26 September 1933, p. 13; 26 October 1933, p. 8. It was also at this time that German Jews began to resign from all German-American organizations. See Davison, "German American," pp. 18-19; interview with Lange.

23. *New York Times*, 20 September 1935, p. 23; *American Hebrew*, 20 September 1935, p. 302; *Jewish Examiner*, 11 October 1935, p. 3.

24. The German government made an effort to influence the non-Nazi German-American organizations through various tactics. Advertisements were placed in their publications, propaganda favorable toward Germany was supplied, and reduced rate trips to Germany were provided. There were a number of German government agencies whose main purpose was to appeal to German-Americans and other Germans living abroad (Diamond, *The Nazi Movement*, pp. 194-99, 228; Frye, *Nazi Germany*, p. 54).

25. McCormack-Dickstein Committee, *Hearings*, 73 Cong., 2d sess., 1934, pp. 112-13; *New York Times*, 9 January 1943, p. 15; interview with Lange; *Roland News*, March 1937, p. 7; *Yorkville Advance*, 20 May 1937, p. 6; Diamond, *The Nazi Movement*, p. 169; German-American Bund Commands, no. 26, 15 December 1939, in German-American Bund Folder, ADL (this is a series of orders from Bund headquarters to its members).

26. Knobloch, "Nazi Bund Movement," p. 33; *New York Times*, 12 July 1939, p. 13; *Roland News*, August 1939, p. 4; interview with Lange. A split occurred in the Steuben Society over the Nazi issue, since some officers were more sympathetic to Nazi ideology than others. Gustav W. M. Wieboldt, New York State chairman, had publicly criticized the Bund not only for its divisive tactics but also for its un-American principles. Theodore Hoffmann, national chairman, who criticized only the Bund's tactics and who had complained to Hitler about this organization, also had supported in 1934 one faction of the Bund against another during an intraparty split in an effort to eliminate the Bund leaders who were criticizing the Steuben Society. There are suggestions that had

Hoffmann's favorite won the intraparty conflict, he would have supported the idea of the two organizations' joining forces. However, even with Hoffmann's attitude, the *Steuben News* did not support the Nazi racial philosophy (Diamond, *The Nazi Movement*, pp. 169–74; *New York Times*, 28 November 1934, p. 12; 3 December 1934, p. 18; 11 December 1934, p. 17; *American Hebrew*, 30 August 1935, p. 262: *DGFP*, series C, 3: 1116).

27. *Steuben News*, November 1936, p. 3; Davison, "German American," p. 15.

28. *Staats-Zeitung*, 6 March 1934, p. 6 (see also *New York Times*, 28 March 1933, p. 12); see, for example, *Staats-Zeitung*, 12 July 1935, p. 1, for a report on Berlin Riots.

29. *New York Times*, 28 March 1933, p. 13; J. Joseph Huthmacher, *Senator Robert F. Wagner and the Rise of Urban Liberalism* (New York: Atheneum, 1968), p. 268; Davison, "German American", p. 14; *American Hebrew*, 11 May 1934, p. 532; *Jewish Examiner*, 15 February 1935, p. 1; *New York Times*, 7 September 1935, p. 5; transcription of radio address by Grigat, 16 September 1935, in LGP, Box 2546.

30. Erroneous judgment—when "incorrect inferences are drawn from known facts"—is considered another unrealistic component of conflict (Robin M. Williams, Jr., *The Reducation of Intergroup Tensions* [New York: Social Science Research Council, 1947], Bulletin 57, pp. 40–41).

31. Alfred V. Solomon to editor, *American Hebrew*, 27 October 1933, p. 398; *Jewish Examiner*, 12 January 1934, p. 12.

32. Information on the controversy within the Jewish community over the boycott is from the following articles by Moshe Gottlieb: "The First of April Boycott and the American Jewish Community," *American Jewish Historical Quarterly* 56 (June 1968): 521–23, 528, 554; "The Berlin Riots of 1935 and Their Repercussions in America," *American Jewish Historical Quarterly* 59 (March 1970): 323–27; "In the Shadow of War: The American Anti-Nazi Boycott Movement in 1939–1941," *American Jewish Historical Quarterly* 62 (December 1972): 146–57.

33. George H. Gallup, *The Gallup Poll, 1935–1971*, 3 vols. (New York: Random House, 1972), 1: 130.

34. Transcript of Administrative Committee Meeting of the American Jewish Congress, 4 September 1934, Stephen Wise Papers, American Jewish Historical Society, Waltham, Massachusetts (Wise Papers hereafter cited as SWP); *Jewish Examiner*, 3 April 1934, p. 8; 12 October 1934, pp. 1, 8; 3 April 1934, p. 8; 7 December 1934, p. 1; 8 July 1938, p. 4; 7 October 1938, p. 1; Joseph Tenenbaum, *The Nazi Menace in the United States* (New York: American Jewish Congress, 1934), p. 9, in American Jewish Congress Papers, American Jewish Historical Society; *American Hebrew*, 27 October 1933, p. 389; Mary Glendon to editor, 24 November 1933, p. 30; 15 December 1933, p. 95; 9 November 1934, p. 505; 30 September 1938, p. 3; *New York Times*, 19 October 1933, p. 14; *Brooklyn Jewish Center Review*, June 1935, p. 1; May 1936, p. 1; May 1938, p. 1; *Jewish Veteran*, October-November 1937, p. 11; *New York Jewish News*, 15 October 1937, p. 4; *B'nai B'rith Magazine*, October 1933, p. 3. Numerous letters requesting investigations can be found in Joint Boycott Council Papers, New York Public Library, New York City.

35. *Staats-Zeitung*, 17 November 1933, p. 1; *American Hebrew*, 24 November 1933, p. 24; National Council of the Steuben Society of America to La Guardia, 28 April 1934, LGP, Box 2564 (see also *Steuben News*, May 1933, p. 1; August 1936, p. 5; February 1937, p. 3); *Steuben News*, May 1936, p. 8.

36. *New York Times*, 10 May 1934, p. 22; Knobloch, "Nazi Bund Movement," p. 34; Diamond, *The Nazi Movement*, pp. 137–39, 230; German-American Bund, *Free America!*, p. 4, in American Jewish Committee Files.

37. The DKV stickers were imported from Germany. See Department of Justice,

"Outline of Evidence against the German-American Bund," 1942, p. 69 in German-American Bund Folder, ADL; Diamond, *The Nazi Movement*, pp. 230, 281. See also *New York Times*, 28 March 1934, p. 19; 9 April 1937, p. 1.

38. Diamond, *The Nazi Movement*, pp. 137–39, 230.

39. Interview with Lange; interview with Rabbi Joseph H. Lookstein, New York City, 27 April 1973; *Jewish Examiner*, 20 April 1934, p. 12. During the 1930s Lookstein was the Rabbi of Congregation Kehilath Jeshurun in Yorkville which was just down the street from the New York Turn Verein where the Bund used to meet and from Bund headquarters.

40. *Jewish Examiner*, 13 April 1934, p. 1; Tenenbaum, *Nazi Menace*, p. 9.

41. *New York Times*, 15 May 1934, p. 15.

42. *Jewish Examiner*, 7 December 1934, p. 1; 7 September 1934, p. 26; interview with Lange.

43. Daniel S. Day, "American Opinion of German National Socialism, 1933–1937" (Ph.D. diss., University of California, Los Angeles, 1958), p. 2; Margaret Norden, "American Editorial Response to the Rise of Adolph Hitler," *American Jewish Historical Quarterly* 59 (March 1970): 290; Dodd and Dodd, *Ambassador*, p. 52; *DGFP*, Series C, 4: 474, 515; Series D, 1: 650, 664; New York State Branch, Catholic Central Verein of America, *Proceedings of the Annual Convention*, 1935, pp. 6, 34, 47–48; *Roland News*, May 1936, p. 2; June 1936, p. 2; Federation of German Workers Clubs to Vito Marcantonio, 18 March 1936, Vito Marcantonio Papers, New York Public Library, New York City (Marcantonio Papers hereafter cited as VMP); *New York Times*, 14 December 1936, p. 13.

44. By September 1937, according to a Gallup poll, 58 percent of Americans answered yes, 24 percent stated no and 18 percent had no opinion when asked if they thought Nazis in the United States were a menace to the country (Hadley Cantril, ed., *Public Opinion 1935–1946* [Princeton, New Jersey: Princeton University Press, 1951], p. 166). The German government was well aware of the increasingly hostile American reaction to the Bund. This led them in 1938 to order once again all German citizens in the Bund to resign (*DGFP*, Series D, 1: 664–65, 675, 709; 4: 675–78.

45. *DGFP*, Series D, 1: 719; Manfred Jones, *Isolationism in America 1935–1941* (Ithaca, N. Y.: Cornell University Press, 1966), p. 210; Bell, *In Hitler's Shadow*, p. 69; *DGFP*, Series D, 1: 664, 4: 675–78; Frye, *Nazi Germany*, p. 89; Bell, *In Hitler's Shadow*, pp. 64–65, 81–82; *New York Times*, 21 April 1938, p. 1; *DGFP*, Series D, 1: 719; 6: 34–35. A Fortune survey in October 1937 "found 62 percent of Americans neutral in their attitude toward Germany." After the Munich Conference in September 1938, which decided the fate of Czechoslovakia, Americans were no longer neutral: 56 percent now supported an economic boycott of Germany. (Jonas, *Isolationism*, p. 212). On the McNaboe Committee see chapter 5, note 9, below.

46. *Steuben News*, August 1938, p. 3; November 1941, p. 2; *New York Times*, 4 October 1937, p. 16; 3 October 1938, p. 1. The Steuben Society had made its intentions known to the German Ambassador to the United States (Hans Dieckhoff) as early as January 1938. Dieckhoff noted that Hoffmann of the Steuben Society had visited him to state that his organization would publicly disavow the Bund. The actual public disavowal, however, took many months. Perhaps the delay was caused by Dieckhoff, who might have urged a postponement of a public denunciation until he could attempt to eliminate the Bund. Dieckhoff prodded the German government to cut its connections with the Bund and direct German citizens to withdraw from the organization. Although both were done, the Bund still survived. The Steubenites therefore went ahead with their planned attack, with, most likely, little pressure from the Foreign Ministry to desist (*DGFP*, Series D, 1: 673, 677).

47. *Steuben News,* October 1938, pp. 3–5; *New York Times,* 9 October 1938, p. 39 (Hoffmann was still national chairman of the Steuben Society at this time); *Steuben News,* October 1938, pp. 5, 3; Diamond, *The Nazi Movement,* p. 321; *New York Times,* 15 September 1938, p. 9; 3 October 1938, p. 1; *DGFP,* Series D, 1: 710; *New York Times,* 3 October 1938, p. 1.

48. *DGFP,* series C, 4:565–67, 568–70; series D, 1:650; Frye, *Nazi Germany,* p. 61.

49. *New York Times,* 23 November 1938, p. 13; Sander A. Diamond, "The Kristallnacht and the Reaction in America," *YIVO Annual of Jewish Social Science* 14 (1969):198–202; "Digest of Public Opinion," *Contemporary Jewish Record* 2 (January 1939):41–43; *DGFP,* series D, 4:639–41; *Forward,* 15 November 1938, p. 4; Gallup, *Gallup Poll,* 1:128. A Fortune poll revealed that support for a boycott of German goods had jumped from 56 percent in favor in September 1938 to 61 percent after November 1938 to 65 percent after Germany absorbed Czechoslovakia in March 1939. Jonas, *Isolationism,* p. 212.

50. Bell, *In Hitler's Shadow,* p. 84; Diamond, *The Nazi Movement,* p. 170 n. 21, 277; *Staats-Zeitung,* 15 November 1938, p. 8; 7 December 1938, p. 1.

51. Dieckhoff stated in 1938 that fear of an anti-German crusade had caused the German-American community to reassert its Americanism and reject Germany's advances (Diamond, *The Nazi Movement,* p. 291).

52. *Staats-Zeitung,* 23 November 1938, p. 1; *New York Times,* 23 November 1938, p. 13; *Staats-Zeitung,* 7 December 1938, p. 1.

53. *New York Times,* 22 November 1938, p. 5. See also Victor Ridder to Lehman, 26 April 1940, HLP.

54. Address of Anton Weidman to the German and Austrian War Veterans in the United States, 2 July 1938, in HLP; *Roland News,* May 1938, p. 2; June 1939, p. 3; *New York Times,* 23 August 1939, p. 9; *Volksfront,* 4 March 1939, p. 1.

55. *American Hebrew,* 23 September 1938, p. 5; *Jewish Examiner,* 23 September 1938, p. 1; *American Hebrew,* 25 November 1938, p. 1; *New York Times,* 29 March 1939, p. 24.

56. Interview with Lookstein; *Steuben News,* September 1939, p. 3; October 1940, pp. 3, 8; *Staats-Zeitung,* 12 March 1938, p. 8; 14 March 1938, p. 8; 15 March 1938, p. 1; *New York Post,* 30 April 1938, in Noah Greenberg Collection; *Staats-Zeitung,* 16 March 1939, p. 10; 18 March 1939, p. 8; *New York Times,* 8 June 1943, p. 23; 7 October 1943, p. 21; 20 June 1945, p. 25; *Steuben News,* April 1936, p. 1; April 1938, p. 3; November 1938, p. 3; *New York Times,* 3 October 1938, p. 1. See chapter 6 for the German attitude after the outbreak of war.

57. *Irish World,* 25 July 1934, p. 4; *Gaelic American,* 21 March 1936, p. 4; 2 September 1939, p. 4. See also chapter 6 and note 4 for the Irish attitude after the outbreak of war.

58. To insure that American Catholics would accept the Nazi government, the German consulate in New York financed the publication of an English translation of the concordat. This document was then sent to Catholic priests in America (Frye, *Nazi Germany,* p. 37).

59. F. K. Wentz, "American Catholic Periodicals React to Nazism," *Church History* 31 (December 1962):401, 404–5, 408, 417; Celtic Circle, Brooklyn, to Lehman, 3 April 1933, HLP; George Q. Flynn, *Roosevelt and Romanism: Catholics and American Diplomacy, 1937–1945,* (Westport, Conn.: Greenwood Press, 1976), p. 13. The *Catholic News* also criticized Germany at this time because of the anti-Catholic actions, but notably this paper, unlike the *Brooklyn Tablet,* attacked Germany for its anti-Semitism. Revealing the influence of the German Catholics (Henry and Charles H. Ridder published this paper),

the *Catholic News* took a strong stand in its editorials and articles against Germany's anti-Jewish policies at the same time that the German-American community was doing so (*Catholic News,* 16 July 1938, p. 2; 10 December 1938, p. 10; 17 December 1938, p. 4; 20 January 1940, p. 8).

60. Dies Committee, *Hearings,* 4, 76 Cong., 1st sess., 1939, pp. 3765–66, 3888, 3946; *Appendix,* part 4, 77 Cong., 1st sess., 1941, p. 1466; Department of Justice, "Outline of Evidence," p. 89; "Report on Bund Activities," German-American Bund Folder, ADL; German-American Bund Commands, no. 27, 15 January 1940, in German-American Bund Folder, ADL; Diamond, *The Nazi Movement,* pp. 318–20. A number of anti-Semites had direct ties with the German government and were being supplied with propaganda materials (Frye, *Nazi Germany,* p. 92; Diamond, *The Nazi Movement,* pp. 193–94). See also chapter 8, below, and note 38 for discussion on Bund-Mobilizer meeting in Bronx.

61. *Il Progresso,* 18 July 1934, p. 8-S; 29 July 1934, p. 8-S; 9 January 1938, p. 8-S; 20 February 1938, p. 8-S; 27 August 1939, p. 8-S.

62. Department of Justice, "Outline of Evidence," p. 89; Dies Committee, H. Rept. 2, 76th Cong., 1st sess., 1939, p. 110; *Jewish Examiner,* 21 April 1939, p. 1; Diamond, *The Nazi Movement,* p. 319; John P. Diggins, *Mussolini and Fascism: The View from America* (Princeton, New Jersey: Princeton University Press, 1972), p. 105; Columbian League of Kings County to Lehman, 29 March 1933, HLP; interview with Charles S. Zimmerman, 30 March 1973, New York City; Resolution of American Sons of Italy Grand Lodge, 3, 4 December 1938, VMP; A. Palmeri to editor, *Jewish Examiner,* 14 April 1939, p. 4; *New York Times,* 6 June 1933, p. 15; 31 January 1934, p. 4; 8 September 1935, p. 29; 4 March 1937, p. 25; 16 March 1937, p. 1; 3 May 1937, p. 21; 15 November 1938, p. 5; 19 November 1938, p. 4; 21 November 1938, p. 4; 22 November 1938, p. 6; 10 December 1938, p. 1.

63. Quoted in William F. Whyte, *Street Corner Society* (Chicago: University of Chicago Press, 1943), p. 274.

64. Copy of interview with Gregario Morabito by Rev. Silvano Tomasi, New York City, 28 March 1969; interview with Leonard Covello, New York City, 20 February 1969; Marcantonio to William Feinberg, 12 May 1937, VMP; "Survey of Italian Fascism in New York," n.d., LGP, Box 2675; Diggins, *Mussolini,* pp. 108–9.

65. Diggins, *Mussolini,* pp. 90–94; Alan Cassels, "Fascism for Export: Italy and the United States in the Twenties," *American Historical Review* 69 (April 1964):707–11.

66. Dies Committee, H. Rept. 2, 76 Cong., 1st sess., 1939, pp. 114–16; "Report on National United Italian Associations," United States Attorney General's Office to Charles Poletti, 24 July 1940, Poletti Papers; "Survey of Fascist (Italian) Activities in New York," n.d., pp. 1–3, 12, in James Finn Papers, privately held; M.B. Schnapper, "Mussolini's American Agents," *Nation,* 15 October 1938, pp. 374–76; "The War of Nerves: Hitler's Helpers," *Fortune,* November 1940, pp. 86, 110; Diggins, *Mussolini,* pp. 94–95.

67. Interview with Covello, 20 February 1969; Robert Ferrari, *Days Pleasant and Unpleasant in the Order Sons of Italy in America* (New York: Mandy Press, 1926), p. 92; Diggins, *Mussolini,* p. 95.

68. Interview with Zimmerman. Antonini was also a vice-president of the ILGWU and later became state chairman of the American Labor Party. Others among the Italian anti-Fascist labor leaders were Vanni Montanna and Salvatore Ninfo of the ILGWU and Girolamo Valenti of the Amalgamated Clothing Workers Union.

69. Diggins, *Mussolini,* pp. 112–14.

70. Ibid., p. 116. Approximately eighty of the 129 Italian-language newspapers in the United States supported Fascism, whereas only about twelve of the 178 German-

American newspapers supported Nazism ("Foreign-Language Press," *Fortune*, November 1940, pp. 92, 102).

71. Giovanni E. Schiavo, *Italian-American History*, 2 vols. (New York: The Vigo Press, 1947), 1:535; Diggins, *Mussolini*, pp. 182–90; *Staats-Zeitung*, 4 October 1935, p. 2B. For a discussion on Italian-Irish relations as they were affected by the events of the 1930s, see chapter 5, below.

72. *American Hebrew*, 9 March 1934, p. 317; 21 September 1934, pp. 353, 364; 1 December 1934, p. 101; *Jewish Examiner*, 2 February 1934, p. 1; 9 February 1934, p. 1; *New York Times*, 18 September 1933, p. 12.

73. M. B. Schnapper, "Mussolini's American Agents," p. 374; Diggins, *Mussolini*, pp. 202, 302.

74. *Il Grido della Stirpe*, 15 May 1937, p. 3; *New York Times*, 5 June 1933, p. 3.

75. *New York Times*, 11 August 1936, p. 4; 26 May 1937, p. 1; 1 July 1937, p. 7; 17 February 1938, p. 4.

76. Ibid., 31 July 1938, IV:5; 3 August 1938, p. 13; 2 September 1938, p. 1; 11 September 1938, IV:5; 7 October 1938, p. 10; 8 October 1938, p. 7; 11 November 1938, p. 1; 11 January 1939, p. 14; 28 February 1939, p. 6; Raul Hilberg, *The Destruction of the European Jews* (Chicago: Quadrangle Books, 1961), pp. 414–16, 421–32.

77. Roberto Farinacci was a member of the Fascist Grand Council, former secretary of the party, and editor of *Il Regime Fascista* (Stephen Wise to Ferdinand Pecora, 3 December 1936, SWP).

78. *Brooklyn Jewish Center Review*, September 1938, p. 1; *Forward*, 2 September 1938, editorial page.

79. *New York Jewish News*, 9 September 1938, p. 4; *American Hebrew*, 23 September 1938, p. 4; *Jewish Examiner*, 29 July 1938, p. 1; 2 September 1938, p. 1; J. David Delman, "Jewish News and Notes," *Jewish Veteran*, November 1938, p. 18.

80. *American Hebrew*, 14 October 1938, p. 3; *Jewish Examiner*, 12 August 1938, p. 1; *Forward*, 3 September 1938, editorial page; *Jewish Examiner*, 23 September 1938, p. 3.

81. Generoso Pope to Wise, 7 July 1937, SWP; *Il Progresso*, 1 August 1938, p. 6; 28 August 1938, editorial page; 25 December 1938, editorial page; Dominick Sorrenti to editor, 2 September 1938, editorial page.

82. Marcantonio to Charles Kreindler, 14 December 1938, VMP; Marcantonio to Santo Modica, 22 February 1939, VMP; *Jewish Examiner*, 23 September 1938, p. 3; *New York Times*, 8 October 1938, p. 7; 9 October 1938, p. 38; 10 December 1938, p. 1; 12 December 1938, p. 3; 13 June 1939, p. 9; Joseph Tigani to Wise, 9 October 1938, SWP; *American Hebrew*, 29 July 1938, p. 10; *New York Times*, 21 November 1938, p. 7.

83. Joseph W. Anania, "Report on the Interdependence of Italians and Jews living in New York City and the Effects of the Recent Italian Governmental Decrees on Relations between Italians and Jews in New York City," prepared for the American Jewish Committee, 25 November 1938, pp. 4–24, 27, in American Jewish Committee Files. See also J.C.M. to editor, *Brooklyn Tablet*, 23 July 1938, p. 6, and Salvatore Marturano to editor, *Brooklyn Tablet*, 25 February 1939, p. 8.

84. *Il Progresso*, 28 August 1938, editorial page; 11 September 1938, editorial page; *New York Times*, 8 October 1938, p. 7; 8 September 1938, p. 4; 3 October 1938, p. 23.

85. The United States government also brought pressure on Mussolini to cease his anti-Semitic activities. Diggins, *Mussolini*, pp. 354–55; Philip V. Cannistraro and Theodore P. Kovaleff, "Father Coughlin and Mussolini: Impossible Allies," *Journal of Church and State* 13 (Autumn 1971): 436 n. 27, 437; *Il Mondo*, August 1939, p. 1.

86. *Il Grido della Stirpe*, 2 July 1938, p. 2; 9 July 1938, p. 2; 8 October 1938, p. 2;

26 November 1938, p. 2; 10 December 1938, p. 2; 17 December 1938, p. 2. This newspaper was published from 1923 until it was closed by the United States Government on 13 December 1941.

87. Mary Testa, "Anti-Semitism Among Italian-Americans," *Equality* 1 (July 1939): 27–28; Anania, "Report on the Interdependence," p. 4; American Jewish Committee, "Memorandum on Front Meetings, 1938," in American Jewish Committee Files. Also see the discussion on Christian Front in chapter 5.

88. Marcantonio to Santo Modica, 22 February 1939, VMP; Circular of American Sons of Italy Grand Lodge, 1 June 1939, VMP; *New York Times,* 13 June 1939, p. 9.

89. Vincenzo Beltrone, "The Jewish Question in Italy," *Il Grido della Stirpe,* 12 November 1938, p. 2; 26 November 1938, p. 2; *Jewish Examiner,* 29 July 1938, p. 1.

90. Diggins, *Mussolini,* pp. 343–44.

91. The factors which muted the explosive issue did the same to other points of friction between Italians and Jews.

CHAPTER 5. COMMUNISM, COUGHLINISM, AND THE CHURCH

1. *Brooklyn Tablet,* 25 April 1942, p. 1.

2. Ibid., 19 July 1930, p. 1; David J. O'Brien, *American Catholics and Social Reform: The New Deal Years* (New York: Oxford University Press, 1968), p. 82; Edward C. McCarthy, "The Christian Front Movement in New York City, 1938–1940" (M.A. thesis, Columbia University, 1965), pp. 135–39.

3. Gary T. Marx, *The Social Basis of the Support of a Depression Era Extremist: Father Coughlin,* monograph 7 (Berkeley, California: Survey Research Center, University of California, 1962), p. 60; O'Brien, *American Catholics,* p. 180. Among the various religious groups, Catholics indicated "the greatest approval of Coughlin both in the absolute per cent approving and in the ratio of approvers to disapprovers." The Lutherans also indicated support in that they were the only group, "with the exception of the Catholics, in which the approvers outnumber the disapprovers." In descending order of per cent approval of the radio priest, Lutherans followed Catholics (Marx, *Social Basis,* pp. 13–14).

4. Seymour Martin Lipset, "Three Decades of the Radical Right: Coughlinites, McCarthyites, and Birchers," in *The Radical Right,* ed. Daniel Bell (New York: Doubleday and Company, Anchor Books, 1964), p. 386; Marx, *Social Basis,* pp. 21–34, 50–52, 62, 67–72, 93.

5. David H. Bennett, *Demagogues in the Depression: American Radicals and the Union Party, 1932–1936* (New Brunswick, N. J.: Rutgers University Press, 1969), pp. 6, 58, 222; Samuel Lubell, *The Future of American Politics,* 3d ed., rev. (New York: Harper and Row, 1965), p. 143; James P. Shenton, "The Coughlin Movement and the New Deal," *Political Science Quarterly* 73 (September 1958): 360–66. One cannot assume that Coughlin was supported by a majority of either the Irish or German Catholics, since many in both communities denounced him. However, he received considerable and vocal support from these people and in New York City particularly among the Irish. Support for Coughlin in the City was weaker in the German community than among the Irish both before and after Coughlin became openly anti-Semitic in 1938 (interview with Paul O'Dwyer, New York City, 9 August 1973; New York State Branch, Catholic Central Verein of America, *Proceedings of the Annual Convention,* 1935, p. 13; *Roland News,* April 1935, p. 6; June 1935, p. 5; *Steuben News,* August 1936, p. 3; *Staats-Zeitung,* 16 January 1940,

p. 8). The *Catholic News* took a neutral position on Coughlin, in contrast to the strongly Coughlinite *Brooklyn Tablet*. In Philadelphia this also seems to have been true "since what little support the Charles Coughlin–backed Union Party received in Philadelphia [in 1936] appears to have been almost exclusively Irish" (John Shover, "The Emergence of a Two-Party System in Republican Philadelphia, 1924–1936," *Journal of American History* 60 [March 1974]: 999 n. 35; see also note 32, below.)

6. On a national basis Coughlin did not attract a majority of his followers to anti-Semitism (Marx, *Social Basis,* pp. 107–9).

7. On opinion concerning the general Communist threat see New York State Branch, Catholic Central Verein, *Proceedings,* 1932, p. 8; 1933, pp. 4–8; 1937, p. 5; 1939, p. 24. The Brooklyn local federation particularly noted in 1939 that it was active in fighting Communistic activities, which had grown in number and intensity in their area. *Catholic News,* 20 November 1937, p. 4; 16 July 1938, p. 4; 28 October 1939, p. 12; 11 November 1939, p. 12; 30 August 1941, p. 8; *Irish World,* 19 July 1930, p. 4; 16 July 1938, p. 4; 30 September 1939, p. 4; *Brooklyn Tablet,* 29 September 1928, p. 10; 17 February 1940, p. 10; Scanlan, "From the Managing Editor's Desk," *Brooklyn Tablet,* 26 August 1939, p. 9. The German community as a whole was not at first as united in acknowledging the threat of Communism and the need for a vigorous counterattack as were the Irish. Victor Ridder of the *Staats-Zeitung* did not initially recognize the danger of Communism. As Works Progress Administrator of the City in 1935, Ridder refused to begin an investigation of Communist activities in the W.P.A. (As he stated, "We are not going to waste time to find out whether a man is a Communist.") By 1937, however, he was much more concerned about the menace of this "ism." Dr. Frederick H. Knubel, president of the United Lutheran Church, stated in 1936 that although Communism presented a real peril to the Church, the threat did not necessitate hysterical action (*New York Times,* 18 October 1935, p. 3; 16 October 1936, p. 23; 18 April 1937, p. 1; 21 February 1938, p. 20). See also *Steuben News,* August 1936, p. 5; *Roland News,* November 1935, p. 3; October 1936, p. 4.

8. *Catholic News,* 1 January 1938, p. 4; 12 February 1938, p. 4; International Catholic Truth Society to Lehman, 2 February 1938; Catholic War Veterans, St. Albans Post no. 10, to Lehman, 15 February 1938; Ancient Order of Hibernians, Division no. 3, Kings County, to Lehman, 15 February 1938; Celtic Circle of Kings County to Lehman, 18 February 1938, HLP; *New York Times,* 21 February 1938, p. 20; Advertisement in *Brooklyn Tablet,* 22 January 1938, p. 4, asking readers to send letters and petitions to Lehman.

9. Isaacs was aware of Gerson's Communist affiliation before the appointment but felt that as long as he was qualified for the job there should be no question of his remaining in the position. La Guardia agreed to allow Isaacs to make the decision. However, in 1941, according to Isaacs, the mayor refused to support him for renomination to the borough presidency because of this decision. La Guardia was afraid of losing the anti-Gerson and anti-Communist Catholic vote (Stanley Isaacs, "Reminiscences" [Oral History Project, Columbia University, 1950], pp. 92–94, 133; *New York Times,* 23 December 1937, p. 17; 29 July 1941, p. 11). As a result of the Gerson appointment and Nazi activity, the McNaboe Committee, created by the New York State Legislature, began to investigate un-American activities. The result of its investigation was the Devany law, passed in November 1939, which barred Communists and fascists from public office, civil service, and teaching.

10. There was also suspicion that other Communists besides Gerson were in city government. See *Irish World,* 21 May 1938, p. 4; see also chapter 7, on La Guardia and the Communist issue. It was essentially the Irish press which regarded La Guardia in this way. Neither the Italian nor German press attacked the mayor for Communist sympathies.

The *Staats-Zeitung* even continued to support him. See chapter 7, discussion on 1937 and 1941 mayoralty elections and *Staats-Zeitung,* and *Brooklyn Tablet,* 6 November 1937, p. 10; *Gaelic American,* 17 September 1941, p. 4. La Guardia was always regarded more harshly in the Irish than in the German community since he symbolized to the Irish their loss of power in the City.

11. George Q. Flynn, *American Catholics and the Roosevelt Presidency 1932–1936* (Lexington, Ky.: University of Kentucky Press, 1968), pp. 174, 195, 197, 202–6, 225; O'Brien, *American Catholics,* pp. 78, 83, 170–71.

12. *New York Times,* 18 April 1937, p. 1; 17 May 1937, p. 11; 21 February 1938, p. 20; *Social Justice,* 10 May 1937, p. 5; *New York Times,* 14 August 1938, p. 31; 1 July 1938, p. 1; interview with Charles S. Zimmerman, 30 March 1973, New York City; Nathan Glazer, *The Social Basis of American Communism* (New York: Harcourt, Brace and World, 1961), pp. 105, 113, 138–39, 143. Browder testified before the McNaboe Committee.

13. See, for example, *Brooklyn Tablet,* 29 September 1928, p. 10.

14. Ibid., 16 January 1937, p. 8; Sheldon Marcus, *Father Coughlin: The Tumultuous Life of the Priest of the Little Flower* (Boston: Little, Brown and Company, 1973), p. 140; *Catholic News,* 27 August 1938, p. 4; O'Brien, *American Catholics,* pp. 108–11 (see also New York State Branch, Catholic Central Verein, *Proceedings,* 1937, p. 42; 1939, p. 39); *Brooklyn Tablet,* 23 March 1940, p. 10. German Catholics, although also concerned about the increase in government power, supported the New Deal relief programs throughout this period (New York State Branch, Catholic Central Verein, *Proceedings,* 1933, p. 35; 1937, p. 44; 1938, p. 35; 1939, pp. 33–34; 1941, p. 31).

15. *Brooklyn Tablet,* 23 March 1940, p. 20.

16. Scanlan, "From the Managing Editor's Desk," 17 January 1931, p. 11; Scanlan, 15 April 1939, p. 11; Scanlan, 6 January 1940, p. 11; *Brooklyn Tablet,* 11 June 1938, p. 11. Scanlan and the *Irish World* noted a trend toward Communism in the federal government when Roosevelt appointed Robert Lovett, an editor of the *New Republic,* to the position of government secretary for the Virgin Islands (Scanlan, "From the Managing Editor's Desk," 13 May 1939, p. 11; *Irish World,* 20 May 1939, p. 4).

17. For opinion on Mexico see *Irish World,* 27 October 1934, p. 4; 3 November 1934, p. 4; 28 January 1939, p. 4. The Brooklyn and New York local federations of the Catholic Central Verein as well as the state body adopted resolutions protesting the treatment of Catholics in Mexico (New York State Branch, Catholic Central Verein, *Proceedings,* 1935, pp. 28–29, 41).

18. J. David Valaik, "American Catholics and the Spanish Civil War, 1931–1939" (Ph.D. diss., University of Rochester, 1964), pp. 113–15; *Social Justice,* 16 January 1939, p. 7.

19. George H. Gallup, *The Gallup Poll, 1935–1971,* 3 vols. (New York: Random House, 1972), 1:132; *Time,* 23 January 1939, p. 36; Lipset, "Three Decades," pp. 385–86; Marx, *Social Basis,* pp. 83–84, 93–94. People supported Coughlin for various reasons and did not necessarily agree with him on all his political positions.

20. Tabulations on this poll indicating national origin of respondents were supplied by the Roper Public Opinion Research Center, Williams College. The poll was numbered AIPO 147 (2 February 1939).

21. On the basis of the ethnic press and organizations, had German Catholics rather than all Germans been the respondents in this poll, support for Franco would probably have registered higher. See New York State Branch, Catholic Central Verein, *Proceedings,* 1937, pp. 6, 21; 1938, p. 6; 1939, p. 33; *Staats-Zeitung,* 22 July 1936, p. 2B; *Catholic News,* 18 September 1937, p. 4; 16 October 1937, p. 4; *Il Progresso,* 28 July 1936, p. 8-S; 9 August 1936, p. 8-S; *Irish World,* 21 January 1939, p. 4; 28 January 1939,

p. 4; 18 February 1939, p. 4; 19 August 1939, p. 4; *Brooklyn Tablet,* 20 February 1937, p. 9; 28 January 1939, p. 7; Scanlan, "From the Managing Editor's Desk," 26 August 1939, p. 9.

22. Interview with Paul O'Dwyer; William V. Shannon, *The American Irish* (New York: The Macmillan Company, 1963), pp. 303, 305. Coughlin pictured himself as a defender of the faith and was able to win support on this point. However, among the Irish and German Coughlinites, there was also an anticlerical attitude evident in their attacks on the clergy who dared to criticize the radio priest. Essentially, these Coughlinites were selective in their defense of the Church, supporting or attacking those forces seen as saving or destroying Catholicism and themselves. Coughlin was regarded as a saviour, and all those who criticized him—including other clergy—were considered misguided enemies of the Church (Wilfrid Parsons, "Father Coughlin: The Aftermath," *America,* 29 June 1935, pp. 275–77; Shenton, "The Coughlin Movement," pp. 366–69. Also see the discussion later in this chapter under the heading "The Christian Front" and note 56.

23. Will Herberg, *Protestant-Catholic-Jew,* rev. ed. (New York: Doubleday and Company, 1960), pp. 146–47; *Irish World,* 3 October 1937, p. 4; 1 July 1939, p. 4 (see also 11 March 1939, p. 4; *Light,* September 1939, p. 2); *Social Justice,* 30 January 1939, p. 8.

24. *Jewish Examiner,* 26 April 1935, p. 4; Samuel Dickstein, "Reminiscences" (Oral History Project, Columbia University, 1950), pp. 35–36; *Jewish Examiner,* 24 March 1939, p. 4; *American Hebrew,* 26 April 1940, p. 3; Rev. Edward F. Brophy to Rabbi Louis Gross (editor of *Jewish Examiner*) 15 December 1939, reprinted in *Brooklyn Tablet,* 20 January 1940, p. 12. The difference in opinion between the two groups is noted by a January 1939 Gallup poll which asked respondents to state their preference for either fascism or Communism. The Catholic response showed 66 percent choosing fascism and 34 percent Communism. Among Jews, 33 percent chose fascism and 67 percent chose Communism. It has been suggested that respondents who chose fascism had Mussolini in mind (John P. Diggins, *Mussolini and Fascism: The View From America* [Princeton, New Jersey: Princeton University Press, 1972], pp. 337–39).

25. Stephen Wise to Morris Rothstein, 9 December 1941, SWP.

26. Moses Rischin, *The Promised City: New York's Jews 1870–1914* (Cambridge, Massachusetts: Harvard University Press, Corinth Books, 1964), pp. 42–44. For a discussion of Jews and Communism see Glazer, *Social Basis of American,* pp. 105, 130, 137–39, 143, 146–47, 152–67. Many Jews were opposed to Communism and to working with the Communists. The Jewish Labor Committee in 1938 rejected the cooperation of Communist groups in fighting anti-Semitism. Jews also showed sensitivity about this link. In 1935 the American Jewish Committee, Jewish Labor Committee, and B'nai B'rith issued a joint statement assailing the concept of a connection between Jewry and Communism. In 1938 an American Jewish Federation to Combat Communism and Fascism was formed in order to show that Jews also opposed Communism.

27. Valaik, "American Catholics and the Spanish Civil War," p. 244; *New York Times,* 5 April 1938, p. 11 (see also *Jewish Examiner,* 23 April 1937, p. 4; 27 January 1939, p. 4; Isadore Krigsman to editor, 2 September 1938, p. 4); Robert A. Rosenstone, "The Men of the Abraham Lincoln Battalion," *Journal of American History* 54 (September 1967):334 (see also *Jewish Examiner,* 17 February 1939, p. 7).

28. The Jewish support of the Loyalists tended to confirm, for some people, this group's Communist sympathies. Scanlan noted that "the lining up of Jews ... with the loyalist anarchists and Communists ... is a more fearful indictment than any Father Coughlin ever uttered" (Scanlan, "From the Managing Editor's Desk," 4 February 1939, p. 11).

29. References in the Irish press linking Jews to Communist and anti-Catholic influ-

ences actually appear as early as 1919, although infrequently at that point. Beginning in 1933 the number of such references increases. See Scanlan, "From the Managing Editor's Desk," 6 December 1919, p. 4; Scanlan, 14 October 1933, p. 9; *Brooklyn Tablet*, 22 February 1919, p. 4; 9 September 1933, p. 7; 7 October 1933, p. 9; 14 October 1933, p. 7; 28 October 1933, pp. 1, 9.

30. On Coughlin's influence see, for example, James O'Donnell to editor, *Brooklyn Tablet*, 17 December 1938, p. 9. On religious anti-Semitism see Alson J. Smith, "The Christian Terror," *Christian Century*, 23 August 1939, p. 1017.

31. As Covello noted, "the Italians were concerned about Communism, but not particulary so" (interview with Leonard Covello, New York City, 20 February 1969). For some Italian-American comment on Communism, see Carlo D'Alva to editor, *Il Progresso*, 3 November 1940, editorial page; Salvatore Cipolletti to editor, 6 November 1940, editorial page; John Guattroni to editor, 10 November 1940, editorial page.

32. The *Catholic News*, in contrast to the *Brooklyn Tablet*, included both editorials denouncing anti-Semitism and articles favorable to the Jews. The *Staats-Zeitung* and *Il Progresso*, in contrast to the *Gaelic American* and the *Irish World*, rejected anti-Semitism. See *Catholic News*, 16 July 1938, p. 2; 6 August 1938, p. 4; 10 December 1938, p. 10; 17 December 1938, pp. 3-4; 20 January 1940, p. 8; *Staats-Zeitung*, 15 November 1938, p. 8; 7 December 1938, p. 1; 16 January 1940, p. 8; *Il Progresso*, 1 August 1938, p. 6; 28 August 1938, editorial page. Also, observers such as the Italian ambassador to the United States noted, "The impact of Father Coughlin's words is mainly among the Irish masses" (quoted in Philip V. Cannistraro and Theodore P. Kovaleff, "Father Coughlin and Mussolini: Impossible Allies," *Journal of Church and State* 13 [Autumn 1971]: 438).

33. Maurice S. Sheehy to Isadore Hershfield, 30 May 1935, SWP; Marcus, *Father Coughlin*, pp. 83, 126; Marx, *Social Basis*, 97-98; O'Brien, *American Catholics*, pp. 171, 266, n. 44; *Social Justice*, 28 August 1939, p. 6; 4 September 1939, p. 10; 15 January 1940, pp. 3, 6; John O'Hara to editor, 3 May 1937, p. 13.

34. Coughlin in his newspaper also linked the Jews to Communism because of their support of the Loyalists during the Spanish Civil War and repeatedly asked why the Jews do not seem interested in speaking out against Communism (*Social Justice*, 20 February 1939, p. 7; 4 September 1939, p. 10). See also 9 January 1939, p. 8.

35. *Irish World*, 24 December 1938, p. 4; see also 3 December 1938, p. 4; Scanlan, "From the Managing Editor's Desk," *Brooklyn Tablet*, 26 November 1938, p. 11; *Brooklyn Tablet*, 3 December 1938, p. 1; Mary Duff to editor, 3 June 1939, p. 3; William M. Ryan to editor, 1 July 1939, p. 8; Dick O'Brien to editor, *Irish World*, 24 December 1938, p. 4.

36. T. Fitzpatrick to editor, *Social Justice*, 6 February 1939, p. 17; Patrick Walsh to editor, 27 February 1939, p. 17; *Brooklyn Tablet*, 28 January 1939, p. 3; *Catholic News*, 10 December 1938, p. 5; 17 December 1938, p. 3; Marcus, *Father Coughlin*, p. 165; George Britt, "Poison in the Melting Pot," *Nation*, April 1, 1939, p. 375.

37. Even among Catholics who opposed anti-Semitism there was resentment that only Jews seemed to receive sympathy and support. O'Brien, *American Catholics*, p. 174; *Irish World*, 3 November 1934, p. 4; *Brooklyn Tablet*, 25 March 1938, p. 3; 11 June 1938, p. 10; 22 April 1939, p. 1; 29 July 1939, p. 9; Scanlan, "From the Managing Editor's Desk," 19 November 1938, p. 11; Scanlan, 3 December 1938, p. 11. See also *Irish World*, 27 October 1934, p. 4; Scanlan, "From the Managing Editor's Desk," 14 October 1933, p. 9; Scanlan, 4 August 1934, p. 9; Scanlan, 31 December 1938, p. 9; Scanlan, 6 January 1940, p. 11; *Brooklyn Tablet*, 25 August 1934, p. 1; John Coughlin to editor, 25 August 1934, p. 6; 13 February 1937, p. 9; Benedict Fitzpatrick to editor, 28 October 1939, p. 8; H.J. Sullivan to editor, 27 January 1940, p. 8; 3 February 1940, p. 1.

Although it was quickly forgotten by the Coughlinites, the Jews did protest against the persecution of Catholics in Mexico, and there was some indication of a willingness among the Jews to support a boycott of Mexican goods (*Jewish Examiner*, 30 November 1934, p. 6; *Brooklyn Tablet*, 1 December 1934, p. 1).

38. O'Brien, *American Catholics*, pp. 171–72. Father Coughlin's Friends, *An Answer to Father Coughlin's Critics* (Royal Oak, Mich.: The Radio League of the Little Flower, 1940), pp. 9–14. Coughlin's supporters claimed that there was no evidence of anti-Semitism in his speeches. Father Curran noted that such accusations were "a rehash of what is being said by the leftist leaders of the country" (*New York Times*, 24 July 1939, p. 3).

39. Among the prominent Catholics supporting Coughlin were Herbert O'Brien, Justice of the Queens County Domestic Relations Court; Bernard T. D'Arcy, active in the Holy Name Society and Knights of Columbus in his diocese; William Goodwin, Democratic district leader of the fourth assembly district in Queens; Patrick Scanlan of the *Brooklyn Tablet*; and Father Edward Lodge Curran, head of the International Catholic Truth Society and Chaplain of the Kings County branch of the Ancient Order of Hibernians. Coughlin's continued support among various Catholic clergymen is attested to by a banquet held for him in 1941 in Brooklyn in honor of the twenty-fifth anniversary of his ordination to the priesthood. "Seated at the Dias and throughout the banquet hall were hundreds of priests not only from the Brooklyn Diocese, but from all over the Greater City" (*Gaelic American*, 5 July 1941, p. 1; see also *Brooklyn Tablet*, 26 February 1938, p. 4, and *Social Justice*, 2 January 1939, p. 11).

40. In the concept of Catholic Action, the laity would work under the direction of the Church hierarchy. The laity was first to be instructed in the Church's teachings and then organized to fulfill the goals of the program (which remained vague). Education of the laity included formal instruction as well as study and discussion groups on Catholic social principles.

41. *Social Justice*, 23 May 1938, p. 8; 20 June 1938, p. 5; 27 June 1938, p. 23; 11 July 1938, p. 23. The leader of the Front later claimed that the cause of the organization can be found "in the pages of Father Coughlin's Weekly, Social Justice" (John F. Cassidy to Christian Brother, 1939, in American Jewish Committee Files, New York City). *Social Justice* and the *Brooklyn Tablet* were sold at Front meetings.

42. *Brooklyn Tablet*, 13 August 1938, p. 2; McCarthy, "Christian Front," pp. 8–9. The Front also began to appear in other cities, such as Boston, Philadelphia, Pittsburgh, Jersey City, and Newark.

43. The organizers for the Front at this point were Jack and Harry Thorne and Marcel Honoré, musicians who were worried about Communist and Jewish influence in their union (McCarthy, "Christian Front," pp. 12–13; Dale Kramer, "The American Fascists," *Harper's Magazine*, September 1940, p. 384).

44. McCarthy, "Christian Front," pp. 13–14; American Jewish Committee, "Report on the Christian Front," 1939, in American Jewish Committee Files. In 1936 Cassidy had been chairman of a local branch of Coughlin's National Union for Social Justice and in late 1938, among his other activities, had led a Christian-American Citizens Committee against Communism.

45. McCarthy, "Christian Front," pp. 11–15; American Jewish Committee, "Memorandum on Front Meetings, 1938," in American Jewish Committee Files. July 1938 was the time when the Italian-Jewish conflict was beginning (see chapter 4, discussion on Italian anti-Semitism).

46. The membership of the Front has been estimated to be as low as 2,000 and as high as 38,500 in the New York City area. However these estimates were never verified (American Jewish Committee, "Report on the Front,"; *New York Times*, 15 January 1940, p. 3).

47. Theodore Irwin, "Inside the Christian Front," *Forum* 103 (March 1940):106–7; handbill of Christian Labor Front, in American Jewish Committee Files; *Equality,* October 1939, p. 11; "Christian American Jew Baiting," *Christian Social Action,* September 1939, pp. 107–8.

48. McCarthy, "Christian Front," p. 99; Irwin, "Inside the Christian Front," p. 106; "New York Meeting," *Commonweal,* September 1, 1939, p. 428; Alson J. Smith, "Coughlin's Platoons," *New Republic,* 30 August 1939, p. 97; Alson J. Smith, "The Christian Terror," p. 1018; Donald S. Strong, *Organized Anti-Semitism in America* (Washington D.C.: American Council on Public Affairs, 1941), p. 67; "What is the Christian Front?" *Propaganda Analysis,* 20 January 1940, p. 56. Members of the German-American Bund and Italian Fascist organizations were not allowed to join the Front since it styled itself as strictly an American organization. However, Bundists, Fascists, and Frontists cooperated with each other.

49. *New York Times,* 17 January 1940, p. 14; 18 January 1940, p. 3; 9 February 1940, p. 1; 14 February 1940, p. 1; 15 February 1940, p. 6. "New York Meeting," *Commonweal,* p. 428; Irwin, "Inside the Christian Front," pp. 106, 108; Strong, *Organized Anti-Semitism,* pp. 67–68; "Christian American Jew Baiting," *Christian Social Action,* pp. 104, 113; "What is the Christian Front?" *Propaganda Analysis,* p. 56.

50. McCarthy, "Christian Front," pp. 78, 99; American Jewish Committee, "Report on the Front"; John F. Cassidy to editor, *Brooklyn Tablet,* 19 August 1939, p. 6; "Christian American Jew Baiting," *Christian Social Action,* p. 101; "What is the Christian Front?" *Propaganda Analysis,* p. 56.

51. American Jewish Committee, "Memorandum on Front Meetings, 1938"; "Christian American Jew Baiting," *Christian Social Action,* p. 113.

52. *Brooklyn Tablet,* 7 October 1939, p. 14; Christian Front Pamphlet, in American Jewish Committee Files; Irwin, "Inside the Christian Front," p. 107; *Christian Front News Bulletin,* 24 May 1940, in American Jewish Committee Files; Christian Front Handbill, 1940, in American Jewish Committee Files; Christian Front Pamphlet in American Jewish Committee Files; American Jewish Committee, "Memorandum on Front Meetings, 1938"; *Brooklyn Tablet,* 7 October 1939, p. 14.

53. Christian Front Pamphlet, 1938, in American Jewish Committee Files; Alson J. Smith, "The Christian Terror," p. 1017.

54. See chapter 8 for a description of Front activities against the Jews in a number of neighborhoods. During the last six months of 1939 there were 238 arrests at Front outdoor meetings. Of these, 112 were for illegal activities in connection with anti-Semitism, and 126 were for illegal activities in connection with opposition to the anti-Semitism (*New York Times,* 23 December 1939, p. 6; 15 February 1940, p. 6).

55. *Brooklyn Tablet,* 23 September 1939, p. 8; Handbill, 1939, in American Jewish Committee Files; *Social Justice,* 20 February 1939, p. 2; 31 July 1939, p. 3; American Jewish Committee, "Report on the Front"; *Light,* August 1938, p. 12; *Gaelic American,* 9 March 1940, p. 3; "Father Coughlin's Trojan Horse in the Catholic World," *Equality,* March 1940, pp. 27, 31; McCarthy, "Christian Front," p. 56; Marcus, *Father Coughlin,* p. 9; *New York Post,* 9 February 1940, in American Jewish Committee Files; *Brooklyn Tablet,* 17 February 1940, p. 10; 4 May 1940, p. 22; McCarthy, "Christian Front," p. 80. Years later Patrick Scanlan would still refer to the Front as "a patriotic organization" (Patrick Scanlan to author, 4 January 1973). The *Catholic News* remained silent on the Front, neither attacking nor supporting it.

56. *New York Times,* 25 May 1940, p. 19; McCarthy, "Christian Front," p. 132. The selective anticlerical attitude of the Coughlinites was evident at a Christian Mobilizer meeting (a spin-off of the Front) in which their leader, Joseph McWilliams, commented that Coughlin was the only priest preaching Christ's gospel and that the other clergy were misguided. The selective militancy of Coughlin's followers is best illustrated by the fact

that the Frontists and Mobilizers were anti-Jewish even after the Pope had condemned anti-Semitism. These Coughlinites defined for themselves what was needed to defend the Church, and this definition was based on the realistic and unrealistic components of ethnic conflict (Lawrence Phelan, "An Evening with the Mobilizers," *Commonweal* March 22, 1940, p. 472).

57. "Christian American Jew Baiting," *Christian Social Action,* p. 104; John Roy Carlson (pseud.), *Under Cover: My Four Years in the Nazi Underworld of America* (New York: E.P. Dutton, 1943), p. 77.

58. Essentially, McWilliams had tried to take advantage of Front popularity in order to build a personal organization loyal to himself. His real aim was political power, and he used the ethnic tensions as his drawing card. In 1940 the Mobilizers became the American Destiny Party, and McWilliams was their candidate for Congress in the Yorkville area. See chapter 8, discussion on McWilliams in Yorkville. See also Dies Committee, *Executive Hearings,* 4, 76th Congress, 3d Session, 1939–40, p. 1505; *PM,* 12 June 1941, p. 19.

59. *New York Post,* 28 August 1939 in ADL Files; McCarthy, "Christian Front," p. 48; *Social Justice,* 13 November 1939, p. 5; McCarthy, "Christian Front," p. 69, n. 108; *New York Times,* 22 January 1940, p. 3; McWilliams was not Catholic, although many thought he was (*Jewish Examiner,* 27 October 1939, p. 3; 10 November 1939, p. 1; *Brooklyn Tablet,* 2 September 1939, p. 6).

60. Phelan, "An Evening," p. 472; "Christian American Jew Baiting," *Christian Social Action,* p. 106; Smith, "Coughlin's Platoons," p. 97; Phelan, "An Evening," p. 470; Dies Committee, *Executive Hearings,* 4, p. 1507; Non-Sectarian Anti-Nazi League Pamphlet, LGP, Box 2539; Dies Committee, *Executive Hearings,* 4, p. 1508; Phelan, "An Evening," pp. 470–72. For more on the Mobilizers' campaign of violence, see chapter 8.

61. Of the eighteen, one was released immediately and the others were charged not only with conspiracy to overthrow the government but also with conspiracy to steal government property.

62. The defendants claimed that the bombs were supposed to be too weak to kill anyone. The idea was only to incite a Jewish-Communist reaction, not necessarily to kill people. The actual degree of violence contemplated in relation to the bombings is a disputed point. See *New York Times,* 15 January 1940, p. 1; 25 April 1940, p. 12; 30 April 1940, p. 8; 3 May 1940, p. 8; *Brooklyn Eagle,* 15 January 1940, p. 6.

63. *Brooklyn Eagle,* 15 January 1940, p. 6; *Brooklyn Tablet,* 20 January 1940, p. 18. *New York Times,* 15 January 1940, p. 1; 6 April 1940, p. 1; 30 April 1940, p. 8; *Brooklyn Eagle,* 15 January 1940, p. 6. On the U.S. arms embargo see chapter 6; the Coughlinites feared that this repeal would draw America into war.

64. Information on the plot and the sequence of events was provided by the defendants in statements to the F.B.I. at the time of arrest, by an F.B.I. informant in the group, by F.B.I. agents who had recordings of various conversations of the defendants gathered at some of their conspiratorial meetings, and by a witness who had heard two of the defendants talking in a bar about killing the Jews and overthrowing the government. Although some of the alleged plotters admitted to discussing and planning for these events, they denied that they were actually involved in a conspiracy. They stated first that this plan was strictly a defensive one and was not to go into effect unless a Communist Revolution appeared imminent. Secondly, the defense (and most of the defendants) claimed that William Bishop and Denis Healy, the F.B.I. informant, had masterminded the plot and led the others astray. The defense accused them of having been planted by the Russian government, the American Communist Party, and high United States officials to disgrace the Front. Cassidy and the others were therefore pictured as dupes of Bishop and Healy. When Bishop took the stand, however, he blamed everything on Healy, stating

that there had been no group called the Action Committee. (Actually, Healy had joined the Action Committee a few months after it was organized and therefore had nothing to do with its formation.) The bombs and guns, Bishop said, were to be used for peaceful purposes. An unsubstantiated claim was also made that Cassidy had agreed to go along with Bishop in forming the Action Committee only because he was suspicious of him and wanted to watch him. Supposedly Cassidy had disagreed with Bishop over the latter's excessive emphasis on violence and his idea of taking over the government. The prosecution did not accept this defense claim, since Cassidy had said nothing to the F.B.I. about this when he was arrested. It was mentioned only in the trial. Although Cassidy was acquitted, doubt about his role remained. Four years later the Brooklyn Appellate Division barred him from practicing law, noting that "according to the evidence before us, the applicant deliberately advocated and counseled the unlawful formation of armed units for use against what he considered subversive elements, and he advocated that if the Government failed to act promptly these units should take the law into their own hands." See *New York Times*, 6 April 1940, p. 1; 19 April 1940, p. 10; 25 April 1940, p. 12; 30 April 1940, p. 8; 3 May 1940, p. 8; 17 May 1940, p. 13; 5 June 1940, p. 12; 12 June 1940, p. 26; 19 June 1940, p. 24; 15 November 1944, p. 29.

65. It was noted that three of those involved had become interested in the Front "as a result of local friction arising between partisan groups during the Spanish Civil War." Another individual had joined the Front because he was influenced by Coughlin and felt that he was joining a crusade sanctioned by the Church (*New York Times*, 16 January 1940, p. 3; *New York Post*, 9 February 1940, in American Jewish Committee Files).

66. The government contended that Bishop's real name was William Hrnecek, a native of Austria who had come to the United States in 1926; he claimed otherwise. It was also unknown whether he was a member of the Front, although he had spoken at Front meetings (*New York Times*, 15 January 1940, p. 1; 16 January 1940, p. 3; 20 January 1940, p. 3; 3 May 1940, p. 8; 17 May 1940, p. 13; *Brooklyn Eagle*, 15 January 1940, p. 4).

67. How their goals were to be accomplished against such great odds did not seem to concern those involved. The weapons confiscated included fifteen partly made bombs, eighteen cans of explosive material with which to make bombs, seventeen rifles, one shotgun, and various small arms, plus ammunition. However, the group did plan to enlarge their force and arms (*New York Times*, 15 January 1940, p. 1; 19 June 1940, p. 24; 25 June 1940, p. 1).

68. *Brooklyn Tablet*, 20 January 1940, p. 10; *Irish World*, 27 January 1940, p. 1; *Brooklyn Tablet*, 20 January 1940, p. 18; *Gaelic American*, 9 March 1940, p. 3 (see also 21 June 1941, p. 3); *Irish Echo* editorial, quoted in *Social Justice*, 29 January 1940, p. 3. Paul O'Dwyer also observed that the Front received strong support in the Irish community (interview with Paul O'Dwyer).

69. *Staats-Zeitung*, 16 January 1940, p. 8. The *Staats-Zeitung* was not the only one to see Coughlin's influence behind the plot. See *New Republic*, 22 January 1940, p. 99; *Commonweal*, 26 January 1940, p. 293. Coughlin attacked and disavowed the Front upon learning of the arrests, presumably because he feared that people would think he was involved in the conspiracy. However, finding this stand to be unpopular among his supporters, he quickly reversed himself, offered a vigorous defense of those arrested, and claimed that it was "opposition to Communism" which was on trial (*Social Justice* 22 January 1940, p. 3; 29 January 1940, pp. 1, 4; *Irish World*, 27 January 1940, p. 1; McCarthy, "Christian Front," p. 54).

70. *Catholic News*, 27 January 1940, p. 26; 20 January 1940, p. 8; *Il Progresso*, 20 January 1940; 23 January 1940; 29 January 1940.

71. Marx, *Social Basis*, pp. 13–15; McCarthy, "Christian Front," p. 38; Myra

Dinnerstein, "Roosevelt's Purge of John J. O'Connor" (M.A. thesis, Columbia University, 1963), pp. 133–34; see also *Jewish Examiner*, 9 December 1938, p. 12; 19 January 1940, p. 4; Saul Cohen to editor, 2 June 1939, p. 4; 4 August 1939, p. 4; *Brooklyn Jewish Center Review*, January 1939, p. 5; *American Hebrew*, 9 June 1939, p. 4; *B'nai B'rith Magazine*, February 1940, p. 176. See chapter 8 for further description of Jewish reaction to the Front.

72. Charles J. Tull, *Father Coughlin and the New Deal* (Syracuse: Syracuse University Press, 1965), pp. 202–3; O'Brien, *American Catholics*, p. 173; *New York Times*, 25 April 1939, p. 21; O'Brien, *American Catholics*, p. 173.

73. Tull, *Father Coughlin and the New Deal*, pp. 179–86, 237; Marcus, *Father Coughlin*, pp. 142–46, 161. Attempts by various elements in the Church hierarchy to control Coughlin continued nevertheless (Harold L. Ickes, *The Secret Diary of Harold L. Ickes*, 3 vols. (New York: Simon and Schuster, 1954), vol. 3, *The Lowering Clouds*, p. 382; Cannistraro and Kovaleff, "Father Coughlin and Mussolini," pp. 441–42.

74. Interview with Gerald L. Carroll, 27 February 1973, New York City (Carroll was on the executive board of this committee); *Voice for Human Rights*, September 1939, pp. 1–3; November 1939, p. 11.

75. Scanlan, "From the Managing Editor's Desk," *Brooklyn Tablet*, 8 July 1939, p. 9; Scanlan, 22 July 1939, p. 9; Scanlan, 16 September 1939, p. 11; Scanlan, 10 January 1940, p. 11; William Ryan to editor, *Brooklyn Tablet*, 5 August 1939, p. 8; Anna Crosby to editor; 16 September 1939, p. 8; George Fitzgerald to editor, 16 September 1939, p. 8 (see also *Social Justice*, 28 August 1939, p. 6); *PM*, 7 January 1944, p. 9; 21 January 1944, p. 10; *Jewish Examiner*, 4 February 1944, p. 3.

76. *Jewish Examiner*, 2 February 1940, p. 4.

77. McCarthy, "Christian Front," pp. 116–21. Spellman chose to remain silent on the Front even after he was specifically urged to take a stand. See "An Open Letter to Archbishop Spellman," *Equality*, October 1939, pp. 7–8.

78. Bishop Molloy did offer during this period some vague statements opposing intolerance and hatred (*American Hebrew*, 3 November 1939, p. 1; *New York Times*, 27 September 1940, p. 19). The *American Hebrew* was thankful for even this meager response.

79. *Bronx and Washington Heights Jewish Review*, 13 January 1944, p. 1. For Jewish reactions to anti-Semitic incidents see, for example, *Forward*, 31 December 1943, editorial page; 4 January 1944, editorial page; *Jewish Examiner*, 18 February 1944, p. 4; *PM*, 11 January 1944, p. 12.

80. *Gaelic American*, 11 March 1944, p. 1; *Brooklyn Tablet*, 8 January 1944, p. 1. The *Gaelic American* took a position similar to that of the *Tablet*, shrugging off anti-Semitism and speaking instead of anti-Christianity (*Gaelic American*, 15 January 1944, p. 2; 22 January 1944, p. 1; 5 February 1944, p. 6).

81. *Catholic News*, 8 January 1944, p. 8; 15 January 1944, p. 10; 22 January 1944, p. 10.

82. Ibid., 5 February 1944, p. 1; *Gaelic American*, 12 February 1944, p. 1; *New York Post*, 14 January 1944, p. 5. For a more detailed discussion on how Catholic cooperation finally helped to control anti-Semitism, see chapter 8, under "Conflict Resolution: Washington Heights."

83. Interview with Paul O'Dwyer; interview with Leonard Covello, 20 February 1969; Caroline F. Ware, *Greenwich Village, 1920–1930* (Boston: Houghton Mifflin Company, 1935), pp. 128, 130–31, 137. It seems that by this decade an easing of the Irish-Italian conflict occurred in other cities as well, with politics being the main area of continued rivalry and hostility. Another possible area of competition was that for position and influence within the Catholic Church. However, my efforts to secure information on

this rivalry proved fruitless. I was allowed to search through parts of the Diocese of Brooklyn archives but found no pertinent material relating to this or any other question. Other attempts to get this information—for example, by contacting various clergymen for interviews—also were unsuccessful. Still, judging from the previous experiences of these two groups in the Church, it is likely that this competition did exist to some extent. It is perhaps worthy of note that not until 1968 was an Italian-American (Francis J. Mugavero) named to lead a Catholic diocese in New York State (Brooklyn) (William F. Whyte, "Race Conflicts in the North End of Boston," *New England Quarterly* 12 (December 1939): 637–40).

84. Scanlan, "From the Managing Editor's Desk," 17 December 1938, p. 11. Over the generations the Italians were becoming more like the Irish in their religious practices. This too may have played a role in the new attitude on the part of the Irish. (see Nicholas J. Russo, "The Religious Acculturation of the Italians in New York City [Ph.D. diss., St. John's University, 1968], pp. 295–98). At the dinner for Bishop Molloy, he was presented with a decoration by the Italian Consul General in New York for having shown "deep sympathy and understanding for the New Rome, the New Italy, the Italy of today" (*Catholic News,* 17 December 1938, p. 3). *Social Justice* also defended Fascism and encouraged anti-Semitism among the Italians. For example, Italy's racial policies were defended on the basis that "most Jews were anti-Fascist." Moreover, Mussolini was hailed as "Man of the Week" by the paper in 1938 (*Social Justice,* 27 March 1939, p. 11; 23 May 1938).

85. Scanlan, "From the Managing Editor's Desk," *Brooklyn Tablet,* 17 December 1938, p. 11. See also 11 June 1938, p. 10, for an editorial opinion.

86. Salvatore A. Marturano to editor, *Brooklyn Tablet,* 25 February 1939, p. 8.

CHAPTER 6. GOING TO WAR

1. Manfred Jonas, *Isolationism in America 1935–1941* (Ithaca, New York: Cornell University Press, 1966), pp. 212–214, 215. A September 1939 Gallup poll found that 82 percent of those polled felt that Germany was to blame for the war. Only 3 percent blamed England and France. A Fortune poll in October 1939 stated that 83.1 percent of the American people desired a victory for England and France, and only 1 percent preferred that Germany win (ibid., p. 212). According to the results of a Gallup poll taken in November 1941, New York City was "more isolationist than the country as a whole" (*New York Times,* 8 November 1941, p. 34).

2. *Irish World,* 17 May 1941, p. 4. Paul O'Dwyer also noted that the desire to avoid getting into the war, based on the anti-British feeling, was strong in the Irish-American community (interview with Paul O'Dwyer, 9 August 1973, New York City).

3. *Gaelic American,* 18 January 1941, p. 4. See also 11 January 1941, p. 1. The *Tablet* warned particularly against following those "who would place us again, with India, Canada and Northern Ireland, under the English Crown" (*Brooklyn Tablet,* 18 October 1941, p. 10).

4. The German embassy, recognizing the hostility to England in the Irish-American community, tried to cultivate their support in order to bring pressure on Roosevelt to stop his aid to the allies program. However, Hans Thomsen, the German Chargé d'Affaires noted in 1941 that the Irish now perceived Germany differently from the way they had during World War I, when they had viewed Germany as a liberator. Now, he stated, the Irish were worried that Germany's war with England would create difficulties for Ireland and, owing to the clergy's influence, did not support National Socialism for ideological

reasons. However, the German embassy was active among the Irish-American press. The *New York Enquirer* worked closely with the Germans and served as their propaganda outlet in the Irish community. (William Griffin, the publisher of this paper, was indicted for sedition in 1942). Thomsen also mentioned that the *Enquirer* had provided for Embassy cooperation with such papers as the *Gaelic American*. Contacts with Coughlin and *Social Justice* also were maintained as a way of winning over the Irish. *DGFP*, series D, 11:1213–14.

5. *Brooklyn Tablet*, 23 September 1939, p. 1.

6. *Catholic News*, 16 September 1939, p. 3; *Brooklyn Tablet*, 19 August 1939, p. 3; 4 January 1941, p. 4; *Gaelic American*, 4 January 1941, p. 6; 19 April 1941, p. 1; *New York Times*, 3 April 1939, p. 18; 2 October 1939, p. 10; 24 October 1940, p. 9; 4 November 1940, p. 22; *Light*, September 1939, p. 2.

7. *Brooklyn Tablet*, 9 September 1939, p. 1; Patrick Scanlan, "From the Managing Editor's Desk," *Brooklyn Tablet*, 21 October 1939, p. 11; *Catholic News*, 9 September 1939, p. 12; 23 September 1939, p. 12; *New York Times*, 24 October 1940, p. 9.

8. Information on this poll, which was financed by the America First Committee, is contained in American Friends of Irish Neutrality Papers, St. John's University, New York City.

9. *Gaelic American*, 30 August 1941, p. 1; Mark Lincoln Chadwin, *The Warhawks: American Interventionists before Pearl Harbor* (Chapel Hill: University of North Carolina Press, W. W. Norton and Company, 1970), pp. 146–47; *New York Times*, 29 June 1941, p. 10.

10. *New York Times*, 28 October 1940, p. 5; 9 November 1940, p. 3.

11. Chadwin, *The Warhawks*, p. 148; *Irish World*, 11 October 1941, p. 4; 18 October 1941, p. 1; *Brooklyn Tablet*, 15 November 1941, p. 2; 22 November 1941, p. 7; 6 December 1941, p. 2.

12. Interview with Paul O'Dwyer. A Gallup poll taken in January 1941 asked whether Ireland should give up her neutrality and let England use Irish bases and ports. Irish-Americans answered 40 percent yes, 52 percent no, and 8 percent undecided as compared to the general public's response of 63 percent yes, 16 percent no, and 21 percent undecided. In February 1942, with America now in the war, Irish-Americans were asked whether they would like to see Ireland permit allied use of its ports. This time 72 percent answered yes, 21 percent no and 7 percent were undecided. Although the percent answering yes was less than the national average of 90 percent, it indicated a shift in Irish-American opinion on the question, although not until after American entry. *New York Times*, 22 February 1941, p. 12.

13. *Irish World*, 6 September 1941, p. 1; *Gaelic American*, 28 December 1940, p. 1; 1 February 1941, p. 1; 1 November 1941, p. 1.

14. Sheldon Marcus, *Father Coughlin: The Tumultuous Life of the Priest of the Little Flower* (Boston: Little, Brown and Company, 1973), p. 175.

15. *Jewish Veteran*, April 1941, p. 18; *Jewish Examiner*, 18 April 1941, p. 1; 15 August 1941, p. 1; *PM*, 12 June 1941, p. 12; Lawrence Phelan, "An Evening with the Mobilizers," *Commonweal*, March 22, 1940, p. 472.

16. *New York Times*, 8 February 1941, p. 1. O'Brien was also chairman of the Catholic Laymen's Committee for Peace, of which William Leonard, chairman of the Brooklyn chapter of America First, was secretary.

17. John Roy Carlson (pseud.), *Under Cover: My Four Years in the Nazi Underworld of America* (New York: E.P. Dutton, 1943), p. 260; *PM*, 12 June 1941, p. 10; Wayne S. Cole, *America First: The Battle Against Intervention, 1940–1941* (New York: Ferrar, Straus and Giroux, 1953), p. 135; *PM*, 25 May 1941, p. 19; 12 June 1941, p. 10; *Herald Tribune*, 20 May 1941 in *American Jewish Committee Press Clippings*, YIVO

Institute for Jewish Research, New York City; *New York Times,* 24 May 1941, p. 1. The *Tablet* carried numerous advertisements soliciting contributions to America First. See also Scanlan, "From the Managing Editor's Desk," 27 September 1941, p. 11.

18. Cole, *America First,* pp. 86–87. The Catholic Laymen's Committee for Peace, led by a Coughlinite, was formed in response to the German attack on Russia and its implications for American involvement. See *Brooklyn Tablet,* 20 September 1941, p. 1; *Gaelic American,* 15 November 1941, p. 4.

19. Cole, *America First,* pp. 136–37; Michael Sayers and Albert E. Kahn, *Sabotage! The Secret War Against America* (New York: Harper and Brothers, 1941), p. 207.

20. Interview with Paul O'Dwyer.

21. The Front and other active anti-Semitic isolationist groups in New York City remained predominantly Irish. There are also no reports of German-Jewish confrontation over this issue on the neighborhood level.

22. *Staats-Zeitung,* 4 September 1939, p. 6; *New York Times,* 5 September 1939, p. 10; New York State Branch, Catholic Central Verein of America, *Proceedings of the Annual Convention,* 1939, pp. 3, 40; *Roland News,* May 1939, p. 6; interview with Ward Lange, 14 December 1972, New York City; *Steuben News,* September 1939, p. 1; June 1940, p. 6; *New York Times,* 12 June 1939, p. 6.

23. *Staats-Zeitung,* 23 February 1941, p. 1 (on the Steuben Society's views, see *Steuben News,* February 1941, pp. 1, 3; March 1941, p. 4); *Staats-Zeitung,* 2 March 1941, p. 1; 11 March 1941, p. 6 (the America First Committee's attack on the lend lease bill also centered on the fear that it would give Roosevelt too much power); ibid., 22 February 1941, p. 6.

24. *Steuben News,* May 1940, p. 1; August 1940, p. 1; December 1940, p. 3; *Staats-Zeitung,* 11 December 1940, p. 6; 22 June 1940, p. 6. The *Staats-Zeitung,* which had been temporarily banned in Germany because of its earlier anti-Nazi statements, now began to publish items from the Trans-Ocean News Service, under German government control, which presented news with "the German viewpoint." The United States government closed Trans-Ocean along with the German consulates on 16 June 1941. *DGFP,* series D, 8:432.

25. German-American Bund, *Program of the National Convention,* August 1941 in German-American Bund Folder, ADL; Geoffrey S. Smith, *To Save a Nation: American Countersubversives, the New Deal and the Coming of World War II* (New York: Basic Books, 1973), pp. 151–52; Sander A. Diamond, *The Nazi Movement in the United States 1924–1941* (Ithaca, New York: Cornell University Press, 1974), p. 326.

26. Smith, *To Save a Nation,* p. 229, n. 5.

27. *New York Times,* 9 May 1941, p. 12; Cole, *America First,* p. 104; Hans Thomsen, the German chargé d'affairs in the United States, had urged the Foreign Ministry in 1939 to avoid giving any indication of support for the American isolationists, since they were already under suspicion of working for Hitler. He felt that obvious backing would weaken the isolationist movement. However, this request did not prevent the German government from covertly aiding the America First Committee and the No Foreign Wars Committee and from helping to organize the Make Europe Pay War Debts Committee and the Islands for War Debts Committee. The Bund, which often disregarded Thomsen's suggestion, remained the most obvious Nazi tie to the isolationist cause (*DGFP,* Series D, 8:127; 11:949–50; *New York Times,* 9 October 1941, p. 1; German-American Bund Commands, no. 23, 8 September 1939; no. 41, 20 January 1941—both in German-American Bund Folder, ADL).

28. Steuben Society of America, *20th Anniversary and Testimonial Steuben Day Banquet,* 17 September 1939 (New York: Steuben Society of America, 1939); *Staats-Zeitung,* 2 September 1939, p. 6; 22 May 1940, p. 8; *Volksfront,* 9 September 1939, p. 1;

Roland German-American Democratic Society of New York to La Guardia, 5 September 1939, Box 2674, LGP; Roland German-American Democratic Society to Members, 1 June 1940, HLP.

29. *New York Times,* 15 June 1940, p. 8; 2 January 1941, p. 6; 3 March 1941, p. 5; 28 July 1941, p. 6; 4 August 1941, p. 4; interview with Robert F. Wagner, Jr., 8 March 1973, New York City; Chadwin, *The Warhawks,* p. 187; J. Joseph Huthmacher, *Senator Robert F. Wagner and the Rise of Urban Liberalism* (New York: Atheneum, 1968), pp. 269–70; *New York Times,* 20 May 1940, p. 40. Included in the German-American Congress for Democracy was, for example, Eugene Grigat's Friends of German Democracy (see chapter 4, discussion on early German-American anti-Nazis).

30. *Steuben News,* August 1941, p. 4; *New York Times,* 15 September 1940, p. 47; see also 12 July 1939, p. 13, for similar comments about the German-American Conference; and see the discussion on Victor Ridder's difficulties with a similar charge in chapter 4.

31. *New York Times,* 4 March 1941, p. 22. This became increasingly true as Nazi spies were captured. One ring, discovered in 1941, included some German-Americans from Queens. Others arrested were former Bund members (ibid., 31 August 1941, p. 16; 31 December 1941, p. 9).

32. *Steuben News,* April 1941, p. 4; German-American Conference Relief Fund, *Annual Report, 1940,* p. 3; *New York Times,* 28 July 1941, p. 6; August B. Recholtz to La Guardia, 8 October 1941, Box 2546, LGP. See also New York State, Department of Labor, Bureau of Research and Statistics, *Survey of Industries and Employment,* 1941, pp. 2–3. This report noted discrimination in employment related to defense.

33. *Steuben News,* July 1940, p. 1.

34. John P. Diggins, *Mussolini and Fascism: The View From America* (Princeton, New Jersey: Princeton University Press, 1972), pp. 345–46.

35. *Il Progresso,* 3 September 1939, p. 8; 5 September 1939, p. 10; 10 September 1939, p. 8; 3 September 1939, p. 1.

36. *New York Times,* 11 June 1940, p. 1; see chapter 7, discussion on the impact which this statement had on Roosevelt's Italian support.

37. *Il Progresso,* 7 June 1940, p. 1; see also 11 June 1940, p. 1; 23 June 1940, p. 1. Some of the organizations that restated their loyalty to America were the Order of the Sons of Italy in America, the American Sons of Italy Grand Lodge, the United Italian-American League (representing 500 Italian-American civic, religious, social, and political organizations in New York State), and the Columbia Associations of New York City (representing Italian-Americans in civil service). Individuals included such notables as Luigi Antonini and Charles Poletti (*New York Times,* 12 June 1940, p. 18; 14 June 1940, p. 10; 16 June 1940, p. 19; 28 June 1940, p. 15; 13 October 1940, p. 30; Columbia Associations of New York City to Roosevelt, 12 October 1940, Franklin D. Roosevelt Papers, OF233A, Franklin D. Roosevelt Library, Hyde Park, New York).

38. *New York Times,* 14 June 1940, p. 10; Diggins, *Mussolini,* p. 350; *New York Times,* 12 June 1940, p. 17. The idea for the Italian Emergency Committee had been suggested by Antonini (Luigi Antonini to La Guardia, 12 June 1940, LGP, Box 2675).

39. *Il Mondo,* August 1940, p. 1; Diggins, *Mussolini,* pp. 343–47.

40. *Il Progresso,* 11 June 1940, p. 1; 24 June 1940, p. 2; 22 June 1940, p. 2; 22 June 1940, p. 6; 24 June 1940, p. 2; 25 June 1940, p. 6; 27 June 1940, p. 6.

41. There were a number of complaints concerning discrimination against Italians by this time (Italian Bronx Community House to Lehman, 18 March 1941, HLP; Louis Franchi to La Guardia, 30 April 1941, and Armand Sabatini to La Guardia, 30 April 1941, LGP, Box 2546). Pressure on Pope from outside sources is illustrated by the American government's initiation of an investigation of his activities in 1941 (Diggins, *Mussolini,*

pp. 347–48). In addition, the Italian consulates and agencies in the United States were closed in June 1941.

42. *Il Progresso,* 25 March 1941, p. 10; 2 March 1941; 14 April 1941, in Roosevelt Papers, PPF 4617. Harold L. Ickes, *The Secret Diary of Harold L. Ickes,* 3 vols. (New York: Simon and Schuster, 1954), vol. 3, *The Lowering Clouds,* pp. 463–64, 477. Pope even tried to become a member of and give a contribution to the interventionist Fight for Freedom Committee at this time. His application and contribution were rejected because of his earlier pro-Fascist position. This committee supported all aid to the Allies including war (Chadwin, *The Warhawks,* pp. 219–20.

43. *Il Progresso,* 12 September 1941, p. 10.

44. *New York Times,* 23 June 1940, p. 13; 24 June 1940, p. 17; 17 February 1941, p. 7; 30 October 1941, p. 18; *Jewish Veteran,* January 1941, p. 6; July 1941, p. 4; *Jewish Examiner,* 21 February 1941, p. 1 (see also *New York Times,* 5 January 1941, p. 35, and 19 January 1941, p. 34, on the favorable response of Rabbis in New York City to the President's policies); Chadwin, *The Warhawks,* p. 178.

45. *New York Times,* 24 June 1940, p. 34; 6 May 1940, p. 6. Rabbi Wise was involved in the organizational meeting of the New York Chapter of the Committee to Defend America by Aiding the Allies. This chapter merged with the New York Chapter of the Fight for Freedom Committee in August 1941 and urged all-out American participation in the war.

46. Cole, *America First,* pp. 131–32; *New York Times,* 25 May 1941, p. 3; *Jewish Veteran,* September–October 1941, p. 18; Chadwin, *The Warhawks,* pp. 213–15; *Jewish Veteran,* December 1940, p. 8; *Jewish Review,* December 1941 (see also *American Hebrew,* 17 January 1941, p. 1; *Jewish Examiner,* 21 February 1941, p. 1; 4 July 1941, p. 4).

47. *New York Times,* 12 September 1941, p. 2; 13 September 1941, p. 1.

48. Ibid., 20 September 1941, p. 5; *Brooklyn Eagle,* 19 September 1941, in American Jewish Committee Press Clippings, YIVO Institute for Jewish Research, New York City; *New York Times,* 20 September 1941, p. 5 (see also *Jewish Veteran,* September–October 1941, p. 18).

49. The Keep America Out of War Congress also attacked the anti-Jewish aspects of the speech (*New York Times,* 21 September 1941, p. 27); *Chicago Herald-American,* 17 September 1941, in American Jewish Committee Press Clippings; *Brooklyn Tablet,* 27 September 1941, p. 1.

50. *New York Times,* 21 September 1941, p. 12.

51. Ibid., 12 December 1941, p. 22; *Steuben News,* January 1942 (see, for example, the front page letter to Roosevelt); *New York Times,* 11 January 1942, p. 27; 21 November 1943, p. 7; interview with Ward Lange, 14 December 1972; *Steuben News,* April 1942, p. 2.

52. *Steuben News,* February 1943, pp. 1–2; April 1943, p. 1; August 1943, p. 1; September 1943, p. 1; February 1944, p. 1; August 1944, p. 1 (see also *New York Times,* 21 May 1943, p. 7; 4 July 1943, p. 11); *Steuben News,* February 1944, p. 2. For information on the Peace Now movement see Dies Committee, *Report on the Peace Now Movement,* H. Rept. 1161, 78 Cong., 2d sess., 1944.

53. *Il Progresso,* 12 December 1941, p. 1; 14 December 1941, pp. 3, 9; 21 December 1941, p. 16 (see also Pope to Stephen T. Early, 16 December 1941, Roosevelt Papers, PPF 4617); *New York Times,* 12 December 1941, p. 22; *Brooklyn Eagle,* 12 September 1942, p. 2; Italian-American Labor Council, *First Annual Report,* 1941–1942. This council was organized on 20 December 1941 as a central body of Italian-American organized workers. Luigi Antonini was president.

54. New York State War Council, Committee on Discrimination in Employment,

Report, 24 September 1942, Poletti Papers; Department of Labor, *Survey of Industries and Employment,* p. 2. One of the main reasons for the formation of the Italian-American Labor Council was to prevent discrimination against their ethnic group.

55. The government did not remove the enemy alien classification from non-citizen German-Americans, although curfew restrictions were eliminated in December 1942.

56. *Il Progresso,* 13 December 1941, p. 10; Pope to Stephen T. Early, 16 December 1941, Roosevelt Papers, PPF 4617; *New York Times,* 12 December 1941, p. 22. La Guardia was one of the first to note the theme that Italy was under the control of Germany and in reality a conquered nation (*New York Times,* 8 May 1941, p. 11).

57. Diggins, *Mussolini,* pp. 403, 405. At this time Pope also began his rapprochement with Roosevelt, which culminated in their meeting in October 1944. See Henry F. Pringle to William D. Hasset, 13 March 1943; Roosevelt Papers, PPF 4617; Memorandum for James M. Barnes, Eugene Casey, Jonathan Daniels and David Niles, 4 April 1944, ibid. See also chapter 7, note 75. On the divisiveness in the Italian-American community concerning the future of Italy, see Diggins, *Mussolini,* pp. 402–21.

58. *Gaelic American,* 13 December 1941, p. 1; *Brooklyn Tablet* 13 December 1941, p. 1; *Irish World,* 20 December 1941, p. 4. For an indication of Irish-American opinion after American entry see n. 12 this chapter. The American Friends of Irish Neutrality disbanded on 13 December 1941 in order to focus their attention on winning the war (Publicity Release, 13 December 1941, American Friends of Irish Neutrality Papers).

59. *New York Post,* 28 March 1944; *Herald Tribune,* 2 May 1944, in American Jewish Committee Press Clippings; *Gaelic American,* 4 December 1943, p. 4.

60. Marcus, *Father Coughlin,* p. 205.

CHAPTER 7. WINNING THE VOTES

1. O'Brien was mayor at the time, having won a special election in 1932 to complete James J. Walker's term. Immediately following Walker's resignation McKee had been acting mayor until the special election could be held.

2. The Recovery party had been organized at the request of Roosevelt, who instructed Ed Flynn, Democratic leader of Bronx County, and Jim Farley to persuade McKee to run, with probable help from the White House. The president was angry at Tammany for not supporting his nomination the previous year and wished to secure control of the New York City Democratic organization (Jeremiah Mahoney, "Reminiscences" (Oral History Project, Columbia University, 1949), p. 129; Paul Windels, "Reminiscences" (Oral History Project, Columbia University, 1949–1950), p. 79; Edward Flynn, "Reminiscences" (Oral History Project, Columbia University, 1950), p. 19; *New York Times,* 23 October 1933, p. 4; Arthur Mann, *La Guardia Comes to Power 1933* (Philadelphia: J. B. Lippincott Company, 1965), pp. 95–96, 105, 116.

3. Roosevelt never endorsed McKee. Adolf Berle, one of the president's advisors, noted on a number of occasions that Roosevelt was neutral in this campaign and that McKee was not the New Deal candidate. McKee nevertheless pictured himself as such (*New York Times,* 2 November 1933, p. 1; Mann, *La Guardia Comes to Power,* pp. 105, 151; Charles Garrett, *The La Guardia Years: Machine and Reform Politics in New York City* [New Brunswick, N.J.: Rutgers University Press, 1961], p. 109).

4. *New York Times,* 22 October 1933, p. 27; 28 September 1933, p. 2; William E. Ringel to Victor Ridder, 24 July 1934, LGP, Box 2702; *Steuben News,* September 1933, p. 3; *Roland News,* November 1933, p. 5; December 1933, p. 2.

5. *New York Times,* 7 October 1933, p. 17; *Irish World,* 21 October 1933, p. 4;

Gaelic American, 21 October 1933, p. 5 (see also 15 July 1933, p. 4); 14 October 1933, p. 5; Patrick S. Hickey to La Guardia, 25 September 1933, LGP, Box 2717.

6. *Il Progresso,* 5 November 1933, p. 1; Italian-American Civic Association to La Guardia, 15 September 1933, LGP, Box 2715; United Italian-American Democratic Club to La Guardia, 23 September 1933, LGP, Box 2719; Italian Medical Society of Brooklyn to La Guardia, 4 December 1933, LGP, Box 2717; Joseph Graziano to La Guardia, 4 November 1933, LGP, Box 2717. Numerous letters expressing support are scattered throughout the La Guardia papers.

7. Mann, *La Guardia Comes to Power,* p. 140.

8. In 1929, for example, when he was the Republican mayoral candidate, La Guardia had suggested that American soldiers be sent to Palestine to aid the Jews against the Arabs (*New York Times,* 27 August 1929, p. 3; 5 September 1929, p. 2; see also Lawrence H. Fuchs, *The Political Behavior of American Jews* [Glencoe, Illinois: The Free Press, 1956], pp. 156–57). Although La Guardia was part Jewish (his mother was Jewish), this was not known to the general public until later in the decade. Even then, however, neither the Jewish community nor La Guardia himself recognized him as Jewish in any way. By nationality background and culture he was Italian, and by religion an Episcopalian. Later on, when his Jewish heritage was brought up, he remarked, "I never thought that I had enough Jewish blood in my veins to justify boasting of it" (quoted in Arthur Mann, *La Guardia: A Fighter Against His Times, 1882–1933* [Philadelphia: J. B. Lippincott Company, 1959], p. 330).

9. The instability of the Jewish vote prior to 1933 is discussed in Mann, *La Guardia Comes to Power,* p. 142, and Thomas Henderson, "Tammany Hall and the New Immigrants, 1910–1921" (Ph.D. diss., University of Virginia, 1973). On the ethnic composition of the tickets see chapter 3, above.

10. Mann, *La Guardia Comes to Power,* p. 113.

11. Joseph V. McKee, "A Serious Problem," *Catholic World* 101 (May 1915): 210–12. This article was reprinted in the *New York Times* on 17 October 1933, p. 2. According to one of his campaign managers, La Guardia had known about McKee's article and originally had decided not to use it, but finally had done so because of McKee's use of the anti-Semitic issue. The article meanwhile had been removed from all of the city's libraries, and La Guardia's staff had to go to the Congressional Library in order to secure a copy. McKee, according to Nathan Straus, Jr., a prominent Jew who ran as the Recovery party's candidate for president of the board of aldermen, was well aware of the danger of this article. Straus felt that he had been put on the ticket to counteract any political damage among the Jews in case the article was revealed (Paul Windels, "Reminiscences, Additional Interview" (Oral History Project, Columbia University, 1953), pp. 14–17; Nathan Straus, Jr., "Reminiscences" (Oral History Project, Columbia University, 1950), p. 80.

12. *New York Times,* 16 October 1933, p. 8; 17 October 1933, p. 1; Mann, *La Guardia Comes to Power,* pp. 114–15; *New York Times,* 18 October 1933, p. 16.

13. Samuel Untermyer to Herbert Lehman, Felix Warburg, Henry Morgenthau, and Jonah B. Wise, 23 October 1933, HLP; Stephen Wise to Herbert B. Swope, 23 October 1933, SWP.

14. See, for example, Harry B. Kossove to La Guardia, 17 October 1933, LGP, Box 2718; Harry L. Koenig to La Guardia, 18 October 1933, LGP, Box 2718. There are many letters in the La Guardia Papers which comment on this issue.

15. *Jewish Examiner,* 20 October 1933, p. 1; Mann, *La Guardia Comes to Power,* p. 115; *American Hebrew,* 3 November 1933, p. 1; *New York Times,* 23 October 1933, p. 1.

16. *New York Times,* 1 November 1933, p. 3; 2 November 1933, p. 3; Press Release, 1 November 1933, LGP, Box 2716; *Jewish Examiner,* 3 November 1933, p. 8.

17. *New York Times,* 22 October 1933, p. 1. 23 October 1933, p. 6; *Steuben News,* November 1933, p. 1. The *New York Daily News* interpreted O'Brien's action as a political move.

18. Joseph V. McKee Independent Citizens Committee Pamphlet, n.d., LGP, Box 2717; *New York Times,* 26 October 1933, p. 1; O'Brien Pamphlet, n.d., LGP, Box 2717.

19. Socioeconomic data for the election districts was determined from New York Times, Daily News, and Herald Tribune, *New York City Market Analysis* (New York: 1934), and New York Times, Daily News, Mirror, and Journal-American, *New York City Market Analysis* (New York: 1943). In these economic surveys the neighborhoods of New York were analysed by using census tract information gathered from the 1930 and 1940 census. The economic status of each tract and each neighborhood was determined on the basis of annual family expenditure (based on rent or home value information). Census tract and election district boundaries were matched against the maps provided in the *Market Analysis* thus enabling me to secure a class description of the voting units with which I was working.

Because of the Depression, class categorization of the census tracts, and therefore election districts, changed from 1930 to 1940 as many were downwardly mobile. Only the Jewish election districts were represented in all class divisions in 1933 (based on the 1930 census data) and in all but the upper-middle class in the 1937 and 1941 elections (based on the 1940 census data). The Irish election districts in 1933 were represented only in the middle-middle and lower-middle class. In the 1937 and 1941 elections the same Irish election districts were categorized in the lower-middle class and lower class. The German election districts in 1933 were found in upper-middle, middle-middle, and lower-middle-class tracts. In 1937 and 1941 they were in the middle-middle, lower-middle, and lower class. The Italian areas were represented in the middle-middle and lower-middle class as well as the lower class in 1933. For the 1937 and 1941 election they were found in the lower-middle and lower class. Although there were certainly Irish, Germans, and Italians in other class divisions, they could not be found in election districts that were comprised of at least 50 percent of their own group and that retained the same boundaries over the years.

20. In a few election districts where Tammany (but not Democratic) boss control had been diluted, the lower-class Jewish vote went to McKee rather than O'Brien. The McKee vote in the lower-middle-class Jewish areas was 22 percent, and in the lower-class Jewish areas, it was 21 percent.

21. Jewish discontent with Tammany had been revealed in the 1932 special mayoralty election when O'Brien ran far behind Lehman and Roosevelt in Jewish areas. Many Jewish votes went to the Socialist Morris Hillquit (Mann, *La Guardia Comes to Power,* pp. 141–42).

22. Robert Moses, *La Guardia, A Salute and A Memoir* (New York: Simon and Schuster, 1957), pp. 37–41. See also Fuchs, *Political Behavior,* pp. 156–57.

23. Steuben Society of America, *Bulletin,* 5 March 1937, in LGP, Box 758; *New York Times,* 7 March 1937, p. 28; George Britt, "Will Farley Re-elect La Guardia?" *Nation,* 18 March 1936, p. 342; editorial, *Daily News,* 1937, in LGP, Box 758.

24. *New York Sun,* 23 August 1937, in American Jewish Committee Press Clippings, YIVO Institute for Jewish Research, New York City.

25. *Deutscher Weckruf und Beobachter,* 9 September 1937, p. 3; *New York Times,* 10 September 1937, p. 12 (see also *Staats-Zeitung,* 31 October 1937, p. 9); *Steuben News,* 3 June 1937, p. 3. That some resentment against La Guardia existed in the German-American community has been confirmed in an interview with Ward Lange, 14 December 1972, New York City.

26. *Deutsches Volksecho* to La Guardia, 25 August 1937, LGP, Box 2721; *Staats-Zeitung,* 18 September 1937, p. 2B; 4 November 1937, p. 2B.

27. Gustav W. M. Wieboldt, for example, former chairman of the New York State Council of the Steuben Society, was appointed a city magistrate in April 1936 to fill an unexpired term, reappointed in May 1937 for a full term, and elevated to the Court of Special Sessions in 1938.

28. Ernst L. Graue to La Guardia, 21 October 1937, LGP, Box 2721; *Roland News,* October 1937, p. 5.

29. *New York Times,* 5 August 1937, p. 11; 8 August 1937, p. 25.

30. Mahoney political pamphlet, 1937, LGP, Box 2722; The *Morning Journal,* 13 October 1937, p. 12, and the *Day,* 13 October 1937, p. 3, in LGP, Box 2722.

31. For some Jewish comment on the parade see anonymous to La Guardia, 1 November 1937; Sidney Strykes to La Guardia, 28 October 1937; Jewish War Veterans, Borough Park Post, to La Guardia 27 October 1937; Temple Israel, Long Beach, to La Guardia, 28 October 1937; Young Folks Jewish Social Clubs to La Guardia, 26 October 1937; R. Zavolin to La Guardia, 29 October 1937—all in LGP, Box 758.

32. Copy of Goldstein radio address, 26 October 1937, and War Veterans Committee pamphlet, in LGP, Box 758 (see also *Jewish Veteran,* December 1937, p. 14); The *Day,* 1 November 1937, in American Jewish Committee Press Clippings.

33. Press Release, 30 October 1937, LGP, Box 758; *New York Jewish News,* 12 November 1937, p. 7; *Jewish Veteran,* December 1937, p. 14.

34. *Forward,* 3 November 1937, editorial page; 4 November 1937, editorial page; *American Hebrew,* 12 November 1937, p. 1; the *Day,* 1 November 1937, in American Jewish Committee Press Clippings; *New York Jewish News,* 12 November 1937, p. 4; *Forward,* 4 November 1937, editorial page.

35. *New York Times,* 27 August 1937, p. 7; 28 October 1937, pp. 1, 19; 1 November 1937, p. 3; 2 November 1937, p. 1; Mahoney Pamphlet, in LGP, Box 2722; Mahoney advertisement in *Irish World,* 20 October 1937, p. 6. It was the Irish rather than the German Catholics who accused La Guardia of having Communist sympathies (see chapter 5, note 10).

36. Irish American Non-Partisan Committee for La Guardia, Publicity Release, 1937, LGP, Box 2721. Also see chapter 3, discussion on Irish attitudes toward La Guardia.

37. Political Pamphlet in LGP, Box 2721. That this tactic was used was substantiated in an interview with Paul P. Rao, 7 August 1973, New York City. Rao was chairman of the Italian-American Division of the Mahoney Campaign. See also *Yorkville Advance,* 15 January 1937, p. 3, on Rao's comments concerning the mayor's appointments.

38. Political Pamphlet in LGP, Box 2721. Also see chapter 3, discussion on Democrats' efforts to win the Italian vote after 1933.

39. Being a Tammany district leader who was the choice of the other county Democratic organizations, Mahoney could not seriously offer himself as a reformer or good-government candidate.

40. Richard J. Stack to La Guardia, 25 October 1937, LGP, Box 2722.

41. According to one political analyst, the German-Americans, because of Mahoney's and La Guardia's anti-German statements, actually preferred U. S. Senator Royal Copeland. Copeland ran against Mahoney and La Guardia in the Democratic and Republican primaries, respectively, but lost in both. His defeat left this community with little choice. Copeland was Tammany's original selection. He was also associated with an anti-New Deal position (Max Lerner, "Tammany's Last Stand," *Nation,* 11 September 1937, p. 256).

42. *Roland News,* October 1937, p. 5.

43. *Jewish Examiner,* 4 February 1939, p. 4; 7 July 1939, p. 1; 14 July 1939, p. 4; *Jewish Veteran,* January 1940, p. 12; *New York Jewish News,* 3 February 1939, p. 4;

Brooklyn Jewish Center Review, June 1939, p. 1; Abraham Cahan, editor of the *Forward,* to La Guardia, 26 June 1939, LGP, Box 2539; Rabbi Louis Spitz to editor, *American Hebrew,* 28 July 1939, p. 7; *Equality,* September 1939, pp. 14–15.

44. *New York Times,* 21 July 1939, p. 5; 23 December 1939, p. 6. The Mayor may actually have thought the situation was under control, since two of his undercover agents reported in November 1939 that anti-Semitism was no longer an acute problem. This was a premature conclusion, since just two months later, in January 1940 the Front was involved in a spectacular treason plot (see chapter 5). The Mobilizers continued to be active through 1940, and the Front reappeared in 1941. For the report of the undercover agents see Nathan Frankel and Byrnes McDonald, ''Final Report to Mayor from Committee to Investigate Anti-Semitic Groups in New York City—Confidential,'' 6 November 1939, LGP, Box 2539.

45. The police also arrested people who unlawfully interfered with the anti-Semitic speakers (*New York Times,* 23 December 1939, p. 6; 15 February 1940, p. 6). In cases of picketing and strikes (and presumably other forms of protest), La Guardia was of the opinion that if the malcontents were allowed to demonstrate freely, they would not resort to violence (Garrett, *The La Guardia Years,* p. 386).

46. O'Dwyer was speaking about Herbert O'Brien, a leading Coughlinite, whom La Guardia had appointed as a justice in the Queens County domestic relations court (*New York Times,* 19 September 1941, p. 1).

47. Ibid., 27 October 1941, p. 10; 21 October 1941, p. 19; 22 October 1941, p. 17; O'Dwyer pamphlet in LGP, Box 2735.

48. Murray E. Plager to La Guardia, 22 October 1941, LGP, Box 2546; *Jewish Examiner,* 31 October 1941, p. 4; 29 March 1940, p. 4. William O'Dwyer suggested in an interview years later that the mayor had not wanted to eliminate the Front because he had wanted to avoid antagonizing Catholics and at the same time had wanted to use this issue to win Jewish support. O'Dwyer noted that La Guardia ''could always shake his fist at Hitler, or say something dramatic, and hold onto the Jews, who in the main were not alert to what La Guardia was doing to them with the Christian Front.'' Also, as O'Dwyer stated, the mayor benefited from the Front because it kept the Jews and Irish divided and therefore split the Democratic party in certain areas (William O'Dwyer, ''Reminiscences'' (Oral History Project, Columbia University, 1960–62), 4: 670–72; 1: 151–52.

49. *New York Times,* 23 October 1941, p. 15; La Guardia to Murray E. Plager, 24 October 1941, LGP, Box 2546; *New York Times,* 28 October 1941, p. 19; Trade Union Committee to Elect Labors' Candidates, Pamphlet, LGP, Box 2729; *New York Times,* 20 October 1941, p. 20.

50. *New York Times,* 15 October 1941, p. 1; 19 October 1941, p. 37; interview with Paul O'Dwyer, New York City, 9 August 1973; *New York Times,* 19 September 1941, p. 1.

51. Interview with Paul O'Dwyer. Less than a week after O'Dwyer's attack on the anti-Semites, the Coughlinites formed the American Rock Party on a platform of isolationism and anti-Communism. They decided to run as their candidate William J. Goodwin, Democratic district leader of the fourth assembly district in Queens, a member of the editorial board of the *Tablet,* and a man who was extremely active in the Coughlin movement and anti-war crusade. However, the elections board voided the nominating petition of this party because of an insufficient number of signatures. The lack of signatures most likely was the result of the time element, since this was a hastily organized party which was not even suggested until after the campaign had begun. The party's followers probably voted for O'Dwyer—at least, before O'Dwyer's attack, this group was pictured as being ready to support his candidacy. Immediately before the election, *Social Justice* excused O'Dwyer's critical statements by noting that he was forced to say those things because of Jewish pressure. Therefore the go ahead to vote for O'Dwyer was given

(*New York Times,* 24 September 1941, p. 16; 22 October 1941, p. 16; *Social Justice,* 3 November 1941, p. 7).

52. *New York Times,* 19 September 1941, p. 1; 14 October 1941, p. 20. See chapter 5, note 9, for more on the Gerson issue.

53. The *Day,* 13 October 1941, in LGP, Box 2735.

54. *New York Times,* 25 October 1941, p. 10; 31 October 1941, p. 46; 3 November 1941, p. 13; 4 November 1941, p. 19; 26 October 1941, p. 36; *American Hebrew,* 31 October 1941, p. 4.

55. La Guardia had faced a strong challenge in the Republican primary from John R. Davies mainly on the question of the mayor's support for an interventionist foreign policy. He had also antagonized Republican voters by enrolling as a member of the American Labor party.

56. *New York Times,* 2 January 1941, p. 6; 12 February 1941, pp. 1, 9; 11 September 1941, p. 15; 26 October 1941, p. 22.

57. *New York Times,* 8 November 1941, p. 34. The Roosevelt percentage vote in 1940 correlated a high .777 (r^2 = .604) with the La Guardia percentage vote in 1941, indicating a strong relationship. They were drawing their votes from the same election district constituency. The votes in the Jewish election districts for example were strongly for Roosevelt and La Guardia and show an almost complete identity of support with little variance. See also *Gaelic American,* 17 September 1941, p. 4; 18 October 1941, p. 2.

58. *Staats-Zeitung,* 1 November 1941, p. 6.

59. *New York Times,* 31 October 1941, p. 24.

60. See the discussion on Democrats and Italians in chapter 3, and the discussion on Mahoney and the Italian vote earlier in this chapter.

61. Interview with Rao; telephone interview with Leonard Covello, 22 June 1972; telephone interview with Alfred Santangelo, 5 July 1972. However, *Il Progresso* could still boast upon La Guardia's election that Italians were advancing and demanding more respect, although, as in 1937, the paper did not endorse any mayoral candidate (11 November 1941, p. 6).

62. Although economic conditions had improved by November 1941, there was surely still resentment in these areas related to the recent economic hardships, which in some cases still continued.

63. Edward C. Banfield and James Q. Wilson, *City Politics* (Cambridge, Massachusetts: Harvard University Press, Vintage Books, 1963), p. 55. Although appealing to the fears and frustrations of the various ethnic groups, the Democrats did not want to encourage a situation which would destroy their party in certain neighborhoods. They therefore tried to eliminate the more overt manifestations of conflict, such as the street meetings, while still continuing their narrow ethnic appeals (see chapter 8, discussion on South Bronx).

64. The Lehman campaigns for governor involved the issue of anti-Semitism. For example, a whispering campaign was directed against Lehman in 1938. Moreover, Lehman charged in that year that the Republicans were waging a campaign of racial and religious intolerance. However, according to Dewey, Lehman would use the tactic of waving the "bloody shirt" of anti-Semitism toward the end of every campaign in an effort to smear his opponents (*New York Times,* 6 November 1938, p. 1; Thomas E. Dewey and Rodney Campbell, ed., *Twenty Against the Underworld* [New York: Doubleday and Company, 1974], pp. 415, 435). See chapter 3, discussion on 1938 campaign.

65. Myron I. Scholnick, "The New Deal and Anti-Semitism in America" (Ph.D. diss., University of Maryland, 1971), pp. 112, 123, 126–30.

66. Ibid., pp. 172, 184, 186–87; *New York Times,* 29 September 1940, p. 39. There was some truth in the statement that the German government favored a Willkie victory.

The German embassy, for example, tried to defeat Roosevelt through the publication of materials on Poland which appeared to show the president's desire for war. See *DGFP*, series D, 9:48, 57; 10:48–49; Alton Frye, *Nazi Germany and the American Hemisphere* (New Haven: Yale University Press, 1967), pp. 132–33.

67. Robert A. Divine, *Foreign Policy and U. S. Presidential Elections 1940–1948* (New York: New Viewpoints, 1974), pp. 60, 73; *New York Times*, 29 September 1940, p. 39.

68. Scholnick, "The New Deal," pp. 188, 192, 198–202; Divine, *Foreign Policy*, pp. 50–51; *New York Times*, 28 August 1940, p. 1; 6 October 1940, p. 1; Divine, *Foreign Policy*, pp. 66–67, 82.

69. *Staats-Zeitung*, 4 November 1940, p. 6; Dorothy Thompson, quoted in Divine, *Foreign Policy*, p. 73.

70. The importance of the foreign policy issue in the 1940 election is noted in a report, submitted to Roosevelt in 1941, entitled "Research Project on the Influence of Nationality Groups on Election Returns" and containing information on New York. Louis Bean was director of the project which compiled the report. In 1944 Bean and others published an article which contained parts of the 1941 report. Both studies note a shift away from Roosevelt between 1932 and 1940, particularly between 1936 and 1940, by German and Italian voters. Bean stated that this shift could not be explained by economic factors. Further analysis, based on national sample survey data (American Institute of Public Opinion) for 1936, 1940, and 1944, is contained in an unpublished report by Robert T. Bower and Leo Srole. This study notes a decrease in the percentage Democratic vote among Italian and Irish voters in 1936, 1940, and 1944 and an increase among Jewish voters (Germans were not included in this study). The report states, however, that variables other than ethnicity (e.g., economic status) played a significant role in determining this vote. While this is true (since upper- and middle-income individuals are less likely to vote Democratic than are those in the lower economic categories), economic rank was not as important as ethnicity in 1940, according to my study, although it did influence voting behavior (see table 15). For example, there was less difference in the way units in the same ethnic grouping were voting than there was among units in the same economic category. The 1941 report is in OF 4351, Franklin D. Roosevelt Papers, Franklin D. Roosevelt Library, Hyde Park, New York, and is discussed in Louis Gerson, *The Hyphenate in Recent American Politics and Diplomacy* (Lawrence, Kansas: University of Kansas Press, 1964), pp. 119–21. For the 1944 study see Louis Bean, Frederick Mosteller, and Frederick Williams, "Nationalities and 1944," *Public Opinion Quarterly* 8 (Fall 1944):371–72. The AIPO Analysis is in Robert T. Bower and Leo Srole, "Voting Behavior of American Ethnic Groups 1936–1944" Bureau of Applied Social Research, Columbia University, 1948.

71. Had the Ethiopian crisis not been settled by the 1936 elections, Roosevelt probably would have lost significant Italian support in that contest. The Italian community was angry at Roosevelt's statements and his intended actions against Italy. Although the Republicans tried to use this issue in 1936, it did little good. Italy had annexed Ethiopia by this time, the League of Nation's economic sanctions had been removed, and the war was old news. An indication that even pro-Fascists were now supporting the president can be observed from the pages of *Il Progresso*. Pope, who accepted the chairmanship of the Italian division of the Democratic National Committee in 1936, hailed Roosevelt in a number of editorials and even noted that the people of Italy were hoping for a Roosevelt victory. See *Il Progresso* 19 October 1936, p. 4; 31 October 1936, p. 6; 2 November 1936, p. 6; Republican political advertisement, 3 November 1936, p. 11; John P. Diggins, *Mussolini and Fascism, The View from America* (Princeton: Princeton University Press, 1972), pp. 302–05.

72. Mark A. Bogart to Marguerite LeHand, 24 October 1940, Roosevelt Papers, OF 233A; Luigi Antonini to Marguerite LeHand, 10 February 1941, Roosevelt Papers, PPF 7382; Alfred F. Beiter to Edward J. Flynn, 1 October 1940, Roosevelt Papers, PPF 2532; Charles Rappina to Roosevelt, 21 October 1940, Roosevelt Papers, OF 233A; Elsa Riccio to Roosevelt, 26 October 1940, Roosevelt Papers, OF 233A; Ralph Manzoni to Marguerite LeHand, 8 October 1940, Roosevelt Papers, OF 233A.

73. *Il Progresso,* 3 November 1940, p. 1. After the election, Pope made sure to mention how hard and loyally Italian-Americans had worked for Roosevelt (*Il Progresso,* 7 November 1940, p. 1).

74. *New York Times,* 13 October 1940, p. 30.

75. *New York Times,* 13 October 1940, p. 22; Divine, *Foreign Policy,* p. 64. After the election Roosevelt continued to woo the Italians. In May 1941 he appointed Paul P. Rao to the position of assistant U.S. Attorney General in charge of customs. Rao was an important figure among Italian Democrats in New York, and the position had been offered in order to make amends for the "stab in the back" speech, which still caused bitterness. Roosevelt and Pope, who were at odds after the publisher's lack of support in 1940, managed to bury the old resentments before the 1944 elections. Roosevelt felt Pope was important for purposes of winning the Italian vote and at Ed Flynn's urging invited Pope to the White House in October 1944 and agreed to permit the publisher to be seen coming out. The president and his political advisors were also concerned about the situation in Italy, after that country's defeat, knowing well that Italian-Americans were watching the president's actions carefully (Interview with Rao; *New York Times,* 30 May 1941, p. 3; Edwin Watson memo to Roosevelt, 9 October 1944, Roosevelt Papers, PPF 4617; William O'Dwyer, "Reminiscences," 5:942–43; Gerson, *The Hyphenate,* p. 127; Diggins, *Mussolini,* pp. 417–18.

76. *Steuben News,* October 1940, p. 1; *New York Times,* 17 October 1940, p. 18.

77. *Gaelic American,* 16 November 1940, p. 4; *PM,* 12 June 1941, p. 17; for examples of political ads, see *Irish World,* 2 November 1940, pp. 3, 6; *Gaelic American,* 2 November 1940, p. 1; 16 November 1940, p. 4; *New Republic,* 26 October 1940, in American Jewish Committee Press Clippings. Based on a Gallup Poll in 1938, there is an indication that the drop in Roosevelt's vote in 1940 was related to a loss of Coughlinite support. For example, "Coughlin supporters who had voted for Roosevelt in 1936 were more likely to have changed their opinion concerning the President [by 1938] than were Roosevelt voters who disapproved of the radio priest." Furthermore, those 1936 Roosevelt voters who still approved of Coughlin in 1938 were more likely than anti-Coughlinites to switch their vote to the Republicans in the 1938 congressional elections. In general more Coughlinites than anti-Coughlinites in 1938 were opposed to Roosevelt. However this opposition decreased as one moved down the income scale. Most of the poor and those on relief who approved of Coughlin also supported Roosevelt, seeing them both as aiding their income class. This might partially explain Roosevelt's high Irish and German vote in 1936 even after Coughlin had come out against the president in New York State. It may also have been a contributory factor to Roosevelt's majority Irish vote in 1940 (Gary T. Marx, *The Social Basis of the Support of a Depression Era Extremist: Father Coughlin,* monograph 7 [Berkeley, California: Survey Research Center, University of California, 1962], pp. 74–76, 79–80, 92; Seymour Martin Lipset, "Three Decades of the Radical Right: Coughlinites, McCarthyites, and Birchers," in *The Radical Right,* ed. Daniel Bell (New York: Doubleday and Company, Anchor Books, 1964), pp. 387–89; *New York Times,* 1 November 1936, p. 48).

78. Geoffrey S. Smith, *To Save A Nation: American Countersubversives, the New Deal and the Coming of World War II* (New York: Basic Books, 1973), pp. 159–60; *PM,* 12 June 1941, p. 17.

CHAPTER 8. IN THE NEIGHBORHOODS

1. Archbishop Mooney in 1942 demanded that Coughlin terminate his nonreligious public activities or leave the priesthood. Coughlin chose the former. *Social Justice*'s second-class mailing privileges were revoked under the Espionage Act of 1917. McWilliams was brought to trial in 1942 along with twenty-five others for sedition. The Bund, after Kuhn's arrest and conviction, was split and weakened. On 11 December 1941, the F.B.I. raided its headquarters and seized its records. Subsequently a number of Bund leaders were brought to trial and convicted for sedition and conspiracy to violate the Selective Service Act.

2. *Brooklyn Jewish Center Review*, January 1944, p. 3.

3. Washington Heights' boundaries are West 158th and 159th streets on the south, Manhattan's borough limits on the north, the Harlem River on the east, and the Hudson River on the west.

4. Background information on this neighborhood comes from the following: Lee Lendt, *A Social History of Washington Heights, New York City* (New York: Columbia–Washington Heights Community Mental Health Project, 1960), pp. 8, 12–14, 17, 54, 58; Protestant Council of the City of New York, Department of Church Planning and Research, *Upper Manhattan: A Community Study of Washington Heights* (New York: Protestant Council of the City of New York, 1954); New York Washington Heights Congregation, *Annual Report,* 1927–28, p. 1.

5. Lendt, *A Social History,* pp. 8, 13–14.

6. Washington Heights Jewish population figures are from C. Morris Horowitz and Lawrence Kaplan, *Jewish Population, New York Area, 1900–1975* (New York: Federation of Jewish Philanthropies, 1959), p. 98. Since Jewish population figures for all New York areas in the 1920s were available only for 1923 and not for a census year, it was necessary to estimate the total population of these areas for 1923 by noting the rate of increase or decrease between 1920 and 1925. Tract data is computed from Walter Laidlaw, ed., *Statistical Sources for Demographic Studies of Greater New York, 1920* (New York: The New York City 1920 Census Committee, 1922), pp. 125–35, which lists foreign-born for each nationality group in each census tract; and Walter Laidlaw, ed., *Population of the City of New York, 1890–1930* (New York: Cities Census Committee, 1932), p. 265, which offers a ratio of native-born persons of foreign or mixed parentage to foreign-born persons, by borough, for each nationality group in 1920. It is possible from this and the Laidlaw 1920 data to get a good estimate of the foreign stock population, by nationality, in each census tract.

7. Lendt, *A Social History,* p. 73; interview data from the leading citizens of Washington Heights was collected as part of the Lendt study. Although these interviews are confidential, Dr. Bruce Dohrenwend of the Social Psychiatry Research Unit, College of Physicians and Surgeons, Columbia University kindly allowed me to submit questions to his staff who then searched through the interviews for appropriate answers and quotations. The confidentiality of the interviews was kept intact in this way since I did not see the interviews, while at the same time I was provided with valuable data from long-time residents of this community that was not utilized in the Lendt study. On information pertaining to early anti-Semitism, interview number 0019 was valuable. These interviews will be hereafter cited as Social Psychiatry interview (with the appropriate number).

8. All Irish, Russian (Jewish), and other ethnic tract figures for 1920 for Washington Heights were computed from Laidlaw, *Statistical Sources,* pp. 125–35, and Laidlaw, *Population of the City of New York,* p. 265. The 1940 data is estimated on the basis of ratios of foreign-born heads of families to total foreign-born, and total foreign-born to native-born of foreign or mixed parentage, for each nationality group, using borough and

tract statistics. See United States, Department of Commerce, Bureau of the Census, *Census Tract Data on Population and Housing, New York City: 1940* (New York: Welfare Council Committee on 1940 Census Tract Tabulations for New York City, September 1942), pp. 149, 153–54; United States, Department of Commerce, Bureau of the Census, *Population: Nativity and Parentage of the White Population, Country of Origin of the Foreign Stock, 1940* (Washington, D.C.: Government Printing Office, 1942), p. 74. This ratio technique is the only possible way to secure even an estimate of Irish and Russian (Jewish) tract populations for 1940. All tract figures and percentages must therefore be considered estimates, although according to neighborhood surveys and data based on larger units than tracts (e.g., health areas) they seem to be accurate.

9. Voter registration data was also considered to determine if there was an Irish presence in the Jewish tracts west of Broadway.

10. The Index of Dissimilarity was 26 for 1920 and 35.5 for 1940. Census block statistics by ethnicity were not available for either 1920 or 1940.

11. All voter registration material comes from various volumes of the City Record, City Record Supplement, *List of Registered Voters*. In this case the volumes for 1910, 1920, 1930, and 1940 were used. This compilation lists registered voters by election district, street, and house number. An identification of the ethnicity of the registered voter was made by considering the person's name. Voters with ethnically doubtful names were not assigned to any group. See chapter 3, note 12. Efforts were made to confirm the name technique through the use of census tract ethnic information and neighborhood social surveys. For example, Irish-sounding names were identified as Irish only on streets within census tracts that were estimated as having an Irish presence and/or which were described by neighborhood surveys as having Irish residents. Although voter registration lists were not the ideal data base to use, it was the only one available for the years under examination. The lack of any city house directories in New York which list residents by street address precluded an attempt to find all residents (not just registered voters) at an address and compare them over the years. While perhaps the voter registration lists are not totally accurate in revealing the exact number of each ethnic group in each house, they are accurate in revealing a group mobility pattern over the years, and this is what I was most interested in finding. The alphabetical city directories, which are arranged by name, end with 1933/34. Telephone directories, which obviously left out many people in the 1930s, particularly in low-income areas, must be used after that date.

12. United States, Department of Commerce, Bureau of the Census, *Housing Block Statistics—Manhattan, 1940* (Washington, D. C.: Government Printing Office, 1941), pp. 37–40; Lendt, *A Social History*, p. 17.

13. Also notable was that the Jews were the proprietors of most of the retail stores in the Heights. See Gerhart Saenger and Harry Shulman, "A Study of Intercultural Behavior and Attitudes among Residents of the Upper West Side" (New York: Mayor's Committee on Unity, 1946), p. 5; New York Times, Daily News, and Herald Tribune, *New York City Market Analysis* (New York: 1934); New York Times, Daily News, Mirror, and Journal-American, *New York City Market Analysis* (New York: 1943).

14. Saenger and Shulman, "A Study of Intercultural Behavior," pp. 4–7.

15. American Jewish Committee, "Report on the Christian Front," 1939, in American Jewish Committee Files, New York City. This lists the principal outdoor meeting locations of the Front.

16. Social Psychiatry interview 0018; Front Pamphlet, 1938, in American Jewish Committee Files; Social Psychiatry interview 0021 noted the resentment Irish Catholics felt toward the movement of German Jewish refugees into the neighborhood because many came with some money and were able to buy small shops.

17. Anti-Defamation League of B'nai B'rith, "Reports and Affidavits on

Washington Heights," in ADL Files, New York City. (hereafter cited as ADL Reports); Social Psychiatry interviews 0018, 0021; New York City, Department of Investigation, *Report on Investigation of Anti-American and Anti-Semitic Vandalism,* 5 January 1944, pp. 18, 125; *New York Post,* 22 December 1943, p. 3; 29 December 1943, p. 3; 14 January 1944, p. 5; *New York Times,* 30 December 1943, p. 19; *New York Sun,* 31 December 1943. Some Protestant churches were also attacked. Only Catholic places of worship were left untouched.

18. These gangs were identified as Irish (Social Psychiatry interview 0021; interview with Ann Lee Jacobs [Raff], 5 April 1973, New York City).

19. This included 161st Street and Amsterdam Avenue, J. Hood Wright Park at 174th Street and Fort Washington Avenue, and the area between 162nd and 163rd Street on Fort Washington Avenue. The Shamrocks operated around Sherman Avenue and Dyckman Street. The influence of the earlier anti-Semites on these juveniles was attested to by Ann Lee Jacobs, who was involved in efforts to rehabilitate the Shamrocks (interview with Jacobs).

20. Interview with Paul O'Dwyer, 9 August 1973, New York City; *New York Times,* 11 January 1944, p. 24.

21. *Voice for Human Rights,* January 1940, p. 14. One Washington Heights resident noted that in the fight with the Front the Irish politicians had a lot to lose politically by speaking out against this organization and Coughlin. Apparently some did so anyway (Social Psychiatry interview 0023).

22. Interview with Jacobs; Social Psychiatry interview 0021.

23. Interview with Jacobs; ADL Reports; *New York Post,* 29 December 1943, p. 3; 30 December 1943, p. 5; *Bronx and Washington Heights Jewish Review,* 13 January 1944, p. 1. Suspicion of the police was also based on their involvement as members of the Front. See chapter 5, discussion on Front occupational breakdown.

24. *Bronx and Washington Heights Jewish Review,* 13 January 1944, p. 1.

25. Department of Investigation, *Report,* p. 13 (see also *New York Post,* 11 January 1944, p. 4); *New York Times,* 30 December 1943, p. 19; *PM,* 7 January 1944, p. 9; *New York Post,* 14 January 1944, p. 5; *New York Post,* 3 January 1944, p. 5; 10 January 1944, p. 4. For La Guardia's earlier actions against anti-Semitic activities, see chapter 7.

26. Interview with Jacobs.

27. Ibid.; Social Psychiatry interview 0012. Ann Lee Jacobs ran the Youth Aid program.

28. Social Psychiatry interview 0021; Lendt, *A Social History,* p. 76; Interview with Jacobs; ADL Reports; *New York Post,* 6 January 1944, p. 4. See chapter 5, regarding how the New York City Catholic Church hierarchy reacted to these incidents. There was still an ambivalence on the part of the Church in relation to condemning anti-Semitism and the remnants of the Front.

29. That the Front and anti-Semitic issue continued to disturb the community is revealed by two political events. Many believed that Jacob Javits' victory over Dan Flynn for Congressman in this area in 1946 was related to Flynn's earlier failure to take a stand against anti-Semitism. Flynn was also bothered during the campaign by the rumor that he had been associated with the Front. In the second case, Paul O'Dwyer noted that when he campaigned in Washington Heights in 1948 for the congressional seat, he was attacked by remnants of the Front because of his earlier opposition to them. (Social Psychiatry interview [no number given]; *New York Times,* 2 August 1946, p. 10; interview with Paul O'Dwyer).

30. The boundary of the South Bronx on the north is approximately 161st Street, running across to Longwood Avenue to Tiffany Street to Whitlock Avenue to Bryant

Avenue to Garrison Avenue; on the south, the East River; on the west, the Harlem River; and on the east, the Bronx and East rivers.

31. Background information on this neighborhood comes from Eleanor Symonds, "Population Shifting in Manhattan" (M.A. thesis, Columbia University, 1924), pp. 4–5, and a telephone interview with James Brown (a long-time resident of the South Bronx), 7 August 1973.

32. Based on information compiled from the *List of Registered Voters, 1910.*

33. Horowitz and Kaplan, *Jewish Population,* p. 100 (see explanation in note 6, above); see also Jewish Welfare Board, "Study of the Educational and Recreational Resources and Needs of the Jewish Community of the Borough of the Bronx," New York, 1924; and Bureau of Jewish Social Research, Jewish Communal Survey of Greater New York, "Report 1, Studies on the New York Jewish Population," 1928.

34. Laidlaw, *Statistical Sources,* pp. 139–69; Laidlaw, *Population of the City of New York,* p. 265; Community Council of Greater New York, Census Tract Tabulations, 1930; Bureau of the Census, *Census Tract Data,* 1940, pp. 15–16; Bureau of the Census, *Population: Nativity and Parentage,* p. 74; *List of Registered Voters,* 1920, 1930, 1940 (see notes 6, 8, and 11 above); interview with Brown; Bronx Council of Social Agencies, "A Study of the Lower Bronx," September 1939, pp. 4–5, 100. Crimmins, Cypress, and Powers avenues were heavily Jewish in the St. Mary's Park area. Also parts of Beekman Avenue, Beech Terrace, Oak Terrace, and St. Mary's Street were Jewish in this section. In the Hunts Point section, those of Russian foreign stock, which did not include all Jews, were 32 percent (1,781) of the population in tract 101 and 29 percent (3,979) of the population in tract 83 in 1940. The percentage Irish in these tracts were 2 percent (412) and 5.4 percent (743) respectively. However, in the area west of St. Ann's, tract 25 was 34 percent Irish foreign stock (3,743) and only 3.9 percent Russian (426); tract 39 was 38 percent Irish (4,659) and 3.6 percent Russian (440) in 1940.

35. *New York Market Analysis,* 1934, 1943. In a health area (number 46) where the Irish predominated, 11.1 percent of the total dwelling units either needed major repairs or had no private bath in 1940. In a predominantly Jewish health area (number 42), the percentage was 2.5 (Department of Commerce, Burgau of the Census, *Housing, Data for Small Areas, 1940* [Washington, D.C.: Government Printing Office, 1942], 1:76; Bronx Council, "A Study of the Lower Bronx," pp. 5, 91–92).

36. Department of Commerce, Bureau of the Census, *Population and Housing, Statistics for Health Areas, New York City, 1940* (Washington, D. C.: Government Printing Office, 1942), pp. 34–35. In Washington Heights a similar breakdown was not possible, since no health area, which consists of a number of census tracts, was predominantly Irish.

37. Except for the Bundists, conflict in this community remained mainly an Irish-Jewish one (Interview with Brown; Florence S. McDonough to Roosevelt, 22 October 1941, Roosevelt Papers, OF 300).

38. The Bund met mainly at Ebling's Casino (156th Street and St. Ann's Avenue) near the German section or at the Triborough Palace (137th Street and Third Avenue) in a mixed but predominantly Irish area, in what were social and propaganda meetings. For example, beginning in 1936, every Thursday the Bund conducted a "Beer Evening" in an effort to camouflage a membership recruitment program as a social evening with free food and drink. They also held street meetings. The Mobilizers met at both the Casino and Palace and were at times provided with Bund guards. The Front met at the Palace ("Report on Bund Activites in the Bronx, Manhattan and Brooklyn," German-American Bund Folder, ADL; Dies Committee, *Hearings,* 4, 76 Cong., 1st sess., 1939, 3765–66, 3888, 3946; *Hearings,* 14, 77 Cong., 1st sess., 1941, 8369; *Hearings, Appendix,* part 4,

77 Cong., 1st sess., 1941, p. 1466; Department of Justice, "Outline of Evidence against the German-American Bund," 1942, p. 89 in German-American Bund Folder, ADL; American Jewish Committee, "Report on the Front." Sander A. Diamond, *The Nazi Movement in the United States 1924–1941* [Ithaca, New York: Cornell University Press, 1974], pp. 245, 319–20).

39. "Report on Bund Activities," ADL.

40. Contemporary observers agree that the Front and Mobilizers influenced the later juvenile anti-Semitic agitators who were active in the 1940s. One Irish girl whose father had been prominent in the Mobilizers was one of the leaders of the vandals in 1943 (Department of Investigation, *Report*, pp. 38–39, 51–52, 66–67, 72, 81, 128).

41. *Voice for Human Rights*, November 1940, p. 8; *Bronx Home News*, 7 May 1939, p. 1; *New York Times*, 14 August 1939, p. 32; 1 September 1939, p. 14; Department of Investigation, *Report*, p. 38; *Bronx Home News*, 7 May 1939, p. 1; *New York Times*, 22 May 1939, p. 2. Front meetings in this area ceased in 1940 after the sedition arrests.

42. Department of Investigation, *Report*, pp. 39, 62–64, 126–28, 135, Appendix C; *New York Times*, 14 August 1939, p. 32; 1 September 1939, p. 14. Contemporary observers of the Front in the South Bronx noted that the effect of the Depression in this area made it a fertile ground for Front growth. Apparently the Depression caused significant discontent and frustration in this neighborhood (*Voice for Human Rights*, November 1940, p. 8).

43. Department of Investigation, *Report*, pp. 128–29.

44. McDonough was active in the Democratic party during the 1930s and later, in the 1960s, became leader of the Bronx County Democratic organization.

45. *Voice for Human Rights*, November 1940, p. 8; *New York Post*, 11 January 1944, p. 5; Lawrence Phelan, "An Evening with the Mobilizers," *Commonweal*, March 22, 1940, p. 471.

46. Florence S. McDonough to Roosevelt, 22 October 1941, Roosevelt Papers, OF 300. Florence McDonough was the wife of Henry McDonough. The effort of the Democrats to crush the overt anti-Semitism may have been due to a desire to avoid a further split between two of their stalwart groups—the Jews and the Irish—which would have been disastrous for the party in certain areas.

47. *New York Times*, 23 October 1939, p. 16; Alson J. Smith, "Coughlin's Platoons," *New Republic*, August 30, 1939, p. 97.

48. *PM*, 11 January 1944, p. 14; *New York Times*, 14 August 1939, p. 32.

49. The boundaries of these areas are as follow: for West Side, 74th to 106th Street, and Central Park West to Riverside Drive; for Fordham, Tremont Avenue on the south, Van Cortland Park South on the north, Gun Hill Road and Bronx Park East on the east, and the Harlem River and Riverdale Avenue on the west; for Highbridge, 161st Street to 170th Street, and Jerome Avenue to Harlem River; for Flatbush, Prospect Park and Lefferts Avenue on the north, Avenue R to Gerritsen Avenue to Avenue X on the south, Remsen Avenue and Ralph Avenue on the east, and Coney Island Avenue on the west.

50. Telephone interview with David Agines (a long-time resident of Highbridge), 16 August 1973; Department of Investigation, *Report*, pp. 13, 15–16, 104; Brooklyn Jewish Community Council, *Summary of Proceedings of the Fourth Annual Convention, 1943*, p. 8. American Jewish Committee, "Report on the Front;" *New York Post*, 31 December 1943, p. 5, 11 January 1944, pp. 4, 11; *PM*, 2 January 1944, p. 12.

51. Department of Investigation, *Report*, p. 16; Mary F. Hall to editor, *Brooklyn Tablet*, 22 April 1939, p. 5; Joseph Sweeney to editor, *Brooklyn Tablet*, 24 February 1940, p. 7 (the Front began to meet on the streetcorners which on other nights were used by the Communists); *New York Times*, 4 November 1941, p. 6; *Brooklyn Eagle*, 10

September 1942, p. 12; Brooklyn Jewish Community Council, *Third Annual Convention*, 1942, p. 4.

52. George Britt, "Poison in the Melting Pot," *Nation*, April 1, 1939, pp. 374-76; Interview with Agines; Sheldon Marcus, *Father Coughlin: The Tumultuous Life of the Priest of the Little Flower* (Boston: Little, Brown and Company, 1973), p. 156; Brooklyn Jewish Community Council, *Fifth Annual Convention, 1944*, p. 7; *PM*, 2 January 1944, p. 12; 4 January 1944, p. 10; Louis E. Yavner, Commissioner of Investigation, *Report to the Honorable F.H. La Guardia on the Administration of Human Relations Programs in New York City Schools*, (New York, 1945).

53. Interview with Rabbi Joseph H. Lookstein, 27 April 1973, New York City; see also chapter 4. Yorkville's boundaries are Central Park to the East River, and 57th Street to 96th Street.

54. McWilliams's Christian Mobilizers became the American Destiny party for the purposes of his campaign.

55. *New York Times*, 18 September 1940, p. 1. Willkie beat Roosevelt in this area because of the war issue. Interview with Robert F. Wagner, Jr., 8 March 1973, New York City.

56. *New York Post*, 8 June 1940 in American Jewish Committee Press Clippings, YIVO Institute for Jewish Research, New York City.

57. Interview with Wagner; interview with Lookstein. It should be noted again that the Front did not permit Bund members to join.

CHAPTER 9. ON ETHNIC CONFLICT

1. On an individual basis, some people may have been drawn into conflict because of psychological needs which had little to do with group tensions. This component of conflict must also be considered but not overstated. As one social scientist commented, "There would be a basis for group conflict even in a world in which there were no sick individuals or sick societies, provided only that groups . . . are operating as distinct entities that are in competition or rivalry for scarce values" (Robin M. Williams, Jr., *Strangers Next Door* [Englewood Cliffs, New Jersey: Prentice-Hall, 1964], p. 357.

2. Allen D. Grimshaw, "Relationships Among Prejudice, Discrimination, Social Tension and Social Violence," *Journal of Intergroup Relations* 2 (Autumn 1961): 303, 307-9.

3. *New York Times*, 7 October 1945, p. 5; 26 June 1947, p. 25; 19 July 1947, p. 11; Christian Front Pamphlet, 1945, in American Jewish Committee Files.

4. Robin M. Williams, Jr., *The Reduction of Intergroup Tensions* (New York: Social Science Research Council, 1947), Bulletin 57, p. 40.

5. Ibid., p. 41.

6. Tamotsu Shibutani and Kian Kwan, *Ethnic Stratification* (New York: The Macmillan Company, 1965), p. 401; Lewis A. Coser, *The Functions of Social Conflict* (Glencoe, Ill.: The Free Press, 1956), pp. 80, 128, 137.

Essay on Sources

The bibliography for this book is actually contained in the footnotes, and any attempt to cite all the sources again would simply be repetitious. Therefore this essay will be used to describe the more important primary sources in order to provide some direction to others who wish to study intergroup relations in America.

Since the conflicts of this period involved the Jewish community so extensively, the Files of the American Jewish Committee (New York) and the Anti-Defamation League of B'nai B'rith (New York) were indispensable. Contained in these files are publications, correspondence, descriptions of meetings and anti-Semitic events, studies, and other material relating to the German-American Bund, Christian Front, Christian Mobilizers, and the anti-Jewish vandalism of the 1940s. Research on any anti-Semitic organizations or manifestations of the twentieth century must begin here. Also useful for understanding the 1940s anti-Jewish events was the New York Department of Investigation's *Report on Investigation of Anti-American and Anti-Semitic Vandalism*, 5 January 1944 (New York Public Library).

The ethnic and general press was an excellent source of information on all aspects of this study. The *Brooklyn Tablet, Irish World and American Industrial Liberator, Gaelic American, New Yorker Staats-Zeitung und Herold, Il Progresso Italo-Americano, American Hebrew, Jewish Examiner, Forward, New York Times, PM,* and many others were used throughout this study. Added to these papers were the organizational publications such as the *Steuben News, Roland News, Brooklyn Jewish Center Review, Jewish Veteran,* and the *Proceedings of the Annual Conventions* of the New York State Branch of the Catholic Central Verein of America.

Manuscript sources which proved especially helpful included the Fiorello H. La Guardia Papers (Municipal Archives and Records Center, New York), Vito Marcantonio Papers (New York Public Library), Herbert H. Lehman Papers (Columbia University), Charles Poletti Papers (Columbia University), Franklin

D. Roosevelt Papers (Franklin D. Roosevelt Library, Hyde Park, New York), and Stephen Wise Papers (American Jewish Historical Society, Waltham, Massachusetts). The La Guardia Papers particularly are invaluable for any study of ethnic politics in the New York of the 1930s and 1940s.

I also used interviews to provide information which could not be found in traditional sources. This included a number of the transcribed interviews of the Columbia University Oral History Project as well as many which I did myself. Of the latter, the most helpful were interviews with Leonard Covello, Ward Lange, Paul O'Dwyer, Paul P. Rao, and Robert F. Wagner.

Among the sources which enabled me to develop my ethnic voter analysis and secure other pertinent information on neighborhoods, the following were especially important: the City Record, City Record Supplement, *List of Registered Voters* for 1910, 1920, 1930, 1932, 1933, 1936, 1937, 1938, 1940, 1941, which list registered voters by election district, street and house number: New York City, Board of Elections, *Maps Showing the Assembly Districts of New York,* 1932–41 (New York Public Library), which actually shows both assembly and election district boundaries; the census publications edited by Walter Laidlaw, *Statistical Sources for Demographic Studies of Greater New York, 1920* (The New York City 1920 Census Committee, 1922) and *Population of the City of New York, 1890–1930* (Cities Census Committee, 1932); and the Bureau of the Census, Sixteenth Census of the United States, *Census Tract Data on Population and Housing, New York City: 1940* (Welfare Council Committee on 1940 Census Tract Tabulations for New York City, 1942), which provides information on foreign-born heads of families for each nationality group. I would also include in this list the unpublished census tract tabulation sheets for 1930 recording foreign stock for each nationality group by tract (Community Council of Greater New York).

Other sources which were helpful for various aspects of this book included the reports and hearings of the House Special Committee on Un-American Activities (McCormack-Dickstein and Dies Committees), which provided information on the Christian Front, Christian Mobilizers, and German-American Bund; and the Department of State, *Documents on German Foreign Policy,* which offered material on Germany's relationship with the Bund and the German-American community, as well as appraisals of American public opinion regarding Nazi Germany.

Finally, I would also like to mention some sources which were particular disappointments. I was allowed to search through parts of the Diocese of Brooklyn Archives but found no useful material. The papers of Cardinal Spellman, housed at the Archdiocese of New York Archives (St. Joseph's Seminary, Yonkers, New York) remain closed. This collection would certainly have been helpful to my study. I hope it is opened for future researchers.

Index